# ORIGINAL NARRATIVES
# OF EARLY AMERICAN HISTORY

REPRODUCED UNDER THE AUSPICES OF THE
AMERICAN HISTORICAL ASSOCIATION

GENERAL EDITOR, J. FRANKLIN JAMESON, PH.D., LL.D., LITT.D.

DIRECTOR OF THE DEPARTMENT OF HISTORICAL RESEARCH IN THE
CARNEGIE INSTITUTION OF WASHINGTON

———————

NARRATIVES OF EARLY VIRGINIA

BRADFORD'S HISTORY OF PLYMOUTH PLANTATION

WINTHROP'S JOURNAL "HISTORY OF NEW ENGLAND"
(2 vols.)

NARRATIVES OF EARLY CAROLINA

NARRATIVES OF EARLY MARYLAND

NARRATIVES OF EARLY PENNSYLVANIA, WEST NEW JERSEY,
AND DELAWARE

NARRATIVES OF NEW NETHERLAND

EARLY ENGLISH AND FRENCH VOYAGES

VOYAGES OF SAMUEL DE CHAMPLAIN

SPANISH EXPLORERS IN THE SOUTHERN UNITED STATES

SPANISH EXPLORATION IN THE SOUTHWEST

NARRATIVES OF THE INSURRECTIONS

NARRATIVES OF THE INDIAN WARS

JOHNSON'S WONDER-WORKING PROVIDENCE

THE JOURNAL OF JASPAR DANCKAERTS

NARRATIVES OF THE NORTHWEST

NARRATIVES OF THE WITCHCRAFT CASES

THE NORTHMEN, COLUMBUS, AND CABOT

# ORIGINAL NARRATIVES
## OF EARLY AMERICAN HISTORY

REPRODUCED UNDER THE AUSPICES OF THE
AMERICAN HISTORICAL ASSOCIATION

General Editor, J. FRANKLIN JAMESON, PH.D., LL.D.

No. 5

# NARRATIVES
# OF EARLY CAROLINA

## 1650—1708

EDITED BY

## ALEXANDER S. SALLEY, JR.

LATE SECRETARY OF THE HISTORICAL COMMISSION OF SOUTH CAROLINA

*WITH TWO MAPS*

*New York*
BARNES & NOBLE, INC.

PRINTED IN THE UNITED STATES OF AMERICA

0875

# CONTENTS

## NARRATIVES OF EARLY CAROLINA

### Edited by Alexander S. Salley, Jr.

v

# CONTENTS

viii CONTENTS

# THE DISCOVERY OF NEW BRITTAINE, 1650

# INTRODUCTION

PRESUMING on the claim that the explorations of Sebastian Cabot gave the British government sovereignty over that portion of North America lying between the 31st and 36th degrees of north latitude, Charles I., on October 30, 1629, granted it to his attorney-general, Sir Robert Heath, for the founding of a province. Sir Robert did nothing in the way of settling his territory, and for thirty years after the grant was made to him very few explorations were made in that country and very little was written about it. One contribution to the subject, however, was a pamphlet published in London in 1651, containing an account by Edward Bland, Abraham Woode, Sackford Brewster, and Elias Pennant of an expedition made by them in August and September, 1650, into that part of the domain of Carolina next to Virginia, to which they gave the name New Britain.

Bland was a merchant of Virginia and in this trading expedition among the Indians he realized that the Christianizing of the Indians and settling of the country would sooner advance the interests of the province of Virginia and the merchants and traders thereof. Upon his return he and his companions petitioned the Assembly of Virginia to be allowed to make discoveries to the southward and to establish settlements and have intercourse with the Indians there. The petition was granted on condition that Bland and his associates, in effecting the settlement, should secure themselves with a hundred able men sufficiently supplied with arms and ammunition.

To advance their undertaking they resorted to the customary plan of publishing a pamphlet designed to attract

3

and interest prospective settlers. They gave an account of each day's movements, with their observations of the topography, condition, and advantages of the country which they had journeyed over and to which they were now inviting settlers to come. This pamphlet, first printed in 1651, was reprinted at New York by Joseph Sabin in 1873.

# THE DISCOVERY OF NEW BRITTAINE, 1650

*The Discovery of New Brittaine, Began August 27, Anno Dom.
1650, by Edward Bland, Merchant, Abraham Woode, Captaine, Sackford Brewster, Elias Pennant, Gentlemen.*
*From Fort Henry, at the Head of Appamattuck River in Virginia,
to the Fals of Blandina, first River in New Brittaine, which
runneth West, being 120. Mile South-west, between 35. and
37. degrees, (a pleasant Country), of temperate Ayre, and
fertile Soyle.*
*London, Printed by Thomas Harper for John Stephenson, at
the Sun below Ludgate. M. DC. LI.*[1]

*To the Honorable, Sir John Danvers, Knight:*[2] *Great Favourer of
the Westerne Plantations, and a Member of the Parliament
of England.*
*Noble Sir:*
    THE great Incouragement that I have found from your
Worthy selfe to propogate the Publique Affaires, as well
Forraigne as Domestique, hath imbolned[3] mee to presume
humbly to present this small Piece of the Discovery of the
Westerne Part of Virginia, wherein you shall finde by the
Industry of the Surveyors of that Part, the great Benefit
that may accrew to the English Plantation; in regard of
the many and severall Commodities that may thence arise,
by reason of the fertility of the Soyle, Nature having provided so plentifully for all things, that with no extraordinary
great Charge it may be effected, to the great Profit, and more
Glory of this English Nation: And whereas your selfe hath
beene, and still are a Chiefe Agent in that, and other Plan-

---

[1] Text of the title-page of the original.

[2] Sir John Danvers (1588-1655) had been a prominent member of the Virginia Company and in 1649 one of the regicide judges of Charles I.

[3] Emboldened.

5

tations, so (under God) you may be a meanes for converting divers of those poor Indians to the Christian Faith. For the World doth take notice you observe the Orators saying; That you were not borne for your selfe, but for your Country: Which that you may ever doe, shall be the Prayer,

    Sir,

Of your most humble servant,

                      J. S.

### To the Reader.

WHO ever thou art that desirest the Advancement of Gods glory by conversion of the Indians, the Augmentation of the English Common-wealth, in extending its liberties; I would advise thee to consider the present benefit and future profits that will arise in the wel setling Virginia's Confines, especially that happy Country of New Brittaine, in the Latitude of 35. and 37. degrees, of more temperate Clymate then [1] that the English now inhabite, abounding with great Rivers of long extent, and encompassing a great part, or most of Virginia's Continent; a place so easie to be settled in, in regard that Horse and Cattle in foure or five dayes may be conveyed for the benefit of Undertakers, and all inconveniencies avoyded which commonly attend New Plantations, being supplied with necessaries from the Neighbourhood of Virginia.

That the Assembly of Virginia (as may be seene by their Order since my returne hereto procured) have conceived a hundred to be a sufficient force and competence for the establishment of that Country in which Tobacco will grow larger and more in quantity. Sugar Canes are supposed naturally to be there, or at least if implanted will undoubtedly flourish: For we brought with us thence extraordinary Canes of twenty-five foot long and six inches round; there is also great store of fish, and the Inhabitants relate that there is plenty of Salt made to the sunne without art; Tobacco Pipes have beene seene among these Indians tipt with Silver, and they weare Copper Plates about their necks: They have two Crops of Indian Corne yearely, whereas Virginia hath but one. What I

[1] Than.

write, is what I have proved; I cordially wish some more then private Spirits would take it into their consideration, so may it prove most advantagious to particular and publick ends; for which so prayeth,

Your faithfull servant,

EDWARD BLAND.

### *October* 20. 1650.  *By the Assembly.*[1]

It is Ordered by the Grand Assembly, that according to the Petition of Mr. Edward Bland, Merchant, that he the sayd Bland, or any other be permitted to discover and seate to the Southward in any convenient place where they discover; and that according to his Petition for furthering his Designes hee bee permitted to have correspondence with the Indians, and also receive the benevolence of the well-affected, and use all lawfull meanes for effecting thereof, provided that they secure themselves in effecting the sayd Designe with a hundred able men sufficiently furnished with Armes and Munition.

JOHN CORKES,[2] *Cler. Dom. Com.*

### *Sir Walter Rawleighs Observation on* 35. *degrees Latitude.*

Paradise was created a part of this Earth, and seated in the lower part of Eden or Mesopotamia, containing also a part of Shinar and Armenia; it stands 35 degrees from the Equinoctiall, and 55 from the North-pole, in a temperate Climate, full of excellent fruits, chiefely of Palme-trees without labour; for whereinsoever the Earth, Nature, and the Sun can most vaunt that they have excelled, yet shall the Palme-tree be the greatest wonder of all their workes: This tree alone giveth unto man whatsoever his life beggeth at Natures hand. The like are also found both in the East and West-Indies as well as in Paradise, which Countries are also blessed with a perpetuall Spring and Summer, etc. Rawleighs *Marrow of History*, Page 42.

---

[1] Of Virginia.
[2] Properly, Corker. "Clericus Domus Communis" = Clerk of the House of Commons.

By how much Adam exceeded all living men in perfection by being the immediate workmanship of God, by so much did that chosen, and particular Garden exceed all the parts of the Universall World in which God had planted the Trees of Life, and Knowledge, Plants onely proper, and belonging to the Paradise, and Garden, of so great a Lord. *Ibid.*, p. 43.

## THE DISCOVERY OF NEW BRITAINE

*August* 27. 1650.   The Right Honorable Sir W. Berkly,[1] Kt. being Governour and Captaine Generall of Virginia, Edw. Bland Merch. Abraham Wood Capt. Elias Ponnant[2] and Sackford Brewster Gent. foure Men, and one Indian named Pyancha, an Appamattuck for our Guide, with two servants, foure Horses and Provision, advanced from Fort Henry, lying on Appamattuck River at the fals,[3] being a branch of James River, intending a South westerne Discovery.

This day wee passed over a branch[4] belonging to Black-water lake, running South east into Chawan River; at that place wee were forced to unlade our Carriages by reason of the great raines lately fallen, which otherwise is very passable for foot, being firm gravelly ground in the bottome, and lieth from Fort Henry 20. miles, and some 12. miles from this place we travelled unto a deepe River called the Nottaway Creeke some 100. paces over sandy bottomes (and with a little labour may be made passeable) unto a Nottaway Town lying some two miles from the River.   Hither we came within night, and by reason of our suddaine approach and hallowing of Robert Farmer servant to Mr. Bland, the Inhabitants ran all away into the Woods, with their Women and Children; therefore by us it was named Farmers Chase. After our arrivall there within a small space of time one Indian man appeared, and finding of us peaceable, and the white flag bore before us by our Guide whom they knew, he made a hallow, and the rest came in from their sculking holes like

---

[1] This is not the proper spelling, Berkeley being the way that Sir William himself and his brother, John, Lord Berkeley, spelled the name.

[2] Pennant.                        [3] Now Petersburg, Virginia.

[4] Presumably Stony Creek.

so many timerous Hares, and shewed us what curtesie they could. About two houres after came to us Oyeocker elder brother to Chounterounte of the Nottaway Kings, who told us that his brother Chounterounte, and other of the Nottaway Kings would come to us next day by Noone, and that the day before Chounterounte and all his men had been a hunting, and it hapned that Chounterounte had shot one of his brothers in the leg, and that thereupon he was gone downewards. We stayed untill next day at Noone but he came not, and then we journyed unto the Towne belonging unto Oyeocker, who kindly invited us thither, and told us he thought that Chounterounte would meet us there, and also of his owne accord proffered us to be our guide withersoever we went. The Land generally to this Towne is Champion, very rich, and the Towne scituate in a rich levell, well timbered, watered, and very convenient for Hogs and Cattle.

*August* 28. We journied with our new entertained Guide Oyeocker, lying betweene South, and South and by West, from the first Towne upon a very rich levell of Land: sixteen miles from this place we came unto the River Penna Mount, being another branch of Chawan River eight miles on the South side it hath very rich Land and Corn-fields on both sides the River, and is about 200. paces wide, and runs out with elbowes: at the place of our passage over this River to this second Towne is shallow upon a Sandy Point, and with a very little labour may be made passeable both for foot and horse, or any Carriage by Land, or pentater with small Boats, and some two miles higher there is a sound passage no deeper then a mans anckle: Within night came Chounterounte unto our Quarters frowning, and with a countenance noting much discontent, downe he sets, and lookes about him, salutes the English with a scornefull posture, and then our Appamattack Guide, and tels him, I am sorry for thee friend, thou wilt be knockt on the head; after this some pause was made before any discourse, expecting the English would begin, but finding us slow, he thus spake: There was a Wainoake Indian told him that there was an Englishman a Cockarous [1] hard by Captaine Floods, gave this Indian Bells, and other petty truck to lay downe to the Tuskarood [2] King, and would

---

[1] Ind. *cawcawaassough*, adviser.            [2] Tuscarora.

have hired him to have gone with him, but the Wainoakes being doubtfull what to doe, went to Captaine Flood for advice, who advised them not to go, for that the Governour would give no licence to go thither; heere upon Chounterounte was by us questioned, when and who it was that had told him so, and if he did know that Wainoake Indian, to which he answered doubtfully, and demanded of us whither we did intend to go; we told him the Tuskarood King had envited us to trade, and our Governour had ordered us to go, and speake with an Englishman amongst them, and to enquire for an English woman cast away long since, and was amongst those Nations. Chounterounte perswaded us to go no further, alleadging there was no English there, that the way was long, for passage very bad by reason of much raine that had lately fallen, and many rotten Marrishes and Swampps there was to passe over, in fine we found him, and all his men very unwilling we should go any further; but we told them, that let the waies and passages be never so bad, we were resolved to go through, and that we were not afraid of him nor his Nation, nor any other, for we intended no injury, and that we must go, for we were commanded by our King; these words caused Chounterounte to assimulate a feare in his countenance, and after delivery of himselfe, at our going away next day, when we had mounted our Horses, Chounterounte came privately unto us, and in a most serious manner intimating unto us, that he loved us, and our Nation, and that he lively apprehended our danger, and that our safety concerned him, for if any accident hapned otherwise then good to us, he should be suspected to have a hand in it, and withall wished us to go no further, for that he certainly knew that the Nations we were to go through would make us away by treachery; we answered him, that we were not afraid to be killed, for that any one of us were able to deale with forty through the protection of our great God, for we were commanded by our King.

*August* 29. We travelled from this second Town to Maharineck,[1] eight miles upon barren Champion Lands, and six miles further is a branch that runnes South west,

[1] The town of the Meherrin Indians, an Iroquoian tribe living on Meherrin River.

with rich Lands upon it; and from thence some six miles
further, is a Brooke some hundred paces over, and runnes
South and a little to the West, on both sides of the Creek:
for fowre miles or thereabouts, is very rich Lands, well Timbered and Watered, and large dry Meadowes, South and by
West: From this Creeke is another, some eight miles off,
that opens it selfe into divers small Guts, made by the inun-
dation of Freshes of Waters; and the passage lies some two
hundred paces from the Path, and this Creek is some ten
miles from Maharinecke Towne, and was by us named New-
combs Forrest.   It was night when we entred into Maharineck, where we found a House ready made for us of Matts;
and Corne stalkes layd in severall places for our Horses, the
Inhabitants standing, according to their custome, to greet
us: and after some discourse with their Werrowance,[1] a Youth,
to whom wee presented severall gifts, we certified them the
cause of our comming was to Trade in way of friendship, and
desired the great men that what Wares or Skins the Town
did afford, might be brought to our Quarters next morning;
and also a measure for Roanoak,[2] which they promised should
be done, and so left us to our selves a while, untill wee had
refreshed our selves with such provisions as they had set
before us, in most plentifull maner;   and afterwards the
great men and Inhabitants came, and performed divers Ceremonies, and Dancings before us, as they used to doe to their
great Emperour Apachancano,[3] when they entertain him
in most solemne maner and friendship.

*August* 30.   Being wearied with our last dayes travell,
we continued at Maharineck, and this day spake with a
Tuskarood Indian, who told us that the Englishman was a
great way off at the further Tuskarood Towne, and wee
hired this Tuskarood Indian to run before, and tell his Werrowance wee intended to lay him downe a present at Hoco-
mowananck, and desired to have him meete us there, and also
wrote to that effect to the Englishman in English, Latine,
Spanish, French and Dutch, the Tuskarood promised in three
dayes to meete us at Hocomawananck.   In the afternoone
came two Indians to our Quarters, one of whom the Mahar-

---

[1] Chieftain.                                  [2] Wampum.
[3] Opechancanough, Powhatan's brother and successor.

inecks told us was the Werrowance of Hocomawnanck River, seemed very joyfull that wee could goe thither, and told us the Tuskarood would have come to us to trade, but that the Wainoakes had spoken much to dishearten them from having any trade with the English, and that they intended divers times to have come in, but were afraid, for the Wainoakes had told them that the English would kill them, or detaine them, and would not let them goe without a great heape of Roanoake middle high, to which we answered that the Wainoakes durst not affirme any such thing to our faces, and that they had likewise spoken much against the Tuskarood to the English, it being a common thing amongst them to villefie one another, and tell nothing but lies to the English.

This day in the morning the Maharineck great men spake to heare some of our guns go off: Whereupon we shot two guns at a small marke, both hitting it, and at so great a distance of a hundred paces, or more, that the Indians admired at it: And a little before night the old King Maharineck came to us, and told us, that the people in the Towne were afraid when the guns went off, and ran all away into the Woods. This night also we had much Dancing.

*August* 31. Wee went away from Maharineck South East two miles to goe over Maharineck River, which hath a bottome betweene two high land sides through which you must passe to get over, which River is about two hundred paces broad, and hath a high water marke after a fresh of at least twenty foot perpendicular by the trees in the breaches betweene the River, and the high land of the old fields. This River is the Southerly last and maine branch of Chawan River, and was by us named Woodford River,[1] and runs to the Eastward of the South. On both sides of Woodford River is very much exceeding rich Land, but especially on the further side towards Hocomawananck. Imediately after the passage over this River, are old Indian fields of exceeding rich Land, that beare two Crops of Indian Corne a yeare, and hath timber trees above five foot over, whose truncks are a hundred foot in cleare timber, which will make twenty Cuts of Board timber a piece, and of these there is abundance.

[1] Now called the Meherrin.

As also exceeding rich Land, full of great Reeds thrice as big as the largest Arrow Reeds we have about our Plantations; this good Land continues for some six miles together unto a great Swampp, and then begins a pyny barren Champion Land with divers Branches and Pecosans, yet very passeable, running South and by West unto a deepe River some a hundred paces over, running South, and a little to the East, which River incloses a small Island which wee named Brewsters Island, some eighteene miles from Woodford River due South, and by West, with very exceeding rich Land on both side of it for some sixe miles together, and this River we also named Brewsters River, it being the first branch of Hocomawananck River:[1] and a little lower downe as the River runs, is such another River as Chickahamine River (which is a mile broad.)

After we had passed over this River we travelled some twenty miles further upon a pyny barren Champion Land to Hocomawananck River, South, and by West: some twelve miles from Brewsters River we came unto a path running crosse some twenty yards on each side unto two remarkeable Trees; at this path our Appamattuck Guide made a stop, and cleared the Westerly end of the path with his foote, being demanded the meaning of it, he shewed an unwillingnesse to relate it, sighing very much: Whereupon we made a stop untill Oyeocker our other Guide came up, and then our Appamattuck Guide journied on; but Oyeocker at his comming up cleared the other end of the path, and prepared himselfe in a most serious manner to require our attentions, and told us that many yeares since their late great Emperour Appachancano came thither to make a War upon the Tuskarood, in revenge of three of his men killed, and one wounded, who escaped, and brought him word of the other three murthered by the Hocomawananck Indians for lucre of the Roanoake they brought with them to trade for Otter skins.  There accompanyed Appachancano severall petty Kings that were under him, amongst which there was one King of a Towne called Pawhatan, which had long time harboured a grudge against the King of Chawan, about a yong woman that the

[1] Roanoke River.  The explorers apparently went to its mouth and then returned.

King of Chawan had detayned of the King of Pawhatan: Now it hapned that the King of Chawan was invited by the King of Pawhatan to this place under pretence to present him with a Guift of some great vallew, and there they met accordingly, and the King of Pawhatan went to salute and embrace the King of Chawan, and stroaking of him after their usuall manner, he whipt a bow string about the King of Chawans neck, and strangled him; and how that in memoriall of this, the path is continued unto this day, and the friends of the Pawhatans when they passe that way, cleanse the Westerly end of the path, and the friends of the Chawans the other. And some two miles from this path we came unto an Indian Grave upon the East side of the path: Upon this Grave there lay a great heape of sticks covered with greene boughs, we demanded the reason of it, Oyeocker told us, that there lay a great man of the Chawans that dyed in the same quarrell, and in honour of his memory they continue greene boughs over his Grave to this day; and ever when they goe forth to Warre they relate his, and other valorous, loyall Acts, to their yong men, to annimate them to doe the like when occasion requires. Some foure miles from Hocomawananck is very rich Champian Land: It was night when we came to Hocomawananck River and the Indian that came with us from Woodford River, and belonged to Hocomawananck, would have had us quartered upon the side of a great Swampp that had the advantage of severall bottomes of the Swampp on both sides of us, but we removed to take our advantage for safety, and retreate, in case any accident should happen, which at that time promised nothing but danger, for our Guides began to be doubtfull, and told us, that the Hocomawananck Indians were very treacherous, and that they did not like the countenances, and shape well; this place we named Pyanchas Farke: about three houres after we had taken up our Quarters, some of the Inhabitants came, and brought us roasting ears, and Sturgeon, and the Hocomawananck Indian that came with us from Woodford River, came not unto us untill next day, but his Warrowance told us before wee came from Woodford, hee could not come untill that day at night. The next day morning after our comming to Hocomawananck the Inhabi-

tants seemed to prepare us a house: But we about eight of
the clock set forward to goe view the place where they killed
Sturgeon, which was some six miles from the place where we
quartered by Pyanchas Parke, where there is a River running
very deep South, exceeding deepe, and foure hundred paces
broad. The high water marke of this River between both
sides of the River perpendicular, from the top of the Banck to
the River, is forty five foot upon a fresh; this River was
by us named Blandina River: from Pyanchas Parke to the
place where they kill Sturgeon is six miles up the River running Northerly, and all exceeding rich Land: Both upwards
and downewards upon the River, at this place where they
kill Sturgeon are also the Falls, and at the foot of these Falls
also lies two Islands in a great Bay, the uppermost whereof
Mr. Blande named Charles Island, and the lowermost Captaine Wood named Berkeley Island: on the further side of
these Islands the Bay runs navigable by the two Islands sides:
Charles Island is three miles broad, and foure miles long,
and Berkeley Island almost as big, both in a manner impreg-
nable by nature, being fortified with high Clefts of Rocky
Stone, and hardly passeable, without a way cut through
them, and consists all of exceeding rich Land, and cleare
fields, wherein growes Canes of a foot about, and of one yeares
growth Canes that a reasonable hand can hardly span; and
the Indians told us they were very sweet, and that at some
time of the yeare they did suck them, and eate them, and
of those we brought some away with us. The Land over
against Charles Island we named Blands Discovery, and the
Land over against Berkeley Island we named Woods journy,
and at the lower end of Charles Island lies a Bay due South
from the said Island, so spatious that we could not see the
other side of it: this bay we called Pennants Bay and in
the River between Charles Island, and the maine Land lies
a Rocky Point in the River, which Point comes out of Charles
Island, and runs into the middle of the River: this Point
we named Brewsters Point, and at this Point only, and no
other is there any place passeable into Charles Island, and
this Brewsters Point runs not quite from Charles Island
to the maine Land, but when you come off the maine Land
to the Rivers side, you must wade about fifty paces to come

upon the Point, and if you misse the Point on either side, up or downe the River, you must swim, and the River runs very swift. Some three miles from the River side over against Charles Island is a place of severall great heapes of bones, and heere the Indian belonging to Blandina River that went along with us at the Fals, sat downe, and seemed to be much discontented, insomuch that he shed teares; we demanded why those bones were piled up so curiously? Oyeocker told us, that at this place Appachancano one morning with 400. men treacherously slew 240. of the Blandina River Indians in revenge of three great men slaine by them, and the place we named Golgotha; as we were going to Blandina river we spake to Oyeocker our Guide to lead us the way, and he would not; but asked our Appamattuck Guide why we did not get us gone, for the Inhabitants were jealous of us, and angry with us, and that the Runner we sent to the Tuskarood would not come at the day appointed, nor his King, but ran another way, and told the Indians that we came to cut them off; whereupon our Appamattuck Guide stepped forth, and frowning said, come along, we will go to see the Falls, and so led the way, and also told us that the Woodford Indians lied, and that Indian that came to us, which the Woodford Indian said was the King of Blandina River, was not the Werrowance of Blandina River; whereupon we resolved to return (having named the whole Continent New Brittaine) another way into our old path that led to Brewsters River, and shot off no guns because of making a commotion, adding to the Natives feares. At Blandina River we had some discourse with our Appamattuck Guide concerning that River, who told us that that branch of Blandina River ran a great way up into the Country; and that about three dayes journy further to the South-West, there was a far greater Branch so broad that a man could hardly see over it, and bended it selfe to the Northward above the head of James River unto the foot of the great Mountaines, on which River there lived many people upwards, being the Occonacheans and the Nessoneicks, and that where some of the Occonacheans lived, there is an Island within the River three dayes journy about, which is of a very rich and fertile soile, and that the upper end of the Island is fordable, not above knee deepe, of a stony bottome, running very swift, and the other side very deepe and navigable: Also we found many of the people of Blandina River to have beards, and both there, and at Woodford River we saw many very old men, and that the Climate according to our opinions was far more temperate then ours of Virginia, and the Inhabitants full of Children; they also told us that at the bottome of the River was great heapes of Salt; and we saw among them Copper, and were informed that they tip their pipes with silver, of which some have been brought into this Country, and 'tis very probable that there may be Gold, and other Mettals amongst the hils.

*September* 1. About noone from Woods Journey wee travelled some six miles North East, unto the old Path that leads to Brewsters River: within night we quartered on the other side of it, and kept good watch: this Path runnes from Woods Journey north and by East, and due North.

*September* 2. In the morning about eight of the clocke, as every one was mounted, came to our quarters Occonnosquay, sonne to the Tuskarood King, and another Indian whom he told was a Werrowance, and his Kinseman, with the Runner which wee had sent to the Tuskarood King, who was to meet us at Blandina that night; the Kings sonne told us that the English man would be at his house that night, a great way off; and would have had us gone backe with him, but we would not, and appointed him to meete us at Woodford River where hee came not, wee having some suspition that hee came from Woodford River that night, and that our Runner had not beene where we had sent him, through some information of our Nottaway guide, which afterwards proved true, by the Relation of the Werrowance of Blandina River, whom about fowre howres after wee had parted with the Kings son, wee met on the way comming from Woodford River with a company of men, thinking he should have found us at Blandina River that night, according to his order and promise; with whom falling into discourse, he told us that the King of the Tuskaroods son, and our Runner were the night before at Woodford River; but the Kings son told us he came from Blandina River, and beyond, and hearing wee were gone before he came, he had travelled all night from Blandina River to overtake us. This day about Noone we came to Woodford River Towne, and tarried there that night, we found the old Werrowance, and all his great men gone, yet had courteous quarter; but not without great grounds of suspition, and signes that they were angry at us: at our coming back to Woodford River we had information that some Spies of Wainoake had been there a little before we came, and that the King of Wainoake and Chounterounte had sent Runners to all the Nations thereabouts, informing them that the English were come to cut them off, which we supposed to be some greater Politicians then Indian Consultations, who had some private ends to themselves, and minded nothing lesse then a publick good; for we found that the Runner whom we imployed to carry our message to the Tuskarood King, ran to the Waynoakes, and he whom the Woodford Indians told us was the Werrowance of Blandina River, was a Woodford Indian, and no Werrowance, but done of purpose to get something out of us, and we had information that at that time there were other English amongst the Indians.

*September* 3. By breake of day we journied from Woodford River to a path some eight miles above Pennants Mount running North, and by East and North, North, East, which was done by the advice of our Appamattuck Guide, who told us that he was informed that some plots might be acted against us, if we returned the way that we came, for we told Chounterounte we would returne the same way againe: And this information our Guide told us he had from a woman that was his Sweet-heart belonging to Woodford River. This day we passed over very much rich, red, fat, marle Land, betweene Woodford River Towne, and the head of Pennants Mount, with divers Indian fields; the head of which River abounds much with great Rocks of Stone, and is two hundred paces over, and hath a small Island in it named Sackfords Island. Betweene Pennants Mount River head, and the head of Farmers Chase River is very much exceeding rich, red, fat, marle land, and Nottaway and Schockoores old fields, for a matter of sixe miles together all the trees are blowne up or dead: Heere it began to raine, and some six miles further we tooke up our quarters, and it proved a very wet night.   At the first other Nottaway old fields, we found the Inhabitants much perplexed about a gun that went off to the Westward of them, the night before wee came thither, which our Appamattuck Guide conceived were the Wainoake Spies, set out there to prevent our Journyings, and we found severall Agers about the place where the Indians told us the gun went off.

*Septemb.* 4.   About 8 of the Clock we travelled North North-East some six miles, unto the head of Farmers Chase River, where we were forced to swimm our horses over, by reason of the great rain that fell that night, which otherwise with a little labour may be made very passable.   At this place is very great Rocky stones, fit to make Mill-stones, with very rich tracts of Land, and in some places between the head of Farmers Chase River and Black water Lake, is ground that gives very probable proofe of an Iron, or some other rich Mine.   Some sixteen miles from Farmers Chase, North, and by East, and North, North-East, lies Black water Lake, which hath very much rich land about it, and with little labour will be made very passable.   From Black Water Lake we did travell to the old fields of Manks Nessoneicks, and from thence some 12 miles N. N. East we came unto Fort Henry about the close of the Evening, all well and in good health, notwithstanding from the time we had spoken with Chounterounte at Pennants Mount, we every night kept a strickt watch, having our Swords girt, and our Guns and Pistols by us, for the Indians every night where we lay, kept a strict guard upon us.

The Discoverers, *viz.*

Mr. Edward Blande, Merchant.
     Abraham Wood, Captaine.
Mr. Elias Pennant.
Mr. Sackford Brewster.
     Robert Farmer, Servant to Mr. Blande.
     Henry Newcombe, Servant to Captaine Wood.
Guides. { Oyeocker, a Nottaway Werrowance.
         { Pyancha, an Appamattuck War Captaine.

# FRANCIS YEARDLEY'S NARRATIVE OF
# EXCURSIONS INTO CAROLINA, 1654

# INTRODUCTION

BEGINNING with the second half of the seventeenth century, information about the province of Carolina, which Charles I. had founded in October, 1629, when he granted all of the territory between the 31st and 36th degrees of north latitude to Sir Robert Heath for a province to be known as Carolina, was acquired and distributed by voyagers and explorers with more frequency than had been the case in the preceding years. Following the appearance of Edward Bland's *Discovery of New Brittaine* in 1651, came a letter from Francis Yeardley, of Virginia, to John Ferrar, Esq., of Little Gidding in Huntingdonshire, England, who had been a prominent member, and for a time deputy treasurer, of the Virginia Company. The letter, dated May 8, 1654, gives a narrative of several excursions into that part of Carolina adjacent to Virginia by some of his employees and neighbors.

Francis Yeardley, the author of this narrative, was the son of Sir George Yeardley, who had been thrice (1616–1617, 1618–1621, and 1626–1627) governor of Virginia. He was born in Virginia about 1622, being one of three children, the other two being a brother, Argall, born about 1620, and a sister, Elizabeth, born about 1618.[1] Upon reaching manhood he became quite prominent in the affairs of Virginia, being for some time a colonel of militia and in 1653 a member of the House of Burgesses for Lower Norfolk.[2] About this time chance brought him into possession of the information contained in his letter, and his philanthropic nature induced

---

[1] J. C. Hotten, *Original Lists of Persons . . . who went from Great Britain to the American Plantations*, 1600–1700, p. 222.

[2] W. G. Stanard, *Virginia Colonial Register* (Boston, 1900), p. 70.

him to transmit it to Mr. Ferrar in the hope that it might be a means of advancing interest in the territory known as Carolina and at the same time bringing about a betterment of the Indians in that quarter. The letter was printed in 1742 in the *State Papers of John Thurloe*, II. 273-274.

# FRANCIS YEARDLEY'S NARRATIVE OF
# EXCURSIONS INTO CAROLINA, 1654

VIRGINIA, LINNE-HAVEN, this 8th May, 1654.

*Sir,*

MY brother Argol Yardley hath received many letters
from you, with animadversions and instructions to encourage
him in the prosecution of better designs than that of tobacco,
but myself never any: yet the honour I bear you, for your
fervent affections to this my native country, commands me
in some measure to give you an account of what the Lord
hath in short time brought to light, by the means of so weak
a minister as myself; namely, an ample discovery of South
Virginia or Carolina, the which we find a most fertile, gallant,
rich soil, flourishing in all the abundance of nature, especially
in the rich mulberry and vine, a serene air, and temperate
clime, and experimentally rich in precious minerals; and
lastly, I may say, parallel with any place for rich land, and
stately timber of all sorts; a place indeed unacquainted with
our Virginia's nipping frosts, no winter, or very little cold
to be found there. Thus much for the country; the manner
and means in the discovery follows: In September last, a
young man, a trader for beavers, being bound out to the
adjacent parts to trade, by accident his sloop left him; and
he, supposing she had been gone to Rhoanoke, hired a
small boat, and with one of his company left with him came
to crave my licence to go to look after his sloop, and sought
some relief of provisions of me; the which granting, he set
forth with three more in company, one being of my family,
the others were my neighbours. They entered in at Cara-
toke,[1] ten leagues to the southward of Cape Henry, and so
went to Rhoanoke island; where, or near thereabouts, they
found the great commander of those parts with his Indians a

---

[1] Currituck Inlet.

hunting, who received them civilly, and shewed them the ruins of Sir Walter Ralegh's fort, from whence I received a sure token of their being there.  After some days spent to and fro in the country, the young man the interpreter prevailed with the great man, and his war-captains, and a great man of another province, and some other Indians, to come in and make their peace with the English, which they willingly condescended [1] unto; and for the favour and relief I extended to the interpreter in his necessity, in gratitude he brought them to me at my house, where they abode a week, and shewed much civility of behaviour.  In the interim of which time, hearing and seeing the children read and write, of his own free voluntary motion he asked me, (after a most solid pause, we two being alone), whether I would take his only son, having but one, and teach him to do as our children, namely in his terms, to speak out of the book, and to make a writing; which motion I most heartily embraced; and with expressions of love, and many presents, crediting with cloaths, dismissed him.  At his departure he expressed himself desirous to serve that God the Englishmen served, and that his child might be so brought up; promising to bring him in to me in four moons, in which space my occasions calling me to Maryland, he came once himself, and sent twice to know, if I was returned, that he might bring his child; but in my absence, some people, supposing I had great gains by commerce with him, murmured, and carried themselves uncivilly towards them, forbidding their coming in any more; and by some over-busy justices of the place, (my wife having brought him to church in the congregation), after sermon, threatened to whip him, and send him away.  The great man was very much afraid, and much appalled; but my wife kept him in her hand by her side, and confidently and constantly on my behalf resisted their threatenings, till they publickly protested against me for bringing them in; but she worthily engaged my whole fortunes for any damage should arise by or from them, till my return; which falling out presently after, I having by the way taken my brother in with me for the better prosecution of so noble a design, immediately I dispatched away a boat with six hands, one being a carpenter, to

[1] In the sense of "agreed."

build the king an English house, my promise at his coming
first, being to comply in that matter. I sent 200 *l.* sterling
in trust, to purchase and pay for what land they should like,
the which in little time they effected, and purchased, and
paid for three great rivers, and also all such others as they
should like of southerly; and in solemn manner took possession of the country, in the name, and on the behalf, of the
commonwealth of England; and actual possession was solemnly
given them by the great commander, and all the great men of
the rest of the provinces, in delivering them a turf of the earth
with an arrow shot into it; and so the Indians totally left
the lands and rivers to us, retiring to a new habitation, where
our people built the great commander a fair house, the which
I am to furnish with English utensils and chattels. In the
interim, whilst the house was building for the great emperor of Rhoanoke, he undertook with some of his Indians,
to bring some of our men to the emperor of the Tuskarorawes,
and to that purpose sent embassadors before, and with two of
our company set forth and travelled within two days journey
of the place, where at a hunting quarter the Tuskarorawes
emperor, with 250 of his men, met our company, and received
them courteously; and after some days spent, desired them
to go to his chief town, where he told them was one Spaniard
residing, who had been seven years with them, a man very
rich, having about thirty in family, seven whereof are negroes;
and he had one more negro, leiger [1] with a great nation called
the Newxes. He is sometimes, they say, gone from thence a
pretty while. Our people had gone, but that the interpreter
with overtravelling himself fell sick; yet the Tuskarorawe
proffered him, if he would go, he would in three days journey
bring him to a great salt sea, and to places where they had
copper out of the ground, the art of refining which they have
perfectly; for our people saw much amongst them, and some
plates of a foot square. There was one Indian had two
beads of gold in his ears, big as rounceval peas; and they
said, there was much of that not far off. These allurements
had drawn them thither, but for the interpreter's weakness,
and the war, that was between a great nation called the
Cacores, a very little people in stature, not exceeding youths

[1] Resident.

of thirteen or fourteen years, but extremely valiant and fierce in fight, and above belief swift in retirement and flight, whereby they resist the puissance of this potent, rich, and numerous people. There is another great nation by these, called the Haynokes, who valiantly resist the Spaniards further northern attempts. The Tuskarorawe told them, the way to the sea was a plain road, much travelled for salt and copper; the salt is made by the sea itself, and some of it brought in to me. After the Tuskarorawe could not prevail, but our people would return, he sent his only son with a great man his tutor, and another great man, and some other attendance with them; and when they came to the rest of our company, the house being done and finished, the Rowanoke with the Tuskororawe prince, and sundry other kings of the provinces, in all some forty-five in company, together with our six men, on May-day last arrived at my house. The Rowanoke brought his wife with him, and his son, to be baptized. It fell out happily, that my brother and many other friends were met at my house. The only present brought us was the turf of earth with the arrow shot into it, which was again solemnly delivered unto me, and received by me, in the name, and on the behalf, of the commonwealth of England, to whom we really tender the sure possession of this rich and flourishing place; hoping only, that our own properties and our pains will not be forgotten. There is no man hath been at a penny charge but myself, and it hath already cost me 300 *l.* and upwards; and were my estate able, I should hope to give a better account of my well-wishes to a general good. My hopes are, I shall not want assistance from good patriots, either by their good words or purses. Tuesday the third of May, the Rowanoke presented his child to the minister before the congregation to be baptized, which was solemnly performed in presence of all the Indians, and the child left with me to be bred up a Christian, which God grant him grace to become! At their departure, we appointed a further discovery by sea and land, to begin the first of July next. God guide us to his glory, and England's and Virginia's honour!

Sir, if you think good to acquaint the states with what is done by two Virginians born, you will honour our country.

I have at this instant no present worthy your acceptance, but an arrow that came from the Indians inhabiting on the South-sea, the which we purpose, God willing, to see this summer, *non obstante periculo.* I am lastly, Sir, a suitor to you, for some silk-worms eggs, and materials for the making of silk, and what other good fruits, or roots, or plants, may be proper for such a country. Above all, my desire is to the olive, some trees of which could we procure, would rejoice me; for wine we cannot want with industry. Thus desiring to kiss your hands, with the fair hands of my virtuous country-woman, the worthily to be honoured Mrs. Virginia Farrar,[1] I humbly take leave, and ever remain, Sir,

Your true honourer, and affectionate

servant to be commanded,

Francis Yardley.

For the worshipfull John Farrar, Esq; at his mannor of Little Gidding in Huntingdonshire.

---

[1] Daughter of John Ferrar. "Mrs." was in the seventeenth century used of unmarried ladies. A map of Virginia by her is reproduced in Winsor's *Narrative and Critical History of America,* III. 465.

A RELATION OF A DISCOVERY, BY
WILLIAM HILTON, 1664

# INTRODUCTION

On March 20, 1662/3, King Charles by letters patent granted to eight Proprietors—the Earl of Clarendon, the Duke of Albemarle, Lord Craven, Lord Berkeley, Lord Ashley (afterward Earl of Shaftesbury), Sir George Carteret, Sir William Berkeley, and Sir John Colleton—a province to be called Carolina, extending from latitude 31° to 36° N. and from the Atlantic to the Pacific. In this province the Proprietors were to have the right to institute government, to appoint officers, and, with the assistance of the freemen, to make laws. By a new charter of June 30, 1665, the bounds of the province were extended to run from 29° to 36° 30′ N.

About the time when the first charter was granted, Captain William Hilton, of the island of Barbados, already a populous and important colony, made a voyage to the coast of what is now North Carolina and, upon his return, gave a favorable account of the country about the Charles (Cape Fear) River. Some New Englanders who had previously been sent to settle at Cape Fear to raise cattle departed about this time and made contrary reports as to the condition of the country. In consequence of these reports many citizens of Barbados united and sent out a second expedition under Captain Hilton, as commander and commissioner, Captain Anthony Long, and Peter Fabian, to explore the coast of Carolina southward from Cape Fear to latitude 31° north. The expedition sailed from Spikes (Speights) Bay August 10, 1663, in the ship *Adventure*. On August 12 the "Adventurers," as the promoters of the expedition were called, addressed to the Lords Proprietors a petition requesting that these Barbadian adventurers, some two hundred in number, might be permitted to purchase from the Indians and hold under the Proprietors a tract of a thousand square miles in Carolina, to be called the Corporation of the Barbados Adventurers, and that they might have certain powers of self-government.[1] Their agents, Thomas Modyford and Peter Colleton, suggested that these powers might be like those of a municipal corporation in England, e. g., Exeter.

To the petition of the adventurers the Proprietors answered on September 9, stating that they had "given directions to Col. Modyford and Peter Colleton, to treat with them concerning the premises, not receding from the substance of their declaration."[2]

In the meantime Hilton's expedition reached the coast of Carolina August 26, 1663, and explored the coast of what is now South Carolina from the Combahee River southward to Port Royal, sailing up the Combahee about six leagues and also entering the great harbor of Port Royal.

While in that quarter they rescued several Englishmen who had been shipwrecked near there some time previously, had reached land at that point, and had fallen into the hands of the Indians. The Spaniards at St. Augustine had heard of the peril these shipwrecked Englishmen were in and had sent a party to aid them, but Hilton arriving at a propitious moment they readily relinquished their undertaking to the Englishman.

Hilton next sailed to the coast of what is now North Carolina and explored the country in and about the Cape Fear River. He and his associates then returned to Barbados and wrote an account of their explorations. Shortly

[1] Colonial Entry Book no. 20 (MS.), Public Record Office, London, 10–11; Calendar of State Papers, Colonial, 1661–1668, p. 153; Colonial Records of North Carolina, I. 39–42; Collections of the South Carolina Historical Society, V. 10–11.

[2] Colonial Entry Book no. 20, 12–13; Calendar of State Papers, Colonial, 1661–1668, pp. 161–162; Collections of the South Carolina Historical Society, V. 16–18.

thereafter Modyford and Colleton, representing the Lords Proprietors, presented a set of proposals for the encouragement of settlers for the territory "Southwards or Westwards of Cape Romana in the Province of Carolina." The narrative of the explorers and the proposals of the agents of the Lords Proprietors were printed in London in 1664. The favorable account given by Hilton and his associates, and the liberal inducements offered to settlers by the agents of the Proprietors in their proposals, induced many settlers to go to South Carolina a few years later, and the early records of the province show that the terms of the proposals were faithfully kept toward those who settled in the territory prescribed during the time specified.

Under the terms of the proposals every subscriber to the expedition fund who had paid, or should pay within two months after the date of the proposals, and every subscriber to the public stock, was entitled to five hundred acres of land for every thousand pounds of sugar subscribed.

The adventurers elected treasurers for their fund, and a certificate from one of the treasurers acknowledging the receipt of a contribution was subsequently recognized as sufficient basis for the granting of the prescribed amount of land to the contributor presenting such certificate.

Hilton's expedition was of great assistance to the Lords Proprietors of Carolina in their work of settling their province. Not only did it interest the "adventurers" who sent it out, but the publication of the narrative concerning it and the accompanying proposals induced hundreds of excellent people to settle in Carolina, as is shown by the extant land records of South Carolina.

The pamphlet has been reprinted several times: in 1884 as an appendix to the *Year Book* of the city of Charleston; in 1897 in the fifth volume of *Collections of the South Carolina Historical Society*; and in 1907 in *The Genesis of South Caro-*

*lina*, by Hon. William A. Courtenay. The pamphlet of 1664 is described in Allibone's *Dictionary of American Authors* as "liber rarissimus."

Hilton's name has been preserved in the nomenclature of South Carolina by a promontory extending into Port Royal Sound at the mouth of the Port Royal River known as Hilton Head, and by an island from which this head juts out, known as Hilton Head Island.

# A RELATION OF A DISCOVERY, BY WILLIAM HILTON, 1664

*A Relation of a Discovery lately made on the Coast of Florida,
(From Lat. 31. to 33 Deg. 45 Min. North-Lat.)
By William Hilton Commander, and Commissioner with Capt.
Anthony Long, and Peter Fabian, in the Ship Adventure,
which set Sayl from Spikes Bay, Aug. 10. 1663. and was
set forth by several Gentlemen and Merchants of the Island
of Barbadoes.
Giving an account of the nature and temperature of the Soyl,
the manners and disposition of the Natives, and whatsoever
else is remarkable therein, together with Proposals made
by the Commissioners of the Lords Proprietors, to all such
persons as shall become the first Setlers on the Rivers, Harbors, and Creeks there.
London, Printed by J. C. for Simon Miller at the Star neer the
West-end of St. Pauls, 1664.*[1]

*A true Relation of a Voyage, upon discovery of part of the Coast
of Florida, from the Lat. of 31 Deg. to 33 Deg. 45 m. North
Lat. in the Ship Adventure, William Hilton Commander, and
Commissioner with Captain Anthony Long and Peter Fabian;
set forth by several Gentlemen and Merchants of the Island
of Barbadoes; sailed from Spikes Bay, Aug. 10. 1663.*[2]

AFTER Sixteen days of fair weather, and prosperous winds,
Wednesday the 26 instant, four of the clock in the Afternoon,
God be thanked, we espied Land on the Coast of Florida,
in the lat. of 32 deg. 30 min. being four Leagues or thereabouts to the Northwards of Saint Ellens,[3] having run five hun-

[1] Title-page of original.  [2] Heading of original, p. 1.
[3] The name by which the Spaniards then designated Port Royal. Port
Royal was the name given by Jean Ribault, the French explorer, when he reached
it on his voyage of exploration in 1562.

37

dred and fifty Leagues; and to the Westward of the Meridian of Barbadoes, three hundred thirty and one Leagues. This Evening and the Night following we lay off and on: Thursday the 27th instant, in the morning, we stood in with the Land, and coasted the Shoar to the Southward, Ankering at Nights, and sending our Boat out a Mornings, till we came into the lat. of 31 deg. but found no good harbour that way. On Sunday the 30th instant, we tacked, and stood Northward: and on Wednesday the second of September, we came to an Anchor in five fathoms at the mouth of a very large opening of three Leagues wide, or thereabouts, in the lat. of 32 deg. 30 min. and sent our Boat to sound the Channel. On Thursday the third, we entered the Harbour, and found that it was the River Jordan,[1] and was but four Leagues or thereabouts N. E. from Port Royal, which by the Spanyards is called St. Ellens:[2] within Land, both Rivers meet in one. We spent some time to sound the Chanels both without and within, and to search the Rivers in several branches, and to

---

[1] The harbor was doubtless St. Helena Sound and the river the Combahee. Professor William J. Rivers, one of the most accurate of our historians, says (*A Sketch of the History of South Carolina*, foot-note, pp. 16–17), "The reiterated statement in our authors, that the 'Jordan' is the Combahee, I am not prepared to adopt, after a close examination of the accounts of early voyages, old maps and charts, and a comparison of Indian names that have been handed down to us. If, however, we believe that Cutisi-chiqui was the old name of Silver Bluff, the Jordan could not have been far from the Savannah river." At the time Professor Rivers wrote (1856) Sandford's narrative was inaccessible to him, and he probably did not examine Hilton's, for their location of the Jordan certainly identifies it as the Combahee.

[2] Professor Rivers (*ibid.*, p. 15), speaking of the Spanish expedition from Hispaniola to the coast of what is now South Carolina in 1520, also says: "They entered a bay, a cape of which they named St. Helena, and a river in its vicinity they called the Jordan." The name St. Helena has been preserved in that vicinity to the present time, and St. Ellen's was probably another form of writing the same name. Formed by Port Royal River, Morgan River, and several creeks and inlets is St. Helena Island, a large and fertile island that has played no inconspicuous part in the history of South Carolina. In 1712 a parish (an ecclesiastical and legislative sub-division of the province of South Carolina) was laid off contiguous thereto and inclusive thereof and named St. Helena's Parish. By the constitution of 1865 the parishes were abolished as political sub-divisions of South Carolina and St. Helena's passed out of existence. A large sound extending from the mouth of the Coosaw to the mouth of the Combahee also bears the name St. Helena.

view the Land. On Saturday the fifth of September, two Indians came on Board us from the N. E. shoar, whom we entertained courteously, and afterwards set them on shoar. On Sunday the sixth, several Indians came on Board us, and said they were of St. Ellens; being very bold and familiar; speaking many Spanish words, as, *Cappitan, Commarado,* and *Adeus.*[1] They know the use of Guns, and are as little startled at the firing of a Peece of Ordnance, as he that hath been used to them many years: they told us the nearest Spanyards were at St. Augustins, and several of them had been there, which as they said was but ten days journey; and that the Spanyards used to come to them at Saint Ellens, sometimes in Canoa's within Land, at other times in small Vessels by Sea, which the Indians describe to have but two Masts. They invited us to come to St. Ellens with our Ship, which they told us we might do within Land. Munday the 14 September, our Long-Boat went with twelve hands within Land to St. Ellens. On Wednesday the 16th, came five Indians on board us; one of them pointing to another, said, he was the Grandy Captain of Edistow [2]: whereupon we took especial notice of him, and entertained him accordingly, giving him several Beads, and other trade that pleased him well: He invited us to bring up our Ship into a branch on the N. E. side, and told us of one Captain Francisco, and four more English that were in his custody on shoar; whereupon we shewed him store of all Trade, as Beads, Hoes, Hatchets and Bills, etc., and said, he should have all those things if he would bring the English on board us; w^ch he promised

---

[1] *Capitan, camarado, adios,*=captain, comrade, adieu.

[2] Edisto was the name applied by the Indians to the country adjacent to the lower part of the river that now bears that name. The Indian name for the river itself was Ponpon. The Edisto is formed by two branches, North Edisto and South Edisto, which have their sources in the sand hills of the middle section of South Carolina. These rivers unite about seventy-five miles above the sea. About fifteen or twenty miles from the sea the river forks again, the south fork being known as South Edisto and the north fork as Dawhoo River. Dawhoo unites with Wadmalaw River and forms the North Edisto. The island formed by these forks and the sea is known as Edisto Island, and is noted for producing the finest grade of long staple cotton known to the cotton trade. The main river for fifteen or twenty miles of its course through Colleton County is still called Ponpon. The North Edisto of the sea forks was called Grandy in Hilton's time.

should be done the next day. Hereupon we wrote a few lines to the said English, fearing it to be a Spanish delusion to entrap us. In the dark of the same Evening came a Canoa with nine or ten Indians in her with their Bowes and Arrowes, and were close on board before we did discern them: We haled them, but they made us no answer, which increased our jealousie: So we commanded them on board, and disarmed them, detaining two of them prisoners, and sending away the rest to fetch the English; which if they brought, they should have theirs again. At length they delivered us a Note written with a coal, which seemed the more to continue our jealousie, because in all this time we had no news of our long-boat from St. Ellens, which we feared was surprized by the Indians and Spanyards. But to satisfie us that there were English on shoar, they sent us one man on board about twelve of the clock in the Night who related to us the truth of the matter, and told us they were cast away some four or five leagues to the Northward of the place we then rode, on the 24th of July past, being thirteen persons that came on shoar, whereof three of them were kill'd by the Indians. On Thursday the 17th of September the Long-boat returned from St. Ellens, which presently we sent on shoar to fetch the other English, the Indians delivering us three more; and coming aboard themselves, we delivered them their two men. Then we demanded of the chief Commander where the rest of our English were: he answered, Five were carried to St. Ellens, three were killed by the Stonohs,[1] and the other man we should have within two dayes. We replyed to him again, That we would keep him and two more of his chief men,[2] till we had our English that were yet living; and promised them their liberty, with satisfaction for bringing us the English. Now to return to the businesse of our Design; the entertainment we had at S. Ellens put us in great fear of the Indians treachery; for we observed their continual gathering together,

---

[1] The name of the Stono tribe has also been preserved in the name of a river, which separates James Island and John's Island, two of the coastal islands near Charleston.

[2] These were Shadoo, Alush, and one who escaped. Hilton took the first two to Barbados with him, but they subsequently returned to their homes.

and at last began with stern-look'd countenances to speak roughly to us, and came to search our mens Bandileers [1] and pockets; yet inviting us to stay that night with them: but we made a sudden retreat to our Boat, which caused the Indian King to be in a great rage, speaking loud and angry to his men; the drift of which discourse we understood not. That which we noted there, was a fair house builded in the shape of a Dove-house, round, two hundred foot at least, compleatly covered with Palmeta-leaves, the wal-plate being twelve foot high, or thereabouts, and within lodging Rooms and forms; two pillars at the entrance of a high Seat above all the rest: Also another house like a Sentinel-house, floored ten foot high with planks, fastned with Spikes and Nayls, standing upon substantial Posts, with several other small houses round about. Also we saw many planks, to the quantity of three thousand foot or thereabouts, with other Timber squared, and a Cross before the great house. Likewise we saw the Ruines of an old Fort, compassing more than half an acre of land within the Trenches, which we supposed to be Charls's Fort, built, and so called by the French in 1562, etc. [2] On Monday, September 21. one English youth was brought from St. Ellens aboard us by an Indian, who informed us that there were four more of their company at St. Ellens, but he could not tell whether the Indians would let them come to us: For saith he, Our Men told me, that they had lately seen a Frier and two Spanyards more at St. Ellens, who told them they would send Soldiers suddenly to fetch them away. This day we sayled up the River with our Ship to go through to St. Ellens. On Tuesday the 22 instant, three Indians came on board; one of them we sent with a Letter to the English Prisoners there. On Wednesday the 23d, we sent out Boat and Men to sound the Chanel, and finde out the most

---

[1] A bandoleer was a broad belt or baldric slung over the shoulder.

[2] Charles Fort was located on the eastern side of an island between the Broad and Port Royal rivers which was subsequently named Parris Island in honor of Alexander Parris, for many years public treasurer of the province of South Carolina. Its ruins are still to be seen there at the point where Pilot's Creek enters Port Royal River. The ruins here described were probably the remains of some structure used by Spanish priests from St. Augustine who had been trying to convert the Indians in this quarter some years before.

likely way to St. Ellens with our Ship by Combeheh.[1] In the mean time came many Canoa's aboard us with Corn, Pumpions, and Venison, Deer-skins, and a sort of sweet-wood. One of our men looking into an Indian basket, found a piece of Spanish Rusk: it being new, we demanded of the Indian where he had it; who said, of the Spaniards. In the interim, while we were talking, came a Canoa with four Indians from St. Ellens, one standing up, and holding a paper in a cleft stick; they told us they had brought it from the Spanish Captain at St. Ellens. We demanded how many Spaniards were come thither; who said, Seven, and one English-man: We received their Letter writ in Spanish, but none of us could read it: We detained two of the chiefest Indians, one of them being the Kings Son of S. Ellens,[2] and that kept one of the English prisoners; the other two we sent away with a Letter to the Spaniard, wherein we gave him to understand, that we understood not his letter; and told the Indians, when they brought the English, they should have their men again, with satisfaction for their pains. On Thursday, 24 instant, we sayling further up the River to go through, at last came to a place of fresh water, and Anchored there, sending our Boat ashoar with a Guard to get water. Towards night came the first Indian that we sent to St. Ellens with a letter to the English, who brought us another letter from the Spaniards, and an Answer of ours from the English, writ in the Spaniards letter. The Spaniard sent us a quarter of Venison, and a quarter of Pork, with a Complement, That he was sorry he had no more for us at that time. We returned him thanks, and sent him a Jug of Brandy; and withal, that we were sorry we understood not his letter. This night about twelve of the Clock we had a most violent gust of winde, but of no long continuance. On Friday 25 September, we weighed, and returned down the River six leagues, or thereabouts, because we perceived the Indians had gathered themselves in a Body from all parts thereabouts, and moved as the Ship did: and being informed by an Indian that the Spaniards would be there the next day; we took in Fire-wood, and continued there

---

[1] Combahee (pronounced Cumbee) is the name by which the river called Jordan by the Spaniards is now known.

[2] Wommony. He was also taken to Barbados, but returned to his home.

that night, at which time one of our Indian Prisoners made
his escape by leaping over-board in the dark. On Saturday
the 26. we weighed, and stood down to the Harbours mouth,
and stayed there till Monday the 28. In all which time came
no one to us, though we stay'd in expectation of their coming
continually; therefore put out to Sea, concluding their intentions not to be good. Being out of the River Jordan, we
directed our course S. W. four leagues or thereabouts for
Port-Royal, to sound the Chanel without from the poynts
of the Harbour outwards; for we had sounded the Harbour
within from the points inward when our Boat was at St.
Ellens: And now being athwart the Harbours mouth, we sent
our Boat with the Mate and others, who found the N. E.
and E. N. E. side of the opening of Port-Royal to be Sholes
and Breakers to the middle of the opening; and three leagues
or thereabouts into the Sea, from the side aforesaid, is unsafe
to meddle with: but the S.W. and W. side we found all bold
steering in N. N. W. two or three miles from the S. W. shoar,
sayling directly with the S.W. head-land of the entrance of
Port-Royal: the said head-land is bluft, and seems steep, as
though the trees hung over the water: But you must note,
that if you keep so far from the S.W. side, that you stand in
N. N. W. with the bluft head aforesaid, you shall go over the
Outskirt of the E. N. E. sholing, and shall have but three or
four fathom for the space of one league or thereabouts, and
then you shall have six and seven fathoms all the way in:
But if you borrow more on the S.W. side, till you have brought
the S. W. head of the Entry to bear N. N. E. you shall have a
fair large Chanel of six, seven, and eight fathoms all the way
in, and then five, six, seven and eight fathoms within the
Harbour, keeping the Chanel, and standing over to the Northward: we supposed that it flows here as at the River Jordan,
because they are but four leagues asunder, and flows S. E.
and N.W. seven foot and half, and sometimes eight foot perpendicular: the Mouth of Port-Royal lyes in 32 deg. 20 min.
lat. Now as concerning the entrance of the River Jordan,
lat. 32 deg. 30 min. or thereabouts, you shall see a range of
Breakers right against the opening, two or three leagues off
the S. W. Point; which you must leave to the Northward,
and steer in with the said S. W. Point, giving a range of

Breakers that runs from the said Point a small birth, and you
shall have two, three, and four fathoms at low water; and
when you come one mile from the Point aforesaid, steer over
directly to the N. E. Point, and you shall have six or seven
fathom all the way.    Within the N.W. Point is good Anchor-
ing: you shall have five fathoms fair aboard the shoar: and
you shall have five, six, seven, and eight fathoms, sayling all
along upon the River, ten leagues, and a large turning Chanel:
It flows here S. E. and N. W. seven foot and a half, and eight
foot at common Tydes.    The River Grandy, or as the Indians
call it Edistow, lyes six leagues or thereabouts from the River
Jordan, and seems to be a very fair opening:  but because
the chief Indian of that Place was on board us, and the Countrey all in Arms, we not knowing how the winde might crosse
us, it was not thought fit to stay there:  But some of those
English that had lived there, being Prisoners, say, that it is
a very fair and goodly River, branching into several branches,
and deep, and is fresh water at low Tide within two leagues
of the Mouth; it seeming to us as we passed by, a good entrance
large and wide, lat. 32 deg. 40 min. in or thereabouts.    Now
our understanding of the Land of Port-Royal, River Jordan,
River Grandie, or Edistow, is as followeth:  The Lands are
laden with large tall Oaks, Walnut and Bayes, except facing
on the Sea, it is most Pines tall and good:  The Land generally, except where the Pines grow, is a good Soyl, covered
with black Mold, in some places a foot, in some places half a
foot, and in other places lesse, with Clay underneath mixed
with Sand;  and we think may produce any thing as well
as most part of the Indies that we have seen.    The Indians
plant in the worst Land, because they cannot cut down the
Timber in the best, and yet have plenty of Corn, Pumpions,
Water-Mellons, Musk-mellons:  although the Land be over-
grown with weeds through their lazinesse, yet they have two
or three crops of Corn a year, as the Indians themselves inform
us.    The Country abounds with Grapes, large Figs, and
Peaches;  the Woods with Deer, Conies, Turkeys, Quails,
Curlues, Plovers, Teile, Herons;  and as the Indians say, in
Winter, with Swans, Geese, Cranes, Duck and Mallard, and
innumerable of other water-Fowls, whose names we know
not, which lie in the Rivers, Marshes, and on the Sands:

Oysters in abundance, with great store of Muscles; A sort of fair Crabs, and a round Shel-fish called Horse-feet [1]; The Rivers stored plentifully with Fish that we saw play and leap. There are great Marshes, but most as far as we saw little worth, except for a Root that grows in them the Indians make good Bread of. The Land we suppose is healthful; for the English that were cast away on that Coast in July last, were there most part of that time of year that is sickly in Virginia; and notwithstanding hard usage, and lying on the ground naked, yet had their perfect healths all the time. The Natives are very healthful; we saw many very Aged amongst them. The Ayr is clear and sweet, the Countrey very pleasant and delightful: And we could wish, that all they that want a happy settlement, of our English Nation, were well transported thither, etc.

From Tuesday the 29th of September, to Friday the second of October, we ranged along the shoar from the lat. 32 deg. 20 min. to the lat. 33 deg. 11 min. but could discern no Entrance for our Ship, after we had passed to the North-wards of 32 deg. 40 min. On Saturday the third instant, a violent storm came up, the winde between the North and the East; which Easterly windes and fowl weather continued till Monday the 12th. By reason of which storms and fowl weather, we were forced to get off to Sea to secure our selves and ship, and were horsed by reason of a strong Current, almost to Cape Hatterasse in lat. 35 deg. 30 min. On Mon-day the 12th aforesaid we came to an Anchor in seven fathom at Cape Fair-Road, and took the Meridian-Altitude of the Sun, and were in the lat. 33 deg. 43 min. the winde con-tinuing still Easterly, and fowl weather till Thursday the 15th instant; and on Friday the 16th, the winde being at N. W. we weighed, and sailed up Cape Fair-River, some four or five leagues, and came to an Anchor in six or seven fathom; at which time several Indians came on Board, and brought us great store of Fresh-fish, large Mullets, young Bass, Shads, and several other sorts of very good well-tasted Fish. On Saturday the 17th, we went down to the Cape to see the English Cattle, but could not finde them, though we rounded

[1] Clams.

the Cape: And having an Indian Guide with us, here we rode till the 24th instant; the winde being against us, we could not go up the River with our Ship; in which time we went on shoar, and viewed the land of those quarters. On Saturday we weighed, and sayled up the River some four leagues or thereabouts. Sunday the 25th, we weighed again, and towed up the River, it being calm, and got up some fourteen leagues from the Harbours mouth, where we mored our Ship. On Monday the 26 October, we went down with the Yoal [1] to Necoes, an Indian Plantation, and viewed the Land there. On Tuesday the 27th, we rowed up the main River with our long-Boat and twelve men, some ten leagues or thereabouts. On Wednesday the 28th, we rowed up about eight or nine leagues more. Thursday the 29th was foul weather, of much rain and winde, which forced us to make Huts, and lye still. Friday the 30th, we proceeded up the main River, seven or eight leagues. Saturday the 31, we got up three or four leagues more, and came to a Tree that lay athwart the River: but because our Provisions were neer spent, we proceeded no further, but returned downward the remainder of that day; and on Monday the second of November, we came aboard our Ship. Tuesday the third, we lay still to refresh ourselves. On Wednesday the 4th, we went five or six leagues up the River to search a branch that ran out of the main River towards the N. W. In which branch we went up five or six leagues: not liking the Land, we returned on board that night about midnight, and called that place Swampy-branch. Thursday the fifth instant, we staid aboard; on Friday the 6th we went up Greens River, the mouth of it being against the place we rode with our Ship. On Saturday the 7th, we proceeded up the said River some fourteen or fifteen leagues in all, and found that it ended in several small branches; the Land for the most part being marshy and swamps, we returned towards our ship, and got aboard in the night: Sunday the 8th instant we lay still, and on Monday the 9th we went again up the main River, being well provided with Provisions and all things necessary, and proceeded upwards till Thursday noon 12th instant, at which time we came to a place where two Islands were in the middle

[1] Yawl.

of the River, and by reason of the crookednesse of the River
at that place, several Trees lay athwart both branches, which
stopped up the passage of each branch, that we could proceed
no further with our Boat; but we went up the River side by
land some three or four miles, and found the River to enlarge
it self: So we returned, leaving it as far as we could see up a
long reach running N. E. we judging our selves from the
Rivers mouth North near fifty leagues; we returned, viewing
the Land on both sides the River, and found as good tracts
of land, dry, well wooded, pleasant and delightful as we have
seen any where in the world, with great burthen of Grasse
on it, the land being very level, with steep banks on both
sides the River, and in some places very high, the woods
stor'd with abundance of Deer and Turkies every where; we
never going on shoar, but saw of each also Partridges great
store, Cranes abundance, Conies, which we saw in several
places; we heard several Wolves howling in the woods, and
saw where they had torn a Deer in pieces. Also in the River
we saw great store of Ducks, Teile, Widgeon, and in the
woods great flocks of Parrakeeto's;[1] the Timber that the woods
afford for the most part consisting of Oaks of four or five
sorts, all differing in leaves, but all bearing Akorns very good:
we measured many of the Oaks in several places, which we
found to be in bignesse some two, some three, and others
almost four fathoms; in height, before you come to boughs
or limbs, forty, fifty, sixty foot, and some more, and those
Oaks very common in the upper parts of both Rivers; Also
a very tall large Tree of great bignesse, which some do call
Cyprus, the right name we know not, growing in Swamps.
Likewise Walnut, Birch, Beech, Maple, Ash, Bay, Willough,
Alder and Holly; and in the lowermost parts innumerable
of Pines, tall and good for boards or masts, growing for the
most part in barren sandy ground, but in some places up
the River in good ground, being mixed amongst Oaks and
other Timber. We saw several Mulberry-trees, multitudes of
Grape-Vines, and some Grapes which we did eat of. We
found a very large and good tract of Land on the N. W. side
of the River, thin of Timber, except here and there a very
great Oak, and full of Grasse, commonly as high as a mans

---

[1] The Carolina paroquet, now almost extinct.

middle, and in many places to his shoulders, where we saw many Deer and Turkies; also one Deer with very large horns, and great in body, therefore called it Stag-Park: it being a very pleasant and delightful place, we travelled in it several miles, but saw no end thereof. So we returned to our Boat, and proceeded down the River, and came to another place some twenty five leagues from the Rivers mouth on the same side, where we found a place no lesse delightful than the former; and as far as we could judge, both Tracts came into one. This lower place we called Rocky-point, because we found many Rocks and Stones of several bignesse upon the Land, which is not common. We sent our Boat down the River before us; our selves travelling by Land many miles, were so much taken with the pleasantnesse of the Land, that travelling into the woods so far, we could not recover our Boat and company that night. On Sunday the morrow following we got to our Boat, and on Monday the 16th of November, we proceeded down to a place on the East-side of the River some twenty three leagues from the Harbours mouth, which we call'd Turkie-Quarters, because we killed several Turkies thereabouts. We viewed the Land there, and found some tracts of good Land, and high, facing upon the River about one mile inward, but backwards some two miles all Pine-land, but good pasture-ground: we returned to our Boat, and proceeded down some two or three leagues, where we had formerly viewed, and found it a tract of as good Land as any we have seen, with as good Timber on it. The banks of the River being high, therefore we called it High-Land Point. Having viewed that, we proceeded down the River, going on shoar in several places on both sides, it being generally large Marshes, and many of them dry, that they may more fitly be called Medows: the wood-land against them is for the most part Pine, and in some places as barren as ever we saw Land, but in other places good Pasture-ground: And on Tuesday the 17th instant, we got aboard our Ship, riding against the mouth of Green's River, where our men are providing wood, and fitting the Ship for the Sea: In the interim, we took some view of the Land on both sides of the River there, finding some good Land, but more bad, and the best not comparable to that above. Friday the 20th instant was foul

weather, yet in the Afternoon we weighed, and went down
the River some two leagues, and came to Anchor against the
mouth of Hilton's River, and took some view of the Land
there on both sides, which appeared to us much like unto
that at Green's River. Monday 23. we went with our Long-
boat well victualled and manned up Hilton's River; and when
we came three leagues or thereabouts up the said River, we
found this and Green's River to come into one, and so continued for four or five leagues, which causeth a great Island
betwixt them. We proceeded still up the River, till they parted
again, keeping up Hilton's River on the Lar-board side, and
followed the said River five or six leagues further, where we
found another large branch of Green's River to come into
Hilton's, which maketh another great Island. On the Starboard side going up, we proceeded stil up the River some
four leagues, and returned, taking a view of the Land on
both sides, and now judge our selves to be from our ship
some eighteen leagues W. and by W. One league below this
place came four Indians in a Canoa to us, and sold us several
baskets of Akorns, which we satisfied for, and so left them;
but one of them followed us on the shoar some two or three
miles, till he came on the top of a high bank, facing on the
River, we rowing underneath it, the said Indian shot an
Arrow at us, which missed one of our men very narrowly,
and stuck in the upper edge of the Boat, which broke in pieces,
leaving the head behind. Hereupon we presently made for
the shoar, and went all up the bank except four to guide
the Boat; we searched for the Indian, but could not finde
him: At last we heard some sing further in the Woods,
which we thought had been as a Chalenge to us to come and
fight them. We went towards them with all speed, but
before we came in sight of them, we heard two Guns go off
from our Boat, whereupon we retreated with all speed to
secure our Boat and Men: when we came to them, we found
all well, and demanded the reason of their firing the Guns:
they told us that an Indian came creeping on the Bank as
they thought to shoot at them, therefore shot at him a great
distance with Swan-shot, but thought they did him no hurt,
for they saw him run away. Presently after our return to
the Boat, while we were thus talking, came two Indians to

us with their Bows and Arrows, crying *Bonny, Bonny*: we took their Bows and Arrows from them, and gave them Beads, to their content. Then we led them by the hand to the Boat, and shewed them the Arrow-head sticking in her side, and related to them the businesse; which when they understood, both of them manifested much sorrow, and made us understand by signes, that they knew nothing of it: so we let them go, and marked a Tree on the top of the bank, calling the place Mount-Skerry. We looked up the River as far as we could discern, and saw that it widened it self, and came running directly down the Countrey: So we returned, and viewed the Land on both sides the River, finding the banks steep in some places, but very high in others. The banks sides are generally Clay, and as some of our company doth affirm, some Marle. The Land and Timber up this River is no way inferiour to the best in the other, which we call the main River: So far as we discovered, this seems as fair, if not fairer than the former, and we think runs further into the Countrey, because there is a strong Current comes down, and a great deal more drift-wood. But to return to the business of the Land and Timber: We saw several plats of Ground cleared by the Indians after their weak manner, compassed round with great Timber-Trees; which they are no ways able to fall, and so keep the Sun from their Corn-fields very much; yet nevertheless we saw as large Corn-stalks or bigger, than we have seen any where else: So we proceeded down the River, till we found the Canoa the Indian was in who shot at us. In the morning we went on shoar, and cut the same in pieces: the Indians perceiving us coming towards them, run away. We went to his Hut, and pulled it down, brake his pots, platters, and spoons, tore his Deer-skins and mats in pieces, and took away a basket of Akorns: So we proceeded down the River two leagues, or thereabouts, and came to another place of Indians, bought Akorns and some Corn of them, and went downwards two leagues more: at last we espied an Indian peeping over a high bank: we held up a Gun at him; and calling to him, said, *Skerry*: presently several Indians appeared to us, making great signes of friendship, saying, *Bonny, Bonny*, and running before us, endeavouring to perswade us to come on shoar; but we answered them with stern countenances, and said, *Skerry*, taking up our guns, and threatening to shoot at them; but they cryed still *Bonny, Bonny*: And when they saw they could not prevail, nor perswade us to come on shoar, two of them came off to us in a Canoa, one padling with a great Cane, the other with his hand; they came to us, and laid hold of our Boat, sweating and blowing, and told us it was *Bonny* on shoar, and at last perswaded us to go ashoar with them. As soon as we landed, several Indians, to the number of near forty lusty men, came to us, all in a great sweat, and told us *Bonny*: we shewed them the Arrow-head in the Boatsside, and a piece of the Canoa which we had cut in pieces: the chief man of them made a large Speech, and threw Beads into our Boat, which is a signe of great love and friendship; and made us to understand, when he heard of the Affront which we had received, it caused him to cry: and now he and his men were come to make peace with us, making signes to us that they would tye his Arms, and cut off his head that had done us that abuse; and for a further testimony of their love and good will towards us, they presented to us two very handsom proper young Indian women, the tallest that we have seen in this Countrey; which we supposed to be the Kings Daughters, or persons of some great account amongst them. These young women were ready to come into our Boat; one of them crouding in, was hardly perswaded to go out again. We presented to the King a Hatchet and several Beads, also Beads to the young women and to the chief men, and to the rest of the Indians, as far as our Beads would go: they promised us in four days to come on board our Ship, and so departed from us. When we left the place, which was presently, we called it Mount-Bonny, because we had there concluded a firm Peace. Proceeding down the River two or three leagues further, we came to a place where were nine or ten Canoa's all together; we went ashoar there, and found several Indians, but most of them were the same which had made Peace with us before: We made little stay there, but went directly down the River, and came to our Ship before day. Thursday the 26th of November, the winde being at South, we could not go down to the Rivers mouth: but on Friday the 27th, we weighed at the mouth of Hilton's River.

and got down one league towards the Harbours mouth. On Sunday the 29th, we got down to Crane-Island, which is four leagues or thereabouts above the Entrance of the Harbours mouth. Now on Tuesday the first of December, we made a purchase of the River and land of Cape-Fair, of Wattcoosa, and such other Indians as appeared to us to be the chief of those parts: they brought us store of Fresh-fish aboard, as Mullets, Shads, and other very good Fish: this River is all Fresh-water fit to drink. Some eight leagues within the mouth, the Tide runs up about thirty-five leagues,[1] but stops and riseth a great deal farther up; it flowes at the Harbours mouth S.E. and N. W. six foot at Neap-Tides, and eight foot at Spring-Tides: the Chanel on the Easter-side by the Cape-shoar is the best, and lyes close aboard the Cape-land, being three fathoms at High-water, in the shallowest place in the Chanel just at the Entrance; but as soon as you are past that place half a Cables length inward, you shall have six or seven fathoms, a fair turning Chanel into the River, and so continuing four or five leagues upwards; afterwards the Chanel is more difficult in some places six or seven fathoms, four or five, and in other places but nine or ten foot, especially where the River is broad. When the River comes to part, and grows narrow, there is all Chanel from side to side in most places; in some places you shall have five, six, or seven fathoms, but generally two or three, Sand and Oaze. We viewed the Cape-land, and judged it to be little worth, the Woods of it shrubby and low, the Land sandy and barren; in some places Grass and Rushes, and in other places nothing but clear sand: a place fitter to starve Cattel in our judgement, then to keep them alive; yet the Indians, as we understand, keep the English Cattle down there, and suffer them not to go off the said Cape, as we suppose, because the Countrey-Indians shall have no part with them, and as we think, are fallen out about them, who shall have the greatest share. They brought aboard our Ship very good and fat Beef several times, which they could afford very reasonable; also fat and very large Swine, good cheap penny-worths: but they may

[1] The punctuation should apparently be, "all fresh water fit to drink, some eight leagues within the mouth. The tide runs up about thirty-five leagues, but," etc. The author is still speaking of the Cape Fear River.

thank their friends of New-England, who brought their Hogs
to so fair a Market. Some of the Indians brought very good
Salt aboard us, and made signes, pointing to both sides of the
Rivers mouth, that there was great store thereabouts. We
saw up the River several good places for the setting up of
Corn or Saw-mills. In that time as our businesse called us
up and down the River and Branches, we kill'd of wild-fowl,
four Swans, ten Geese, twenty nine Cranes, ten Turkies, forty
Duck and Mallard, three dozen of Parrakeeto's, and six or
seven dozen of other small Fowls, as Curlues and Plovers, etc.

Whereas there was a Writing left in a Post at the Point
of Cape Fair River, by those New-England-men that left
Cattel with the Indians there, the Contents whereof tended
not only to the disparagement of the Land about the said
River, but also to the great discouragement of all those that
should hereafter come into those parts to settle: In Answer to
that scandalous writing, We whose names are under-written
do affirm, That we have seen facing on both sides of the
River, and branches of Cape-Fair aforesaid, as good Land,
and as well Timbered, as any we have seen in any other part
of the world, sufficient to accommodate thousands of our
English Nation, lying commodiously by the said River.

On Friday the 4th of December, the winde being fair, we
put out to Sea, bound for Barbadoes; and on the 6th day
of January, 166¾, we came to Anchor in Carlisle-Bay;[1] and
after several known apparent dangers both by Sea and Land,
have now brought us all in safety to our long-wish'd-for and
much desired Port, to render an Accompt of our Discovery,
the verity of which we aver.

ANTHONY LONG.<br>
WILLIAM HILTON.<br>
PETER FABIAN.

### A Copy of the Spanyard's first Letter.

I am come to this Town of Infidel-Indians, to seek some
English, which my Governour and Captain-General, Don

---

[1] The chief roadstead of Barbados.

Alonso de Arangows, de Colis,[1] Cavallier, and Knight of the Order of St. James, for his Majesty, had notice that there was a Ship lost in that Port in which you are, that the men might not run any hazard of their lives, as those with me here have. Don Adeleyers, with the Governor of the Garison of S. Augustine, are gone to ransome and free the Subjects of the King your Master, Charles the Second: Wherefore I advise you, that if these Indians (although Infidels and Barbarians) have not killed any of the Christians, and do require as a gift or courtesie for those four men, four Spades, and four Axes, some Knives, and some Beads, and the four Indians which you have there, you deliver them, and that for their sakes that shall sayl on this Coast: you may send a Boat, who when she comes athwart the Port of St. Ellens, may hoist an Ancient [2] twice or thrice, and I will do the same. The shortnesse of the dispatch I desire, for I want provision for my Soldiers, and the way is large. Your Servant desires you would give me a speedy Answer; and what may be done in your service, I shall do very willingly: And if you have none that can interpret the Spanish Tongue, you may write in your own, for here are your Countrey-men that can understand it: but if you can, let it be in Spanish.

From the Capt. ALANSO ARGUELES.[3]

From St. Ellens the 22 of Sep-
    temb. 1663.


*The Copies of our Letters sent to the English and Spaniards at St. Ellens, with the Answer of Mr. William Davis, and the Spaniards also, here inclosed.*

*Loving Friends and Country-men,*
    Wee are come up the River with our Ship, and are resolved to come through by Combiheh, to St. Ellens, and to get you away by fair means, or otherways. If that will not do, we have five of your company already: and the Captain of Edistow, and one more are Prisoners with us, whom we intend to keep till we have rescued all the English Prisoners out of

---

[1] Don Alonso Aranjuez y Cotes, governor of Florida.
[2] Ensign.        [3] Alonso de Arguelles.

the hands of the Indians. Send us word by this Bearer what you know concerning the Spanyards; for the youth Morgan tells us that the Spanyards are come with Soldiers to fetch you away. Fail not to inform us how things are. Nothing else at present, but remain

Your friend and Servant<br>
WILL. HILTON.

From on Board the *Adventure,*
    Septemb. 21. 1663.


*An Answer to the Spanyards Letter not understood.*

*Honoured Sir,*

Whereas wee received a Letter from you, the Contents whereof we understand not, because none of us could read Spanish: Our businesse is to demand and receive the English Prisoners from the hands of the Indians, and then they shall have their Indians which we have detained on Board, with satisfaction for their pains. We understand not at present that we have any businesse with you. Not else at present, but remain

Your Friend and Servant in what I may,<br>
WILL. HILTON.

From on Board the *Adventure,*
    Septemb. 23. 1663.
To his honoured Friend the Spanish
   Captain at St. Ellens.


*An Answer to Mr. William Davis his Lines written to us in
the Spanyard's Letter, Viz.*

*Mr. William Davis,*

Wee received your Lines in the Spanish Letter, but hear nothing of your coming to us. Let your Keepers send you, and that without delay; for you may assure them, That we will be gone, and carry the Indians away with us, except they send the English suddenly on Board, and then they shall have their Indians upon our receipt of the English. Not else at present, but thank the Spanish Captain for the Pork and Venison he sent us. Remain

Your loving Friend
WILL. HILTON.

From on Board the *Adventure,*
September 24. 1663.
To Mr. William Davis at St. Ellens.

*Sir,*
Wee have received your second Letter, and give you no Answer, for the Reason mentioned in our former Letter to you. Please to inform the Indians, That if they bring not the English Prisoners on Board us without further delay, we are resolved to carry their Indians we have on Board away: But if they will bring the English, they shall have theirs, with satisfaction. Also we thank you for your Venison and Pork. Not else at present, but remain

Sir,
Your Friend and Servant in what I may
WILL. HILTON.

From on Board the *Adventure,*
Septemb. 24. 1663.
To his Honoured Friend, the Spanish
Captain at St. Ellens.

## A Copy of the Spanyard's second Letter.

My Governour and Capt. General, as soon as he had News that a Ship, by Nation English, was lost in that Port in which you now are, sent me with Soldiers of the Garison of St. Augustine in Florida, as they have at other times done, to free them from death; for which cause I came to this Port of St. Ellens, where I found all these Indians in a fright, fearing that you will do them some mischief: So having found four men of those that were lost, I thought good to advise you, that you might carry them in your company, giving some gifts to those Indians which they desire; which is, four Spades, four Axes, some Knives, and some Beads. This they desire, not as payment, but onely as an acknowledgment of a kindness for having saved their lives; which they have always done as Naturals who have given their obedience to the King our Master. And they do also desire you to let go those four Indians which are there: You may send a Boat when you discover the Points of St. Ellens; may hoist an Ancient two or three times, and I will do the same. I desire your Answer may be sodain; for I am scarce of Provisions, and the way is somewhat long: and if you have no body who understands Spanish, you may write in English, for here are your Countreymen who will interpret it.

By the Captain ALANSO ARGUILES.
From St. Ellens, Septemb.
    23. 1663.

*Proposals made to all such Persons as shall undertake to become the first Setlers on Rivers, Harbours, or Creeks, whose Mouth or Entrance is Southwards or Westwards of Cape St. Romana in the Province of Carolina, and execute the same at their own hazard and charge of Transportation, Ammunition, and Provisions, as is hereafter expressed, etc.*

## I.

*Imprimis,* It is agreed and consented to by us Thomas Mudyford, and Peter Colleton, Esquires, who are impowered by the Lords Proprietors to treat in their behalf; That in consideration of the good service which Captain Anthony Long, Captain William Hilton, and Mr. Peter Fabian have done in making so clear a Discovery on that Coast, They shall each of them enjoy to them and their Heirs for ever one thousand Acres of Land apiece upon the said River, Harbour, or Creeks, on such places as they shall desire, not taken up before.

## II.

*Item,* To Master Pyam Blowers, and Master John Hancock, five hundred Acres apiece, in manner as aforesaid.

## III.

*Item,* To all the Sea-men and Adventurers in the said Ship, one hundred Acres apiece in manner as aforesaid.

## IV.

*Item*, To every person that hath subscribed and paid, or hath subscribed and shall pay within two moneths next after the Date hereof, unto the Treasurer appointed by the Committee for defraying the Charge of the late Discovery,[1] and towards the publique Stock, five hundred Acres of Land, besides what they are otherwayes to receive and enjoy each for every thousand pounds of Sugar, and so for greater or lesser quantity proportionably, to possesse and enjoy the same in manner as aforesaid; the said Adventurers having promised, That the severall and respective Persons above-intended, shall within five years next ensuing, have one Person white or black, young or old, transported at their Charge as aforesaid, on that or some other parcel of Land in the Province, for every hundred of Acres of Land that is or shall be due to them for their adventures as aforesaid: But when once taken up, to settle the same within one year after it is once taken up, or lose the Land.

## V.

*Item*, To every Person that goes, or sends an Agent at his or their own cost with the first Ship or Fleet, or within six weeks next after the first Ship or Fleet that shall be set out from this Island (none to be accompted as first Setlers but such as do send in the first Fleet) Armed with a good Firelock, ten pounds of Powder, and twenty pounds of Bullet, or Lead, and Victualled for six moneths, shall have one hundred Acres of Land, and the like quantity of Acres for every Manservant that he carrieth so armed and provided, to the person at whose charge they shall be transported as aforesaid.

---

[1] Between April 16, 1672, and December 11, 1679 (see *Warrants for Lands in South Carolina*, 1672–1679, Columbia, S. C., 1910), warrants for five hundred acres of land each were issued to the following persons for their "disbursm^ts. on the discovery of this Province by Cap^t: Hilton": John Godfrey and George Thompson, May 11, 1672; Thomas Clutterbuck, of Barbados, June 8, 1672; Thomas Norvill and Bartholomew Reese, September 30, 1672. John Godfrey also received a warrant, September 5, 1674, for two hundred acres of land for coming himself and bringing one servant under the terms of the fifth proposal. The early land records of South Carolina show many people settled under the terms of the other proposals.

## VI.

*Item,* To every person that shall second the first Under-takers, that is to say, shall go within two months next after those that are accompted as first Setlers, armed and provided as aforesaid, seventy Acres of Land, and seventy Acres for every Man-servant that he or they shall carry or send Armed and provided as aforesaid.

## VII.

*Item,* To every person provided as aforesaid, that shall go within two years after the first undertakers, fifty Acres of Land, and as much to him or them for every Man-servant he or they shall carry or send, armed and provided as aforesaid.

## VIII.

*Item,* To every Free-woman above the age of twelve years, that shall go, or be carried thither within the first five years, forty Acres of Land.

## IX.

*Item,* To all Male-Children above the age of fourteen years, the same quantity that is allowed to Free-men, and on the same Conditions.

## X.

*Item,* The Lords Proprietors will grant unto every Parish one hundred Acres of Land for the Church and other publique uses.

## XI.

*Item,* To every person that hath subscribed, and shall pay to the above-mentioned Discovery, who shall go or send an Agent within the first five years next after the first Setlers, forty Acres of Land; and as much to them for every Man-servant they shall carry or send within that time armed and provided as aforesaid, and the like quantity for all others so transporting themselves or servants within the first three years, who are not Subscribers.

## XII.

*Item,* To every Man-servant that shall go with the first Undertakers, fifty Acres of Land; and to such as go with the second Adventurers thirty Acres, and for all other servants that shall go within the first five years, twenty Acres, and for every Woman-servant ten Acres, to become due at the Expiration of the first Term of their servitude in that Countrey.

## XIII.

*Item,* To the Owner of every Negro-Man or Slave, brought thither to settle within the first year, twenty acres; and for every Woman-Negro or Slave, ten acres of Land; and all Men-Negro's, or slaves after that time, and within the first five years, ten acres, and for every Woman-Negro or slave, five acres.

## XIV.

*Item,* That all the before-mentioned parcels of Land given, or to be given, allotted or granted to any person or persons whatsoever, shall be held and enjoyed to them, their Heirs and Assigns for ever, in free and common Soccage, according to the Tenure of East-Greenwich within the County of Kent, within the Kingdom of England (and not *in Capite,* or by Knights-service) paying as a fine once for all to the Lords Proprietors, or their Agents impowered to receive the same, one half-peny per acre for every Acre of Land that is or shall be taken up as aforesaid, or the value of the said half-peny per Acre, when the person who is to receive it shall receive his Deed or Copy of Record for his Land so taken up; and in lieu of all, and all manner of Rents, Services, Fines, Taxes and Impositions whatsoever, one ear of Indian Corn for every hundred acres of Land so taken up, at a certain time and place prescribed, if lawfully demanded.

## XV.

*Item,* It is further agreed, That every person shall or may take up their Land, or any part thereof, where they please, in any place not before taken up: Provided they do therein submit to such Method as the Governor and Council for the time being shall judge most safe and convenient.[1]

## XVI.

*Item*, That the Lords Proprietors shall grant to the Free-Holders the Priviledge of choosing an annual Assembly, wherein by the consent of the said Lords, or their Delegates, they shall be impowered to make Lawes, and them confirm, publish, and abrogate, as in the great Charter is expressed; and that the Assembly may lawfully, without the consent of the Governour, complain to the said Lords of such Grievances as lye upon the People.

## XVII.

*Item*, That forasmuch as the Lords Proprietors or their Delegates may not be at all times there present, to consent to such Lawes as are or shall be thought necessary; In such Case all Lawes and Orders made by the Governour, Council and Assembly, shall be in force untill the Denyal thereof by the Lords Proprietors shall be to them signified under their Hands in Writing.

## XVIII.

*Item*, That the said Free-Holders shall have the freedome of Trade, Immunity of Customes, and Liberty of Conscience, and all other Priviledges made good unto them as amply and as fully as is at large expressed in the great Charter granted to the said Lords Proprietors from His Majesty.

[1] The governor and council of South Carolina for many years directed the surveyor general, in their warrant for a tract of land, not to lay it off "within the compass of any lands heretofore layd out or marked to be layd out for any other person or Towne nor prejudiciall to any such lines or bounds and if the same happen upon any navigable River or any River capable of being made navigable" to "allow only the fifth part of the depth thereof by the waterside."

A BRIEF DESCRIPTION OF THE PROVINCE OF
CAROLINA, BY ROBERT HORNE (?), 1666

# INTRODUCTION

THIS brief description of Carolina was first published in London in 1666 and was one of several pamphlets published with the view of increasing the value of the Lords Proprietors' real estate. It was printed for Robert Horne, but it is uncertain whether he wrote it or not. While it described the settlements in North Carolina it described the climate, soil and other natural conditions of the entire province so favorably that it materially aided the Proprietors in securing settlers for the lower part of the province as well as for the upper part. It was reprinted in *Historical Collections of South Carolina*, by B. R. Carroll (New York, 1836). The original pamphlet contained a crude and incorrect map of Carolina which Carroll did not reproduce in his reprint, but which is in a manner reproduced in Hawks's *History of North Carolina*, Vol. II.

# A BRIEF DESCRIPTION OF THE PROVINCE OF CAROLINA, BY ROBERT HORNE ( ?), 1666

*A Brief Description of the Province of Carolina, on the Coasts of Floreda, and more perticularly of a New Plantation begun by the English at Cape Feare, on that River now by them called Charles-River, the 29th of May, 1664.*
*Wherein is set forth the Healthfulness of the Air; the Fertility of the Earth, and Waters; and the great Pleasure and Profit will accrue to those that shall go thither to enjoy the same. Also, Directions and advice to such as shall go thither whether on their own accompts or to serve under another. Together with a most accurate Map of the whole Province.*
*London, Printed for Robert Horne in the first Court of Gresham-Colledge neer Bishopsgate-street. 1666.*[1]

### A Brief Description of the Province of Carolina, Etc.

CAROLINA is a fair and spacious Province on the Continent of America: so called in honour of His Sacred Majesty that now is, Charles the Second,[2] whom God preserve; and His Majesty hath been pleas'd to grant the same to certain Honourable Persons, who in order to the speedy planting of the same, have granted divers privileges and advantages to such as shall transport themselves and Servants in convenient time; This Province lying so neer Virginia, and yet more Southward, enjoys the fertility and advantages thereof; and yet is so far distant, as to be freed from the inconstancy of the Weather, which is a great cause of the unhealthfulness thereof; also, being in the latitude of the Barmoodoes[3] may expect the like healthfulness which it hath hitherto enjoy'd, and doubtless there is no Plantation that ever the English went upon, in all respects so good as this: for though

---

[1] Title-page of original.   [2] See *post*, p. 140, note.   [3] Bermudas.

Barmoodoes be wonderful healthy and fruitful, yet is it but a Prison to the Inhabitants, who are much streightned for want of room, and therefore many of them are come to Carolina, and more intend to follow.[1] There is seated in this Province two Colonies already, one on the River Roanoak (now called Albemarle River) and borders on Virginia; the Other at Cape Feare, two Degrees more Southerly; of which follows a more perticular Description.

This Province of Carolina is situate on the main Continent of America, between the degrees of 30. and 36. and hath on the North, the South part of Virginia; on the South is bounded by the 30 degree of Latitude not yet fully discovered; on the East is Mare Atlanticum, part of the great Ocean; and on the West the wealthy South Sea is its Confines.

### The perticular Description of Cape Feare.

In the midst of this fertile Province, in the Latitude of 34 degrees, there is a Colony of English seated, who Landed there the 29 of May, *Anno* 1664. and are in all about 800 persons, who have overcome all the difficulties that attend the first attempts, and have cleered the way for those that come after, who will find good houses to be in whilst their own are in building; good forts to secure them from their enemies; and many things brought from other parts there, increasing to their no small advantage. The entrance into the River, now called Cape-Feare River, the situation of the Cape, and trending of the Land, is plainly laid down to the eye in the Map annexed. The River is barred at the entrance, but there is a Channel close abord the Cape that will convey in safety a ship of 300 Tons, and as soon as a ship is over the Bar, the River is 5 or 6 fathom deep for a 100 miles from the Sea; this Bar is a great security to the Colony

---

[1] The same reason for desiring the opening up of Carolina to settlers was given by the Barbadian "adventurers" when they sent out the second Hilton expedition. Believing that Barbados was overcrowded, they not only wanted Carolina opened up to settlers, but believed that settlers of Carolina could there produce "wine, oil, currants, raisind, silks, etc., the planting of which will not injure other Plantations, which may very well happen if there were a very great increase of sugar works or more tobacco, ginger, cotton, and indigo made than the world will vent." *Calendar of State Papers, Colonial,* 1661–1668, p. 157.

against a forreign Invasion, the channel being hard to find by those that have not experience of it, and yet safe enough to those that know it.

## The Earth, Water, and Air.

The Land is of divers sorts as in all Countryes of the world, that which lyes neer the Sea, is sandy and barren, but beareth many tall Trees, which make good timber for several uses; and this sandy gound is by experienced men thought to be one cause of the healthfulness of the place: but up the River about 20 or 30 mile, where they have made a Town, called Charles-Town,[1] there is plenty of as rich ground as any in the world. It is a blackish mold upon a red sand, and under that a clay, but in some places is rich ground of a grayer colour, they have made Brick of the Clay, which proves very good; and Lime they have also for building. The whole Country consists of stately Woods, Groves, Marshes and Meadows; it abounds with variety of as brave Okes as Eye can behold, great Bodies tall and streight from 60 to 80 foot, before there be any Boughs, which with the little under-wood makes the Woods very commodious to travel in, either on Horseback or a foot. In the barren sandy ground grow most stately Pines, white and red Cedars, Ash, Birch, Holly, Chesnut and Walnut-trees of great growth and very plentiful: There are many sorts of fruit Trees, as Vines, Medlars, Peach, Wild Cherries, Mulbury-Trees, and the Silk-worm breeding naturally on them, with many other Trees for Fruit and for Building, for Perfume and for Medicine, for which the English have no name; also several sorts of Dying Stuff, which may prove of great advantage; The Woods are stored with Deer and Wild Turkeys, of a great magnitude, weighing many times above 50l. a piece,[2] and of a more pleasant tast than in England, being in their proper climate; other sorts of Beasts in the Woods that are good for food; and also

[1] This short-lived Charles Town on Cape Fear River should not be confounded with the later and permanent Charles Town on Ashley River.

[2] There are many wild turkeys still left in parts of both North Carolina and South Carolina, but none that will approach in size the birds here described, and the oldest hunters in either state cannot recall ever having seen one of such size. A wild turkey of twenty-five pounds would now be considered unusually large.

Fowls, whose names are not known to them. This is what they found naturally upon the place; but they have brought with them most sorts of seeds and roots of the Barbadoes which thrive very well, and they have Potatoes, and the other Roots and Herbs of Barbadoes growing and thriving with them; as also from Virginia, Barmoodoes, and New-England, what they could afford: They have Indico, Tobacco very good, and Cotton-wool; Lime-trees, Orange, Lemon, and other Fruit-Trees they brought, thrive exceedingly: They have two Crops of Indian-Corn in one year, and great increase every Crop; Apples, Pears, and other English fruit, grow there out of the planted Kernels: The Marshes and Meadows are very large from 1500 to 3000 Acres, and upwards, and are excellent food for Cattle, and will bear any Grain being prepared; some Cattle both great and small, which live well all the Winter, and keep their fat without Fodder; Hogs find so much Mast and other Food in the Woods, that they want no other care than a Swine-herd to keep them from running wild.[1] The Meadows are very proper for Rice,[2] Rape-seed, Lin-seed, etc., and may many of them be made to overflow at pleasure with a small charge. Here are as brave Rivers as any in the World, stored with great abundance of Sturgeon, Salmon, Basse, Plaice, Trout, and Spanish Mackrill, with many other most pleasant sorts

[1] There are ranges in the Low-Country of South Carolina where the same conditions, both as to cattle and hogs, still exist.

[2] Several of the early promoters of the settlement of Carolina suggested or advised the cultivation of rice, and that their efforts were not in vain is attested by the fact that within a few years after the first settlements had been made in the province a considerable quantity of rice was being raised annually. By 1691 it had become such an industry in South Carolina that the General Assembly of the province, on September 20, passed an act securing patent rights in his invention to Peter Jacob Guerard, who had "lately invented and brought to perfection, a Pendulum Engine, which doth much better, and in lesse time and labour huske rice, than any other heretofore hath been used within this Province." The statement often found in works on South Carolina that Landgrave Thomas Smith, while governor of South Carolina (1693–1694), introduced the cultivation of rice into the province by obtaining a bag of seed from Madagascar and planting it in his garden and distributing the seed so raised is shown by this and many other records to be more or less fiction. The warrants for lands show that Landgrave Smith and his family arrived in South Carolina July 10, 1684, and at that time rice was already a commodity produced in the province.

of Fish, both flat and round, for which the English Tongue hath no name. Also, in the little Winter they have, abundance of Wild Geese, Ducks, Teals, Widgeons, and many other pleasant Fowl; and (as it is said before) the Rivers are very deep and navigable above 100 miles up; also there are wholsome Springs and Rivulets. Last of all, the Air comes to be considered, which is not the least considerable to the well being of a Plantation, for without a wholsom Air all other considerations avail nothing; and this is it which makes this Place so desireable, being seated in the most temperate Clime, where the neighbour-hood of the glorious Light of Heaven brings many advantages, and his convenient distance secures them from the Inconvenience of his scortching beams. The Summer is not too hot, and the Winter is very short and moderate, best agreeing with English Constitutions. Cape Feare lyes about 34 degrees from the Equator, the Nights nor Days are so long, when at longest as in England, by somewhat above two hours. A remarkable Instance of the Healthfulness of the Place, is, That at the first setting down of the Colony, when they had no house nor harbour, but wrought hard all day, in preparing Wood to build, and lay in the open Air all night, yet not one of them was ill, but continued well all the time; they Sympathize most with the Barmoodoes, which is the healthfullest spot in the World, and yet the last year they had a Feaver and Ague that troubled them much, which also was at Cape-Feare, but was not dangerous to any that took care of themselves, and had things convenient. This place had been aimed at many years since. Sir Walter Rawleigh had a design to have planted it. Those of the Barmoodoes, whose Habitations are too streight for them, have with longing desire waited for the discovery of this place that is neer their own Latitude, where they may expect the same healthfulness they do now enjoy, which is now perfected as to the first Settlement, and wants nothing but a diligent prosecution of so noble an Enterprize.

If therefore any industrious and ingenious persons shall be willing to pertake of the Felicites of this Country, let them imbrace the first opportunity, that they may obtain the greater advantages.

### The chief of the Privileges are as follows.

*First*, There is full and free Liberty of Conscience granted to all, so that no man is to be molested or called in question for matters of Religious Concern; but every one to be obedient to the Civil Government, worshipping God after their own way.

*Secondly*, There is freedom from Custom, for all Wine, Silk, Raisins, Currance, Oyl, Olives, and Almonds, that shall be raised in the Province for 7. years, after 4 Ton of any of those commodities shall be imported in one Bottom.

*Thirdly*, Every Free-man and Free-woman that transport themselves and Servants by the 25 of March next, being 1667. shall have for Himself, Wife, Children, and Men-servants, for each 100 Acres of Land for him and his Heirs for ever, and for every Woman-servant and Slave 50 Acres, paying at most $\frac{1}{2}d$. per acre, *per annum*, in lieu of all demands, to the Lords Proprietors: Provided always, That every Man be armed with a good Musquet full bore, 10*l*. Powder, and 20*l*. of Bullet, and six Months Provision for all, to serve them whilst they raise Provision in that Countrey.

*Fourthly*, Every Man-Servant at the expiration of their time, is to have of the Country a 100 Acres of Land to him and his heirs for ever, paying only $\frac{1}{2}d$. per Acre, *per annum*, and the Women 50. Acres of Land on the same conditions; their Masters also are to allow them two Suits of Apparrel and Tools such as he is best able to work with, according to the Custom of the Countrey.

*Fifthly*, They are to have a Governour and Council appointed from among themselves, to see the Laws of the Assembly put in due execution; but the Governour is to rule but 3 years, and then learn to obey; also he hath no power to lay any Tax, or make or abrogate any Law, without the Consent of the Colony in their Assembly.

*Sixthly*, They are to choose annually from among themselves, a certain Number of Men, according to their divisions, which constitute the General Assembly with the Governour and his Council, and have the sole power of Making Laws, and Laying Taxes for the common good when need shall require.

These are the chief and Fundamental privileges, but the Right Honourable Lords Proprietors have promised (and it is their Interest so to do) to be ready to grant what other Privileges may be found advantageous for the good, of the Colony.

Is there therefore any younger Brother who is born of Gentile blood, and whose Spirit is elevated above the common sort, and yet the hard usage of our Country hath not allowed suitable fortune; he will not surely be afraid to leave his Native Soil to advance his Fortunes equal to his Blood and Spirit, and so he will avoid those unlawful ways too many of our young Gentlemen take to maintain themselves according to their high education, having but small Estates; here, with a few Servants and a small Stock a great Estate may be raised, although his Birth have not entituled him to any of the Land of his Ancestors, yet his Industry may supply him so, as to make him the head of as famous a family.

Such as are here tormented with much care how to get worth to gain a Livelyhood, or that with their labour can hardly get a comfortable subsistance, shall do well to go to this place, where any man what-ever, that is but willing to take moderate pains, may be assured of a most comfortable subsistance, and be in a way to raise his fortunes far beyond what he could ever hope for in England. Let no man be troubled at the thoughts of being a Servant for 4 or 5 year, for I can assure you, that many men give mony with their children to serve 7 years,[1] to take more pains and fare nothing so well as the Servants in this Plantation will do. Then it is to be considered, that so soon as he is out of his time, he hath Land, and Tools, and Clothes given him, and is in a way of advancement. Therefore all Artificers, as Carpenters, Wheelrights, Joyners, Coopers, Bricklayers, Smiths, or diligent Husbandmen and Labourers, that are willing to advance their fortunes, and live in a most pleasant healthful and fruitful Country, where Artificers are of high esteem, and used with all Civility and Courtesie imaginable, may take notice, that

There is an opportunity offers now by the Virginia Fleet, from whence Cape Feare is but 3 or 4 days sail, and then a small Stock carried to Virginia will purchase provisions at a

---

[1] As apprentices.

far easier rate than to carry them from hence; also the freight of the said Provisions will be saved, and be more fresh, and there wanteth not conveyance from Virginia thither.

If any Maid or single Woman have a desire to go over, they will think themselves in the Golden Age, when Men paid a Dowry for their Wives; for if they be but Civil, and under 50 years of Age, some honest Man or other, will purchase them for their Wives.

Those that desire further advice, or Servants that would be entertained, let them repair to Mr. Matthew Wilkinson, Ironmonger, at the Sign of the Three Feathers, in Bishopsgate-Street, where they may be informed when the Ships will be ready, and what they must carry with them.

Thus much was convenient to be written at present, but a more ample Relation is intended to be published in due time.

A RELATION OF A VOYAGE ON THE COAST
OF THE PROVINCE OF CAROLINA, 1666,
BY ROBERT SANDFORD

# INTRODUCTION

FOLLOWING up their activity in behalf of Carolina in sending out an expedition to the coast of Carolina under Captain
William Hilton, in August, 1663, and in obtaining, soon
thereafter, liberal concessions for settlers from the Lords
Proprietors,[1] the Barbadian planters next took up, in that
same year, the project of establishing a settlement near Cape
Fear on the coast of what is now North Carolina. This undertaking they accomplished the next year. The settlement was
made on the Charles (Cape Fear) River in May, 1664, and
was called Charles Town.[2] Colonel John Yeamans, an influential planter of Barbados, and Lieutenant-Colonel Robert
Sandford, formerly of Surinam and later of Barbados, were
of great assistance to the Proprietors in this enterprise,[3] and,
when the settlement was organized by the Proprietors into a
government under the name of Clarendon County, they appointed Sandford secretary and register of Clarendon County,
November 14, 1664,[4] and on January 11, 1664/5, they appointed Colonel John Yeamans lieutenant-general and governor of Carolina.[5] On account of the previous activities of the
latter in behalf of Carolina Sir John Colleton had given the

---

[1] *Ante*, pp. 35, 57–61.

[2] *Calendar of State Papers, Colonial*, 1661–1668, pp. 154–155, 157, 160, 161–
162; *Collections of the South Carolina Historical Society*, V. 1, 13, 53; W. J.
Rivers, *A Sketch of the History of South Carolina*, pp. 335–337; *Colonial Records
of North Carolina*, I. 43–46.

[3] *Calendar of State Papers, Colonial*, 1661–1668, pp. 267, 379; *Collections
of the South Carolina Historical Society*, V. 56.

[4] *Calendar of State Papers, Colonial*, 1661–1668, p. 254; *Colonial Records of
North Carolina*, I. 71–72.

[5] *Colonial Records of North Carolina*, I. 95–97.

other Proprietors "a good character of his abilities and
loyalty . . . with an assurance that he will vigorously attempt
the settling of a Colony to the southward of Cape Romania,"
and the Proprietors induced the King "to confer the honor of
a Knight baronet upon him and his heirs," which was done
January 12, 1664/5.[1]

The Proprietors having instructed Governor Yeamans to
place a colony in that part of the province of Carolina southward and westward of Cape Romania, he organized an expedition in Barbados in 1665 to explore the lower coast of Carolina
to select a proper site.   His fleet, consisting of a fly boat of
150 tons, a small frigate and a sloop, sailed from Barbados in
October, 1665.   Early in November the fleet reached the
mouth of Charles (Cape Fear) River.   In attempting to enter
the river without a pilot, during a gale, the fly boat was
stranded and destroyed, all on board, of whom Sir John was
one, reaching the shore in safety, but the greater part of their
provisions and clothes and of the arms, powder, and other
military stores sent by the Proprietors for the defence of the
proposed settlement were lost.

Governor Yeamans found the settlers at Charles River in
such a needy condition that he sent the sloop to Virginia to
secure provisions for them, and himself returned to Barbados
in the frigate.   Before leaving he directed that should the
sloop miscarry in its voyage to Virginia the vessel of Captain
Edward Stanyarne, then in the harbor, but bound for Barbados, should be hired by Sandford for his use in making the

---

[1] Sir John Yeamans was the eldest son of John Yeamans (died in 1645), a
brewer, of Bristol, England; was born at Bristol and was baptized at St. Mary
Redcliffe, February 28, 1611.  He attained the rank of colonel in the Royalist
army.  About 1650 he settled in Barbados and engaged in planting.  The minutes
of the council of Barbados from July, 1660, to March, 1664, show that he was a
member of that body during that period.  *Dictionary of National Biography,*
biographies of Robert Yeamans and Sir John Yeamans; *The South Carolina
Historical and Genealogical Magazine,* XI. 107–122; *Calendar of State Papers,
Colonial,* 1574–1660, pp. 484, 494; 1661–1668, pp. 1, 46, 154, 169, 195.

explorations, in case Captain Stanyarne returned before the sloop. On its return voyage from Virginia the sloop was wrecked on Cape Lookout and two of its men were lost. While returning from Barbados Captain Stanyarne went deranged and jumped overboard and was drowned. His vessel, in charge of his survivors, reached Charles River in due season and Sandford assumed charge thereof and started out, June 14, 1666, to explore the lower coast, as he had been directed to do by Governor Yeamans. Nearly a month later, July 12, 1666, he returned to Charles River and landed at Charles Town. He at once addressed a letter to the Lords Proprietors, enclosing an account of his expedition. Accompanying his letter and narrative was a corroborative statement by the officers who accompanied him, dated July 14, 1666. These three documents were among the papers of the Lords Proprietors retained by the Earl of Shaftesbury (Lord Ashley), which passed from one of his successors to the next until the late Earl of Shaftesbury (the ninth earl, who died in 1886) deposited them in the British Public Record Office. They constitute "No. 7" of "Bundle 48" of "Section IX." of "Shaftesbury Papers." An abstract of these papers was published as section 1243 of the *Calendar of State Papers, Colonial*, 1661–1668 (by W. Noel Sainsbury, of the British Public Record Office), in 1880. Soon thereafter such of the "Shaftesbury Papers" as related to South Carolina were transcribed by Mr. Sainsbury for the city council of Charleston, at the instance of Hon. William A. Courtenay, the then mayor of Charleston. Mr. Courtenay used these transcripts in preparing his address for the centennial celebration in 1883 of the one-hundredth anniversary of the incorporation of Charleston, and subsequently printed some of them as appendices to the annual *Year Book* of Charleston. Sandford's narrative was published in the issue for 1885. Subsequently the city council (at the suggestion of Mr. Courtenay) presented the

transcripts of the Shaftesbury papers to the South Carolina
Historical Society and they were published in volume V. of
*Collections of the South Carolina Historical Society,* Sandford's
voyage covering pages 57–82 thereof. In 1907 it was reprinted in Mr. Courtenay's *The Genesis of South Carolina.*

Robert Sandford, the author of this narrative, was an
Englishman who, some years prior to August 17, 1662, along
with other Englishmen, settled on the river Surinam, where
they established a government "subject to the laws of England, elective in the people, who yearly were to appoint all
members thereof." One Byam, having been elected to the
head of this government three successive years, according to
the constitution, built up a strong party about him, and, over-
ruling the smaller faction, decreed the continuance in power
of his party, claiming as his authority for so doing, a proclamation by the King, which, however, he refused to show. Dissatisfaction with Byam for exacting a heavy imposition upon the
people and for calling the colony into arms, and a quarrel over
a Dutch shallop seized as a prize, precipitated a rebellion
against his authority. He seized all who had disputed his
authority and brought them to trial by court-martial. The
prisoners who pleaded not guilty, without being heard, were
hurried away in irons and then fined and exiled. Sandford
was one of those so fined and banished. He proceeded to
England, where his complaints, dated August 17, 1662, were
laid before His Majesty's Privy Council, September 12, 1662.[1]

Sandford next settled in Barbados, where he "gained a
very advantageous employment under Sir Jas. Drax." He
was a member of the Assembly of Barbados in 1663 when that
body became engaged in a quarrel with Lord Willoughby, the
governor of Barbados. With Speaker Farmer and two other
members he was seized under a warrant from the governor
and imprisoned for high treason. Finding no witnesses

[1] *Calendar of State Papers, Colonial,* 1661–1668, pp. 104, 108.

against them the Council ordered them discharged, but, through the contrivance of Willoughby, Farmer and Sandford were sent aboard the governor's ship and taken to England, where they laid their grievances before the King and Council.[1]

Sandford next attracted the attention of the Lords Proprietors of Carolina, who consulted him in regard to the settlement of their province. He and Henry Vassall dined with the proprietors August 22, 1664, and among the items entered on the expense account of the Proprietors is one for this dinner to Sandford and Vassall at the meeting with them "about a treaty w$^{th}$ them Conserneing Carolina."[2] In November following Sandford was appointed secretary and register of Clarendon County, as heretofore recited, and repaired to the Charles River settlement, and in 1665 was in the assembly of Clarendon County. The next year he made the explorations here described.

[1] *Ibid.*, pp. 364–366, 584.

[2] *Ibid.*, p. 379; Transcripts of Letters and Documents in the British Public Record Office relating to South Carolina (MS.), I. 2 (in the office of the Histor'cal Commission of South Carolina); *Collections of the South Carolina Historical Society*, V. 56–57.

# A RELATION OF A VOYAGE ON THE COAST OF THE PROVINCE OF CAROLINA, 1666, BY ROBERT SANDFORD

*A Relation of a Voyage on the Coast of the Province of Carolina, Formerly called Florida, in the Continent of the Northern America, from Charles River near Cape Feare, in the County of Clarendon, and the Lat. of 34 Deg:, to Port Royall, in the North Lat: of 32 Deg: begun 14th June, 1666;*

*Performed by Robert Sandford, Esq*$^{re}$*, Secretary and Chiefe Register for the Lords Proprietors of their County of Clarendon, in the Province aforesaid.*

*To the Right Hono*$^{ble}$ *Edward, Earle of Clarendon, Lord High Chancellor of England; George, Duke of Albemarle, Capt.-Gener*$^{ll}$ *of all his Maj*$^{ties}$ *forces in the Kingdome of England, Scotland and Ireland and Master of the Horse; Wm. Lord Craven; John Lord Berkeley; Anthony Lord Ashley, Chancellor of the Excheq*$^{r}$*; S*$^{r}$ *George Cartrett, Vice-Chamberlaine of His Maj*$^{ties}$ *Household; S*$^{r}$ *Wm. Berkeley, Knt., and S*$^{r}$ *John Colleton, Knt. and Baronett, The true and absolute Lords Proprietors of all the Province of Carolina:*

*Right Honor*$^{ble}$,

IT is not presumption but Duty that presents this Narrative (however rude and imperfect) to soe Illustrious, I had rather say a Constellation than a Corporation; the matter related was performed under your Auspice in your Country and by your servant. It measures to you, my Lords, (as his foot did Hercules) the greatnes of your Soveraignes Guift, and to the World the greatness of your trust and favour with him. It shews you in Prospective how lasting a Renowne you may adde to your already most glorious Names, How boundles a Grandeur to your longest Posterity.   None indeede but God and the King can move your hearts to doe these great things for yourselves and Nation.   Yett that such a Notion be effected may and shall bee the prayers of, Right Hono^ble,

With all submission, readiness and fidelity,

Your Lord^ppes servant,

Rob. Sandford.

## The Port Royal Discovery.

The Right Hono^ble the Lords Proprietors of the Province of Carolina, in prosecution of his sacred Ma^ties pious intentions of planting and Civillizing those his towns and people of the Northerne America, which Neighbour Southward on Virginia (by some called Florida) found out and discovered by S^r Sebastian Cabott in the yeare 1497 att the Charges of H. 7, King of England, etc., Constituted Sir John Yeamans Baronett their Lt.-Generall, with ample Powers for placeing a Colony in some of the Rivers to the Southward and Westward of Cape St. Romana,   Who departing from the Island Barbados in Octob. 1665 in a Fly-boate of about 150 Tonns, accompanyed by a small Friggatt of his owne and a Sloope purchased by a Comon purse for the service of the Colonyes, After they had beene separated by a great storme att Sea (wherein the Friggatt lost all her Masts and himselfe had like to have foundred, and were all brought together againe in the beginning of November to an anchor before the Mouth of Charles River neere Cape Feare in the County of Clarendon, part of the same province newly begunn to be peopled, and within the Lt.-Gen^lls Commission),   They were all blowne from their anchors by a suddaine violent Gust, the Fly-boat S^r John was in narrowly escapeing the dangerous shoales of the Cape.   But this proved but a short differrence of their fate, ffor returning with a favourable wind to a second viewe of the entrance into Charles River, but, destituted of all pilates, save their own eyes (which the flattering gale that conducted them did alsoe delude by covering the rough visage of their objected dangers with a thick veile of smooth waters) they stranded their vessel on the Middle ground of the harbours mouth, to the Westward the Channell, where the Ebbe presently left her, and the wind with its own multeplyed forces and the auxiliaryes of the tide of flood beat her to peeces.

The persons were all saved by the Neighbourhood of the shore, but the greatest part of their provision of Victualls, clothes, etc., and of the Magazine of Armes, powder and other Military furniture shipped by the Lords Proprietors for the defence of the designed Settlement perished in the waters. The Lt.-Gen[ll] purposed at first imediately to repair his Friggatt (which together with the Sloope gote safely into the River when the Fly-boate was driven off) and to send her backe to Barbados for recruits whilest himselfe in person attended the yssue of that discovery which I and some other Gentlemen offered to make Southwards in the Sloope. But when the great and growing necessityes of the English Colony in Charles River (heightened by this disaster) begann clamourously to crave the use of the Sloope in a Voyage to Virginia for their speedy relief, S[r] John altered that his first resolution, and permitting the Sloope to goe to Virginia retorned himselfe to Barbados in his Friggatt. Yett that the designe of the Southerne settlement might not wholy fall, Hee conditioned with the freighters of the Sloope that in case shee miscarryed in her Virginia voyage they should hire Capt. Edward Stanyarn's[1] vessell (then in their harbour but bound for Barbados) to performe the Discovery, and left a Comission with mee for the effecting it upon the retorne of the Sloope or Stanion, which should first happen.

The Sloope in her comeing homeward from Virginia loaden with Victuall being ready by reason of her extreme rottennes in her timbers to sinke was driven on shoare by a storme in the night on Cape Lookout (the next headland to the North and Eastward of Cape Feare and about 20 Le. distant); her men all saved except two, and with many difficultyes brought by their boate through the great sound into Albemarle River neere the Island Roanoake (within this same Province of Carolina) to the English plantation there.

[1] The correct spelling of this name is Stanyarne and it is pronounced as if spelled Stanion. It will be observed that Sandford spelled it in three different ways—all wrong—in two paragraphs.

Capt. Stanyon in returning from Barbados, weakely maned and without any second to himselfe driven to and agen on the Seas for many weekes by contrary winds and conquered with care, vexation and watching, lost his reason, and after many wild extravagancyes leapt overboard in a frenzye, leaveing his small Company and Vessel to the much more quiett and constant, though but little more knowing and prudent conduct of a child, who yett assisted by a miraculous Providence after many wanderings brought her safe to Charles River in Clarendon, her desired Port and Haven.

I had now a Vessell to performe my Southerne Expedition but disfurnished of a Master and none here skilled in Navigation to be persuaded to the Voyage, least therefore a worke soe necessary to promote the settlement of this Province should be poorely left without an attempt, Myselfe undertooke the Office, though noe better capacitated for it then a little reading in the Mathematicks had rendred mee with the helpe of a fewe observations made whilst a passenger in some late Sea Voyages to divert their tedium.

On the 14th June 1666 I entered on my charge, neere six months after the date of my Commission (soe long had theise various accidents detained mee), and on the 16th I left Charles River sayling Westward with a faire gale att East alongst that goodly and bold bay which on her two Capes, Feare and Romania, as on two hornes, procures all dangers of Flatts and shoales from her owne more gentle bosome. To make her yett more signall I named her Berkly Bay from the Right Hon^{ble} John Lord Berkly and S^r Wm. Berkly, two of her noble Lords Proprietors.

I was accompanyed by Capt. George Cary, Lt. Samuell Harvy, Lt. Joseph Woory, Ens. Henry Brayne, Ens. Richard Abrahall and Mr. Tho. Giles, and severall other inhabitants of the County of Clarendon [1] to the number of 17 besides myselfe (and the shipps Company, which alas were but two men and a boy). With mee I tooke a smale shalloope of some three tonns belonging to the Lords Proprietors and appointed by the Lt.-Gen^ll for that service, in which I placed Ens.

---

[1] Of these Cary, Harvey, Brayne, and Giles had been members of the assembly of Clarendon County in 1665. *Collections of the South Carolina Historical Society*, V. 60, 61.

Henry Brayne of some Experience in Sea matters [1] and two other men, soe reserveing Eighteene of all sorts in the biggest vessel, whose burden alsoe exceeded scarce fiveteene Tonns.

The 19th in the night it being very cloudy and darke and hee att our helme unawares bringing our Vessell astayes, we lost Company of our Shalloope. The 22d about 7 o'clock in the morning wee made the land and a fair River to Leward of us (haveing beene driven out to Sea by a Southwest winde from the 18th to the 21st, when a strong Easterly gale brought us in with the shoare againe). Wee bore up to this River and a great way kept our depth of six and five fathom water without any signe of breakers. Att length it shoaled, and Wee could plainely discerne a breach in the Eastern board. The River when wee first made it bore N. W. by W. of us, and by this time we had brought it to N. W. by N.: being therefore come into two fath. water and judging our selves on the banke of the visible Easterne shoalings Wee steered more Westerly and presently deepened our Water to three fathom and soe upwards. But the wind being at East and the Water ebbing, if wee had gonne more Westerly Wee could not have luff'd in; Wherefore I resolved (Noe breach appearing all before mee) to runn in directly with the River which nowe bore N. N. W., and in standing in that Course one heeve of the lead Wee had but 11 foot water, but the next was two fathom, which depth and betweene that and two fathom and a halfe continued a great while, and as we approached the Westerne point of the Entrance it deepened soe that those

---

[1] And also with "the portugall language." After this expedition he was a "greate encourager" of the Carolina "designe" and in 1669 was given command of the Proprietors' frigate *Carolina*, and settled at Ashley River with the first colony to settle in what is now South Carolina in 1670. In that year he claimed to have "the best stock of any three men in the Collony" and asked for 5,000 acres of land "for the monys, sugars servant and else that I was out at Cape Faire and for my first discoverie with Coll. Sandford." He commanded the *Carolina* until 1671, when Lord Ashley declared that he was "not satisfied with Brain in any of the voyages he hath made." He was in Carolina in 1672, and on January 30, 1676/7, received a warrant for 1,100 acres of land. He evidently died in South Carolina, as an inventory of his estate is among the records of the court of ordinary of the province. *Collections of the South Carolina Historical Society*, V. 88, 141, 142, 143, 150, 157, 215, 216, 317, 340, 476; *Warrants for Lands in South Carolina*, 1672–1679, pp. 124–125.

aboard the point Wee found five and six fathom water and soe upwards to nine fathom all the way in. It was halfe Ebbe at least when Wee entred, and I am very much persuaded that if Wee had gonne soe farr Westerly as till the River had borne North or N. N. E., wee had found a much deeper Channell, for though it blew a very fresh gale att East (which here is alongst shore and somewhat upon the Westerne Coast), yett we could not discerne any appearance of Flatts at all to the Westward.

Being come about foure or five miles within the River I anchored, and a Canoa with two Indians came presently aboard mee and told mee that was the Country of Edistoh, and that the chiefe towne or seate of the Casique was within on the Westerne shoare somewhat lower downe towards the Sea, by which relation I guessed this to be the same River that some English in a former discovery mentioned by the name of Grandy (if it be not rather the French Gironde [1]) and only sawe of att Sea but entered not; that it might noe longer remaine under an uncertaine distinction I called it from the name of my Lieutenant, Harvy Haven. It lyes about 32 d. 3 m. and the markes to knowe it by as you come from Sea are these: The North East side is a bluffeland, rounding from the River and stretching East into the Sea, hence a lodge of breakers runn out South before the Harbour's mouth, on which wee borrowed when wee made such shoale water in our Entrance. The Southwest side makes a sharpe lowe flat point bare of trees, a pretty way from the Entrance West, and then shews a hammocke or two of thicke shrubby trees. From this point the Coast tends S.W. and then W.S.W. Just within the Entrance is a shewe of a faire Creeke on the Starboard side and another on the West or larbor⌐ ⌐le. Almost oposite from the uper side of the East side C Marsh Island runns out West and Southerly almos⌐ River, Edged to the Seaward with a banke of O⌐ discernable a good way to Sea as you come fr⌐

---

[1] The North Edisto. Ribault, the French explorer, r
this coast after the rivers of France. B. R. Carroll, in ↑
of South Carolina, I. xxxiv, gives a comparative list of t↑
ous. He gives the Grande as the Broad, which is, of
town was on the island now known as Edisto Isla·

ward, and particularly meett with two lowe trees which in
the offing and before the Oyster banke is discovered seeme as
Vesieble riding within the River.  It flowes here East and
West neere eight foote perpendicular at spring tides.  The
Woods on each side entring, to us seemed to consist most of
live Oake, the land levell, of an habitable height generally,
with steepe redd bankes here and there appeareing over the
Marshes, on which in many places wee could see the fields of
Maiz greenly florishing.

The next day, being the 23rd June, I went with my boate
into a Creek on the East shoare opposite to where the Vessell
rode, a very faire and deepe Creeke or River goeing North
and Easterly to appearance a long way.[1]  Being gone about
a mile up I landed and, according to my instructions, in presence of my Company took a formall possession by turffe and
twigg of that whole Country from the Lat. of 36 deg. North
to 29 d. South and West to the South Seas by the name of
the Province of Carolina, for Our Soveraigne Lord Charles the
Second, King of England, and his heirs and successors, and to
the use of the Right Hono[ble] Edward, Earle of Clarendon,
George, Duke of Albermarle, William Lord Craven, John
Lord Berkeley, Anthony Lord Ashley, S[r] George Cartrett,
S[r] William Berkeley and S[r] John Colleton, their heirs and
assigns, according to the Letters Patents of Our Soveraigne
Lord the King.  I ranged a little on either side this Creeke,
passed through severall fields of Maiz or Indian Corn, and
following the guidance of a small path was brought to some of
the Indians Habitations.  I found all the land that I passed
over, whether I went back or alongst the side of the Creeke,
a rich fatt soyle, black mould on the topp and under mixt
with a soft redd marle, which and a stiffe Clay I after found
the most generall foundation of all the land.  Noe Swamps,
noe Sandy land.  On the Outside of the woods some single
scattring Pine trees, but of the sort which is called Spruce.
The rest and the Generallity of the timber being Oak, Maple,
Ash, Wallnutt, Popler, Bayes, and the trees tall and straight
but not very large, growing closer together than I have seene
in any other part of this Province (the reason I guesse of their
being so slender).  They are for the most part a well seized

[1] Bohicket Creek.

building timber, and some fewe wee sawe of Oak and Maple
that would beare three or foure foot over a very great burthen
upon the ground; and much of it of such growth as wee
knowe to be an excellent feeding for Cattle, and so thick and
high that it made our travelling very tedious.

The next day I went some miles up the maine River, and
finding a creek alsoe on the East side [1] which opened some
groves of Pine trees to our veiwe I putt in there purposely to
see that sort of Land, and found this if any the Swamps of
this Country, for this Creeke carryed us into Low broken
Marshes and Islands of these pine trees lying almost levell
with the water. Wee landed on some of them, found them
firme and dry (though severall dayes and but the very night
before wee had store of raine) and without any signes of
haveing ever beene overflowed. Yett they are seemingly soe
seated as that great store of raine and frequent must necessarily
stand in them. The pines are all spruce; the soyle a fatt
blacke mould with a scarce discernable mixture of sand
founded alsoe either on marle or Clay as the other lands and
bearing a very great burthen, and though on the outside Wee
sawe only pine trees yett being entered the Wood wee found
also Oake and severall other timber trees of a very large seize.
Att a venture wee called these kind of lands pine swamps.
But I esteeme them a very proffitable tillable ground, and
some of my Company did after this see an Indian planted
field of this sort which they told me bore as tall Maiz as any.
We rowed a long way up the Creeke, and besides these swamps
sawe and ranged through very spacious tracts of rich Oake
land, and yett Wee were not past the Oyster bankes and frequent heepes of shells, nor the salt water. Att my returne
downe the River I sent some ashoare to range on the West
side who did instantly affirme that the lands there were of an
equall excellency with the best of those Wee had other where
viewed, and that they believed itt an impossible injunction to
be putt to march to the end of the tracts. Being therfore
well satisfyed with the successe of our discovery hitherto, I
wayed and stood downe the River intending a short stay att
the landing place neerest to the cheife Seate of Edistowe
which the Indian had intreated of mee that they might with

[1] Ladinwah Creek.

the lesser trouble come aboard mee to trade. When Wee were here a Capt. of the Nation named Shadoo (one of them which Hilton had carryed to Barbados [1]) was very earnest with some of our Company to goe with him and lye a night att their Towne, which he told us was but a smale distance thence. I being equally desirous to knowe the forme, manner and populousnesse of the place, as alsoe what state the Casique held (fame in all theire things preferring this place to all the rest of the Coast) and foure of my Company, *vizt:* Lt. Harvy, Lt. Woory, Mr. Thomas Giles and Mr. Henry Woodward, forwardly offring themselves to the service, haveing alsoe some Indians aboard mee who constantly resided there night and day, I permitted them to go with this Shadoo. They retorned to me the next morning with great Comendations of their entertainment, but especially of the goodnesse of the land they marcht through and the delightfull situation of the Towne. Telling mee withal that the Cassique himselfe appeared not (pretending some indisposition) but that his state was supplyed by a Female, who received them with gladnes and Courtesy, placeing my Lt. Harvey on the seat by her.[2] Their relation gave myselfe a Curiosity (they alsoe assuring mee that it was not above foure Miles off) to goe and see that Towne: And taking with mee Capt. George Cary and a file of men I marched thitherward followed by a long traine of Indians, of whome some or other always presented himselfe to

[1] P. 40, *supra.*

[2] By a deed, dated March 10, 1675, "the Casseques naturall borne Heires and sole owners and Proprietors of great and the lesser Cassoe lying on the River of Kyeawah the River of Stonoe and the freshes of the River of Edistoh," for themselves, their "subjects and Vassalls" conveyed the "said parcell and parcells of land called by the name and names of great and little Cassoe with all the Timber on said land and all manner of the appurtenances any way belonging to any part or parts of the said land or lands" to the Lords Proprietors of Carolina. The deed is signed (with marks and seals) by the great cassique, three lesser cassiques, eleven Indian captains and fourteen women captains, the consideration being "a valuable parcell of cloth, hatchetts, Beads and other goods and manufactures." It is probable that the signatures of the women were secured to serve the purpose of a renunciation of dower, the deed being otherwise legally executed. Seven white men witnessed it. (Records of the Register of the Province of South Carolina, 1675–1696, p. 10—a manuscript volume in the office of the Historical Commission of South Carolina.) Numbers of other similar deeds executed later by Indians and signed by their women captains are on record in South Carolina.

carry mee on his shoulders over any the branches of Creekes
or plashy corners of Marshes in our Way.   This walke though
it tend to the Southward of the West, and consequently leads
neere alongst the Sea-Coast,   Yett it opened to our veiwe soe
excellent a Country both for Wood, land and Meadowes as
gave singular satisfaction to all my Company.   Wee crossed
one Meadowe of not lesse then a thousand Acres, all firme
good land and as rich a Soyle as any, clothed with a ffine
grasse not passing knee deepe, but very thick sett and fully
adorned with yeallow flowers; a pasture not inferiour to any
I have seene in England.   The wood lands were all of the
same sort both for timber and mould with the best of those
we had ranged otherwhere, and without alteration or abate-
ment from their goodnes all the way of our March.   Being
entered the Towne wee were conducted into a large house of
a Circular forme (their generall house of State).   Right against
the entrance way a high seate of sufficient breadth for half a
dozen persons on which sate the Cassique himselfe (vouch-
safeing mee that favour) with his wife on his right hand (shee
who had received those whome I had sent the evening before).
Hee was an old man of a large stature and bone.   Round the
house from each side the throne quite to the Entrance were
lower benches filled with the whole rabble of men, Women and
children.   In the center of this house is kept a constant fire
mounted on a great heape of Ashes and surrounded with little
lowe furrows.   Capt. Cary and my selfe were placed on the
higher seate on each side the Cassique, and presented with
skinns, accompanied with their Ceremonyes of Welcome and
friendshipp (by stroaking our shoulders with their palmes and
sucking in theire breath the whilst).   The Towne is scituate
on the side or rather in the skirts of a faire forrest, in which at
severall distances are diverse feilds of Maiz with many little
houses straglingly amongst them for the habitations of the
particular families.   On the East side and part of the South
it hath a large prospect over meadowes very spatious and delightfull.   Before the Doore of their Statehouse is a spacious
walke rowed with trees on both sides, tall and full branched,
not much unlike to Elms, which serves for the Exercise and
recreation of the men, who by Couple runn after a marble
bowle troled out alternately by themselves, with six foote

staves in their hands, which they tosse after the bowle in their race, and according to the laying of their staves wine or loose the beeds they contend for; an exercise approveable enough in the winter, but some what too violent (mee thought) for that season and noonetime of the day. From this walke is another lesse aside from the round house for the children to sport in. After a fewe houres stay I retorned to my Vessell with a greate troope of Indians att my heeles, the old Cassique himselfe in the number, who lay aboard mee that night without the society of any of his people, some scores of which lay in boothes of their own imediate erecc̄on on the beach.

While I lay here I had perfectly understood that the River went through to another more Westerly, and was passable for our Vessell, and alsoe that it was not much more then a tides worke through, this increased my desire of passing this way. Especially being persuaded that this next River was Jordan (Hilton intimateing as much in his Journall and Mapp),[1] Wherefore on the 27th of June, with the helpe of the tide of flood (the winde being contrary) I turned upp the River, so having oportunity to try the whole Channell, which I found generally five, and between that and six fathume deepe and bold home to each shoare till wee were come about 10 miles from the Harbours mouth, when the River was contracted between the Marshes. Yett here (except in one or two places where some flatts narrowed the passage) wee seldome found less than five fathum water. The River being narrowe and variously winding, noe Gale would att any time serve us long, so that wee were forced for the most part to towe through, and that often against the winde, which proved very tedious; nor could we passe but by day, which with lying two tides a ground to stopp some Leakes, made it Sunday morning the first of July before wee came into the next Westerly River,[2] and by it into the Sea again, though by the Travers I tooke of our Course I found it performable with light boates in one tide of flood and an Ebbe. The passage is generally betweene drowned marshes, a great breadth be-

---

[1] There are two considerable rivers lying between the North Edisto and the Jordan (Combahee): the South Edisto and the Ashepoo.

[2] They evidently passed through Dawhoo River to the South Edisto.

tweene the River and wood, especially on the Island side. On
the East or maine side of the Marsh is much narrower, and in
many places the River runns close under the banke of wood
land, which wee had the oportunity to view, and found it to
continue its excellency without change or diminution. The
Indians alsoe that inhabitt the inner parts of it assureing us
that it was all alike. The next Westerly River is a pretty
faire river, not less broad than Harvey Haven, but its Channell more crooked, narrowe and shallowe. The West side of
itt (as wee found afterwards) is but a necke of land, having a
Creeke or two which seeme to goe through into the West
River. It is for the Generallity drowned Marshes alsoe yett
in some places the banke is high, Crowned here and there with
smale ground of wood, consisting of dry plantable Land,
surrounded a good space with a firme Meadowe or pasture
Land, and presenting most delectable Seates for summer
recesses. I did a little wounder to see the Sea and noe apparent open passage first to the Westward as I expected (still
imaginning this to be the River Jordan). And when I was
come out of it into the Sea, and sawe none of these marks
which Hilton had prefixed to Jordan I was in a great puzzle
to know where wee were gott, Nothing of the Coast makeing
like those drafts which Hilton had given of itt. But the winde
first dying into a calm and then again blowing contrary, with
some Menaces of an Evening storme, I putt into the River
againe, and being anchored went a shoare on the East point of
the Entrance, where I found Shadoo (the Capt. of Edistow,
that had been with Hilton att Barbados), and severall other
Indians come from the Towne by Land to see for our comeing
forth, of whome I asked whether this was the River which
Hilton was in. They told me noe, but itt was the next River.
This assured mee that Jordan was yett further, and that
Hilton had noe knowledge of this River and soe could not lay
it downe. I demanded the name of this River. They told
mee Edistowe still, and pointed all to be Edistowe quite home
to the side of Jordan, by which I was instructed that the Indians assigne not their names to the Rivers but to the Countryes and people. Amongst these Indians was one who used
to come with the Southern Indians to trade with us att Charles
Towne in Clarendon, and is knowne by the name of Cassique.

Hee belongeth to the Country of Kiwaha,[1] and was very earnest with mee to goe with my Vessell thither, assuring mee a broad deep entrance,[2] and promising a large welcome and plentiful entertainment and trade.  I told him I must first goe to Port Royall, and that in my retorne I would see his Country; but for his better security hee would needs accompany mee to Port Royall, and soe be my pilate (as hee made mee understand) for their River.  And presently hee sent away his companion to give notice to the cheife Cassique of the place of my intention that hee might prepare for my comeing, and himself went on board with mee.  That Evening blewe a storme of winde att S.W. (the frequent Somer storm on this Coast) soe violent that (though in the River) I durst not trust to my ordinary roade, but kept my sheet anchor under foot.

With the riseing of the morne I weighed and stood out to Sea, haveing an easie gale at N.E. and a Tide of Ebbe.  My Course out lay S. E. between two bankes of shoales lesse then half a mile distant.  I chose rather to keepe in the Sounding of the Easterne than of the West Flatts, both because the winde was Easterly and soe I could beare up from them when I would, and alsoe because haveing both in goeing out and comeing in the day before borrowed on the Westerne shoalings, I should by this Easterly Course take knowledge of the whole Channell.  I was scarce shott a mile without the Eastermost point of the Entrance but the winde wholly left mee, and the Ebbe (which the flatts on either side makeing soe faire a land, I expected should sett directly out to Sea) did runn with soe strong a Current over the Easterne Sands that att the second heave of my lead I was cast from two fathum into six foot water, and I drewe fine into a rowling Sea on the very edge of a breach.  I had no way but imediately to lett fall one anchor, soe to stay the Vessell from precipitating on her ruine whilst I might carry forth another anchor to warpe her into deepe water.  The first was presently downe, but to gett out the

[1] Kiawah (pronounced Keewah).

[2] The present Charleston Harbor.  Kiawah was the Indian name of the present Ashley River and the country adjacent thereto.  The pride which the cassique of Kiawah took in his harbor and his country was responsible for the settling there of the first English colony in South Carolina.  The same pardonable pride in the place is still characteristic of the inhabitants of the Kiawah country.

second, which way to confirme our safety, proved hughesly
difficult.   We lay in soe tumbling a Sea that our boate could
not bee brought to our bowe without danger of staveing.   I
had but two men with mee entred to Sea labour, and the most
spirrited and active part of my Company were Gentlemen but
little used to any labour.   One of the Seamen must necessarily
stay within board to deliver the Anchor and Cable that was to
be carryed out.   However the danger made every one give
his best helpe, and with much adoe the boate is brought to the
bowe and the Anchor putt into her, but all our strength could
not stemme that tide of Ebbe which had hurried us into the
perill, and must therefore be encountred in the way to bring
us out, but a storne wee fall against the whole force of our
Oares.   A second attempt is made with doubled strength, but
one breakes his Thoales, another his Oare, and nowe cumbred
with our owne uslesse number in a boate of scarce equall
seize wee became rather weaker then att first, yett wee have
no other way left but this to prevent our wreake (Heaven not
yeilding us one breath of aide).   Therefore to worke wee goe
againe and refix our boate, but in theise past fruitless perform-
ances soe much time had beene spent as had given the Ebbing
tide a further advantage against us, to the almost perfecting
our destruction, for by this time the Vessell by her repeated
stroakes as it were to rescue herself from those inhospitable
sands, gave us warning that her condition was well neere
desperate, yett out goes our boate againe, and God mercifully
improved our strength to the getting forth an Anchor, though
not much further then our Vessell's length, yett soe farre as
brought us into two fathum water, the banke on which wee
had grounded proving steepe to, by reason of which wee the
more easily wrought ourselves out of those unkinde embraces,
and to the praise of the Almighty Deliverer were snatcht from
either an instant descending into the open Gorge of the un-
sated Ocean, or the more slowe and painfull progresse to our
ends in a naked Exposure amongst Nations whose piety it is
to be barbarous and Gallantry to be inhumane.   This ill entertainment made us brand the place with the name of Port
Perill.   It lyes in the Lat. of 32 d. 25 m. or thereabouts; and
may be knowne when you are in the very Entrance by its
Easterne point, which is a lowe point of Land bare of trees or

other growth save a fewe stragling shrubbs, hence the River
goes in N. N. W. and N. W. by N., a smale Creeke running in
East just within the point. The Coast hence to the Eastward
tends neerest E. by N. with Sandy bayes, and appeares even
and bluffe, with trees when you are in the Offing. The Westerne
part of the Entrance lyes within as in a deepe bay, and beare
from the East point N. N. by W. or W. N. W. about two
miles. It is a bare sandy bay, with a fewe shrubs next the
River [1] and thinne scatring Pine trees. More Southerly the
Coast thence Westward tends S. S. W., and all betweene this
and Jordan shewes with severall hummacks like broken land
or Islands when you are off before itt, and especially next to
Port Perill appears a wide opening as of a River, but it is
nothing but bare sandy bayes or Oyster bankes with lowe
Marshes behinde them.[2] Jordan, or as wee now call it
Yeamans Harbour from the name of our Lt.-Generall, opens
about two Leagues to the Westward of this between two
bluffe lands, from the Westermost of which the North East
end of an Island (which from Capt. Cary wee named Cary
Island [3]) runns out E. S. E. and makes all the Coast between
it and Port Perill lye in the forme of a deepe bay. All between Yeamans Harbour and Port Perill are shoales and
foule ground, which from the West point of Port Perill runne
out S. E. before the mouth of Yeamans Harbour to almost
an even range with the outermost face of Cary Island. From
the East point of Port Perill a rowe of breakers range themselves
parrallell with the Westerne shoales, and were the same which
had like to have proved soe fatall to us at our comeing out,
thence neere a League within Port Perill are three distinct
groves of trees elevated on pretty high bankes with lowe
Marshes in each intervall. They lye neere E. and West, and
when you are so farre South and Westerly as that the lowe
sandy point off the Entrance wholy disappeares these shewe
themselves as though the mouth of the River were betweene
two bluffe lands with a round woody Island in the middle of
itt. In steering in if you come from the South and Westward,

---

[1] The Ashepoo, lying about halfway between South Edisto Inlet (through
which the South Edisto empties into the sea) and the mouth of the Combahee
(Jordan).

[2] St. Helena Sound.                    [3] The Hunting Islands.

keepe East in three fathum water till you bring this seeming
Island to touch the Easterne bluffe, head and then stand in
N. W. by N. and N. W. with the head land, rather takeing
the Soundings of the Easterne flatt then of the W. if the winde
will permitt, and you will have two fathum water little more
or lesse all the way in att lowe water. As you come neere in
you will discerne the Easterne lowe sandy point between you
and that bluffe land and the sandy bayes along the Easterne
Coast. Steering in with that sandy point and you will deepen
and have five fathum water close aboard it.

After we were gott cleare of the Sands, the Ebbe being
donne and the Gale springing up, wee made Sayle and stood
out to Sea, but wee were not gott farre ere the winde shifted
to South East, and the flood sett soe strong into the narrowe
bay that wee could neither board it out nor gaine to the Westward of the Shoales which lye before Yeamans Harbour soe to
runne in there, wherefore I came to an Anchor in three fathum
water till the Ebbe at least might helpe us to worke out against
the winde. Whilst wee rode here wee espyed to our great
rejoyceing the Shalloope whome wee left the 19th of June in
the night. She was come forth of Yeamans Harbour, and stood
to and againe before the Southwest Coast, betweene it and
Cary Island, to shewe herself, not being able to come out to
us for the same reason that kept us imbayed. Wee alsoe
fired a gunn and putt out our Colours to lett her knowe that
wee sawe her, but could not gett to her for the flatts that
interposed.

To goe into Yeamans Harbour Hilton's direction is (and
itt seemed true to mee as I lay before itt, though I went not
in) to goe in on the West side of the shoalings which are
opposite to the mouth thereof and which are contiguous
with the flatts of Port Perill, giving a ledge of breakers that
lye before the Southwest Cape of the Entrance a smale birth,
and soe to steere with the North East land of the Entrance,
and the least depth he sayes is two fathum at lowe water,
and soe upwards to six or seaven fathum when you come neere
under the said Easterne Land. But I have understood since
from Ens. Brayne that between that ledge of breakers which
lye before the Southwest Cape and the end of Cary Island
is a Channell, which hee affirmes has about three fathum

water where shoalest, which alsoe when you are past that
ledge of breakers sett over to the North East land of the
Harbours mouth.  The Ebbe now beginning to make wee
weighed and plyed off to Sea with some difficulty, boarding
it out of the dangerous and foule bay wherein till about
three Leagues from shoare the deepest water wee could finde
was scarce three fathum, and in our turning wee generally
into a fathum and a halfe on each side, and this though it
was high water a place to be attempted with Care when
the winde is off as now it is.  By night wee were gott cleere
of all danger into six and seaven fathum water.  I stood off
and on all night, and in the morning found my self off the
Sea board side of Cary Island.  In the middle betweene two
openings this Island fills up almost the whole space betweene
Yeamans Harbour and Port Royall.  To seaward it makes an
even smooth land, pretty bluffe, with trees, and tends South
West and North East about three Leagues in length.  It
shewes two smale openings neere equi-distant from either
end and from each other.  From the Westermost opening att
Westward the Coast is bold Five fathum water; within half
a league of the shoare more Easterly it is not soe deepe.

The morning was Calme, and soe continued till about
two a Clock afternoon, when a fresh gale sprang up att North
East, which in a short time opened to us Woory Bay and
the mouth of Port Royall.  Woory Bay, of Lt. Woory, is
made by the South Westerly end of Cary Island [1] and the
Southermost Cape or head land without Port Royall, called
from the first discoverer Hilton Head, which is the farthest
land in sight as you come from the North East along by the
end of Cary Island, whence it beares neerest S. W. and is
bluffe, with trees large and tall, which as you approach them
seeme to looke their topps in the Sea.  Port Royall mouth
seems opens in the bottome of this bay neerest to the Westerne
side thereof; the opening is wide, little lesse then two leagues,
the Westermost land of it running out almost South to Hilton
Head, and laying in like a halfe bent bowe.  Makeing the
West side of Woory Bay from the East side of Port Royall
the land tends away East Northerly into Giles Streights [2]

[1] Chaplin's Island, westernmost of the Hunting Islands.
[2] Trenchard's Inlet.

(the passage on the backside of Cary Island named soe from
Mr. Thomas Giles) and formes the bottum of Woory Bay.
Before this part of the Coast and the end of Carey Island,
in all the Easterly part of the bay, its shoales and very uneven
ground unsafe to meddle with towards the Eastermost angle
of it; oposite to the entrance into Giles Streights, lyes a
Sand Hill pretty high, with some smaller about it, visible a
good distance off in comeing from the Westward.  As you
part from Cary Island steere away S. W. with Hilton Head
and you will come thwart the Channell of Port Royall, which
you will finde by the deepning of your water from five to
seaven fathum and upward.  It lyes neerer towards the
West land, and runns in N. N. W. towards the Easterne land
of the Entrance (by us called Abrahall Point [1]), having seldom
so little as seaven fathum water.  All the way in the shoales
in the East part of the bay lye poynting out a good way
to Sea, therefore it will be safe for shipps of burthen to keepe
out till they have brought Hilton Head to beare about N. N. E.
from them.  When I had opened Woory Bay sayling S. W.
along by the end of Cary Island, I had brought the Sand Hills
within a Steerne of mee.  I luffed into the bay to try the
Soundings of that Eastermost part of itt, and after a little
while came on the shoalings, and found them soe uneven that
it was ordinary to differ two fathum in the heave of a lead.
Being therefore satisfyed with the dangerousnes of this part
of the bay, I bore up againe and stood away with Hilton Head
crosse some of the shoales till I came to seaven, eight and
to about tenn fathum water.  Then I steered away with the
body of the West land betweene Hilton Head and the Entrance
of Port Royall, and shoale my water by degrees to six fathum
(which depth continued a good while) and att length to five
and foure fathum and to three within lesse then a mile of the
wood side.  Then I brought my tacks aboard and stood
North Easterly to gett into the Channell againe, and after
some time deepened my water to five, six and seaven fathum.
I then steered away with the East land of the River within
Abrahall Point, still deepning my water, till at length the
Ebbe being strong and wee makeing fresh way against it
with a large winde, I could not for a good space strike ground

[1] Bay Point.

with my leads. About midnight the third of July I came to an Anchor within the River [1] in seaven fathum water (the least depth I could then finde) a little above the Entrance into Brayne Sound,[2] or the passage which goes through to Yeamans Harbour, soe called from Ens. Brayne, who twice sailed itt. I would advise all who enter Port Royall to goe in upon the Soundings on the West side of the Channell till they come a good way within Hilton Head, that side being the evenest ground and freest from all danger. They may keepe in six and seaven fathum all the way in, and then as they steere more Easterly towards Abrahall Point they will finde itt much deeper. It flowes here E. S. E.

The next morning I removed opposite to the principall Indian Towne and there anchored before itt, where I had not ridd long ere the Cassique himself came aboard mee with a Canoa full of Indians, presenting mee with skinns and bidding mee welcome after their manner. I went a shoare with him to see their Towne which stood in sight of our Vessell. Found as to the forme of building in every respect like that of Eddistowe, with a plaine place before the great round house for their bowling recreation, att th'end of which stood a faire woodden Crosse of the Spaniards ereccon. But I could not observe that the Indians performed any adoracon before itt. All round the Towne for a great space are severall fields of Maiz of a very large growth. The soyle nothing inferiour to the best we had seen att Eddistowe, apparently more loose and light, and the trees in the woods much larger and rangd at a greater distance, all the ground under them burthened exceedingly, and amongst it a great variety of choice pasturage. I sawe here besides the great number of peaches which the more Northerly places doe alsoe abound in, some store of figge trees very large and faire, both fruite and plants, and diverse grape vines which though growing without Culture in the very throng of weedes and bushes were yett filled with bunches of grapes to admiracon. It was noe smale rejoyceing to my Company (who began to feare that after Edistowe they should see nothing equally to content them) to finde here not only a River so much superiour to all others

[1] Broad River above the entrance of the Port Royal River.
[2] Port Royal River.

on the Coast Northward, but alsoe a Country which their
fancyes though preengaged could scarce forbeare to preferre
even that which but a little before they had concluded peere-
lesse. The Towne is scited on an Island [1] made by a branch
which cometh out of Brayne Sound and falleth into Port
Royall about a mile above where wee landed,[2] a scituaçon
not extraordinary here, rather the whole Country is nothing
else but severall Islands made by the various intervenings
of Rivers and Creekes, yett are they firme good Lands (excepting what is Marsh) nor of soe smale a sieze, but to con-
tinne many of them thousands of acres of rich habitable wood
land, whose very bankes are washed by River or Creek, which
besides the fertillity adde such a Comodiousnesse for portage
as few Countryes are equally happy in.

After a few hours stay to view the land about the Towne,
I retorned to my Vessell and there found Ens. Brayne with
his Shalloope, come that morning through Brayne Sound [3]
from Yeamans Harbour, att the mouth of which wee had
seene him two days before. He told mee that the same
morning that I made Harvey Haven he came in with the
shoare more to the Estw'd and sayled along it till towards
Evening, when hee entred Yeamans Harbour supposing it
Port Royall, and not findeing mee there nor any knowledge
of mee, and guessing that I might be more Southerly hee
came through to Port Royall and acquainted himselfe with
Wommony the Cassiques sone (who had alsoe been att Barbados) [4] whome hee easily prevailed with to beare him Company from place to place into severall Creeks and branches
betweene this and Yeamans Harbour, soe becoming both his
Guide and proteccon that hee had by this meanes a large
leasure and oportunity of veiwing all that part of the Country, which hee did soe loudly applaud for land and rivers
that my Companies Comendaçons of Eddistowe could scarce
out noise him. Sufficiently satisfyed with this relation (confirmed by those with him) I resolved to loose noe time in a
second search of that parte, but to goe a tides worke up the
maine River and see the body of the Country, and att my
retorne to enter a faire Creek on the West shoare opposite

[1] Parris Island.
[2] Pilot's Creek. Ribault called it Chenonceau.
[3] And Morgan River. [4] See pp. 40, 90.

to where the Vessell rode,[1] and soe to veiwe that side which
Ens. Brayne had not medled with, being the more desirous
alsoe to trye this Creek because the Indians reported that it
lead to a great Southerne River which peirceth farre into the
Continent,[2] and I suppose may be the Frenchmans River
May, or the Spaniards St. Matthias. With the Flood therefore and a favorable fresh Gale of winde I sayled up the River
in the Shalloope neere thirty miles, passed where it divides
itselfe into two principall branches, the Westermost of which[3] I
went upp, and conceiveing myselfe nowe high enough I landed.
Here I found the Ground presently within to rise into a pretty
hill, and as I ranged further I crossed severall fine falls and
riseings of land and one brooke of sweete water which rann
with a mourmoring course betweene two hills, a rarity towards
the sea Coast (to which our former searches had beene con-
fined in which wee had not seene any fresh water but in wells,
which inconveinency was not to be borne with were it not
to be healved by the easie sinking of wells every where).
The land here was such as made us all conclude not onely a
possibility that Eddistowe might be, but a certainty that it
was exceeded by the Country of Port Royall. Being fully
tired with our March through a ranke growth of vines, bushes
and grass, which every where fettered our leggs and pre-
claimed the richnes of the soyle, I retired to my boate, and
with the Ebbe towards our Vessell wee passed diverse faire
Creekes on each side the River but entred none, haveing not
much time to spare, and being satisfyed by the sorts of wood
wee sawe and the banks that the land was all of like goodness to what we had already veiwed (only in one place the
land seemeing lower then usuall and with a great mixture of
pine or rather spruce). I went in there, and after I was somewhat within the woods found it very plashy and water standing
everywhere in holes about ankell deepe or deeper, caused as
I think by the late raine which had fallen somewhat plenti-

[1] Scull Creek.

[2] Savannah River, called by the Indians Westoboo and by the Frenchmen
May. The name May is still preserved in that section in the name of a river
lying between the Broad and Savannah rivers.

[3] It is uncertain whether the "two principall branches" here referred to are
Whale Branch and the main river above the entrance of Whale Branch or the
Tulifinny and Coosawhatchie, which form the Broad.

fully, for there appeared noe signe of constant swampishnes
(as in the Cipresse swamps more Northerly) nor anything
that might discourage the manureing it.  The morning was
pretty faire spent ere I came downe to the Vessell againe,
wherefore I made haste and changed my Company and then
crossed the River into that Westerne Creeke I spoke of,
which after three or four miles opened into a great sound [1]
full of Islands of different sizes Southwards.  It went into
the Sea by two or three out letts in our sight Westward.  We
still opened newe branches, some bigger, some lesse, like
those wee had already passed and found to crumble the
Continent into Islands.  I spent the remainder of this day
and the best part of the next in this sound, went a shoare on
Severall Islands, found them as good firme land as any wee
had seene, exceedingly timbred principally with live Oake
and large Cedar and Bay trees then any I had seene before
on all the Coast.  In one of them wee entred a pleasant Grove
of spruce, shadeing a very cleare pasture of fine grasse in
which wee rouzed a brave heard of Deere, and thence called
it the Discoverer's Parke.[2]  This Island continnes some hundred of acres, and both wood and Marsh, proper for planting,
grazeing and for feeding swine, and all the Islands of this
Sound that were in our veiwe (some few smale ones excepted that were onely Marsh) are in all appeareance alike
good, proportionable to their biggnes with high bankes richly
crowned with timber of the largest size.  So that of what we
sawe in this Sound onely might be found habitations for thousands of people with conveniencyes for their stock of all kinds
in such a way of accomodaçon as is not comon.  And if the
Sound goe through to such a great River as the Indians talk
off (which seems very probable) it will putt in addiçonall
value upon the Settlem$^{te}$ that shal be made in it.  It abounds
besides with Oyster bankes and such heapes of shells as which
noe time cann consume, butt this benefitt it hath but in
comon with all the Rivers betweene this and Harvey Haven,
which are stored with this necessary materiall for lime for
many ages, and lying soe conveniently that whatever neer
River or Creeke you cann thinke fitt to sett a house there
you may place your lime kill alsoe and possibly in the banke
just by or very neere finde clay for your bricke tile, and the

[1] Calibogue Sound.          [2] Bull's Island, Beaufort County.

great and frequent sculls [1] of fish wee mett with gives us ex-
pectaçon of advantage and employment that way alsoe.   In
sume we could see of nothing here to be wished for but good
store of English Inhabitants, and that wee all heartily prayed
for.   I gave my name the Honour of calling this Sound by it,
and doe believe that if this place be setled by us, it may hence
receive a longer duraçon then from any accesse within the
reach of a rationall hope.

Within night I retorned to the Vessell, and the next day
being the 7th of July I tooke in some fresh water purposing
that night to leave Port Royall and retorne homeward, haveing
in the discovery [2] already made, exceeded all our owne and
therfor confident to answere all other expectaçons, besides
each mans proper occasion hastened him, and the Consideration of the Charge of the Vessell hired att five and twenty
pounds sterling per month made us earnest not to detaine
her a minute of time unnecessarily.   Wee alsoe designed ourselves some daies to see the Country of Kywaha, one of whose
Inhabitants remained still with us for that only purpose.
But a little before night the Cassique of Port Royall came
aboard and brought with him a propper young fellowe whome
hee made mee to understand to bee his Sister's sonne.   Hee
demanded of mee when I would retorne thither, and shewing
mee the moone asked whether within three times of her com-
pleating her orbe, I told him noe, but in tenn menthes I
would.   Hee seemed troubled att the length of time and
as it were begged me to come in five.   But I continued my
first given number.   Att length hee gave mee this young
fellowe, told mee hee should goe and retorne with mee and
that I must clothe him, and then hee asked mee when I would
sayle.   I told him presently that night, but hee very much
importuned mee to stay until the next day that hee might
prepare mee some venison, and made signes as hee parted
that if in the morning hee should not see mee hee should Crye,
and soe hee left mee and the Indian with mee.   I was somewhat pleased with the adventure, haveing before I came on
the Discovery wished that if I liked the Country I might
prevaile with the Indians to lett one of their Naçon goe with
mee, I leaveing an English man in their roome for the mutuall
learning their language, and to that purpose one of my Com-

---

[1] Schools.                    [2] Meaning "exploration."

pany Mr. Henry Woodward, a Chirurgeon, had before I sett
out assured mee his resolucon to stay with the Indians if I
should thinke convenient,[1] wherefore I resolved to stay till
the morning to see if the Indians would remaine constant in
this Intencon, according to which I purposed to treate further with them on the morrowe, therefore I went a shoare
to their Towne, tooke Woodward and the Indian with mee
and in presence of all the Inhabitants of the place and of
the fellows relacons asked if they approved of his goeing along
with mee. They all with one voyce consented. After some
pause I called the Cassique and another old man (his second
in authority) and their wives, and in sight and heareing of
the whole Towne delivered Woodward into their charge, telling them that when I retorned I would require him att their
hands. They received him with such high testimonyes of
Joy and thankfullnes as hughely confirmed to mee their great
desire of our friendshipp and society. The Cassique placed
Woodward by him uppon the Throne, and after lead him forth
and shewed him a large feild of Maiz which hee told him
should bee his, then hee brought him the Sister of the Indian
that I had with mee telling him that shee should tend him and
dresse his victualls and be careful of him that soe her Brother
might be the better used amongst us. I stayed a while being
wounderous civilly treated after their manner, and giveing
Woodward formall possession of the whole Country to hold as
Tennant att Will of the right Hono^ble the Lords Proprietors, I
retorned aboard and imediately weighed and fell downe.

An Indian that came with mee from Edistowe with Intencon to goe no further then Port Royall seeing this kindnes
and mutuall obligation betweene us and the people of this
place, that his Nacon or tribe might bee within the League,
voluntarily offered himselfe to stay with mee alsoe, and
would not bee denyed, and thinking that soe hee should be the
more acceptable hee caused himselfe to be shoaren on the
Crowne, after the manner of the Port Royall Indians, a fashion
which I guesse they have taken from the Spanish Fryers,

---

[1] Dr. Woodward had probably conceived the idea of making himself very
useful to the Lords Proprietors by a careful study of the country and the Indians.
This he did now and in after years, and the splendid Indian trade which was subsequently built up and carried through the port of Charles Town was due in no
small measure to his enterprise. See his relation, *post*, pp. 125 seq.

thereby to ingratiate themselves with that Naçon; and indeed all along I observed a kinde of Emulaçon amongst the three principall Indians of this Country (*vizt.*) those of Kywaha, Eddistowe and Port Royall concerning us and our Freindshipp, each contending to assure it to themselves and jealous of the other though all be allyed, and this notwithstanding that they knewe wee were in actuall warre with the Natives att Clarendon and had killed and sent away many of them, ffor they frequently discoursed with us concerning the warre, told us that the Natives were noughts, their land Sandy and barren, their Country sickly, but if wee would come amongst them Wee should finde the Contrary to all their Evills, and never any occasion of dischargeing our Gunns but in merryment and for pastime.

The 10th of July in the morning I was fayre before the River that leadeth into the Country of Kywaha, but the Indian of the place who undertooke to bee my Guide, and stayed all this while with mee for that onely purpose, would not knowe it to be the same, but confidently and constantly affirmed to mee that it was more Easterly, and att length when I was almost neere enough to goe in, with greate assurance and joy hee shewed mee a head land not farre off which hee affirmed the entrance to bee. This confidence of his made mee stand away, but by that time I had sayled some two Leagues. Hee sawe his error when it was too late, for nowe the winde was soe that I could not fetch the River againe, and if it had beene fayre I was sure not to enter it before night, and I did not like the complexcon of the Heavens soe well as to trye that night upon the Coast.

The River lyes in a bay [1] betweene Harvey Haven and Cape St. Romana, wherein wee found 7 or 8 fathum water very neere the shoare, and not the least appearance of shoales or dangers in any part of itt. It shewes with a very faire large opening cleare of any fflatts or barreing in the Entrance onely before the Easterne point wee sawe a breach but not farre out. I persuade myselfe that it leads into an Excellent Country, both from the Comendaçon the Indian give itt and from what I saw in my ranging on the Easterne part of Harvey Haven the next Neighbouring land to this. Wherefore in hopes that it may prove worthy the Dignity I called it the

[1] Charleston Harbor.

River Ashley, from the Right Hon[ble] Anthony Lord Ashley,
and to take away every little remaine of forraigne title to
this Province, I blotted out the name of St. Romane putt
before the next Easterly Cape, and writt Cape Cartrett in the
roome,[1] to evidence the more reall right of S[r] George Cartrett,
as hee is a Lord Proprietor of Carolina.

The 12th of July about noon I entred Charles River, and
before darke night landed att Charles Towne in the County of
Clarendon, to the great rejoiceing of our friends, who yett
received not our persons more gratefully then they did the
sound Comendaçons which they heard from every one of us
without one dissonant note of that never enough to be valued
Country which wee had seene and searcht, in which may be
found ample Seats for many thousands of our Nation in a
Sociable and comfortable Vicinity, secured from any possible
general and from all probable particle Massacres, with such
other accomodaçons to boote as scarce any place cann
parralell, in a clime perfectly temperate to make the habi-
taçon pleasant, and where such a fertile Soyle cannot faile
to yeild soe great a variety of Produccons as will not onely
give an absolute selfe subsistance to the place without all
manner of necessary forraigne dependance, but alsoe reach a
trade to the Kingdome of England as great as that shee has
with all her Neighbours, and render our Soveraigne Lord the
King within his owne Dominions and the Land possessed by
his Naturall English subjects universall Monarch of the
Traffique and Comodity of the whole World.

ROBT. SANDFORD.

For a further Confirmaçon hereof take this Testimoniall
given of this Country by the Principall Gentlemen with mee
in this Discovery, who have attested under their hands as
much as I have sayd, and yett noe more then what thousands had they beene there would alsoe have affirmed—

*Clarendon*
     *in*
*Carolina*—

Wee whose names are hereunto subscribed haveing accompanied Lt.-Colo[ll] Robert Sandford in a Voyage of Discovery

----

[1] But Cape Romain it remains to this day.

on the Coast and Rivers of this Province to the Southward and Westward of Cape St. Romane as farre as the River Port Royall, and being all of us persons well experienced in the nature and quallity of the severall Soyles in these Regions, and some of us by means of our Travells throughly acquainted with most part of America, Northerne and Southerne Continent and Islands, doe hereby declare and Testefie to the whole world that the Country which wee did search and see from the River Grandy, nowe Harvey Haven, to Port Royall inclusive, doth for richnes and fertillity of soyle, for Excellency of Rivers, havens, Creekes and sounds, for aboundance of good Timber of diverse sorts, and many other requisites both to land and Sea building, and for sundry rare accomodaçons both for Navigation and Plantaçon Exceed all places that wee knowe in proporçon of our Naçon in the West Indies, and wee doe assure Our selves that a Colony of English here planted, with a moderate support in their Infant tendency, would in a very short time improve themselves to a perfect Common Wealth, Injoying a Self sufficiency of all the principall Necessaryes to life and abounding with a great variety of Superfluity for the Invitaçon of foraigne Comerce and trade, and which for its Scite and produccons would be of more advantage to our Native Country, the Kingdome of England, and to the Grandeur of Our Soveraigne Lord the King, his Crowne, and dignity then any (wee may say all) his other Dominions in America.

And wee doe further avouch that this Country may bee more securely settled and cheaply defended from any the attempts of its native Inhabitants then any of those other places which our Countrymen have refined from the Dross of Indian Barbarisme.

In Witness whereof wee have hereunto sett our hands this 14th of July, 1666.

> HENRY BRAYNE.
> RICH'D ABRAHALL.
> THOMAS GILES.
> GEORGE CARY.
> SAM'LL HARVEY.
> JOSEPH WOORY.

# LETTERS OF EARLY COLONISTS, 1670

# INTRODUCTION

In consequence of the high praise which Sandford gave the Lords Proprietors of Carolina of the country about Port Royal after his explorations in that vicinity in 1666 they determined to effect a settlement there, and organize a government for that part of their province which lay southward and westward of Cape Carteret (Romain). Accordingly, in August, 1669, they sent out from England a fleet of three vessels (the *Carolina*, the *Port Royal* and the *Albemarle*), under Joseph West, with about one hundred and fifty settlers for Port Royal. The fleet reached Barbados in October, but while there it was struck by a gale and the *Albemarle* was wrecked. The *Three Brothers*, a shallop, was employed at Barbados to take the place of the *Albemarle* and the fleet proceeded on its way. The *Port Royal* subsequently parted from the other vessels and in January, 1670, was cast away near Abaco, one of the Bahama Islands. The passengers all reached the shore by the aid of the small boat and built a boat in which they reached Eleuthera, another of the Bahama Islands, where they hired a shallop and sailed to New Providence, whence most of them obtained transportation to Bermuda, which the other two vessels had already reached. At Bermuda a sloop was procured to take the place of the *Port Royal* and the fleet proceeded on its way.[1]

The fleet soon encountered bad weather again and the *Three Brothers* was separated from the other vessels and did

[1] *Year Book* of the city of Charleston, 1883, appendix; *Collections of the South Carolina Historical Society,* V.; McCrady's *History of South Carolina under the Proprietary Government.*

not reach Carolina until the latter part of May, 1670. On May 15, on account of bad weather, it was forced to put in at the island of St. Catharine. Among its passengers was Maurice Mathews, who prepared a narrative of the adventures of the vessel from this time until it reached Carolina. This narrative was sent to Lord Ashley and was among those of his papers deposited in the British Public Record Office some years ago by his descendant, the late Earl of Shaftesbury. It bears the following endorsement by John Locke, the famous philosopher, then secretary to Lord Ashley: "Mr. Mathews relacon of S$^t$ Katherina Ashley River 70."[1]

Among the passengers in the *Carolina* was Nicholas Carteret, who prepared a narrative of the adventures of his party from February 26, 1670, when the fleet left Bermuda, until the arrival of the *Carolina* and the Bermuda sloop at Ashley (Kiawah) River, where a settlement was made in April, 1670. This narrative was also among the papers of Lord Ashley deposited in the British Public Record Office by his descendant, and bears the following endorsement by Locke: "M$^r$ Carterets relation of their Planting at Ashley River 70."[2]

In a letter, dated at Albemarle Point (the name which the settlers had given to their settlement on Ashley River) June 27, 1670, Joseph West, who was in command of the fleet containing the settlers on its passage over, and who was now deputy for the Duke of Albemarle (George Monck), gave Lord Ashley a narrative of events at Albemarle Point (subsequently Charles Town) from May 28, 1670, to that date. This letter was another of Lord Ashley's papers deposited in the British Public Record Office by his descendant. It is endorsed by Locke: "Joseph West—27 June 70 To my L$^d$ Ashley. Ashley River."[3]

---

[1] *Collections of the South Carolina Historical Society*, V. 169–171.
[2] *Ibid.*, pp. 165–168.        [3] *Ibid.*, pp. 173–174.

When Joseph West left England with the fleet containing the settlers for Port Royal he took with him a commission for a governor of that part of Carolina lying southward and westward from Cape Carteret (Romain) and instructions to Sir John Yeamans, who had apparently relinquished the governorship of Carolina upon his return to Barbados from Cape Fear in 1666, to fill it out with his own name as governor if he desired the position, or, in case he did not desire it, that of any one else he might choose. At Barbados Sir John joined the fleet and sailed with it to Bermuda. There he filled out the commission with the name of William Sayle, an old man who had been a colonel in the British army and had subsequently been governor of Bermuda. Governor Sayle proceeded to Carolina with the fleet and assumed the government. In a communication to Lord Ashley, dated at Albemarle Point September 9, 1670, the Governor and Council gave the Proprietors a statement of occurrences in the province for some time previously. This narrative was also one of the papers of Lord Ashley deposited in the British Public Record Office.[1]

These narratives by several of the first settlers of South Carolina were among the "Shaftesbury Papers" transcribed from the originals in the British Public Record Office about 1882 by Mr. W. Noel Sainsbury for the city of Charleston. Portions of them were incorporated into Mayor Courtenay's address at the centennial celebration, in 1883, of the incorporation of Charleston, which was printed in the *Year Book* of Charleston for 1883, and they were printed in full, together with all other transcripts of the "Shaftesbury Papers," in the fifth volume of *Collections of the South Carolina Historical Society* (Richmond, Va., 1897).

[1] *Ibid.*, pp. 178–181.

# LETTERS OF EARLY COLONISTS, 1670

## Mr. Mathews's "relacon" of St. Katherina: [1]

On Saturday May the 15th we came to an anchor in St. Katherina,[2] a place of about the Latt. of 31 degrees, where wee intended to wood and watter. The Indians very freely came aboard whom wee entertained from this day to the 18, they traded with us for beads and old clothes, and gave our people bread of Indian corne, peas, leakes, onyons, deare skins, hens, earthen pots, etc. Upon the 16 day came aboard an Indian, semi-Spaniard, w[th] a present of bread, etc., to our Master, and promised him Porke for truck. Severall of our people had been just at theire houses and told us of brave plantations with a 100 working Indians and that they want nothing in the world. Our Master upon the 17 instant, about 8 in the morning, with his mate and Mr. Rivers, three seamen and one man servant which had been theire just before, went ashoare with truck to buy porke for the sloupes use, theire were two men servants more which went ashore ag[t] the sloupe to cut wood, etc., and one woman with a girle to wash some Linnien at the wattering place, our Master promised to be aboard next tyde, but he came not. We hollowed to them right ashoare about 4 of the clocke but they made no answere. This raised a doubtfull feare in us. That night we kept a strickt watch and next day about 10 of the clock we heard a drume, and presently saw 4 Spaniards armed with muskets

---

[1] Maurice Mathews, the author of this narrative, was an Englishman of good family, his "Uncle's the Chalanors" being friends of Lord Ashley. He sailed from England with his servants in the *Carolina*, but changed to the *Three Brothers* at Barbados. In Carolina he at once took a prominent part in public affairs. *Collections of the South Carolina Historical Society*, V. 332, 362.

[2] An island off the coast of the present State of Georgia. The Spaniards maintained a mission there called Wallie.

and swords—with the drume came downe one of these and
standing behind a tree holding forth a white cloath hailed us
and bid us yield and submit to the soveraignty of Sto. Do-
mingo and told us it were better soe for o$^r$ Capt. was in
chaines.  I holding up a white shirt told him, if we should
have our people, we would depart in peace, but he cryed No,
No, and giveing the word to some in the wood, Indians and
Spaniards, wee received a volley of Musket shott and a cloud
of arrows which the Indians shott upright, and soe they continued for an houre and a half, then they left of, and commanded three of us ashoare.  We told them we would send
one with Letters to them, and sent them a boy ashoare, who
swimed with a note to the Master and another to the fryer,
the note to the fryer treated of free passage with all our people.
The boy they received courteously, cloathing him at the watter
side with deare skins, etc.  A little after, they bid us not use
any armes, and they would the like.  And bid us expect an
answer to o$^r$ letter.  We were glad of this and agreed, but
about half an houre after, they commanded shippe and all
ashoare.  We told them we had neither winde nor boat to
obey them (not a breath of winde stirring) and gave them
faire words, intending with the first winde to gett without
shott, but they fired and shott at us feirecely, then a small
breeze arising of the lande and we with much adoe having
weighed o$^r$ small bower and cut o$^r$ best, hoisted sayle and
away, and came to an anchor out of theire reach; but before
this, I being at the helme, John Hankes (one of the sea men)
shott at them, which made all keep behind trees.  We hauling
out three muskets had not a bullet, till at last we found severall upon the deck, which re-shooting did a little help us, as
we stood to our sailes; but they fired still, but by God's mercy
hit nobody, but our sailes were much damaged.  The next
day about noone we hoisted and away, turneing it out, they
still keeping watch on the shoare.  Saturday May the 19th
we sailed about the shoare with the winde at South, this night
we came to anchor in two fathoms and a halfe watter.  The
next morning we weighed anchor and steered alongst shoare,
about 10 of the clocke we made a cannew coming of the shoare
towards us, which proved to be of 4 Indians, they with signes
of friendship came aboard.  We entertained them courteously.

They told us the place right ashoare from thence was Odistash [1] and as we understood them, told us there were English at Keyawah. They further told us of a Cap⁺en Sheedou, and made signs that he would speak with us, upon this we detained the chiefest of them and sent one ashoare to that persone they spake of, with a Letter to desire him to come aboard without much company. The three Indians that went with our messenger ashoare promised to returne after sun set. About twilight they returned with our messenger and Capt. Sheedou and one Capt. Alush (who were at Barbadoes [2]) and many more. This Sheedou told us that the English with two shipps had been at Port Royall and were now at Keyawah, he further promised us on the morrow to carry [3] us thither. About 9 of the clock came another cannowe, but we sent them after a little stay away, being all too numerous. The next morning we came to saile for Keyawah where we found the Barmudian Sloupe going out a fishing, who piloted us into Keyawah river.

*Mr. Carteret's Relation of their Planting at Ashley River '70.* [4]

Barmuda, Febrʸ 26th, sayling from thence we came up with the land betweene Cape Romana and Port Royall, and in 17 days the weather being faire and the winde not friendly the Longe boate went ashoare the better to informe as to the certainty of the place where we supposed we were. Upon its

[1] Edisto.

[2] Shadoo and Alush. See pp. 40, 90, 101, *supra.*

[3] An instance of the early use in South Carolina of the word carry in this sense. It is now quite commonly used in that sense in South Carolina.

[4] Nicholas Carteret, the author of this narrative, was one of the passengers who sailed from England with his servants on the frigate *Carolina.* In May following the settling of the colony on the Ashley River he made a voyage to Virginia on the *Carolina*, which had been sent thither for supplies, returning in August. In September he went to Barbados in the *Carolina* and was there May 20, 1671, on which date he there witnessed the will of Sir John Yeamans. He held lands at Accabee, an Indian locality on the Ashley River, in 1672. In 1677 the Council issued a warrant to the surveyor-general to lay off 700 acres of land for him, but in 1678 the surveyor-general was directed to lay off the same land for Edward Mayo. *Collections of the South Carolina Historical Society*, V.; *The South Carolina Historical and Genealogical Magazine*, XI. 115; *Warrants for Lands in South Carolina*, 1672-1679, pp. 125, 190.

approach to the land few were the natives who upon the strand made fires and came towards us whooping in theire own tone and manner, making signes also where we should best land, and when we came ashoare they stroaked us on the shoulders with their hands, saying *Bony Conraro Angles*, knowing us to be English by our collours (as we supposed). We then gave them brass rings and tobacco, at which they seemed well pleased, and into the boate after halfe an houre spent with the Indians we betooke ourselves. They liked our company soe well that they would have come aboard with us. We found a pretty handsome channell about 3 fathoms and a halfe from the place we landed to the shippe, through which the next day we brought the shipp [1] to anchor feareing a contrary winde and to gett in for some fresh watter. A day or two after the Governor whom we tooke in at Barmuda [2] with several others went ashore to view the Land here, some 3 Leagues distant from the shipp, carrying along with us one of the eldest Indians who accosted us on the other day, and as we drew to the shore a good number of Indians appeared, clad with deare skins, having with them their bows and arrows, but our Indian calling out *Appada* they withdrew and lodged theire bows and returning ran up to the middle in mire and watter to carry us ashore, where when we came they gave us the stroaking complim[t] of the country and brought deare skins, some raw, some drest, to trade with us, for which we gave them knives, beads and tobacco and glad they were of the Market. By and by came theire women clad in their Mosse roabs, bringing their potts to boyle a kinde of thickening which they pound and make food of, and as they order it being dryed makes a pretty sort of bread. They brought also plenty of Hickery nutts, a wallnut in shape and taste, onely differing in the thickness of the shell and smallness of the kernell. The Governor and severall others walking a little distance from the watter side came to the Hutt Pallace of his

[1] This was evidently the bay now known as Bull's Bay, and this first landing was evidently made on the north end of Oniseecau, or Bull's Island. The water and country thereabout were known as Seewee, and the local Indians as the Seewee Indians. The name is still preserved in a small bay a few miles west of Bull's Bay.

[2] William Sayle.

Ma<sup>ty</sup> of the place, who meeteing us tooke the Governor on his shoulders and carryed him into the house in token of his chearfull entertainment.  Here we had nutts and root cakes, such as their women useily make, as before, and watter to drink for they use no other lickquor as I can learne in this countrey.  While we were here, his Ma<sup>tye's</sup> three daughters entered the Pallace all in new roabs of new mosse, which they are never beholding to the taylor to trim up, with plenty of beads of divers collours about their necks.  I could not imagine that the savages would so well deport themselves, who coming in according to their age and all to salute the strangers, stroaking of them.  These Indians understanding our business to St. Hellena told us that the Westoes, a rangeing sort of people reputed to be the Mandatoes, had ruinated that place, killed severall of those Indians, destroyed and burnt their habitations and that they had come as far as Keyawah doeing the like there, the Casseeka of which place was within one sleep of us (which is 24 hours for they reckon after that rate) with most of his people whome in two days after came aboard of us.

Leaveing that place, which is called Sowee, carrying [1] the Casseeka of Kayawah with us, a very ingenius Indian and a great linguist in this maine, the winde being very lofty soe that we could not deale with the shoare, we drove to the Southward of Port Royall, where we made a faire opening and findeing by observation and otherwayes the contrary, we stood five minutes to the Northward and soe gott the shipp into Port Royal river (the opening there appeared not to us as Colo<sup>n</sup> Sanford did relate)[2] ag<sup>t</sup> which shoales ley of about five leagues to sea.  W. N. W. Hilton head boare from us when we steared in, and in stearing in W. N. W and N. W. b. W. we had 2 1-2 fathoms at low water with breakers on both sides.  But when you are within you have 5, 6, 7, 8 and 9 fathoms water and a clear river.  I cannot say much of the channel, being but a Landman, but this, the Governor, Capt. Brayne and myself took the Longe boate to goe upon discovery and stood of to sea about 5: or 6: miles close aboard the Northwardmost Breakers.  We had no lesse then 5 fathoms at low water the tyde being spent and the winde proving calm we were forst to

---

[1] See p. 116, note 3.          [2] See pp. 98, 99, *supra*.

make in for the shoare with the tyde of flood.  Leaveing this
to Capt. Brayne, who will give you a more perfect acct. than
I can.  A small kinde of whale, white about the head and
jowle, is very plenty in this river.  In two hours' time I be-
held about 10 or 11 of the kinde, and some pretend and undertake to say to be of the sperme kinde, that were worth the
experim$^t$ to find out the truth of it.  We were two dayes at
anchor ere we could speake with an Indian.  When we did,
they confirmed what we heard at Sowee.  We weighed from
Port Royall river and ran in between St. Hellena and Combohe,
where we lay at anchor.  All the time we staide neare the
place where the distressed Indian sojourned, who were glad
and crying *Hiddy doddy Comorado Angles Westoe Skorrye*
(which is as much as to say) English very good friends, Westoes
are nought.  They hoped by our arrival to be protected from
the Westoes.  Often making signs they would engage them
with their bowes and arrows, and wee should with our guns.
They often brought us veneson and some deare skins w$^{ch}$ wee
bought of them for beads.  Many of us went ashoare at St.
Hellena and brought back word that the land was good land
supplyed with many Peach trees and a competence of timber,
a few figg trees and some cedar here and there and that there
was a mile and a half of cleare land fitt and ready to plant.
Oysters in great plenty, all the islands being rounded with
banks of the kinde, in shape longer and scarcely see any one
round, yet good fish though not altogether of soe pleasant
taste as yo$^r$ Wallfleet oysters.  Here is alsoe wilde Turke
which the Indian brought but is not soe pleasant to eate of as
the tame, but very fleshy and farr bigger.  The sloupe w$^{ch}$
wee have with us, bought at Barmuda, was dispatcht to Kayawah to viewe that land soe much comended by the Casseeka,
brings back a report that that lande was more fit to plant in
than St. Hellena which begott a question, whether to remove
from St. Hellena theither or stay.  Some were of opinion it
were more prudent forthwith to plant provisions where they
were, than betake themselves to a second voyage, though
small, it would not prove a better change, the enterance into
that harbour being as difficult as the other.  The Governor
adhearing for Kayawah and most of us being of a temper to
follow though wee knew no reason for it, imitating the rule of

the inconsiderate multitude cryed out for Kayawah, yet some dissented from it yet being sure to take a new voyage but difident of a better convenience, those that inclyned for Port Royall were looked upon straingely, so thus we came to Kayawah. The land here and at St. Hell[a] is much at one, the surface of the earth is of a light blackish mould, under that is whiter and about 3 or 4 feet is a clay some read w[th] blew vaines and some blew w[th] read vaines, soe is all the land I have seen.

## *Letter of Joseph West.*[1]

ALBEMARLE POYNT[2] AT KYAWAW,
June the 27th, 1670.

*May it Please Yo[r] Lo[p]:*

In my last to yo[r] Lo[p], dated the 28th of May, I gave yo[r] Lo[p] an account by the way of Virginia of our proceedings in Carolina, and how we came to quitt Port Royall and to begin our settlement at Kyawaw. May it please yo[r] Lo[p], since the departure of the ship for Virginia, wee sent the Shallop[3] back againe to St. Katherina, with 2 letters, one for the Governour of St. Augustines, the other for the ffryer at St. Katherina, to demand the men that were detained there by the Spaniards,

---

[1] Joseph West, the writer of this letter, was, July 27, 1669, commissioned by the Lords Proprietors "Governo[r] and Comander in Cheife of o[r] fleet and the persons embarqued in it, bound for Carolina, or that shall embarque in our s[d] fleet before its arriveall in Barbadoes; . . . w[ch] place yo[u] are to execute till another Govern[r] for y[t] parte of o[r] Province y[t] lyes to the Southward or Westward of Cape Carterett shall appeare w[th] Comission under o[r] hands and Great Seale of o[r] Province, to whom yo[u] are then to submitt, and this Comission to become voyd to all intents and purposes." In August he sailed with the fleet for Barbados, stopping on the way at Kinsale, Ireland, to add a few more people to his colonists. At Bermuda he was superseded by Governor Sayle, but received the appointment of deputy to the Duke of Albemarle. In South Carolina he at once took a leading part in public affairs and subsequently served three terms as governor of the province.

[2] Albemarle Point was located on a low bluff, the first high land on the north side of a winding creek, a flat point of dark pine forest projecting into the wide marshes of Ashley River. Across a narrow neck behind the town a palisade and ditch enclosed about nine acres. Beyond this was the village of the Kiawah Indians. *Collections of the South Carolina Historical Society*, V. 173.

[3] *Three Brothers.*

(yo<sup>r</sup> Lo<sup>p's</sup> kinsman, Mr. Rivers, being one of them,) and when the Shallop came thither 2 or 3 of our people went ashoare contrary to orders, without hostage and the ffryer rec<sup>d</sup> them seemingly w<sup>th</sup> much kindness and told them upon his ffaith they should not be wronged.  Whereupon there was 4 of our men went to his house, where he treated them very civilly and told them that our men were at St. Augustines, not as prisoners, but had their liberty about the town and were entertained at an English man's house; but when our men were taking theire leave of the ffryer he, betweene a complement and constraint, detained 2 of them,[1] upon pretence that hee could not lett them goe till hee had an answer from St. Augustines.  Whereupon after 3 days stay our men in the Shallop being informed by the Indians that there were 3 ships at St. Augustines w<sup>ch</sup> would come to surprise the Shallop, were forced to weigh anchor for their security and come for Kyawaw, leaving those two men more behind at the ffryer's house.  Now more yo<sup>r</sup> Lo<sup>p</sup> may please to know that wee are forced to send the Barbadoes Shallop to Bermuda for a supply of provisions, for feare the ship should miscarry at Virginia for we have but 7 weekes provision left and that onely pease at a pint a day a man, the country affording us nothing, w<sup>ch</sup> makes it goe very hard with us, and wee cannot employ our servants as wee would because we have not victualls for them.  Our corne, potatoes and other things doe thrive very well of late, praised be God, but we cannot have any dependance on it this yeare, but if we have kindly supplys now, wee doe not question but to provide for ourselves the next yeare, and that it will prove a very good settlement and answer yo<sup>r</sup> Lo<sup>p's</sup> expectacon, w<sup>ch</sup> is the desire of

Yo<sup>r</sup> Lo<sup>p's</sup>
Most humble and faithfull serv<sup>t</sup>,
JOSEPH WEST.

For the Right Hono<sup>ble</sup>? Anthony Lord Ashley, at
Little Exeter House, in the Strand, London.

[1] Captain Joseph Bailey and John Collins.

*Letter of Governor Sayle and Council.*

ALBEMARLE POINT, Sep<sup>r</sup> 9th, 1670.

*May it Please Yo<sup>r</sup> Honors:*

In observance of our dutyes wee shall not omitt any opportunity of giving yo<sup>r</sup> Honors a faithfull acct. of all our proceedings in this place.  Pursuant thereunto wee here doe offer to yo<sup>r</sup> Honors, that for some time since the dispatch of the *Carolina* from this place to Virginia and the sloop to Bermuda to bring provisions and other supplyes that yo<sup>r</sup> Honors' care had intended for us, wee have been put to purchase our maintenance from the Indians, and that in such small parcells, as we could hardly get another supply before the former was gone, in which time of our so great exigencyes, the Spaniard not being ignorant of it, sent out a party of their Indians ag<sup>t</sup> us, as we received intelligence from the Indians that are our friends, who lay for some time in a place called Stonoe neare our river's mouth untill the *Carolina* ffriggot arrived here, w<sup>ch</sup> was the 22th of Augt. last,[1] in w<sup>ch</sup> time we receiv<sup>d</sup> severall allarums though they never yet came soe far as to action, more than when Mr. Henry Braine came upon the coast and went ashoare[2] in his long boat, thinking to meet with our owne Indians being soe neare the River's mouth. They fired upon him and his company with small shott, notwithstanding that the s<sup>d</sup> Indians had shewed them a white flagg.  But before that time we had put ourselves in a reasonable good posture of receiveing them though they had come much in odds, having mounted our great guns and fortifyed ourselves as well as time and the abilityes of our people would give leave, and moved good courage in our people, besides the assistance of some Indians that were our friends.

After the shipps arrived we sent out a party of our Indians with two of our own people to discover their camp, but when

[1] The *Carolina* reached Virginia June 6 and left there August 8.

[2] On the low, narrow sandy island now called Morris Island.  Behind this island are marshes and beyond the marshes is James Island and behind that the Stono River.  Following the Indian custom that section of country would have been called Stono, which coincides with the statement above as to the location of the hostile Indians.

they expected to come upon them the Spanish Indians were retreated back againe, as our Indians informe us, at the noise of our great gunns, but whether there were any Spaniards among them we cannot yet receive certaine intelligence, other than one, who according to our Indians' description we judge to be a ffryer.   Neither can we as yet know the number of Indians that lay ag$^t$ us, they exceeding the number of an Indian's acct.

The *Carolina's* safe arrivall has very much incouraged our people.   The more for that she has brought us provisions of Indian corne, pease and meale for eight months, soe as wee make no question but (by God's assistance) thoroughly to defend and maintain yo$^r$ Honors' interests and our rights in this place till wee receive a further aid, which wee very much stand in need of.   That soe plantations may be managed and yo$^r$ Honors finde what wee endeavour to persuade, that this country will not deceive yo$^r$ Honors' and others' expecta-c̄ons.   For which purpose wee have dispatched the *Carolina* to Barbadoes, where wee understand are a considerable num- ber of people ready to be shipped for this place, that she may make a returne before winter, w$^{ch}$ will conduce much to the safety of this place and the ease of our people, that have been too much overprest with watching already, and what wee must stand to upon every occasion.   And yet, blessed be God, wee have not lost above foure of our people, who dyed upon distempers usual in other parts, soe far may be yo$^r$ Honors be further convinced of the healthfulnesse of the place.

The stores of all sorts doe very much want a supply, espe- cially cloathing, being all disposed of allready and many of the people unsatisfyed, and the winter is like to prove pretty sharp.   The powder was all damnified, especially when the sterne of the ship broke in, soe as there is a great necessity of ten barrells of powder more.

Wee have received some cowes and hoggs from Virginia, but at an imoderate rate, considering the smalnesse of their growth, 30s. for a hog, a better than w$^{ch}$ may be bought in England for 10s.   If yo$^r$ Honors had a small stocke in Ber- muda from thence may be transported to this place a very good breed of large Cowes, Hoggs and Sheep[1] at farr easier rates.

The Bahama Islands lyeing neare this coast from the latt. 34 to 37, being lately setled, and as yet in no patents, soe far as wee can understand, may be worthy yo[r] Honors' care to take notice of. For from thence wee can be supplyed with salt, and shipps goeing home without freight (if any such should be) may take in a loadeing of Brazellettoe [2] wood.

Wee are in great want of an able minister, by whose meanes corrupted youth might be very much reclaimed and the people instructed in the true religion, and that the Sabbaoth and service of Almighty God be not neglected.

The Israelites' prosperity decayed when their prophets were wanting, for where the Arke of God is, there is peace and tranquility. That the want thereof may never be knowne to yo[r] Honors or this place, are the prayers of,

Yo[r] Honor's most faithfull<br>
Humble servants,<br>
WILLIAM SAYLE,<br>
FLOR. O. SULLIVAN,<br>
STE. BULL,<br>
JOSEPH WEST,<br>
WILL. SCRIVENER,<br>
RALPH MARSHALL,<br>
PAUL SMYTHE,<br>
SAMUEL WEST.

JOS. DALTON, Sec[ry].

[1] Henry Brayne stated, in a letter to Lord Ashley, dated November 9, 1670, that he had "6 head of Cattle that my people have milk enough twice a day" and that he had "there alsoe 7 hoggs," three sheep, 6 geese, 8 turkeys and twelve chickens. *Collections of the South Carolina Historical Society*, V. 215.

[2] Braziletto, resembling brazil wood, and used as a dye-stuff and for cabinet work.

A FAITHFULL RELATION OF MY WESTOE
VOIAGE, BY HENRY WOODWARD, 1674

# INTRODUCTION

IT will be recalled that in the summer of 1666 Robert Sandford, secretary of Clarendon County, Carolina, made a voyage of discovery to Port Royal and vicinity, on the coast of what is now South Carolina, and that upon his departure one of his party, Dr. Henry Woodward, remained there with the Indians.[1] Dr. Woodward spent some time among the natives, by whom he was treated with the greatest consideration, and was able to learn much of the country and of the language, customs, and character of the Indians. After a time the Spaniards, hearing of his presence among the Indians, sent to Port Royal and made him a prisoner and took him to St. Augustine. Soon after this Captain Robert Searle, the buccaneer, surprised the town and released all of the English prisoners there incarcerated. He took Dr. Woodward to the Leeward Islands, where he shipped as surgeon on a privateer in order to defray his expenses to England, as he desired to give Lord Ashley an account of Carolina. The privateer was wrecked near Nevis in a hurricane on August 17, 1669, and Dr. Woodward was cast ashore on that island, and was there when the fleet under Joseph West, bound for Port Royal, stopped there about December 9, 1669. He at once volunteered to join the new colony, was accepted, and returned to Carolina with the fleet. He immediately became a conspicuous figure in the Ashley River colony, and from his knowledge of and influence with the Indians was of great benefit to the government in dealing with them.[2]

[1] See p. 105, *supra*.
[2] *Collections of the South Carolina Historical Society*, V. 190–192, 220, 158–159; *The South Carolina Historical and Genealogical Magazine*, VIII. 29–33.

In October, 1674, some Indians who were strangers to the
people of Charles Town, the name by which the town on the
Ashley River was now known,[1] appeared at the plantation[2]
of the Earl of Shaftesbury (formerly Lord Ashley [3]) near there
for the purpose of trading.   Dr. Woodward's good offices were
called into service and he went up from town to meet them.
He found them to be of the Westo tribe, and determined to
go with them to their country and establish commercial and
friendly relations with them in behalf of the province.   He
departed from the Earl of Shaftesbury's plantation October 10, 1674, and, after attaining a reasonable measure of
success in the expedition, returned to that place November 6,
1674.   On December 31, 1674, he addressed a letter to the
earl giving him an account of the expedition.[4]   This narrative

[1] When the town was first settled upon Ashley River it was called Albemarle
Point, but by an order of Lord Ashley, dated November 1, 1670, it was officially
named Charles Town.  *Collections of the South Carolina Historical Society*, V. 210.

[2] St. Giles, a signiory on the Ashley River, above Charles Town, which subsequently came to be known as Ashley Barony.   The Fundamental Constitutions
of Carolina provided that a signiory and a barony should each consist of 12,000
acres of land.   A signiory was the estate of a Proprietor and each of the eight
Proprietors was entitled to a signiory in each county.   A barony was the estate
of a Landgrave or a Cassique; each Landgrave being entitled to four and each
Cassique to two.   By order of the Grand Council of that part of the province
which lay southward and westward from Cape Carteret (Romain), March 4,
1672/3, a large tract of land on the Ashley River above Charles Town was reserved for the Earl of Shaftesbury, who soon after established a plantation there
and placed it in charge of Andrew Percival, described by the earl as one "Who
hath a Relaçon to my Family."   On March 18, 1675, a formal grant of a signiory
on Ashley River was made to Anthony, earl of Shaftesbury. He called his estate
St. Giles after St. Giles, his family seat in Dorsetshire.  *The South Carolina Historical and Genealogical Magazine*, XI. 75–91.

[3] Anthony Ashley Cooper, son of Sir John Cooper, Bart., of Rockbourne,
Southampton, and Anne, daughter and sole heiress of Sir Anthony Ashley, Knt.,
of Wimborne St. Giles, Dorset, was born July 22, 1621, and succeeded his father
March 23, 1631; was actively engaged in public affairs during the civil wars,
first espousing the royal cause and later that of Parliament and finally aiding in
the Restoration; was elevated to the peerage, by the title of Baron Ashley of
Wimborne St. Giles, Dorset, April 20, 1661, and was advanced to the earldom
of Shaftesbury, April 23, 1672.  His stormy political career is a part of English
history.

[4] *Collections of the South Carolina Historical Society*, V. 456–462.

was among the papers left by the Earl of Shaftesbury and deposited in the British Public Record Office by his descendant some years ago, was one of the papers transcribed for the city council of Charleston by Mr. W. Noel Sainsbury about 1882, and was published in the fifth volume of *Collections of the South Carolina Historical Society* (pp. 456–462) in 1897.

# A FAITHFULL RELATION OF MY WESTOE VOIAGE, BY HENRY WOODWARD, 1674

CAROLINA: Dec<sup>br</sup> 31: 1674

*Right Hono<sup>bl</sup>*

HAVEING received notice at Charles Towne from Mr. Percyvall that strange Indians were arrived at y<sup>r</sup> L<sup>dshps</sup> Plantation, Immediately I went up in the yawle, w[h]ere I found according to my former conjecture in all probability that they were the Westoes not understanding ought of their speech, resolving nevertheless (they having first bartered their truck) to venture up into the maine w<sup>th</sup> them they seeming very unwilling to stay the night yet very desireous that I should goe along w<sup>th</sup> them. The tenth of Oct<sup>ber</sup> being Saturday in the afternoon I accordingly set forth, the weather raw and drizzling, they being ten of them and my selfe in Company. We travelled the remaining part of that afternoon West and by North thorough y<sup>r</sup> L<sup>d</sup>ships land towards the head of Ashley River, passing divers tracks of excellent oake and Hickery land, w<sup>th</sup> divers spatious Savanas, seeming to the best of my judgment good Pastorage. As we travelled this day I saw (as divers other times likewise in my journey) w[h]ere these Indians had drawne uppon trees (the barke being hewed away) the effigies of a bever, a man, on horseback and guns, Intimating thereby as I suppose, their desire for freindship, and comerse w<sup>th</sup> us. The weather continuing wett wee tooke up our quarters, haveing steered exactly by compass from St. Giles Plantation according to the fore named Course. The Indian being diligent in makeing two barke-covered Hutts, to shelter us from the injury of the weather, this night as well as the afternoone proved tedious, having had soe large a vacation from my travels, the diet before almost naturalized now seemed unpleasant, and the ground altogether was uneasy for lodginge. Soe soon as the day appeared wee set

forth steering West and by South. After wee had passed
the head of Ashley River I found the land indifferently good.
In the afternoon wee entered a large tracke of Pines, which
continued untill we came w[th]in two or three miles of that
part of Ædistaw River w[h]ere wee crossed over. The land
seemeth fertyl along the banks of this River, whose head
they report to bee about four score mile up in the main from
the part wee passed, being then twenty mile or something
more distant from w[h]ere divideing himselfe he makes the
pleasant plant[n] of Ædistawe. Here killing a large buck wee
tooke up our rendeavouze w[th] two mile of the river, glad of
the opportunity of lying in two of their hunting hutts. Uppon
Monday morning four of the company went to give notice of
our comeing. Wee following steered West S. West, the land
Piny except along the skirts of small rivulets, many of which
wee passed this day. The weather all over cast. This
evening wee provided shelter, the night proveing extreame
wett. Wee supped w[th] two fatt Turkeys to helpe out w[th]
our parcht corne flower broth. The following day proveing
as bad as the night, wee forsooke not the benefitt of our
hutts. Uppon Wednesday morneing wee sett forth, nothing
at all varying our former course. This day wee had a sight
of Ædistawe River bearing north west by north of us, the
soyle very promiseing, and in some places excellently tymbered.
In the afternoon wee shott a fatt doe which, proportionably
divideing amongst them, was carried along by them for our
better comons at night, quartering along the sides of a pleasant
run. Thursday wee tooke our journey dew West, passing
many large pastorable Savanas, the other land promising very
well. This day wee shott two Bucks. The best of both
w[th] a fatt Turkey wee carried along w[th] us, for our better
accomodation at night. Fryday wee traveled West and by
South, haveing towards three the afternoon a sight of the
mountaines, which bore northwest of us, passing the head
of Port Royall river over a tree, w[h]ere the river intricately
runs through large vallies of excellent land, at the begining
of the adjoyning Hills, along whose banks in a mighty thicke
wood wee tooke up our Quarters. The ensuing day wee
went over many fattigous hills, the land especially the vallies
being excellent good, our course West a little Southwardly.

In the afternoon wee mett two Indians w^th their fowling peeces, sent by their cheife to congratulate my arrivale into their parts, who himselfe awaited my comeing w^th divers others at the Westoe River. The ridge of hills through which the river runs then being in sight bore West and by North. The banks of this river seeme like white chalky cliffs and are at least one hundred foot perpendicular, opposite to which banks uppon a sandy poynt were two or three hutts under whose shelter was their cheife w^th divers others in his company. The two Indians wee met had a canoe ready to pass us over, w[h]ere soe soon as wee landed, I was carried to the Cap^ts hutt, who courteously entertained mee w^th a good repast of those things they counte rarietys amonge them. The river here being very deep w^th a silent current trended North and by West and South and by East nearest. Soe soone as the raine ceased wee sett upp the fertyle banks of this spatious river. Haveing paddled about a league upp wee came in sight of the Westoe towne, *alias* the Hickauhaugau which stands uppon a poynt of the river (which is undoubtedly the river May)[1] uppon the Westerne side soe that the river encompasseth two-thirds thereof. When we came w^thin [sight] of the towne I fired my fowling peece and pistol w^ch was answered with a hollow and imediately thereuppon they gave mee a vollew of fifty or sixty small arms. Here was a concourse of some hundred of Indians, drest up in their anticke fighting garbe. Through the midst of whom being conducted to their cheiftaines house, the which not being capable to containe the crowd that came to see me, the smaller fry got up and uncovered the top of the house to satisfy their curiosity. The cheife of the Indians made long speeches intimateing their own strength (and as I judged their desire of freindship w^th us). This night first haveing oyled my eyes and joynts with beares oyl, they presented mee divers deare skins, setting befoore me sufficient of their food to satisfy at least half a dozen of their owne appetites. Here takeing my first nights repose, the next day I veiwed the Towne, which is built in a confused maner, consisting of many long houses whose sides and tops are both artifitially done w^th

[1] The Savannah River was then known as the May. The Westo town stood on the west side of the river, some distance above the site of Augusta, Georgia.

barke, uppon the tops of most whereof fastened to the ends of
long poles hang the locks of haire of Indians that they have
slaine. The inland side of the towne being duble Pallisadoed,
and that part which fronts the river haveing only a single
one. Under whose steep banks seldom ly less than one
hundred faire canoes ready uppon all occasions. They are well
provided with arms, amunition, tradeing cloath and other
trade from the northward for which at set times of the year
they truck drest deare skins furrs[1] and young Indian Slaves.
In ten daies time that I tarried here I viewed the adjacent
part of the Country. They are Seated uppon a most fruit-
full soyl. The earth is intermingled w$^{th}$ a sparkling substance
like Antimony, finding severall flakes of Isinglass in the
paths. The soales of my Indian shooes in which I travelled
glistened like sylver.[2] The clay of which their pots and pipes
are made is intermingled w$^{th}$ the like substance. The wood
land is abounding w$^{th}$ various sorts of very large straite timber. Eight daies journey from the towne the River hath its
first falls West N. West, w[h]ere it divides it selfe into three
branches,[3] amongst which dividing branches inhabit the
Cowatoe[4] and Chorakae[5] Indians w$^{th}$ whom they are at
continual warrs. Forty miles distant from the towne northward they say lye the head of Ædistaw river being a great
meer or lake.[6] Two days before my departure arrived two
Savana Indians living as they said twenty days journey West
Southwardly from them.[7] There was none here that under-

---

[1] This trade was soon diverted to Charles Town and that town developed
into very nearly, if not quite, the richest and most important trade centre on the
American continent.

[2] Mica scales. Their silvery appearance gave the name Silver Bluff to a
well-known point on the Savannah River in Aiken County, South Carolina.

[3] The Salwege, Tugaloo, and Seneca rivers. The main stream of the Seneca
is known higher up as the Keowee and the main stream of the Tugaloo as the
Chatooga.

[4] Caouitas, or Cowetas, a Muscogee tribe settled on the Salwege 1674–1691,
retiring in the latter year to the Ocmulgee and in 1715 to the Chattahoochee.

[5] The Cherokees, who inhabited that section of South Carolina until the
termination of the Revolutionary War.

[6] The headwaters of the Edisto are east or southeast of this point and there
is nothing like a lake there.

[7] Near the Gulf, west of Appalachicola River. By 1680 they had advanced
to the Savannah and soon pushed the Westo tribe out of the province. They

stood them, but by signes they intreated freindship of the Westoes, showeing that the Cussetaws, Checsaws and Chiokees [1] were intended to come downe and fight the Westoes. At which news they expeditiously repaired their pallisadoes, keeping watch all night. In the time of my abode here they gave me a young Indian boy taken from the falls of that River. The Savana Indians brought Spanish beeds and other trade as presents, makeing signes that they had comerce w[th] white people like unto mee, whom were not good. These they civilly treated and dismissed before my departure. Ten of them prepared to accompany mee in my journey home, returning by the same ways that I came, killing much game w[th] two large she beares uppon the way through much rain the fresshes being mightly encreased. The 5th of nov[br] wee our selfes carrying our trade upon barke logs swam over Ædistaw River and the 6th of that Instant in safety I arrived at yo[r] Hon[rs] Plantation at the Head of Ashley River. For good reasons I permitted them not to enter y[r] Plantation, but very well satisfyed dispatcht them homewards that evening, whom I againe expect in March w[th] deare skins, furrs and younge slaves.

In this relation as in all things else I am
    y[o] L[o] [shipps] ffaithfull Servant
                        HENRY WOODWARD.


Discovery. A ffaithful relation of
my Westoe voiage begun from the head
of Ashley River the tenth of Oct[r] and
finished the sixth of Nov[br] ffollowing.
[Endorsed by Locke]: Carolina. H.
Woodward. To the E. of Shaftesbury
31 Dec. 74.

were good friends of the English. In 1708, says Governor Archdale, they had three towns (near Sand Bar Ferry) and 150 men, but in 1715 they retired to the Creeks.
    [1] The Cusitaws lived about the heads of the Oconee and Salwege rivers; the Chickasaws below Muscle Shoals on the Tennessee River and the Keyokees above. *Collections of the South Carolina Historical Society*, V. 461.

CAROLINA, OR A DESCRIPTION OF THE PRES-
ENT STATE OF THAT COUNTRY, BY
THOMAS ASHE, 1682

# INTRODUCTION

In 1680 His Majesty's ship *Richmond* was sent out for service in American waters. Aboard thereof forty-five French Protestants were sent to South Carolina with a view of settling them there to cultivate silk. The officers of the ship were given instructions from the king to enquire into the state of Carolina while on duty in that quarter. The *Richmond* arrived at Charles Town in April, 1680, and returned to England some time in 1682. In the latter year the following pamphlet, written in the form of a letter to a friend, detailing the natural advantages of that part of Carolina in the vicinity of Charles Town, was published. The authorship is generally credited to Thomas Ashe. The pamphlet is one of several that were designed to advertise the Lords Proprietors' real estate. Its author spent some time in and about Charles Town during the ship's absence from England, and his account of the air, climate, soil, products, commodities, flora, and fauna of the section at that time is quite glowing, but not exaggerated.

In 1836 this pamphlet was reprinted at New York in the first volume of *Historical Collections of South Carolina*, by B. R. Carroll.

# CAROLINA, OR A DESCRIPTION OF THE PRESENT STATE OF THAT COUNTRY, BY THOMAS ASHE, 1682

*Carolina; or a Description of the Present State of that Country, and the Natural Excellencies therof, viz., the Healthfulness of the Air, Pleasantness of the Place, Advantage and Usefulness of those Rich Commodities there plentifully abounding, which much encrease and flourish by the Industry of the Planters that daily enlarge that Colony.*

*Published by T. A. Gent, Clerk on Board his Majesties Ship the* Richmond, *which was sent out in the Year 1680, with particular Instructions to enquire into the State of that Country, by his Majesties Special Command, and Return'd this Present Year, 1682.*

*London, Printed for W. C. and to be Sold by Mrs. Grover in Pelican Court, in Little Britain, 1682.[1]*

## To the Reader.

Reader,

YOU may please to understand, that the first Discovery of this Country was at the Charge of King Henry the Seventh, as you will find in this Book; and that as it hath pleased God to add such a Jewel to the Crown of England, so I doubt not but in a few years it will prove the most Beneficial to the Kingdom in General of any Colony yet Planted by the English, which is the more probable from the great Concourse that daily arrives there, From the other Plantations, as well as from England, Ireland, etc., being drawn and invited thither by the Healthfulness of Air, Delicacy of Fruits, the likelyhood of Wines, Oyls and Silks, and the great Variety of other Natural Commodities within specified, which well

---

[1] Title-page of original.

considered, will sufficiently evidence the Truth of what I
Assert; that I may contribute what lies in my Power for
a further Satisfaction to those Gentlemen that are curious
concerning the Country of Carolina, they may find a small
Description thereof, with a Map of the first Draught, Pub-
lished by Mr. Richard Blome, and Printed for Dorman New-
man, in the Year 1678 in Octavo,[1] and one larger in Mr.
Ogleby's *America*; since the publishing of these, there is by
Order of the Lords Proprietors newly published in one large
Sheet of Paper, a very spacious Map of Carolina, with its
Rivers, Harbors, Plantations, and other Accommodations,
from the latest Survey, and best Informations, with a large
and particular Description of the Entrances into Ashly and
Cooper Rivers; this Map to be sold for 1 *s.* by Joel Gascoyne,
near Wapping Old Stairs, and Robert Green in Budge Row,
London, 1682.[2]

## *A Compleat Discovery of the State of Carolina, in the Year* 1682.

THE Discourses of many Ingenious Travellers (who have
lately seen this part of the West Indies) have for Salubrity
of Air, Fertility of Soyl, for the Luxuriant and Indulgent
Blessings of Nature, justly rendered Carolina Famous. That
since my Arrival at London, I have observed many with
pleasing Idæas, and Contemplations, as if ravisht with Admiration, discourse of its Pleasures: Whilst others more actively
prest and stimulated, have with vehement and ardent Desires
willingly resolved to hazard their Lives, Families, and Fortunes to the Mercy of the Wind, Seas and Storms, to enjoy
the Sweets of so desirable a Being.

Having spent near three Years Abroad, in which time I
had a fair Opportunity of a Survey of great part of our Eng-

---

[1] The reference is to Richard Blome's *Description of the Island of Jamaica,
with the other Isles and Territories in America, to which the English are related*
(London, 1672 and 1678). The account of Carolina in Blome's *Present State
of His Majesty's Isles and Territories in America* (1685) is a mere copy of Samuel Wilson's *Account of the Province of Carolina*, printed next in the present
volume, pp. 161–176, *infra*, while that in the 1687 edition of that work is a
garbled version of the same. The book next mentioned is John Ogilby's *America* (London, 1670, 1671, etc.).

[2] There is a specimen of the Gascoyne map in the Library of Congress.

lish America. You my Worthy Friend, knowing in what
Character I went abroad, and understanding of my being at
Carolina, did obligingly request (that at Leisure) I would col-
lect such Notices of my own whilst there, with those Remarques
and Observations which I had learnt from the most Able
and Ingenious Planters, who have had their Residence on the
place from its first being Coloniz'd: You desiring to be
assured whether the true State of the Country did answer
the Reports of Common Fame. Which in Compliance with,
and in Obedience to your Commands, I have undertaken.

Carolina derives her name either from our present Illustrious Monarch, under whose glorious Auspices it was first
establisht an English Colony, in the Year One Thousand Six
Hundred and Seventy, and under whose benign and happy
Influence it now prospers and flourishes. Or from Charles the
Ninth of that Name King of France, in whose Reign a Colony
of French Protestants were transported thither, at the encouragement of Gasper Coligni, Admiral of that Kingdom; the
place of their first Settlement named in Honour of their Prince
Arx Carolina;[1] but not long after, that Colony, with Monsieur
Ribault their Leader, were by the Spaniard at once cut off

[1] The name was not derived from either source. By letters patent, bearing
date at Westminster October 30, 1629, Charles I. granted to Sir Robert Heath,
his attorney-general, "all that River or Rivelett of Sᵗ Matthew on the South side
and all that River or Rivelett of the great passe on the North side, and all the
lands Tenements and Hereditaments lying, beeing and extending within or between the sayd Rivers by that draught or tract to the Ocean upon the east side and
soe to the west and soe fare as the Continent extands," declaring "that we of our
free grace certain knowledge and meere motion doe thinke fit to erect the sayd
Region Territory and Isles into a Province and by the fulnes of our power and
Kingly Authority for us our heires and successors, we doe erect and incorporate
them into a province and name the same Carolina or the province of Carolina."
Colonial Records of North Carolina, I. 5–13. The name Arx Carolina (Fort
Charles) applied only to Ribault's fort and not to the country, and by the time
of the Heath grant had become merely a theme for antiquarians. When Charles
II. granted the same territory to eight of his "beloved cousins and councellors,"
March 24, 1663, he in his grant applied the same name to it in the same official
words which his royal father had used in the Heath patent in 1629. That the
name applied by Charles I. was regarded by the Lords Proprietors as having
been in force and effect from the date of the Heath grant is attested by the opening words of the first set of their Fundamental Constitutions for Carolina: "Our
Soveraigne Ld. the King haveing out of his royal grace and bounty granted unto
us the province of Carolina," etc.

and destroy'd.[1] Since which, nor French, nor Spaniard have made any Attempt for its Re-Settlement. Carolina is the Northermost part of the spacious and pleasant Province of Florida; it lies in the Northern temperate Zone, between the Latitude of Twenty Nine, and Thirty Six Degrees, and Thirty Minutes: It's bounded on the East, with the Atlantick or Northern, on the West, with the Pacifick or Southern Ocean, on the North, with Virginia, on the South, with the remaining part of Florida. The Air of so serene and excellent a temper, that the Indian Natives prolong their days to the Extremity of Old Age. And where the English hitherto have found no Distempers either Epidemical or Mortal, but what have had their Rise from Excess or Origine from Intemperance. In July and August they have sometimes Touches of Agues and Fevers, but not violent, of short continuance, and never Fatal. English Children there born, are commonly strong and lusty, of sound Constitutions, and fresh ruddy Complexions.[2] The Seasons are regularly disposed according to Natures Laws; the Summer not so torrid, hot and burning as that of their Southern, nor the Winter so rigorously sharp and cold, as that of their Northern Neighbours. In the Evenings and Mornings of December and January, thin congealed Ice, with hoary Frosts sometimes appear; but as soon as the Sun elevates her self, above the Horizon, as soon they disappear and vanish; Snow having been seen but twice in ten Years, or from its first being settled by the English.

The Soil near the Sea, of a Mould Sandy, farther distant, more clayey, or Sand and Clay mixt; the Land lies upon a Level in fifty or sixty Miles round, having scarce the least

---

[1] The French colony at Fort Charles was not destroyed by the Spaniards, but, becoming dissatisfied, returned to France. The second settlement of Frenchmen made under the patronage of Admiral Coligny was made in Florida and that was destroyed by the Spaniards.

[2] As the condition here described continued for many years thereafter, it would seem that the anophele, or malarial mosquito, which has greatly changed conditions in the lower part of South Carolina, is a more recent importation, brought perhaps in slave ships, or evolved from other mosquitos which had been biting negroes with the germs of malaria brought from Africa. The development of the method of cultivating rice by flowing the fields has probably had much to do with the increase of malaria; it has vastly increased the number of mosquito hatcheries, and has interfered greatly with the natural drainage of the country.

Hill or Eminency. It's cloathed with odoriferous and fragrant
Woods, flourishing in perpetual and constant Verdures, viz.
the lofty Pine, the sweet smelling Cedar and Cyprus Trees,
of both which are composed goodly Boxes, Chests, Tables,
Scrittores, and Cabinets. The Dust and Shavings of Cedar,
laid amongst Linnen or Woollen, destroys the Moth and all
Verminous Insects: It never rots, breeding no Worm, by
which many other Woods are consumed and destroyed. Of
Cedar there are many sorts; this in Carolina is esteemed of
equal Goodness for Grain, Smell and Colour with the Bermu-
dian Cedar, which of all the West Indian is esteemed the
most excellent; that in the Caribbe Islands and Jamaica being
of a courser kind, Oyl and the Spirit of Wine penetrating it; but
with this they make Heading for their Cask, which the sharpest
and most searching Liquors does not pierce. With the Berry
of the Tree at Bermudaz, by Decoction, they make a very
wholesome and sovereign Drink. This Tree in the Sacred Writ
is famous, especially those of Lebanon, for their Stately
Stature; but those in the West Indies I observed to be of a
low and humble height. The Sassafrass is a Medicinal Tree,
whose Bark and Leaves yield a pleasing Smell: It profits in all
Diseases of the Blood, and Liver, particularly in all Venereal
and Scorbutick Distempers. There are many other Fragrant
smelling trees, the Myrtle, Bay and Lawrel, several Others to
us wholly unknown. Fruit Trees there are in abundance of
various and excellent kinds, the Orange, Lemon, Pomegranate,
Fig and Almond. Of English Fruits, the Apple, Pear, Plumb,
Cherry, Quince, Peach, a sort of Medlar, and Chesnut. Wallnut Trees there are of two or three sorts; but the Black
Wallnut for its Grain, is most esteem'd: the Wild Wallnut or
Hiquery-Tree, gives the Indians, by boyling its Kernel, a
wholesome Oyl, from whom the English frequently supply
themselves for their Kitchen uses: It's commended for a
good Remedy in Dolors, and Gripes of the Belly; whilst new
it has a pleasant Taste; but after six Moneths, it decays and
grows acid; I believe it might make a good Oyl, and of as
general an use as that of the Olive, if it were better purified
and rectified. The Chincopin Tree bears a Nut not unlike
the Hazle, the Shell is softer: Of the Kernel is made Choco-
late, not much inferiour to that made of the Cacoa.

The Peach Tree in incredible Numbers grows Wild: Of the Fruit express'd, the Planters compose a pleasant refreshing Liquor; the Remainder of the Fruit serves the Hogg and Cattle for Provision. The Mulberry Tree every-where amidst the Woods grows wild: The Planters, near their Plantations, in Rows and Walks, plant them for Use, Ornament and Pleasure: What I observed of this Fruit was admirable; the Fruit there, was full and ripe in the latter end of April and beginning of May, whereas in England and Europe, they are not ripe before the latter end of August. A Manufactory of Silk well encouraged might soon be accomplisht, considering the numerousness of the Leaf for Provision, the clemency and moderateness of the Climate to indulge and nourish the Silk-worm: To make tryal of its Success, was the Intention of those French Protestant Passengers transported thither in His Majesties Frigat the *Richmond* being Forty Five,[1] the half of a greater Number design'd for that place; but their Design was too early anticipated: the Eggs which they brought with them being hatch'd at Sea, before we could reach the Land, the Worms for want of Provision were untimely lost and destroyed.[2] The Olive Tree thrives there very well. Mr. James Colleton, Brother to Sir Peter, one of the Honourable Proprietors, brought an Olive Stick from Fyall, (one of the Western Islands) cut off at both Ends to Carolina, which put into the Ground, grew and prospered exceedingly; which gave so great an Encouragement, that since I left the place, I hear that several more were brought there, there being great

---

[1] From the record of warrants issued for the laying out of lands to settlers within two or three years after the arrival of this French colony we learn that the governor and deputies issued a warrant November 16, 1680, for "a manor of foure thousand acres" to Jacob Guerard, one of the principal promoters of the enterprise, and made a number of lesser grants in the next four years to various persons of French name who were certainly or probably connected with it.

[2] Numerous efforts to raise silk in South Carolina were made at subsequent times and with varying success. Sir Nathaniel Johnson, Knt., undertook its culture during the latter part of the seventeenth century. He called his planta-tion Silk Hope in compliment to his undertaking. About the middle of the eighteenth century Mrs. Elizabeth (Lucas) Pinckney was quite successful in its culture for several years. She once presented to the Princess of Wales (mother of George III.) a dress woven from silk which she had raised, and there is still in the family of her descendants a dress made from silk raised by her.

Hopes, that if the Olive be well improved, there may be expected from thence perhaps as good Oyl as any the World yields.[1]

Vines of divers sorts, bearing both Black and Gray Grapes, grow, climbing their highest Trees, running and over-spreading their lower Bushes: Five Kinds they have already distinguish'd, three of which by Replantation, and if well cultivated, they own, will make very good Wine; some of which has been transported for England, which by the best Pallates was well approved of, and more is daily expected, 't is not doubted, if the Planters as industriously prosecute the Propagation of Vineyards as they have begun; but Carolina will in a little time prove a Magazine and Staple for Wines to the whole West Indies; and to enrich their Variety, some of the Proprietors and Planters have sent them the Noblest and Excellentest Vines of Europe, viz. the Rhenish, Clarret, the Muscadel and Canary, etc. His Majesty, to improve so hopeful a Design, gave those French we carried over their Passage free for themselves, Wives, Children Goods and Servants, they being most of them well experienced in the Nature of the Vine, from whose Directions doubtless the English have received and made considerable Advantages in their Improvements.

Trees for the Service of building Houses and Shipping, besides those and many more which we have not nam'd; they have all such as we in England esteem Good, Lasting, and Serviceable, as the Oak of three sorts, the White, Black and Live Oak, which for Toughness, and the Goodness of its Grain is much esteemed: Elm, Ash, Beech, and Poplar, etc. Into the Nature, Qualities, and Vertues of their Herbs, Roots and Flowers, we had little time to make any curious Enquiry: This we were assured by many of the knowing Planters, that they had Variety of such whose Medicinal Vertues were rare and admirable. The China grows plentifully there, whose Root infus'd, yields us that pleasant Drink, which we know by the Name of China Ale in England: in Medicinal Uses it's far more excellent. Monsieur Tavernier, in his late

---

[1] Olives have been raised in South Carolina in greater or less quantities from its first settlement to the present. In 1837 there was a very severe frost which killed most of the trees then growing, and since then not many have been grown.

Voyages to Persia,[1] observes that Nation, by the frequent
use of Water in which this Root is boyl'd, are never troubled
with the Stone or Gout: It mundifies[2] and sweetens the
Blood: It's good in Fevers, Scurvy, Gonorrhœa, and the
Lues Venerea. They have three sorts of the Rattle-Snake
Root which I have seen; the Comous, or Hairy, the Smooth,
the Nodous, or Knotted Root: All which are lactiferous, or
yielding a Milkie Juice; and if I do not very much in my
Observations err, the Leaves of all these Roots of a Heart
had the exact Resemblance: They are all Sovereign against
the Mortal Bites of that Snake, too frequent in the West
Indies: In all Pestilential Distempers, as Plague, Small
Pox, and Malignant Fevers, it's a Noble Specifick; when
stung, they eat the Root, applying it to the Venemous Wound;
or they boyl the Roots in Water; which drunk, fortifies and
corroborates the Heart, exciteing strong and generous Sweats:
by which endangered Nature is relieved, and the Poyson
carried off, and expelled.

Gardens as yet they have not much improved or minded,
their Designs having otherwise more profitably engaged them
in settling and cultivating their Plantations with good Provisions and numerous Stocks of Cattle; which two things by
Planters are esteemed the Basis and Props of all New Plantations and Settlements; before which be well accomplished
and performed, nothing to any purpose can be effected; and
upon which all Intentions, Manufactories, etc., have their
necessary Dependance. But now their Gardens begin to be
supplied with such European Plants and Herbs as are necessary for the Kitchen, viz. Potatoes, Lettice, Coleworts, Pars-
nip, Turnip, Carrot and Reddish: Their Gardens also begin to
be beautified and adorned with such Herbs and Flowers which
to the Smell or Eye are pleasing and agreable, viz. The
Rose, Tulip, Carnation and Lilly, etc. Their Provision which
grows in the Field is chiefly Indian Corn, which produces a
vast Increase, yearly, yielding Two plentiful Harvests, of
which they make wholesome Bread, and good Bisket, which
gives a strong, sound, and nourishing Diet; with Milk I
have eaten it dress'd various ways: Of the Juice of the
Corn, when green, the Spaniards with Chocolet, aromatiz'd

---

[1] J. B. Tavernier, *Six Voyages* (Paris, 1676-1679).        [2] Clears.

with Spices, make a rare Drink of an excellent Delicacy.[1]
I have seen the English amongst the Caribbes roast the green
Ear on the Coals, and eat it with a great deal of Pleasure.[2]
The Indians in Carolina parch the ripe Corn, then pound it
to a Powder, putting it in a Leathern Bag: When they use it,
they take a little quantity of the Powder in the Palms of
their Hands, mixing it with Water, and sup it off: with this
they will travel several days.  In short, it's a Grain of General Use to Man and Beast, many thousands of both kinds in
the West Indies having from it the greater part of their Sub-
sistence.  The American Physicians observe that it breeds
good Blood, removes and opens Oppellations[3] and Obstruc-
tions.  At Carolina they have lately invented a way of makeing with it good sound Beer; but it's strong and heady: By
Maceration, when duly fermented, a strong Spirit like Brandy
may be drawn off from it, by the help of an Alembick.

Pulse they have of great Variety, not only of what Europe
yield, viz. Beans, Pease, Callavance, Figolaes, and Bonavist,
etc.,[4] but many other kinds proper to the place, and to us
unknown: Green Pease at the latter end of April, at my
being there, I eat as good as ever I did [in] England.  Straw-
berries, Rasberries, Billberries, and Blackberries grow frequently up and down the Woods.  Hemp and Flax thrives
exceeding well; there grows a sort of wild Silk Pods, call'd
Silk-Grass, of which they may make fine and durable Linnen.

What Wheat they have planted has been rather for Experi-
ment and Observation, whether it would be agreeable to the
Soil and Climate, than for any Substance for themselves, or
for Transportation abroad; what they have sown, the Planters assured us grew exceeding well; as also Barly, Mr. Linch[5]
an ingenious Planter, having whilst we were there very good

---

[1] During the war between the United States and the Confederate States
"coffee" made from parched corn was an everyday drink of the Southern people.

[2] This is still done by Southerners, who relish it quite as much now as did
their countrymen of 1682.

[3] Oppilation, *i. e.*, constipation.

[4] Calabashes, figs (?), and kidney beans.

[5] Jonah Lynch, ancestor of Thomas Lynch and his son, Thomas Lynch, Jr.,
both of whom were delegates from South Carolina to the Continental Congress
at the time of the passage of the Declaration of Independence and the latter of
whom signed that document.

growing in his Plantation, of which he intended to make Malt for brewing of English Beer and Ale, having all Utensils and Conveniences for it. Tobacco grows very well; and they have of an excellent sort, mistaken by some of our English Smoakers for Spanish Tobacco, and valued from 5 to 8s. the Pound; but finding a great deal of trouble in the Planting and Cure of it, and the great Quantities which Virginia, and other of His Majesties Plantations make, rendring it a Drug over all Europe; they do not much regard or encourage its Planting, having already before them better and more profitable Designs in Action.[1] Tarr made of the resinous Juice of the Pine (which boyl'd to a thicker Consistence is Pitch) they make great quantities yearly, transporting several Tuns to Barbadoes, Jamaica, and the Caribbe Islands.[2] Indigo they have made, and that good: The reason why they have desisted I cannot learn.[3] To conclude, there grows in Carolina the famous Cassiny,[4] whose admirable and incomparable Vertues are highly applauded and extolled by French and Spanish Writers: It is the Leaves of a certain Tree, which boyl'd in Water (as we do Thea) wonderfully enliven and envigorate the Heart, with genuine easie Sweats and Transpirations, preserving the Mind free and serene, keeping the Body brisk, active, and lively, not for an hour, or two but for as many days, as those Authors report, without any other Nourishment or Subsistance, which, if true, is really admirable; they also add, that none amongst the Indians,

---

[1] A little tobacco was raised in South Carolina continuously from this time until just before the Revolution, when Thomas Singleton came from Virginia and put an impetus to its cultivation which greatly increased its production for many years thereafter. Then its cultivation greatly decreased until about twenty-five years ago, when, through the efforts of F. M. Rogers, of Darlington County, and *The News and Courier*, of Charleston, it once more resumed a conspicuous place among the agricultural products of South Carolina.

[2] Within the next half-century pitch, tar, and turpentine had become three of the most important products exported from Charles Town, which probably led the world in the exportation of those commodities at that time.

[3] The cultivation of indigo was also revived about the middle of the eighteenth century, principally through the efforts of Moses Lindo, a Jew from London and an indigo dealer, who removed to Charles Town and encouraged its cultivation. See the chapter on Moses Lindo in Barnett A. Elzas, *The Jews of South Carolina.*

[4] Cassena or yapon, *ilex cassine.*

but their great Men and Captains, who have been famous
for their great Exploits of War and Noble Actions, are admitted to the use of this noble Bevaridge. At my being
there I made Enquiry after it; but the Ignorance of the
Planter did not inform me. Sponges growing on the Sandy
Shoars, I have gathered good and large; for which Samos in
times past was famous, supposed by the Ancients to be the
only place in the World where they grew: a courser sort I
have seen pull'd up by Fishers, fishing among the Rocks
of the Island of Berbadoes. Ambergrise is often thrown on
their Shoars; a pretious Commodity to him who finds it, if
Native and pure, in Worth and Value It surpasses Gold;
being estimated at 5 and 6 Pound the Ounce, if not adul-
terated. What it is I shall not decide, leaving it to the Judgment of the more Learned, whether it be the Excrement of
the Whale, because sometimes in dissecting and opening
their Bodies it's there discovered.[1] I think as well it may
be argued the Excrements of other Creatures, Birds and some
Beasts greedily desireing and affecting it, especially the Fox,
who eating it, by Digestion it passes through his Body; after
some Alteration it's again recover'd, and is that which we call
Fox Ambergrise. Others, that it is a bitumious Substance,
ebullating or boiling up from the Bottom of the Sea, and float-
ing on the Surface of the Waters, is condensed by the circum-
ambient Air: of which Opinion is the Learned Sennertus.[2]
Some that it is a Plant of a viscous oleaginous Body, really
growing at the bottom of the Sea, the swift and violent Motion
of the Waters in Storms causing an Eradication or Evulsion
of the Plant, forcing it to the adjacent Shoars; that its most
plentifully found after Storms is certain: if true, as an intelligent man informed me, who lived many years at the Bermudaz,
and among the Behama Islands, who saw at the Behama a
piece of Ambergrise weighing thirty pound (for its bigness
famous in those Parts) having perfect and apparent Roots,
equal to the Body in worth and goodness. Others, that it's
the liquid resinous Tears of some odoriferous Tree, hanging
over Seas or Rivers, coagulated in that Form which we find
it. Dr. Trapham, an ingenious Physician in Jamaica, differs

[1] It is in fact a morbid secretion of the liver or intestines of the sperm whale.
[2] A famous German physician (1572–1637).

little from this last opinion, thinking it the Gummous Juice of some Fragrant Plant which grows on Rocks near the Sea, whose Trunks broken by the rude and boysterous Waves, emit that precious Liquor. In Medicinal and Physical uses it has a high esteem, being prescribed in the richest Cordials, admirable in the languishes of the Spirit Faintings, and Deliquium of the Heart; given as the last remedy to agonizing Persons. In Perfumes of Linnen, Wollen, Gloves, etc., there is none esteemed more costly or precious. It's of different Colors, Black, Red, the Nutmeg, and Gray Color are held the best.

The great encrease of their Cattel is rather to be admired than believed: not more than six or seven years past the Country was almost destitute of Cows, Hogs and Sheep, now they have many thousand Head. The Planter in Winter takes no care for their Provision, which is a great Advantage; the Northern Plantations obliging the Planters to spend great part of their Summer to provide Fodder and Provision for their Cattle, to preserve them from starving in the Winter. The Cows the Year round brouzing on the sweet Leaves growing on the Trees and Bushes, or on the wholesome Herbage growing underneath: They usually call them home in the Evening for their Milk, and to keep them from running wild. Hogs find more than enough of Fruits in the Summer, and Roots and Nuts in the Winter; from the abundance of their Feeding, great numbers forsake their own Plantations, running wild in the Woods,[1] the Tyger, Wolf, and wild Cat,[2] by devouring them, oftentimes goes Share with the Planter; but when the Stock encreases and grows strong, the older surround the younger, and boldly oppose, and oftentimes attack their Invaders. Their Sheep bears good Wooll; the Ewes at a time often have 2 or 3 Lambs; they thrive very well, the Country being so friendly to their Natures, that it's observed, they are neither liable or incident to any known Disease or Distemper. Of Beasts bearing Furrs, they have

---

[1] This condition is occasionally to be found in the lower part of South Carolina now.

[2] The only member of the tiger family still to be found in South Carolina is an occasional catamount, the smallest member of the family. The wolf is extinct. Wild cats are still plentiful.

great store of Variety, whose Skins serve the Indians for Cloathing and Bedding, and the English for many uses, besides the great Advantage made of them, by their being sent for England. Deer, of which there is such infinite Herds, that the whole Country seems but one continued Park, insomuch, that I have often heard Captain Matthews, an ingenious Gentleman, and Agent to Sir Peter Colleton for his Affairs in Carolina, that one hunting Indian has yearly kill'd and brought to his Plantation more than an 100, sometimes 200 head of Deer.[1] Bears there are in great numbers, of whose Fat they make an Oyl which is of great Vertue and Efficacy[2] in causing the Hair to grow, which I observed the Indians daily used, by which means they not only keep their Hair clear and pre- served from Vermine, but by the nourishing faculty of the Oyl, it usually extended in length to their middles. There are Bevors,[3] Otters, Foxes, Racoons, Possums, Musquasses,* Hares and Coneys, Squirrels of five kinds, the flying Squirrel, whose delicate Skin is commended for comforting, if applied to a cold Stomack, the Red, the Grey, the Fox and Black Squirrels. Leather for Shoes they have good and well tann'd: The Indians have also a way of dressing their Skins rather softer, though not so durable as ours in England.

Birds the Country yields of differing kinds and Colours: For Prey, the Pelican, Hawk, and Eagle, etc. For Pleasure, the red, copped and blew Bird, which wantonly imitates the various Notes and Sounds of such Birds and Beasts which it hears, wherefore, by way of Allusion, it's call'd the mocking Bird; for which pleasing Property it 's there esteem'd a Rarity. Birds for Food, and pleasure of Game, are the Swan, Goose, Duck, Mallard, Wigeon, Teal, Curlew, Plover, Partridge, the Flesh of which is equally as good, tho' smaller than ours in

---

[1] Deer are still plentiful in the lower part of South Carolina. On one plan- tation where the shooting of does has been long prohibited by the owner a friend of the editor counted fourteen does in one day's hunt and bagged a buck besides.

[2] See p. 132, *supra*. Bears are also plentiful in some sections of the lower part of South Carolina.

[3] Probably the last beaver in South Carolina was killed in Edgefield County about 1888, according to newspaper reports at the time.

* "It's a little creature feeding on Sweet Herbs, whose Codds scent as sweet and strong as Musk, lasting a long time, if handsomely inclosed in Cotton Wooll." (Note in original.)

England.   Pigeons and Parakeittoes.[1]   In Winter huge Flights
of wild Turkies, oftentimes weighing from twenty, thirty, to
forty pound.   There are also great Stocks of tame Fowl, *viz.*
Geese, Ducks, Cocks, Hens, Pigeons and Turkies.   They have a
Bird I believe the least in the whole Creation, named the
Humming Bird;  in bigness the Wren being much superiour,
in magnitude not exceeding the Humble Bee, whose Body in
flying much resembles it, did not their long Bills, between
two and three Inches, and no bigger than Needles, make the
difference.   They are of a deep Green, shadow'd with a Murry,
not much unlike the color of some Doves Necks;  they take
their Food humming or flying, feeding on the exuberant
Moistures of sweet odoriferous Leaves and Flowers.   I have
frequently seen them in many parts of the West Indies, but
never observed them to have any Musical Air, but a loud Note
to Admiration, crying *Chur, Chur, Chur,* etc., which at the
distance of half a mile is plainly heard: their Eggs, of which
they produce three or four young at a time, not unlike small
white Pease: they continue between the Tropiques the whole
year round, as I have observed at Berbadoes and Jamaica;
but I am informed, that in the more Northern parts of America they sleep the whole Winter; at Berbadoes the Jews
curiously skin these little Birds, filling them with fine Sand,
and perfuming their Feathers, they are sent into Europe as
pretty Delicacies for Ladies, who hang them at their Breasts
and Girdles.
    There are in Carolina great numbers of Fire Flies, who
carry their Lanthorns in their Tails in dark Nights, flying
through the Air, shining like Sparks of Fire, enlightning it
with their Golden Spangles.   I have seen a larger sort at
Jamaica, which Dr. Heylin in his Cosmography,[2] enumerates
amongst the Rarities and Wonders of Hispaniola, an Island
under the King of Spain, distant between 20 and 30 Leagues
from Jamaica: These have two Lights above their Eyes, and
a third in their Tails; in dark nights they shine like Candles:

---

[1] In December, 1885, or 1886, the editor saw a passenger pigeon in Orange-
burg County, South Carolina.   Since that time very few have been seen in the
state.   The Carolina paroquet appears to be extinct in South Carolina.   See
Arthur Trezevant Wayne. *Birds of South Carolina* (Charleston, S. C., 1910).

[2] Peter Heylin, *Cosmographie* (London, 1657, and other editions).

for which I have often at a distance mistaken them, supposeing them to have been the Lights of some adjacent Plantation; and in this I have not been the first that has been so deceived. Amongst large Orange Trees in the Night, I have seen many of those Flies, whose Lights have appeared like hanging Candles, or pendant Flambeaus, which amidst the Leaves and ripe Fruit yielded a Light truly glorious to behold: with 3 of these included in a Glass Bottle, in a very dark Night I have read very small Characters: When they are kill'd, their Igneous or Luminous Matter does not immediately, (till half an hour, or an hour after their Deaths) extinguish.[1]

As the Earth, the Air, etc., are enrich'd and replenished with the Blessings of the most High, the Seas and Rivers of the same bounty equally participate in the Variety of excellent and wholesome Fish which it produces, *viz.* Sturgeon, of whose Sounds Iceing-glass,[2] of whose Roes Caviare are made: Mullet, a delicious sweet Fish, of whose Roes or Spawn Botargo is made: Whale, Salmon, Trouts, Bass, Drum, Cat-fish, whose Head and glaring Eyes resemble a Cat; it 's esteem'd a very good Fish; it hath a sharp thorny Bone on its Back, which strikes at such as endeavour to take it: which by Seamen is held venemous: yet I saw one of our Seamen, the back of whose Hand was pierced with it, yet no poysonous Symptoms of Inflammation or Rancor appear'd on the Wound, which quickly heal'd, that I concluded it was either false, or that of this Fish there were more kinds than one: Plaice, Eels, Crabs, Prawns twice as large as ours in England: Oysters of an Oblong or Oval Form; their number inexhaustible; a man may easily gather more in a day than he can well eat in a year; some of which are margiritiferous, yielding bright round Oriental Pearl.

The Tortoise, more commonly call'd by our West Indians the Turtle, are of three sorts, the Hawks-Bill, whose Shell is that which we call the Turtle or Tortoise Shell; the Green Turtle, whose shell being thin is little regarded; but its Flesh is more esteemed than the Hawks-bill Tortoise: The Loggerhead Turtle, or Tortoise has neither good shell or Flesh, so is

---

[1] A firefly swallowed by a toad has been observed to illuminate the whole anatomy of the toad in X-ray fashion.

[2] Isinglass.

little minded or regarded. They are a sort of creatures which live both on Land and Water. In the day usually keeping the Sea, swiming on the surface of the Water, in fair Weather delighting to expose themselves to the Sun, oftentimes falling asleep, lying, as I have seen several times, without any Motion on the Waters, till disturbed by the approach of some Ship or Boat, being quick of hearing, they dive away. In the Night they often come ashore to feed and lay their Eggs in the Sand, which once covered, they leave to the Influence of the Sun, which in due time produces her young ones, which dig their Passage out of the sand immediately making their way towards the Water. At this Season, when they most usually come ashore, which is in April, May and June, the Seamen or Turtlers, at some convenient distance watch their opportunity, getting between them and the Sea, turn them on their Backs, from whence they are unable ever to rise, by which means the Seamen or Turtlers turn 40 or 50 in a night, some of 2, 3, 400 weight: If they are far distant from the Harbor or Market to which they design to bring them, they kill, cutting them to pieces, which Salted they Barrel: This is the way of killing at the Caymana's, an Island lying to the Leeward of Jamaica. Turtle, Barrel'd and Salted, if well conditioned, is worth from 18 to 25 shillings the Barrel. If near their Market or Harbor they bring them in Sloops alive, and afterwards keep them in Crauls, which is a particular place of Salt Water of Depth and Room for them to swim in, pallisado'd or staked, in round above the Waters Surface, where, upon occasion they take them out, and kill them, and cutting them to pieces, sell their Flesh for two pence or three pence the pound: the Belly, which they call the Callope of the Turtle, pepper'd and salted, or roasted and baked, is an excellent Dish, much esteemed by our Nation in the West Indies: the rest of the Flesh boil'd, makes as good and nourishing Broath, as the best Capon in England, especially if some of the Eggs are mixt with it; they are some white, and others of a yellow or golden Colour, in largeness not exceeding a Walnut, wrapt in a thin Skin or Membrane, sweet in Taste, nourishing and wholesome: and of this property, that they never grow hard by boiling: the Liver is black: it freely opens and purges the Body: if little of it be

eaten, it dies the Excrements of a deep black Colour: The
Fat in Color inclines to a Sea Green; in Taste it's sweet
and luscious, equalling, if not surpassing the best Marrow,
if freely eaten it deeply stains the Urine of its Color: It's of
of a very penetrating piercing quality, highly comended in
Strains and Aches: Of it the Turtlers oftentimes make an Oyl,
which in Lamps burns much brighter and sweeter than common Lamp or Train Oyl.   In general,the Flesh is commended
for a good Antiscorbutique and an Antivenereal Diet; many
in the former, and some that have been far gone in Consump-
tions, with the constant use alone of this Diet, have been
thoroughly recovered and cured in 3 or 4 months.   It hath
3 Hearts, by thin Pellicules only separated, which has caused
some to Philosophize on its Amphibious Nature, alluding to
those participating and assimulating Qualities which it has to
the rest of the Universe, it swiming like a Fish, laying Eggs
like a Fowl, and feeding on Grass like an Ox.   This I am
assured of, that after it's cut to pieces, it retains a Sensation
of Life three times longer than any known Creature in the
Creation:   Before they kill them they are laid on their Backs,
where hopeless of Relief as if sensible of their future Condition, for some hours they mourn out their Funerals, the Tears
plentifully flowing from their Eyes, accompanied with passionate Sobs and Sighs, in my Judgment nothing more like than
such who are surrounded and overwhelmed with Troubles,
Cares and Griefs, which raises in Strangers both Pity and
Compassion.   Compleatly six hours after the Butcher has
cut them up and into pieces, mangled their Bodies, I have
seen the Callope when going to be seasoned, with pieces of
their Flesh ready to cut into Stakes, vehemently contract
with great Reluctancy rise against the Knife, and sometimes
the whole Mass of Flesh in a visible Tremulation and Concus-
sion, to him who first sees it seems strange and admirable.
There is farther to the Southward of Carolina, especially about
the Shoars and Rivers of His[pa]niola and Cuba a Fish in
Nature something like the former, call'd the Manacy or Sea-
Cow, of an extraordinary Bigness, sometimes of 1000 pound
weight: It feeds on the Banks and Shoar sides on the grassy
Herbage, like a Tortoise; but that which is more wonderful
of this Creature is, that she gives her young Ones Suck from

her Duggs; she is headed like a Cow, of a green Colour, her Flesh by some esteemed the most delicate in the World, sweeter than the tenderest Veal, sold at Jamaica, where it's sometimes brought for 6d. the pound: It hath a stone in the Head which is a gallant Remedy against the Pains and Dolors of the Stone; so are the Bones of its Body to provoke Urine, when pulveriz'd and exhibited in convenient Liquors. Its Skin makes excellent Whips for Horses, if prudently us'd, which are very serviceable and lasting; with one of these Manaty Strapps, I have seen a Bar of Iron cut and dented: It cuts so severe and deep, that by the Public Authority at Jamaica, Masters are forbidden and prohibited with it to strike their White Servants.

There is in the mouth of their Rivers, or in Lakes near the Sea, a Creature well known in the West Indies, call'd the Alligator or Crocodile, whose Scaly Back is impenitrible, refusing a Musquet Bullet to pierce it, but under the Belly, that or an Arrow finds an easie Passage to destroy it; it lives both on Land and Water, being a voracious greedy Creature, devouring whatever it seizes on, Man only excepted, which on the Land it has not the courage to attacque, except when asleep or by surprize: In the Water it's more dangerous; it sometimes grows to a great length, from 16 to 20 foot, having a long Mouth, beset with sharp keen Teeth; the Body when full grown as large as a Horse, declining towards the Tail; it's slow in motion, and having no Joynt in the Vertebraes or Back Bone, but with its whole length is unable to turn, which renders it the less mischievous; yet Nature by Instinct has given most Creatures timely Caution to avoid them by their strong musky Smell, which at a considerable distance is perceiveable, which the poor Cattle for their own Preservation make good use of: their Flesh cuts very white; the young ones are eatable; the Flesh of the older smells so strong of Musk, that it nauseates; their Stones at least so called, are commended for a rich, lasting perfume.

Mettals or Minerals I know not of any, yet it's supposed and generally believed, that the Apalatean Mountains which lie far up within the Land, yields Ore both of Gold and Silver, that the Spaniards in their running Searches of this Country saw it, but had not time to open them, or at least, for the present were unwilling to make any farther Discovery till their Mines of Peru and Mexico were exhausted, or as others, that they were politically fearful that if the Riches of the Country should be exposed, it would be an Allure to encourage a Foreign Invader, Poverty preserving, Riches oftentimes the cause that Property is lost, usurped and invaded; but whether it be this or that reason time will discover.

The Natives of the Country are from time immemorial, ab Origine Indians, of a deep Chesnut Colour, their Hair black and streight, tied various ways, sometimes oyl'd and painted, stuck through with Feathers for Ornament or Gallantry; their Eyes black and sparkling, little or no Hair on their Chins, well limb'd and featured, painting their Faces with different Figures of a red or sanguine Colour, whether for Beauty or to render themselves formidable to their Enemies I could not learn. They are excellent Hunters; their Weapons the Bow and Arrow, made of a Read, pointed with sharp Stones, or Fish Bones; their Cloathing Skins of the Bear or Deer, the Skin drest after their Country Fashion.

Manufactures, or Arts amongst them I have heard of none, only little Baskets made of painted Reeds and Leather drest sometimes with black and red Chequers coloured. In Medicine, or the Nature of Simples, some have an exquisite Knowledge; and in the Cure of Scorbutick, Venereal, and Malignant Distempers are admirable: In all External Diseases they suck the part affected with many Incantations, Philtres and Charms: In Amorous Intrigues they are excellent either to procure Love or Hatred: They are not very forward in Discovery of their Secrets, which by long Experience are religiously transmitted and conveyed in a continued Line from one Generation to another, for which those skill'd in this Faculty are held in great Veneration and Esteem. Their Religion chiefly consists in the Adoration of the Sun and Moon: At the Appearance of the New Moon I have observed them with open extended Arms then folded, with inclined Bodies, to make their Adorations with much Ardency and Passion: They are divided into many Divisions or Nations, Govern'd by Reguli, or Petty Princes, which our English call Cacicoes.[1] Their Diet is of Fish, Flesh, and Fowl, with Indian Maiz or Corn; their Drink

---

[1] Cassiques.

Water, yet Lovers of the Spirits of Wine and Sugar. They
have hitherto lived in good Correspondence and Amity with
the English, who by their just and equitable Cariage have
extreamly winn'd and obliged them; Justice being exactly
and impartially administred, prevents Jealousies, and main-
tains between them a good Understanding, that the Neighbouring Indians are very kind and serviceable, doing our
Nation such Civilities and good Turns as lie in their Power.

This Country was first discover'd by Sir Sebastian Cabott,
by the order, and at the expence of King Henry VII. from
which Discovery our Successive Princes have held their Claim,
in pursuance to which in the Seventeenth Year of His Majesties
Reign it was granted unto his Grace George Duke of Albe-
marle, unto the Right Honourable Edward Earl of Clarendon,
William Earl of Craven, John Lord Berkley, Anthony Lord
Ashley now Earl of Shaftsbury,[1] to the Honourable Sir George
Carteret, and Sir John Colleton, Knights and Baronetts, to
Sir William Berkeley Knight, with a full and plenipotentiary
Power, to Colonize, Enact Laws, Execute Justice, etc. The
Regalia's of Premier Sovereignty only reserved. The Principal
place where the English are now settled lies scituated on a
point of Land about two Leagues from the Sea, between
Ashly and Cooper Rivers, so named in Honour to the Right
Honourable the Earl of Shaftsbury, a great Patron to the
Affairs of Carolina. The place called Charles Town, by an
express Order from the Lord Proprietors in the Year One
thousand six hundred and eighty, their Ordnance and Ammunition being removed thither from Old Charles Town, which
lay about a League higher from Ashly River, both for its
Strength and Commerce  It's very commodiously scituated
from many other Navigable Rivers that lie near it on which
the Planters are seated; by the Advantage of Creeks, which
have a Communication from one great River to another, at
the Tide or Ebb the Planters may bring their Commodities
to the Town as to the Common Market and Magazine both

---

[1] George Monck was the family name of the Duke of Albemarle; Edward
Hyde that of the Earl of Clarendon; William Craven that of the Earl of Craven;
John Berkeley that of Lord Berkeley, and Anthony Ashley Cooper that of Lord
Ashley. The other three proprietors being only baronets or knights bore only
their family names.

for Trade and Shipping. The Town is regularly laid out into large and capacious Streets, which to Buildings is a great Ornament and Beauty. In it they have reserved convenient places for Building of a Church,[1] Town-House and other Publick Structures, an Artillery Ground for the Exercise of their Militia, and Wharfs for the Convenience of their Trade and Shipping. At our being there was judged in the Country a 1000 or 1200 Souls; but the great Numbers of Families from England, Ireland, Berbadoes, Jamaica, and the Caribees, which daily Transport themselves thither, have more than doubled that Number. The Commodities of the Country as yet proper for England, are Furrs and Cedar: For Berbadoes, Jamaica and the Caribbee Islands, Provisions, Pitch, Tarr and Clapboard, for which they have in Exchange Sugar, Rumm, Melasses and Ginger, etc., such things which are proper and requisite for the Planter to be stored with before he leaves England for his better Settlement there at his Arrival, chiefly Servants: All kind of Iron Work for the clearing of Land, pruning of Vines, for the Kitchen and for Building. Commodities proper for the Merchant to Transport thither for his Advantage, Cloathing of all kinds, both Linnen and Woollen, Hats, Stockins, Shoes; all kind of Ammunition, Guns, Fowling-pieces, Powder, Match, Bullet, Nails, Locks and Knives; all Haberdashers Ware; Cordage, and Sails for Shipping, Spirits and Spices, *viz.*, Cloves, Nitmegs and Cinnamon. Finally, to encourage People to Transport themselves thither, the Lord Proprietors give unto all Masters and Mistresses of Families, to their Children, Men-Servants and Maid-Servants if above sixteen years of Age, fifty to all such under forty Acres of Land to be held for ever, annually paying a Peny an Acre to the Lord Proprietors to commence in 2 Years after it's survey'd.

*Sir*, Thus in an Abstract I have given you the Draught of this excellent Country, begining with its Name, Scituation, etc., and when first settled, regularly proceeding to the Nature

---

[1] At the southeast corner of the streets now known as Meeting and Broad. A church was erected soon after and called St. Philip's. St. Michael's Church now stands on the spot, a new St. Philip's having been built elsewhere at a subsequent date.

of the Soil, Quality of the Air, the Diseases and Longævity of its Inhabitants, the Rarity of its produce in Trees, Fruits, Roots and Herbs, Beasts, Fish, Fowl and Insects; the Nature and Disposition of the Indians, the Progress the English have made since their first Settlement, what Commodities they abound with, in what defective; in all which from the Truth I have neither swerved nor varied: Indeed in some other things I might have farther enlarged and expatiated, which I shall refer to a Personal Discourse, when I have the Honour to wait upon you again; in the mean time I am

Your humble Servant

**T. A.**

AN ACCOUNT OF THE PROVINCE OF
CAROLINA, BY SAMUEL WILSON, 1682

# INTRODUCTION

THE Lords Proprietors of Carolina evidently believed in advertising, if we judge by the frequency (for their time) with which they published pamphlets extolling the virtues of their province as a place for settlers. In 1682 one of these was published in London, giving a history of the Ashley River settlement in Carolina, an account of the natural resources of that part of the province, the advancement which the settlers had made, the methods of obtaining lands there, the necessary articles for settlers to take with them, and the mode of getting there. Its author was Samuel Wilson, who had been secretary to the Earl of Craven, one of the Lords Proprietors, for his Carolina affairs for four years preceding, and had thoroughly familiarized himself with conditions in South Carolina. While the pamphlet is written with the enthusiasm of a partisan, it can be corroborated from many contemporaneous sources, and is good history. It is copied into Richard Blome's *Present State of His Majesty's Isles and Territories in America* (London, 1685) and, in a garbled form, into the 1687 edition of that work.

This pamphlet was reprinted in 1836 in *Historical Collections of South Carolina* (New York), by B. R. Carroll. Carroll's text varies from that of the original pamphlet so often that it would seem that he used a different edition in making his copy, possibly a later edition of the pamphlet.

# AN ACCOUNT OF THE PROVINCE OF CAROLINA, BY SAMUEL WILSON, 1682

*An Account of the Province of Carolina, in America: together with an Abstract of the Patent, and several other Necessary and Useful Particulars, to such as have thoughts of transporting themselves thither. Published for their Information. London: Printed by G. Larkin, for Francis Smith, at the Elephant and Castle in Cornhil. 1682.*[1]

*To the Right Honourable William Earl of Craven Pallatine, and the rest of the true and absolute Lords and Proprietors of the Province of Carolina.*

MAY it please your Lordships,

Finding by my Conversation with People who have an Inclination to try their Fortunes in America, that your Province of Carolina had not its due valuation for want of being made known to the World, and not hearing of any that had undertaken it, I looked upon it as a Duty incumbunt upon me, who have had the Honour to be your Secretary in your Carolina-Affairs now four years, to Publish the ensuing Treatise; whereby is made known the Greatness of your Soveraign's Gift to your Selves, and to the World the Greatness of your Trust and Favour with Him; and to those that have a desire of settling there, to what kind of Countrey and Climate they Transport Themselves: Wherein I have most strictly kept to the Rules of Truth, there not being any thing that I have written in Commendation of your Province, which I cannot prove by Letters from thence now in my possession, and by Living Witnesses now in England.

I should not have been thus presumptuous to adventure upon this Work, and to have crav'd for it your Lordships Patronage,

---

[1] Title-page of original.

had not the Employment I have under you (which hath given me frequent Opportunities of discovering the Humanity and Softness with which you Treat all Those who apply to you, your constant Endeavours for the Good of all those who come under your Government in Carolina, and the great care you have taken by your admirable Constitution of Government, which you have there settled, for the lasting security, peace and well being of all the Inhabitants of your Province) induc'd me to beleive that the same goodness with which you treat others, will be extended to me, and that you will pardon my present presumption, and all the other Imperfections of,

May it please your Lordships,
Your Lordships most Faithful and
Obliged, Humble Servant,
SAMUEL WILSON.

## An Account of the Province of Carolina, in America.

CAROLINA is that part of Florida [1] which lies between twenty nine and thirty six Degrees and thirty Minutes of Northern Latitude: On the East it is washed with the Atlantick Ocean, and is bounded on the West by Mare Pacificum (or the South Sea) and within these bounds is contained the most healthy Fertile and pleasant part of Florida, which is so much commended by the Spanish Authors.

This Province of Carolina, was in the Year 1663 Granted by Letters Pattents in Propriety of his most Gracious Majesty, unto the Right Honourable Edward Earl of Clarendon, George Duke of Albemarle, William Earl of Craven, John Lord Berkely, Anthony Lord Ashly, now Earl of Shaftsbury, Sir George Carteret, and Sir John Colleton, Knights and Barronets, Sir William Berkeley Knight, by which Letters Pattents the Laws of England are to be of force in Carolina: but the Lords

---

[1] While the Atlantic coast of North America was first discovered and partially explored by Sebastian Cabot, it was the Spanish explorer, Juan Ponce de Leon, who gave the name Florida to the southern portion of it, and despite the fact that the English were able to defend their claim to it and gave it the name Virginia, many—even of the British empire—continued to call it Florida long after the English had laid out their provinces and established governments there.

Proprietors have power with the consent of the Inhabitants to make By-Laws for the better Government of the said Province: So that no Money can be raised or Law made, without the consent of the Inhabitants or their Representatives. They have also power to appoint and impower Governours, and other Magistrates, to Grant Liberty of Conscience, make Constitutions, etc., With many other great Priviledges, as by the said Letters Pattents will more largely appear. And the said Lords Proprietors have there setled a Constitution of Government, whereby is granted Liberty of Conscience, and wherein all possible care is taken for the equal Administration of Justice, and for the lasting Security of the Inhabitants both in their Persons and Estates.

By the care and endeavours of the said Lords Proprietors, and at their very great charge, two Colonys have been setled in this Province, the one at Albemarle in the most Northerly part, the other at Ashly River, which is in the Latitude of thirty two Degrees odd Minutes.

Albemarle bordering upon Virginia, and only exceeding it in Health, Fertility, and Mildness of the Winter, is in the Growths, Productions and other things much of the same nature with it: Wherefore I shall not trouble the Reader with a perticular Description of that part; but apply my self principally to discourse of the Collony at Ashly-River, which being many Degrees more Southward than Virginia, differs much from it in the Nature of its Clymate and Productions.

Ashly-River was first setled in April 1670, the Lords Proprietors having at their sole charge, set out three Vessels, with a considerable number of able Men; eighteen Moneths Victuals, with Clothes, Tools, Ammunition, and what else was thought necessary for a new Settlement, and continued at this charge to supply the Collony for divers years after, until the Inhabitants were able by their own Industry to live of themselves; in which condition they have been for divers years past, and are arrived to a very great Degree of Plenty of all sorts of Provisions. Insomuch, that most sorts are already cheaper there, than in any other of the English Collonys, and they are plentifully enough supplied with all things from England or other Parts.

Ashly-River, about seven Miles in from the Sea, divides

it self into two Branches; the Southermost retaining the name of Ashly-River, the North Branch is called Cooper-River. In May 1680, the Lords Proprietors sent their Orders to the Government there, appointing the Port-Town for these two Rivers to be Built on the Poynt of Land that divides them, and to be called Charles Town, since which time about an hundred Houses are there Built,[1] and more are Building daily by the Persons of all sorts that come there to Inhabit, from the more Northern English Collonys, and the Sugar Islands, England and Ireland; and many persons who went to Carolina Servants, being Industrious since they came out of their times with their Masters, at whose charge they were Transported, have gotten good Stocks of Cattle, and Servants of their own; have here also Built Houses, and exercise their Trades: And many that went thither in that condition, are worth several Hundreds of Pounds, and live in a very plentiful condition, and their Estates still encreasing. And Land is become of that value near the Town, that it is sold for twenty Shillings per Acre, though pillaged of all its valuable Timber, and not cleared of the rest, and Land that is clear'd and fitted for Planting, and Fenced, is let for ten Shillings per annum the Acre, though twenty miles distant from the Town, and six men will in six weeks time, Fall, Clear, Fence in, and fit for Planting, six Acres of Land.

At this Town, in November 1680. There Rode at one time sixteen Sail of Vessels (some of which were upwards of 200 Tons) that came from divers parts of the Kings Dominions to trade there, which great concourse of shipping, will undoubtedly in a short time make it a considerable Town.

The Eastern Shore of America, whether it be by reason of its having the great Body of the Continent to the Westward of it, and by consequence the North-west Wind (which Flows contrary to the Sun) the Freezing-Wind, as the North-East is

---

[1] A town was laid out there in 1672, and some of the lots had been granted out and a few had been built upon prior to 1680, when, by order of the Proprietors, the seat of government was removed to the new site, and the removal of the inhabitants rapidly followed. The site of the old town is now upon the plantation of Mr. E. T. Legaré, and the society of Children of the American Revolution has lately erected a stone about a quarter of a mile from the site to mark it. The stone, however, contains the erroneous statement that it marks the *site* of the old town.

in Europe, or that the Frozen Lakes which Lye-in, beyond
Canada, and lye North and West from the Shore, Impregnate
the Freezing Wind with more chill and congealing qualities,
or that the uncultivated Earth, covered for the most part
with large shading Trees, breathes forth more nitrous Vapours,
than that which is cultivated; or all these Reasons together,
it is certainly much more cold than any part of Europe, in
the same Degree of Latitude of thirty nine and forty, and
England and those parts of America about the Latitude of
thirty nine and forty, and more North, though about six
hundred Miles nearer the Sun than England; is notwithstanding many degrees colder in the Winter.

The Author having been informed by those that say they
have seen it, that in those Parts it Freezeth above six Inches
thick in a Night, and great Navigable Rivers are Frozen over
in the same space of time; and the Country about Ashly-
River, though within nine Degrees of the Tropick, hath seldom
any Winter that doth not produce some Ice, though I cannot
yet learn that any hath been seen on Rivers or Ponds, above
a quarter of an Inch thick, which vanisheth as soon as the
Sun is an hour or two high; and when the Wind is not at
North-west, the Weather is very mild. So that the December
and January of Ashly River, I suppose to be of the same
Temperature with the latter end of March, and beginning of
April in England. This small Winter causeth a fall of the
Leaf, and adapts the Country to the Production of all the
Grains and Fruits of England, as well as those that require
more Sun; insomuch, that at Ashly-river the Apple, the Pear,
the Plum, the Quince, Apricock, Peach, Medlar, Walnut, Mulberry and Chesnut, thrive very well in the same Garden together with the Orange, the Lemon, Olive, the Pomgranate,
the Fig and Almond; Nor is the Winter here Cloudy, Overcast
or Foggy, but it hath been observed that from the twentieth
of August to the tenth of March, including all the Winter
Months, there have been but eight overcast days; and though
Rains fall pretty often in the Winter, it is most commonly in
quick Showers, which when past, the Sun shines out clear
again.

The Summer is not near so hot as in Virginia or the other
Northern American English Collonys, which may hardly gain

belief with those that have not considered the reason; which is its neerness to the Tropicks, which makes it in a greater Measure than those Parts more Northward partake of those Breezes, which almost constantly rise about eight or nine of the Clock, within the Tropicks, and blow fresh from the East till about Four in the Afternoon; and a little after the Sea-breeze dys away, there rises a North-wind, which blowing all night, keeps it fresh and cool.  In short, I take Carolina, to be much of the same nature with those Delicious Countries about Aleppo, Antioch, and Smyrna: but hath the Advantage of being under an equal English Government.

Such, who in this Country have seated themselves near great Marshes, are subject to Agues, as those who are so seated in England; but those who are planted more remote from Marshes or standing Waters, are exceeding healthy; insomuch, that out of a Family consisting of never less than twelve Persons, not one hath died since their first Arrival there, which is nine years; but what is more, not one hath been sick in all that time; nor is there one of the Masters of Families that went over in the first Vessels, dead of Sickness in Carolina, except one, who was seventy and five years of Age before he came there,[1] though the number of those Masters of Families be pretty considerable: divers persons who went out of England Ptisical, and Consumptive, have re-cover'd, and others subject in England to frequent fits of the Stone, have been absolutely freed from them after they have been there a short time; nor is the Gout there yet known.  The Ayr gives a strong Appetite and quick Digestion, nor is it with-out suitable effects, men finding themselves apparently more lightsome, more prone, and more able to all Youthful Exer-cises, than in England, the Women are very Fruitful, and the Children have fresh Sanguine Complexions.

The Soyle is generally very fertile, but hath some sandy

---

[1] Paul Smith, who was put down on the list of the passengers in the *Carolina*, one of the ships that brought over the first settlers, as a master, or head of family, died prior to June 29, 1672, when the governor and deputies directed the sur-veyor-general to lay out fifty acres of land to parties who had purchased it of the heirs of Paul Smith, deceased.  Possibly he was the head of family to whom the writer here refers.  See A. S. Salley, Jr., *Warrants for Lands in South Caro-lina*, 1672–1679, pp. 16, 48.

tracts so as to make an agreable variety, but even this Land produceth good Corne and is excellent pasture; Wheat, Rye, Barly, Oates, and Peas, thrive exceedingly, and the ground yeilds in greater abundance than in England, Turnips, Parsnips, Carrots, Potatoes, and Edoes, a substantial wholesome nourishing Root grow well, and all excellent in their kindes, they have near twenty sorts of Pulse that we have not in England, all of them very good food, insomuch that the English Garden Bean is not regarded.

Near the Sea the Trees are not very large, they grow pritty neare together; farther up they are larger, and grow farther asunder, and are in most parts free from Underwood, so that you may see near half a mile amongst the bodyes of large tall timber trees, whose tops meeting make a very pleasing shade, yet hinders not grass, myrtle and other sweet scenting shrubs here and there from growing under them: Amongst these Groves of Timber Trees are here and there Savana's, (or grassy plains) of several magnitudes clear of Trees, which have occasion'd some that have seene them to compare Carolina to those pleasant Parks in England, that have abundance of tall Timber Trees unlop'd, here you may hunt the Hare, Fox, and Deere all day long in the shade, and freely, spur your horse through the Woods to follow the chase.

This Country hath the Oak, Ash, Elm, Poplar, Beech, and all the other Sorts of useful Timber that England hath, and divers sorts of lasting Timber that England hath not, as Cedar white and red, Cypress, Locust, Bay and Laurell Trees, equal to the biggest Oaks, large Mirtles, Hickery, black Wallnut and Pynes big enough to Mast the greatest Ships, and divers other sorts, which I cannot enumerate.

The Woods abound with Hares, Squirrels, Racoons, Possums, Conyes and Deere, which last are so plenty that an Indian hunter hath kill'd nine fatt Deere in a day all shott by himself, and all the considerable Planters have an Indian hunter which they hire for less than twenty shillings a year, and one hunter will very well find a Family of thirty people with as much Venison and Foul, as they can well eat.   Here are also in the woods great plenty of wilde Turkeys, Partridges, something smaller than those of England, but more de[l]icate, Turtle Doves, Paraquetos, and Pidgeons; On the grassy plaines

the whistling Plover and Cranes and divers sorts of Birds un-
knowne in England.

Carolina doth so abound in Rivers, that within fifty miles
of the Sea you can hardly place your self seven miles from a
Navigable River, and divers are navigable for good big Vessels above three hundred miles: [1] The Rivers abound with
variety of excellent Fish, and near the Sea with very good
Oysters, in many of which are Pearl: the Author having seen
Pearl that have been taken out of some of them bigger than
Rouncival Pease and perfectly round. On the Rivers and
brooks are all the winter moneths vast quantitys of Swan,
wild Geese, Duck, Widgeon, Teale, Curlew, Snipe, Shell Drake
and a certaine sort of black Duck that is excellent meat,
and stayes there all the year.[2]

Neat Cattle thrive and increase here exceedingly, there
being perticular Planters that have already seven or eight
hundred head, and will in a few years in all probability, have
as many thousands, unless they sell some part; the Cattle are
not subject to any Disease as yet perceiv'd, and are fat all the
Year long without Fother, the little Winter they have, not
pinching them so as to be perceiv'd, which is a great advantage
the Planters here have of the more Northern Plantations who
are all forc'd to give their Cattle Fother, and must spend a
great part of their Summers Labour in providing three or four
Months Fother for the Cattle in the Winter, or else would have
few of them alive in the Spring, which will keep them from
ever having very great Heards, or be able to do much in Planting any Comodity for Forreign Markets; the providing Winter
Food for their Cattle, taking up so much of their Summers
Labour; So that many Judicious Persons think that Carolina
will be able by Sea, to supply those Northern Collonys, with
salted Beef for their Shipping, cheaper than they themselves
with what is bred amongst them; for, considering that all the
Woods in Carolina afford good Pasturage, and the small Rent

---

[1] There are only three rivers in South Carolina that extend inland from the
sea so much as three hundred miles: the Edisto, the Santee, and the Peedee.
There are about a dozen more that are from fifteen to one hundred miles long
that are navigable by steamers almost to their sources.

[2] The only duck that stays in South Carolina all the year now is the wood
duck, known locally as the summer duck. See Wayne, *Birds of South Carolina.*

that is paid to the Lords Proprietors for Land, an Ox is raised at almost as little expence in Carolina, as a Hen is in England. And it hath by experience been found that Beef will take salt at Ashly-River any Month in the Year, and save very well.

Ewes have most commonly two or three Lambs at a time; their Wool is a good Staple and they thrive very well, but require a Shepherd to drive them to Feed, and to bring them home at night to preserve them from the Wolves.

Hogs increase in Carolina abundantly, and in a manner without any charge or trouble to the Planter, only to make them Sheds, wherein they may be protected from the Sun and Rain, and Morning and Evening to give them a little Indian Corn, or the pickings and parings of Potatoes, Turnips, or other Roots, and at the same time blowing a Horn, or making any other constant noyse, to which being us'd, they will afterwards upon hearing it, repair home, the rest of their Food they get in the Woods, of Masts, and Nuts of several sorts; and when those fail, they have Grass and Roots enough, the ground being never frozen so hard as to keep them from Rooting, these conveniencies breeds them large, and in the Mast time they are very fat, all of which makes the rearing of them so easy, that there are many Planters that are single and have never a Servant, that have two or three hundred Hogs, of which they make great profit; Barbados, Jamaica, and New-England, affording a constant good price for their Pork; by which means they get wherewithal to build them more convenient Houses, and to purchase Servants, and Negro-slaves.

There have been imported into Carolina about an hundred and fifty Mares, and some Horses from New-York and Rhoad-Island, which breed well, and the Coalts they have are finer Lim'd and Headed than their Dams or Sires, which gives great hopes of an excellent breed of Horses, as soon as they have gotten good Stalions amongst them.

Negros By Reason of the mildness of the Winter thrive and stand much better, than in any of the more Northern Collonys, and require less clothes, which is a great charge sav'd.

With the Indians the English have a perfect freindship, they being both usefull to one another. And care is taken by the Lords Proprietors, that no Injustice shall be done them; In order to which they have established a Particular

Court of Judicature, (compos'd of the soberest and most disinterested Inhabitants) to determine all differences that shall happen between the English and any of the Indians, this they do upon a Christian and Moral Consideration, and not out of any apprehension of danger from them, for the Indians have been always so engaged in Wars one Town or Village against another (their Government being usually of no greater extent) that they have not suffered any increase of People, there having been several Nations in a manner quite extirpated by Wars amongst themselves since the English setled at Ashly River: This keeps them so thin of people, and so divided, that the English have not the least apprehensions of danger from them; the English being already too strong for all the Indians within five hundred Miles of them, if they were united, and this the Indians so well know, that they will never dare to break with the English, or do any Injury to any particular person, for fear of having it reveng'd upon their whole Nation.

The Lords Proprietors do at present grant to all persons that come there to Inhabit as follows, viz. To each Master or Mistriss of a Family fifty acres, and to every able son or man servant they shall carry or cause to be transported into Carolina fifty acres more, and the like for each Daughter or woman servant that is marriageable, and for each child, man or woman servant under sixteen years of age, forty acres, and fifty acres of Land to each servant when out of their time, this Land to be injoy'd by them and their Heirs for ever, they paying a Penny an Acre Quit-rent to the Lords Proprietors, the Rent to commence in two years after their taking up their Land. But forasmuch as divers persons who are already Inhabitants of Carolina, and others that have Intentions to transport themselves into that Province, desire not to be cumber'd with paying of a Rent, and also to secure to themselves good large convenient tracts of Land, without being forc'd to bring thither a great number of servants at one time; The Lords Proprietors have been Prevail'd upon, and have agreed to sell to those who have a mind to buy Land, after the rate of fifty pound for a Thousand Acres, reserving a Pepper-Corn per annum Rent when demanded.

The way of any ones taking up his Land, due to him

either by carrying himself or servants into the Country, or by purchasing it of the Lords Proprietors, is after this manner; He first seeks out a place to his mind that is not already possessed by any other, then applyes himself to the Governour and Proprietors Deputys, and shew what rights he hath to Land, either by Purchase or otherwise; who thereupon issue out their Warrant to the Surveyor-General to measure him out a Plantation containing the number of acres due to him; who making Certificate that he hath measur'd out so much Land and the Bounds, a Deed is prepar'd of course, which is signed by the Governour and the Lords Proprietors Deputys, and the Proprietors Seal affixed to it, and Register'd, which is a good Conveyance in Law of the Land therein mention'd to the party and his Heirs for ever.

I have here, as I take it, described a pleasant and fertile Country, abounding in health and pleasure, and with all things necessary for the sustenance of mankind, and wherein I think I have written nothing but truth, sure I am I have inserted no wilful falshood:  I have also told you how men are to have Land that go there to Inhabit.  But a rational man will certainly inquire, When I have Land, what shall I doe with it? what Comoditys shall I be able to produce that will yeild me mony in other Countrys, that I may be inabled to buy Negro slaves (without which a Planter can never do any great matter) and purchase other things for my pleasure and convenience, that Carolina doth not produce?  To this I answer, That besides the great profit that will be made by the vast heards of Cattle and Swine, the Country appears to be proper for the Commoditys following. *viz.*

*Wine.*  There are growing naturally in the Country five sorts of Grapes, three of which the French Vignaroons who are there, judge will make very good Wine, and some of the Lords Proprietors have taken care to send plants of the Rhenish, Canary, Clarret, Muscatt, Madera, and Spanish Grapes, of all which divers Vinyards are planted; some wine was made this year that proved very good both in colour and taste, and an indifferent good quantity may be expected the next year: The Country hath gentle rising hills of fertile sand proper for Vines, and further from the Sea, rock and gravel, on which very good grapes grow naturally, ripen well, and together, and very lushious in taste, insomuch as the French Protestants who are there, and skill'd in wine, do no way doubt of pro- ducing great quantitys and very good.

*Oyl.* There are severall Olive trees growing, which were carryed thither, some from Portugal, and some from Ber- mudas and flourish exceedingly, and the Inhabitants take great care to propagate more, so that in all probability it will be an excellent Oyl-Country.

*Silk.* There is in Carolina great plenty of Mulberry Trees, such as are by experience found to feed the Silk-worm very well, yea as well as the white Mulberry, but there is of that sort also, which are propagated with a great deal of ease, a stick new cut and thrust into the ground, seldom failing to grow, and so likewise if the seed of them be sown.

*Tobacco.* Tobacco doth here grow very well, and is nearer to the nature of the Spanish Tobacco than that of Virginia.

*Indigo.* Indigo thrives well here, and very good hath been made.

*Cotton.* Cotton of the Cyprus and Smyrna sort will grow well, and good plenty of the Seed is sent thither.

*Flax and Hemp.* Thrives exceedingly.

Good plenty of Pitch and Tar is there made, there being particular persons that have made above a thousand barrels.

Here is good plenty of Oake for Pipe staves, which are a good Commodity in the Maderas, Canaryes, Barbados, and the Leeward Islands.

*Sumack.* Sumack growes in great abundance naturally, so undoubtedly would Woad, Madder and Sa-Flower, if planted.

*Drugs.* Jallop, Sassaparilla, Turmerick, Sassafras, Snake- root, and divers others.

In short, This Country being of the same Clymate and Temperature of Aleppo, Smyrna, Antioch, Judea, and the Province of Nanking, the richest in China, will (I conceive) produce any thing which those Countrys do, were the Seeds brought into it.

The Tools that men who goe thither ought to take with them are these, *viz.* An Ax, a Bill, and a Broad Hoe, and grabbing Hoe, for every man, and a cross cut Saw to every four men, a Whip-saw, a set of Wedges and Fraus and Betle-Rings to every family, and some Reaping Hooks and

Sythes, as likewise Nails of all sorts, Hooks, Hinges, Bolts and Locks for their Houses.

The Merchandizes which sell best in Carolina, are Linnen and Woollen, and all other Stufs to make clothes of, with Thread, Sowing Silk, Buttons, Ribbons, Hats, Stockings, Shoes, etc., which they sell at very good rates, and for these goods any man may purchase the Provision he hath need of.

The Passage of a man or woman to Carolina is five Pound, Ships are going thither all times of the year. Some of the Lords Proprietors, or my self, will be every Tuesday at 11 of the clock at the Carolina-Coffee-house in Burching-Lane near the Royal Exchange, to inform all people what Ships are going, or any other thing whatsoever.[1]

[1] Then follows in the pamphlet a seven-page abstract of the patent.

# LETTERS OF THOMAS NEWE, 1682

# INTRODUCTION

AMONG those who settled in South Carolina in the year 1682 was Thomas Newe, who arrived in Charles Town May 12. He was the son of William Newe, butler of Exeter College, Oxford; a man of excellent education, being a graduate of Oxford with the degree of Master of Arts,[1] and well equipped to take a leading part in the affairs of the province, but, unfortunately, he died before the year was out. On December 1, 1682, Governor Morton appointed John Beresford, Esq., administrator of his estate and, at the same time, directed Robert Daniell, Richard Codner, and John Norton to make an inventory and appraisement of his property. The inventory shows that he had accumulated some cattle, household goods and furniture, and some books,[2] and had also run into debt to the extent of £53. 6s. 1d.[3] Three letters which he wrote to his father during his brief sojourn in South Carolina, and which give very interesting accounts of the province at that time, have been preserved. They are to be found in MS. Rawlinson D. 810 in the Bodleian Library at Oxford. MS. Rawlinson D. 810 is a volume of miscellaneous collections partly transcribed from collections of Hannibal Baskerville, of Bayworth, Berks, but chiefly written by his son Thomas, relative to their

---

[1] Foster, in his *Alumni Oxonienses*, p. 1060, has this entry: "Thomas Newe, s. William, of Oxford city, pleb., Exeter Coll., matric. 7 March, 1672–3, aged 17; B. A. 1676, M. A. 1679."

[2] These were Heylin's *Geography*, appraised at £1, a dictionary, at 15s., a Roman history, at £1. 2s., a Greek dictionary, at 5s., and twenty-three other books, at £1. 10s.

[3] Records of the Court of Ordinary of South Carolina, 1672–1692 (MS. in the office of the Historical Commission of South Carolina), pp. 131–132.

family, their friends, and the University of Oxford, and of the most varied nature. Thomas Newe's letters are imbedded in the description of Exeter College, as follows:

*Exeter College.* . . . This Colledge is Capacious and large enough to entertaine and lodge 120 people (so saith Mr. Crabb and Mr. Oliver Schollers in't) but my friend Mr. Newe the present Butler saith it is capacious enough for 150 people. . . .

The Gentlemen which I can remember that have been and now are of my acquaintance in this Colledge are these. . . . Mr. Newe my loving friend and Butler of this Colledge as aforesaid, who had an ingenous son sometimes a Scholler of this House; who went one of the earliest Planters to Carolina whose loss, with his dear father I do much lament as being deprived by his death of further intelligence from those parts; yet to make him live what we can in our Memory take here an account of that plantation, as it came in letters from him before any narrative of that place was put in print.[1]

These letters were used by Professor Charles M. Andrews in his *Colonial Self-Government.* Professor Andrews called the attention of Dr. J. Franklin Jameson, managing editor of the *American Historical Review,* to them, and Doctor Jameson printed them, with an introduction and annotations, in the *Review* for January, 1907 (vol. XII., pp. 322–327).[2]

[1] The pamphlets of both Ashe and Wilson appeared in the same year in which these letters were written, 1682.

[2] The editor has made liberal use here of Doctor Jameson's introduction and notes, and begs to acknowledge his obligation to Doctor Jameson's work.

# LETTERS OF THOMAS NEWE, 1682

May the 17th, 1682, from CHARLES TOWN on
Ashley River by way of Barbadoes in the
*Samuel.*

*Most Honourd Father:*
   THE 12th of this instant by the providence of God after a
long and tedious passage we came to an Anchor against Charles
town at 10 in the night in 3½ fathom water, on the sixth we
made land 60 miles to the South of Ashley River against which
we came the 8 but could not get in by reason of contrary winds
sooner then we did.   We had little or nothing observable in
the whole voyage, but the almost continual S.W. winds.   God
be thanked I had my health very well except a day or two of
Sea sickness but most of the other passengers were much
troubled with the scurvy;   Of 62 that came out of England we
lost 3, two of them were seamen, one dyed of the scurvey, the
other fell overboard, the third was a woman in child bed, her
child died shortly after her.   As for the Countrey I can say
but little of it as yet on my one [own] knowledge, but what I
hear from others.   The Town which two years since had but
3 or 4 houses, hath now about a hundred houses in it, all
which are wholy built of wood, tho here is excellent Brick
made, but little of it.   All things are very dear in the Town;
milk 2 *d* a quart, beefe 4 *d* a pound, pork 3 *d*, but far better
then our English, the common drink of the Countrey is Molos-
sus and water, I don't hear of any mault that is made hear as
yet.   The English Barly and Wheat do thrive very well, but
the Indian corn being more hearty and profitable, the other is
not much regarded.   I am told that there is great plenty of
all things in the Countrey, whither I intend to go as soon as
conveniently I can dispose of my goods, which I fear will not

be soon, nor to such advantage as we expected.[1]  Severall in
the Country have great stocks of Cattle and they sell so well
to new comers that they care not for killing, which is the
reason provision is so dear in the Town, whilst they in the
Country are furnisht with Venison, fish, and fowle by the Indians for trifles, and they that understand it make as good
butter and cheese as most in England.  The land near the sea
side is generally a light and sandy ground, but up in the Country they say there is very good land, and the farther up the
better, but that which at present doth somewhat hinder the
selling [settling] farther up, is a war that they are ingaged in
against a tribe of Barbarous Indians being not above 60 in
number, but by reason of their great growth and cruelty in
feeding on all their neighbours, they are terrible to all other
Indians, of which, there are above 40 severall Kingdoms, the
strength and names of them all being known to our Governer
who upon any occasion summons their Kings in.  We are at
peace with all but those common enemies of mankind, those
man eaters before mentioned, by name the Westos,[2] who have
lately killed two eminent planters that lived far up in the
Country, so that they are resolved now if they can find their
settlement (which they often change) to cut them all off.
There is a small party of English out after them, and the most
potent Kingdome of the Indians armed by us and continually
in pursuit of them.  When we came into Ashley river we found
six small vessels in the Harbour, but great ones may and have
come in by the assistance of a good Pilot, and if they can make
good wine hear, which they have great hopes of, and this year
will be the time of tryall which if it hits no doubt but the place
will flourish exceedingly, but if the vines do not prosper I
question whither it will ever be any great place of trade.  On
Sunday the 14th of this instant a small vessell that came from
Mewis [3] hither, was cast away upon the Bar, but the men and

---

[1] He evidently expected to do as many of the foremost men of South Carolina had done and as many more of them subsequently did.  They accumulated
capital in trade and then took up planting and grew wealthy thereby.

[2] See Woodward's *Westoe Voiage*, pp. 130–134, *supra*, for an account of the
Westoes.  They rose against the English settlements in 1673, 1680, and 1681,
but were defeated each time.  See *Collections of the South Carolina Historical
Society*, V. 461; *Calendar of State Papers, Colonial*, 1681–1685, pp. 508–510.

[3] Nevis.

goods were all saved.   This is the first opportunity I have had
to write since I came from England but I hope to find more
opportunityes here, then I had at Sea, this with my most
humble duty to yourself and my Mother, my kind love to my
sister and Brothers being all from

Your most duetifull and obedient son

THOMAS NEWE

My duty to my Grandmother and my love to all my relations and friends that enquire concerning me.

May 29th, 1682, by way of

Barbados.

*Most Honoured Father:*

The 17th of this Instant by way of Barbados in the *Samuel*,
being the 1ʳˢᵗ opportunity since my departure from England,
I sent you a letter wherein I gave you an account of our safe
arrival, but not of the Voyage, that I leave to my Journall
which I intend to send by the first Ship that goes directly for
England, with my knowledge of the Countrey of which I have
not seen much yet, but one thing I understand (to my sorrow)
that I knew not before, the most have a seasoning, but few
dye of it.   I find the Commonalty here to be mightily dissatisfied, the reason is 3 or 4 of the great ones, for furs and skins,
have furnished the Indians with arms and ammunitions
especially those with whome they are now at War, for from
those they had all or most of their fur, so that trade which 3
or 4 only kept in their hands is at present gone to decay, and
now they have armed the next most potent tribe of the Indians to fight the former, and some few English there are out,
looking after them, which is a charge to the people and a stop
[to] the further setling of the Countrey.[1]   The Soyl is gen-

---

[1] Dr. Henry Woodward had built up a fine trade with the Westo Indians,
in which he was personally interested.   In 1680 the Savannah Indians pushed
eastward from their towns near the Gulf, west of the Appalachicola River, to
the Westoboo (Savannah).   In the same year, the Westoes, in violation of a
treaty they had made with the governor, killed, or captured for slaves, some
Indians of the coastal tribes near Charles Town, and war was declared upon
them by the whites.   Dr. Woodward was accused of having furnished the Westoes
with arms to use against the friendly Indians and prohibited from trading or
negotiating with them.   He was subsequently fined for his conduct, but the

erally very light, but apt to produce whatsoever is put into it.
There are already all sorts of English fruit and garden herbs
besides many others that I never saw in England, and they
do send a great deal of Pork, Corn and Cedar to Barbados,
besides the victualling of severall Vessels that come in here,
as Privateers and others which to do in the space of 12 years
the time from the 1ʳˢᵗ seating of it by the English, is no small
work, especially if we consider the first Planters which were
most of them tradesmen, poor and wholy ignorant of husbandry
and till of late but few in number, it being encreased more the 3
or 4 last years then the whole time before, the whole at presen[t]
not amounting to 4000,[1] so that their whole Business was to
clear a little ground to get Bread for their Familyes, few of
them having wherewithall to purchase a Cow, the first stock
whereof they were furnished with, from Bermudas and New
England, from the later of which they had their horses which
are not so good as those in England, but by reason of their
scarcity much dearer, an ordinary Colt at 3 years old being
valued at 15 or 16 *lis.* as they are scarce, so there is but little
use of them yet, all Plantations being seated on the Rivers,
they can go to and fro by Canoo or Boat as well and as soon
as they can ride, the horses here like the Indians and many of
the English do travail without shoes.   Now each family hath
got a stock of Hogs and Cows, which when once a little more
encreased, they may send of to the Islands cheaper then any
other place can, by reason of its propinquity, which trade alone
will make it far more considerable than either Virginia, Maryland, Pensilvania, and those other places to the North of us.

I desire you would be pleased by the next opportunity to
send me over the best herbalist for Physical Plants in as small
a Volume as you can get.   There was a new one just came out
as I left England, if I mistake not in 8ᵛᵒ. that was much commended, the Author I have forgot,[2] but there are severall in

Lords Proprietors pardoned him.  See *Journal of the Grand Council of South
Carolina,* 1671–1680 (Columbia, S. C., 1907), pp. 84–85.  While hostilities were
on with the Westoes the English furnished the Savannahs with arms with which
to drive out their rivals, the Westoes, which they did in 1681.

[1] See p. 158, *supra.*

[2] Perhaps this was John Ray's *Methodus Plantarum Nova* (London, 1682,
octavo).  If he received the "herbalist" it probably was included in the twenty-
three books appraised in his inventory at £1. 10s.  See p. 179, *supra.*

the Colledge that can direct you to the best.  If Mr. Sessions, Mr. Hobart or Mr. White, should send to you for money for the passage of a servant, whether man or boy that they Judge likely, I desire you would be pleased to send it them, for such will turn to good account here; and if you please to enquire at some Apothecarys what Sassafrass (which grows here in great plenty) is worth a pound and how and at what time of the year to cure it, let me know as soon as you can, for if the profit is not I am sure the knowledge is worth sending for. Pray Sir let me hear by the next how all our friends and relacions do, what change in the Colledge, and what considerable alteracion through the whole Town; I have now nothing more to speak but my desire that you may still retain (what I know you do) that love with which I dayly was blest and that readiness in pardoning whatsoever you find amiss, and to believe that my affections are not changed with the Climate unless like it too, grown warmer, this with my most humble duety to yourself and my mother, my kind love to my sister and Brothers and all the rest of our Friends I rest

Your most dutifull and obedient son,<br>Tho: Newe.

From Charls Town in Carolina.

From Charls Town, August the 23,<br>1682.

*Most Honourd Father.*

In obedience to your commands, I am ready to embrace every opportunity of sending to you, this is the 3rd, The 2 first by way of Barbados, the 1$^{rst}$ of the 17th, the 2$^{nd}$ of the 29th of May, which I hope you will receive long before this comes to your hands.  This place affords little news, nothing worth sending.  The 11th of June a French Privateer of 4 Guns 30 men whereof 10 were English men brought in here a Spanish prize of 16 Guns and a 100 men, which by the Frenchmens confession they had never taken, had it not been for the English, they have allready spent most of it and are providing to be gone againe.

The 30th of July cam an Indian to our Governour and told him that 800 Spaniards were upon their march coming from St. Augustine (a place belonging to our Proprietors about 150

miles to the South of us, where the Spaniards are seated and
have a pretty strong Town) to fall upon the English, upon
which the Council met 3 times and ordered 20 great Guns
that lay at a place where the town was first designed to be
made, to be brought to Charls Town, and sent Scouts at a
good distance (knowing which way they must come) to discover
their strength and the truth of it, which if they had seen anything were to return with all speed, and 700 men were to have
met them, which were to lay in Ambuscade in a Cave, swam[1]
where the Spaniards were to come, through a Marsh, that
every step they would be up to their middle.  Our people
were so far from being afraid that they mightily rejoyced at
the news of it, wishing that they might have some just cause
of War with the Spaniards, that they might grant Commissions to Privateers, and themselves fall on them at St. Augustine.[2] as we understand since this was the ground of the report,
The Spaniards thinking themselves to be abused by a nation
of Indians that lived betwixt them and us, marched out to
cut of that Nation, to which this Indian belonged, which (as
it is usual with the Indians) reported that they were 800,
whereas some of the Privateers have been there, and say that
they are not able to raise above 300 men.  we have 100 Privateers here all shar like though not at the taking of the prize,
which if our Governour would suffer them would fain fall on
the Spaniards at St. Augustine; it is not likely if the Spaniards
were so strong as the Indian reported, that they would send
out such strength against them, For when the English have
any war with a Nation of the Indians tho at 150 miles distance they think 20 English and 30 or 40 friendly Indians to
be a sufficient party.  The Indians are sent before to discover
where the other Indians lay who if they see but [gap in MS.]
of their enemyes they will returne with great speed and greater
fear to the English reporting they saw 200.

The 20th of August I saw a Comet in the North East about
2 hours before day, the 21 it was seen in the west.[3]  Sir of
those goods you gave me of my Brothers, I have sold some,

---

[1] Sic.

[2] "These sentiments were vividly manifested when the Spaniards actually
did attack, in 1686."—Jameson.

[3] Halley's comet was then visible.

and most of them I bought in London, but I can not yet make any returne; for money here is but little and that Spanish which will not go for so much in England by 4 or 5 *s* in the *li*. Our pay is what the Countrey affords, as Corn, Pork, Tar and Cedar, the 3 first are fit only for the Islands. I know not whether the last will pay charges to England it can't be afforded under 30 or 32 *s* profit in London, if you please you may enquire what it will yield in Oxon, and if you think it worth sending, and know how to dispose of it, I will take care to send it by the first, after I know your mind. Sir I have sent to Mr. Sessions for these following goods which are the best I can think of and I desire you, that you would let him have as much money as will buy them. Nuttmegs to the value of 5 *li*, Pepper 50 *s*, Cinnamon 25 *s*, Cloves and Mace 25 *s*, $\frac{1}{2}$ a C of large Beads, blue and white, or white with streaks of blue or black, or blew with beads blew and white, or white with streaks of blew or black, 1 [gap] of blew Duffals, a quarter of a Cask of brandy, $\frac{1}{2}$ doz white Castors, at about 8 or 10 *s* per piece, and one good French hat, 2 or 3 [gap] of fine thread to make lace, 500 small needles and 20 [gap] of that tape which is now in fashion to make lace with, 8 or 10 doz. of knives from 2 *s* 06 *d* to 5 *s* per doz., one good [gap] coat for myself and 2 C[1] of pigeon shot. Sir I desire you with these things to send me $\frac{1}{2}$ C of Shomakers thread and one of my Brothers shop books if you have one that is not used. Sir I beseech you pardon my presumption since 'twas your goodness made me so by your usuall readiness in granting my former requests. Pray present my humble duety to my Mother and my Grandmother, my kind love to my sister and Brothers and the rest of our Relations and be confident that I will be industrious to improve whatsoever you shall commit to my charge and to approve my self

Your most Dutifull and obedient Son,

THOMAS NEWE.

[1] *I. e.*, hundredweight.

# JOURNAL OF ELDER WILLIAM PRATT,
## 1695-1701

# INTRODUCTION

In 1695 a small colony, or "church," as its promoters termed it, was organized in Dorchester, Massachusetts, for the purpose of settling in South Carolina. In the records of the First Church at Dorchester it appears that on October 20, 1695, Joseph Lord, Increase Sumner, and William Pratt were "dismissed" (transferred) from that church for "The gathering of A church for the South Coralina,"[1] and in the same records for two days later the following appears:

ocktober the 22 being ower lecktuer day was sett apart for the ordering of M^r Joseph lord for to be pastuer to A church gathered that day for to goe South Coralina to settell the gospell ther and the names of the men are thes

| | | |
|---|---|---|
| Joshua Brooks | } | of Concord |
| Nathaniel Billings | | |
| William Norman | | Coralina |
| William Adams | | Sudbury |
| Increase Sumner | } | Dorchester |
| William Pratt | | |
| George Foxe | | Reading |
| Simon Daken | | Concord |

thes with M^r. Joseph lord did enter into a most solem Covenant to sett up the ordinances of Jesus Christ ther if the lord caryed them safely thither accordin to gospell truth withe a very large profeson of ther faithe.[2]

William Norman had been living in South Carolina for some years previously. On April 10, 1684, the Governor and Lords Proprietors' deputies had issued a warrant to the sur-

---

[1] *Records of the First Church at Dorchester, New England* (1891), p. 13.
[2] *Ibid.*, p. 109.

veyor-general to lay out 320 acres of land for him; that being the amount allowed to him under a late concession of the Lords Proprietors for the arrival in the province of himself, his wife, his son William, two servants and a negro that had been assigned to him by Matthew English,[1] and the land so allowed was laid out for him on the east side of the Ashley River above Booshoee (Dorchester) Creek, September 22, 1684.[2] It is probable that, being a Congregationalist, he wanted a church of that denomination near him and, for the purpose of securing it, suggested the organization of this colony for South Carolina. The colony, or church, sailed from Boston December 5, 1695, as is shown by the following entry on the records of the First Church at Dorchester:

December 5th, 1695—The church for Carolina set sail from Boston Dec 14th at night the skiff was neer run und[r] water the Stormy wind being so boisterous. They kept a day of pray on board: and safely Landed at Carolina Decemb[r] the 20th the other vessells had a Moneths Passage this but about 14 days.[3]

William Pratt, originally of Weymouth, Massachusetts, removed to Dorchester in that colony in 1690. He is named in the record of the meeting of October 22, 1695, as a member of the "church gathered that day for to goe South Carolina." He kept a journal of the voyage from Boston to South Carolina and of various experiences in South Carolina for some time after his arrival therein. On February 8, 1695/6, he left Charles Town and returned to Massachusetts, where he remained for nearly a year. He again sailed from Boston for South Carolina, January 8, 1696/7, and again he kept a journal of his voyage and of events occurring in South Carolina after his return thither. This journal is now in the hands of one of

---

[1] "Warrants for Lands, 1672–1692" (MS. in office of Historical Commission of South Carolina), p. 296.

[2] *The South Carolina Historical and Genealogical Magazine*, VI. 64–65.

[3] *Records of the First Church at Dorchester, New England* (1891), p. 145.

Elder Pratt's descendants, Mr. Joshua Eddy Crane, librarian of the Taunton Public Library, of Taunton, Massachusetts, who very kindly allowed it to be copied for publication here. Parts of it have been printed heretofore. Rev. James Stacy printed certain portions in his *History of the Midway Congregational Church, Liberty County, Georgia* (Newnan, Ga., 1899), and Mr. Henry A. M. Smith quoted parts of it from Mr. Stacy's work in an article, entitled "The Town of Dorchester, in South Carolina—A Sketch of Its History," in *The South Carolina Historical and Genealogical Magazine* for January, 1905 (vol. VI., no. 1). The entries below, intermixed with recipes, etc., are made on the blank leaves of a pocket almanac. Their order is confused. The arrangement adopted on the following pages is believed to be chronological. All the historical entries are here printed.

Elder Pratt (he became "ruling elder" of the Dorchester, South Carolina, church in 1697) returned to Weymouth after a few years, then removed to Bridgewater, then to Easton, Massachusetts, where he died in 1713. The Puritan church, long maintained in this New England settlement on Ashley River, was in the eighteenth century transferred into Georgia.

# JOURNAL OF ELDER WILLIAM PRATT,
## 1695–1701

On Dec. the 3. 1695. We the Church that was gathered in order to bring the gospel ordinences to South Carolina at this time sum of us went into a longbote to go on board the Brigantine *frindship* of boston in newingland in order to our passing to Carolina but mising the vessell at first we by reason of the strength of the wind could not come up with here again but were constrained to endure the cold 3 or 4 hours before we could get at any land til at length we got to dorchester Neck and from there returned to boston all in safty

December the 5 We set sail in the aforesaid vessell to go on our voyage and haveing a moderate and stedy gale on the saboth evening which was the 8 day of the month and the 4th day of our being upon the sea we were in the latitude of the capes of virginia. this evening the wind began to bluster being at norwast and the day foloing blew hard continually incresing its strengh so that on munday the 9th day of the month, in the evening we wer fain to lie by, i. e. take in all the sails except the main course which being reafed was left to give [*illegible*] as well as to stedy her, the helm being lashed to leward. So we continued til tusday night, and about midnight the wind was risen so high that the vessel had like to have sunk, by reson that that small sail was enough then to run her under water, and had lik to have don it but the seamen made way for the vessel to rise, by furling the mainsail and bearing up before the wind, we were fain to scud thus, excepting sumtimes when the wind abated, as by fits for a short time it did, at which times we lay by as before all the next day and part of the day foloing. either on wedensday or thursday, we agreed to set apart friday to seek the lord by fasting and prayer and to beg of him prosperous winds and

194

weather. on thursday about noon the wind began to fall and the sun to shine out, which it had not don so as that ther mit be any observasion after our going out before, so that on friday we could with sum comfort cary on the work of the day.

On saturday, the 10th day of our voyage, we found that we were got on allmost as far southward as the latitude of 31°, and wanted much westing, for the northwest wind had driven us southestward. on sabbath day which was the 15th day of the month, we were so favered with wind as that we went with great spead, on our course.

On Munday and so forward the wind often shifted, yet not so as to hindr our going on in our desired course tho we could not go w[th] so much speed as we desired. thursday morning, being the 19th day of the month, we came in sight of the land of Carolina, but were by a disappointment hindered from geting in that day: but the next day we got in thro' divine goodness, being the 20th day of desember.

when we cam to the town our vessell fired 3 guns and the peopel to welcom us to the land fired about 9 guns which was more then usiall and when we came to an ancor being in the evening, many of the peopel being worthy gentelmen came on bord us and bid us welcom to Carolina and invited many of us ashore and to ther housis. I was among the rest kindly entertained that night. I keept in Charsltoun about a week and then was caried by water up to m[r] normons. increce Sumnor and I war kindly reseved and entertained by the lady Extol [1] and tho two other men war indevering to get into faviour with the ladey and other neighbers and to obtain the land at ashly rever and, that we mit not obtain it, yet thay could not prevail: for as soon as we came the lady and others of the neigbers did more hily esstem of us then of the other as thay told us and rejoysed at our coming tho ther was no more of the church then increse sumner and I, and after we had discorsed secretly with them, thay war not only very kind to us, but allso used all menes and touk great pains to obtain our setteling upon ashly rever and

[1] Lady Rebecca Axtell, widow of Landgrave Daniel Axtell, whose plantation (Newington) lay on Booshoee Creek. See *The South Carolina Historical and Genealogical Magazine*, VI. 174–176.

that we shuld indever to perswad our pastr and the Church to settel their.

our minister [1] was at this time up at landgrave morttons [2] and som of the church, and others of the chu^ch at Charlstoun. our minister and church war strongly perswaded by the lieut^t generall blak [3] and many others to go to new london to settel, [4] and upon that acount wer perswaded to go to landgrave mortons w^c was neer this place.

about a week after we went by land to Charlstoun and war caryed by water up to land grave mortons, we, many of us together, went to vew the land at newlundon. after two days we returned to land grave morttons.

m^r lord cald me aside and I had much discors with him and when he heard what I had to say consarning ashly rever and conserning new lundon, m^r lord was wholy of my mind and willing to tak up, upon thos condishons that we discorsed about, at ashly rever, which condishons war kept privet, betwen to or 3 of us. when I sougth arnestly to god for wisdom and counsel god was grasious to me, for which I have great caus to prais his name, as well as for many other signol marsys. [5] we keept sumthing secrit from others which was greatly for our benifit.

we came from there to m^r curtesis [6] and from ther to m^r

[1] Rev. Joseph Lord. Graduated from Harvard College in 1691, he probably taught school in Dorchester, Massachusetts, from 1692 to 1695. In the autumn of the latter year he was ordained minister of the emigrating church. After about twenty years in South Carolina he returned to New England. In 1720 he was installed pastor of the church in Chatham, Massachusetts, and died there in 1748. His wife was a daughter of Governor Thomas Hinckley of the Plymouth Colony.

[2] Landgrave Joseph Morton, son of the former Governor Joseph Morton, whom he had succeeded as landgrave upon his death.

[3] Joseph Blake, a nephew of the great English admiral, Robert Blake, and at that time governor of South Carolina. He was subsequently made a landgrave and, having purchased the share of John, Lord Berkeley, in Carolina became a Proprietor in 1698. His plantation (Plainsfield) was on Stono River, near New Cut.

[4] New London, subsequently called Willtown, was a town which had been founded on the Edisto, or Ponpon, River a few years previously. On May 10, 1682, the Lords Proprietors had directed the laying out thereof, directing that it be called London. See *The South Carolina Historical and Genealogical Maga zine*, January, 1909 (X. 20–32).

[5] Signal mercies.                                    [6] Daniel Courtis.

gilbosons.[1] we were very kindly entertained at every place
wher we came, but wher we came we herd of sum of thos that
came from Newingland that had ben giltey of gros miscareges
w[c] was a trobel to us, but m[r] gilbeson cald me aside and
had much discors with me. afterward he told me he was
very glad that I came to Carolina and that he had seen me
and had opertunity to discors with me. he told me he was
much discureged to see the il careg of thos that came from
new ingland, but afterward he was bater satisfied and told
me he did think ther was a great diferenc betwen the parsons[2] that cam from newingland. tho many did manifest
their dislik of bad parsons that came from newingland yet
thay wer glad of the coming of good parsons. we tarried their
2 or 3. days being kindly entertained and when we came
away thay gave us provission for our voyag doun to Charlstoun and wer very kind to us. from thenc we came to governor
blakes wher we wer kindly entertained and we dind with them
and after sum discors with governor blak we came to mrs
bamers[3] wher we lodge all night being very kindly entertained.
next day the peppel being very kind, we had a comfortable
voyag doun to Charlstoun, being the 14th of Janir.[4] the
16th of January was the eleksion day at Charlstoun. after
this m[r] lord and sume of the church came up to ashley rever
and upon the saboth after, being the 26th day of Janry, m[r]
lord precht at m[r] normons hous upon that texte in 8 rom 1
vrs. ther was many that came to hear, of the neigbers round
about and gave diligent atension.

the second day of feburary being sabath day m[r] lord
preched at ashly rever upon that texte 1 pet 3. 18. most
of the neightbors came to hear, all the next neigbrs and
severell parsons came about 10 mils to hear. the sacriment
of the lords supper was administered that day and 2 decons
chosen.

at this time ther was great Joy among the good pepel tho I
have sumtims ben il and afraid of sicknes or of on troble or
other that would happen, yet god hath ben very grasious to
me and hath heard my request from time to time and helped
me and shoed me great marsy and when I was redy to be

[1] James Gilbertson.          [2] Persons.          [3] Mrs. Beamer.
[4] 1696.

discureged many tims god incureged me again and delivered
out of my trobles.

the first day of feburary being the last day of the week
and the sacriment to be administred and many of us wer
to come away on second day morning to Charlstoun to com
to newingland, we set apart sum time in the afternoun to
pray unto god and ther was much of the spirit of good brethe-
ing in that ordinenc and when we touk our leves of our Christian frinds ther was weeping eyes at our departuer and we
had many a blesing from them.

----

the 6th of feburary[1] we went over the water to m[r] revers[2]
and from thenc to m[r] w[m] Russels and 7th day of the month
we traveld about James's island as it is called and saw a place
wher ther seemed to have ben a fort mad for [*illegible*] an
acre of land and the walls about it was made with oister-
shels and earth [*illegible*] that came from north Carolina is
John meers.

----

An account of our Voyage From S° Carrolina to Boston
New England with Capt Hill In the Brigantien *Friendship*.

on Saturday Feb: 8th 1695/6 In the afternoone wee fell
downe as far as the look-out on Suilifunts[3] Island.

----

when I came from newengland to South Carolina with my
family we came out of boston the 8th day of Janeuery in the
year 1696/7 and we sat sail from nantasket, for Carolina, the
11th day the 2nd day of the week. the 15th day of the month,
the 6. day of the week it began to be stormmy wind and Rain,
and the 16 day being the 7th day of the week it began in
the morning to be very violent and we shipt in abundenc of
water. at that time we lost the bolsplet,[4] and it continued very
stormy.   we then sat to praying espesially on saterday night,
but on the saboth we had sum mettegasion but afterward it
gru mor stormmy again and much rain and on the 4th day of
the week being the 20th day of the month about midnight
our mast fel doun.   but in all these trobles ther was much of

----

[1] 1696.
[2] Mr. Rivers.  The name Rivers is still identified with James Island.
[3] Sullivan's.                              [4] Bowsprit.

marsy mixed with it for alltho the wind was very high and stormy yet it was very fair for us, and that we sumtims [had?] sum metigasion espesially after earnest prayer, allso that when our mast fel doun, it fel Right along about the medel of the vesell toward the storn and did not break the pump but fel just by it, the mast being so exceding heavy if falen over the sid of the vesel we mit have ben all lost.

on the 6th day of the week 22nd day of the month, we with the free consent of the master and mat and marchant, we all of us together keept a solum day of fasting and prayer, and on the next day we had calm wether and a comfortable opertunity to gat up an other smal mast which was a great help to us. we had allso a fair wind and on the saboth day we had a frash gal and fair and had much caus to prais god and on munday the wind was fair but so much of a calm that ther was opertunity to lenkthen our mast and mad it beter for sailing. after this much calm wether but fair winds until we came in sight of the land. but god haveing a design to try and prove us furdor and to sho his pour and faithfullnes and yet furder to humble us and to mak us to pris marsys the mor ca[u]sed a violent storm to aris and drive us of from land again for above a fortnite, but on the 23rd of feburary brought us all safe to land, for which we promised to prais his holy name.

------

the 23. day of march in the year 1697.[1] the church and others that wer concarnd did draw loots, the 24th day that all meet together to stak out and mark ther loots in the trading town. on both days when thay meet to gether on thos ocasions ther was love and unity and pece in what was acted.

------

The Reverent Mr Peairpoint[2] dyed, in Charlstown in Carolina the third day of January in the year 1698.
A letel after this ther was many dyed with the smal pox

------

[1] 1696/7. Elder Pratt adopted the "new style" of dating here. For a table showing the result of the drawing of lots see *The South Carolina Historical and Genealogical Magazine*, VI. 73-75.

[2] Rev. Benjamin Pierpont, pastor of the Independent Congregational meeting (White Meeting) in Charles Town. In recording his death Elder Pratt again adopted the "new style" of dating.

that distemper groing mor mortal then before,[1] and the 24th day of feburary foloing ther was a great fire in Charlstown which burnt doun a great part of the town and a few days before the fire ther was an earth quak in Charlstown.

---

### A fast in secret.

the 28 day of august in the year 1699 I keept a day of fasting and prayer in secret alltho at the begining of my entering upon the work of the [day?] I found much unability and discuragings in my self and lettel liklihoud that I shuld hold out to go thorow the work of the day alon.  but at the begining i beged gods help and asistants and god was pleased so to help me so that I hild out comfortablely until it was near night alltho I begun under discuragments yet g[d]. was pleased so to asist and incuragment me afterward as that I was much incuraged and ended the work of the day with much comfort.

---

A fast.   the 20th day of Jun. 1700 the church of christ at dorchest. keep a day of fasting and prayer to seek unto god for rain, the next day it pleased god to send great showers of rain and much refreshed the earth and revived the corn.

The 3rd day of september or, the 4 day [          ][2] 1700 ther was A haurricane in South Carolina.

governer blak dyed the 6th of september 1700.[3]

the 8th day of october in the year 1700 was apointed to chous men for an asembly.

the 25. of Jun. 1701 a day of fasting and prayer for rain.

[1] See McCrady, *History of South Carolina under the Proprietary Government*, 1670–1719, p. 308.

[2] Blank in manuscript.

[3] Langdon Cheves, Esq., in his genealogy of the Blake family in *The South Carolina Historical and Genealogical Magazine* for April, 1900 (I. 153-166), puts it on the 7th.

# LETTER OF EDWARD RANDOLPH TO THE BOARD OF TRADE, 1699

# INTRODUCTION

IN 1698–1699 Edward Randolph, Surveyor-General of His Majesty's Customs for North America, arrived in Charles Town, South Carolina, on one of his official visits. He soon sent a report on his work to the Board of Trade and Plantations, into which he incorporated his personal observations as to conditions in South Carolina, thereby giving his report considerable value as a narrative of contemporaneous history. His account contains some erroneous observations, due, doubtless, to the fact that he had been but a short time in the province and had not become fully conversant with its affairs. He seems, however, to have been very highly impressed with the natural resources, commercial advantages, existing industries, and general prospects of the province, for he not only wrote enthusiastically as to them, but requested that he be allowed to make Charles Town his chief place of residence. It is likely that he saw the ease with which the merchants and planters of South Carolina acquired wealth and desired to "try his fortune."

This report is preserved in the British Public Record Office in the records of the Board of Trade, Proprieties, volume 25, pp. 448 to 459, and a transcript of it constitutes pp. 88–95 of volume 4 of Public Records of South Carolina, a series of transcripts of papers in the British Public Record Office relating to South Carolina, now in the custody of the Historical Commission of South Carolina. It was printed in full by Professor William J. Rivers in *A Sketch of the History of South Carolina* (Charleston, 1856), pp. 443–447, and an abstract of it was printed in volume I. of *Collections of the South Carolina Historical Society* (Charleston, 1857), pp. 210–211.

# LETTER OF EDWARD RANDOLPH TO THE
# BOARD OF TRADE, 1699

*E. Randolph to the Lords of Trade,* 16 *March,* 1698–1699.

*May it please y$^r$ Lordships,*

After a dangerous voyage at Sea, I landed at Charles Town, in the Province of So. Carolina, and soon after my arrival, I administered the Oath to Mr. Jos. Blake, one of the Proprietors and Governor of this Province.[1] But he is not allowed of by his Ma$^{tys}$ Order in Council to be Govr., the Act of Parlt. for preventing frauds being not taken notice of by the Proprietors.[2]

There are but few settled Inhabitants in this Province, the Lords have taken up vast tracts of land for their own use, as in Colleton County and other places, where the land is most commodious for settlement, which prevents peopling the place, and makes them less capable to preserve themselves.[3] As to their civil Governt., 'tis different from what I have met with in the other Proprieties. Their Militia is not above 1500 Soldiers White men, but have thro' the Province generally 4 Negroes to 1 White man, and not above 1100 families, English and French.[4]

[1] About the middle of the year 1696 John Archdale, one of the Proprietors of Carolina and Governor of South Carolina, retired to England, appointing Joseph Blake deputy governor to serve in his stead. By a letter, dated April 25, 1697, the Proprietors appointed him governor. (Public Records of South Carolina, 197–198.)

[2] Parliament had passed an act in 1695, in order to prevent frauds, requiring the consent of the King to such appointments by proprietary governments; the Proprietors of Carolina had appointed Blake without complying with that act.

[3] This was a most pessimistic view. While it is true that the Proprietors had taken up a matter of forty-eight to sixty thousand acres (four or five baronies) for themselves in Colleton County, there were still a few hundred thousand acres of excellent planting lands left in that county.

[4] Estimating one soldier for every five white inhabitants would make the white population of the province 7,500—a number which the editor believes from

Their Chief Town is Charles Town, and the seat of Govt. in this Province, where the Governor, Council and Triennial Parliamt. set, and their Courts are holden, being above a league distance from the entrance to their harbour mouth, w^ch is barred, and not above 17 foot water at the highest tide, but very difficult to come in. The Harbour is called by the Spaniards, St. George; it lyes 75 leagues to the Northward of St. Augustine, belonging to the Spaniards. It is generally laid down in our English maps to be 2 deg., 45 min., within the southern bounds of this Province. In the year 1686, one hundred Spaniards, w^th Negroes and Indians, landed at Edistoe, (50 miles to the southward of Charles Town,) and broak open the house of Mr. Joseph Moreton,[1] then Governor of the Province, and carried away Mr. Bowell,[2] his Brother-in-law, prisoner, who was found murdered 2 or 3 days after; they carried away all his money and plate, and 13 slaves, to the value of £1500 sterling, and their plunder to St. Augustine. Two of the Slaves made their escape from thence, and returned to their master. Some time after, Govr. Moreton sent to demand his slaves, but the Govr. of St. Augustine answered it was done without his orders, but to this day keeps them, and says he can't deliver them up w^thout an ord^r from the King of Spain. About the same time they robbed Mr. Grimball's House, the Sec. of the Province, whilst he attended the Council at Charles Town, and carried away to the value of over £1500 sterl^g. They also fell upon a settlement of Scotchmen at Port Royal, where there was not above 25 men in health to oppose them. The Spaniards burnt down their houses, destroyed and carried away all that they had, because (as the Span^ds pretended) they were settled upon their land, and had they at any time a superior force, they would also destroy this town built upon Ashley and Cooper Rivers.

many years' study of the public records to be about the correct one. The proportion of negroes to whites was nothing like four to one in 1699. It was scarcely two to one. Governor Johnson and his council estimated in 1708 that the total population of the province was 8,180, almost equally divided between whites and negroes. In the same year Oldmixon estimated the population at 12,000. The editor is of opinion that the total population at this time was about 16,000— 7,500 whites and 8,500 negroes.

[1] Joseph Morton. The name is pronounced as if spelled Moreton.

[2] Edward Bowell.

This whole Bay was called formerly St. George's, which they likewise lay claim to. The Inhabitants complained of the wrong done them by the Spaniards to the Lords Proprietors, and humbly prayed them (as I have been truly informed) to represent it to His Ma$^{ty}$, but they not hearing from the Lord Prop$^{rs}$, fitted out two vessels with 400 stout men, well armed, and resolved to take St. Augustine. But Jas. Colleton came in that time from Barbadoes with a Commission to be Govr., and threatn'd to hang them if they proceeded, whereupon they went on shore very unwillingly. The Spaniards hearing the English were coming upon them for the damages, they left their Town and Castle, and fled into the woods to secure themselves. The truth is, as I have been credibly informed, there was a design on foot to carry on a Trade with the Spaniards.

I find the Inhabitants greatly alarmed upon the news that the French continue their resolution to make a settling at Messasipi River, from [whence] they may come over land to the head of Ashley River w$^{th}$out opposition, 'tis not yet known what care the Lords Prop$^{rs}$ intend to take for their preservation. Some ingenious gentlemen of this Province (not of the Council) have lately told me the Deputies have talked of mak$^g$ an Address to the Lords Prop$^{rs}$ for relief, But 'tis apparent that all the time of this French War they never sent them one barrel of powder or a pound of lead to help them. They conclude they have no reason to depend upon them for assistance, and are resolved to forsake this Country betimes, if they find the French are settled at Meschasipi, or if upon the death of the King of Spain these Countries fall into the hands of the French,[1] as inevitably they will (if not timely prevented), and return with their families to England or some other place where they may find safety and protection. It was one of the first questions asked by several of the Chief men at my arrival, whether His Ma$^{ty}$ will please to allow them half pay for 2 or 3 years at furthest, that afterwards they will maintain themselves and

---

[1] In 1699 the death of King Charles II. of Spain was daily expected (he died in 1700), and it was known that his death would be the signal for aggressive movements on the part of the French, whence came the War of the Spanish Succession, called in the colonies Queen Anne's War.

families (if they have any) in making Pitch and Tar and planting of Indian Corn.  His Majesty will thereby have so many
men seasoned to the Country ready for service upon all occasions, five such men will do more service by sea or land then
20 new rais$^d$ men from home, they may be brought hither
in the Virginia outward bound ships, 100 or 150 men in a
year, till they are made up 1000, it will save the charge of
transporting so many another time 2 or 3000 leagues at sea.
I heard one of the Council (a great Indian Trader,[1] and has
been 600 miles up in the Country west from Charles Town)
discourse that the only way to discover the Meschasipi is
from this Province by land.   He is willing to undertake it if
His Ma$^{ty}$ will please to pay the charge w$^{ch}$ will not be above
£400 or £500 at most;  he intends to take with him 50 white
men of this Province and 100 Indians, who live 2 days journey
east from the Meschasipi, and questions not but in 5 or 6
months time after he has His Ma$^{ty's}$ commands and instructions to find out the mouth of it and the true latitude thereof.

The great improvement made in this Province is wholly
owing to the industry and labour of the Inhabitants.   They
have applied themselves to make such commodities as might
increase the revenue of the Crown, as Cotton, Wool, Ginger,
Indigo, etc.   But finding them not to answer the end, they
are set upon making Pitch, Tar and Turpentine, and planting
rice, and can send over great quantityes yearly, if they had
encouragement from England to make it, having about 5,000
Slaves to be employed in that service,[2] upon occasion, but
they have lost most of their vessels, which were but small,
last war by the French, and some lately by the Spaniards, so
that they are not able to send those Commodities to England
for a market, neither are sailors here to be had to man their
vessels.

I humbly propose that if His Ma$^{ty}$ will for a time suspend
the Duties upon Commodities, and that upon rice also, it will

---

[1] James Moore.

[2] This estimate is about right.  This was considerably over half the negro
population of the province.  The remaining slaves were used as servants and
tradesmen and as laborers about Charles Town.  A misprint in Rivers's work
(*A Sketch of the History of South Carolina*) makes this figure 50,000 instead of
5,000.

encourage the Planter to fall vigilantly upon making Pitch and Tar, etc., w$^{ch}$ the Lords Prop$^{rs}$ ought to make their principal care to obtain from His Ma$^{ty}$, being the only way to draw people to settle in their Province, a place of greatest encouragement to the English Navy in these parts of the world.  Charles Town Bay is the safest port for all vessels coming thro' the gulf of Florida in distress, bound from the West Indies to the Northern Plantations; if they miss this place they may perish at sea for want of relief, and having beat upon the coast of New England, New York, or Virginia by a North West Wind in the Winter, be forced to go to Barbadoes if they miss this Bay, where no wind will damage them and all things to be had necessary to refitt them.  My Lords, I did formerly present Your Lordships with proposals for supplying England with Pitch and Tar, Masts and all o$^r$ Naval Stores from New England.  I observed when I were at York in Septr. last, abundance of Tar brot. down Hudson's River to be sold at New York, as also Turpentine and Tar in great quantities from the Colony of Connecticut.  I was told if they had encouragement they could load several Ships yearly for England.  But since my arrival here I find I am come into the only place for such commodities upon the Continent of America; some persons have offered to deliver in Charlestown Bay upon their own account 1000 Barrels of Pitch and as much Tar, others greater quantities provided they were paid for it in Charles Town in Lyon Dollars [1] passing here at 5s. p$^r$ piece, Tar at 8s. p$^r$ Barrel, and very good Pitch at 12s. p$^r$ Barrel, and much cheaper if it once became a trade. The season for making those Commodities in this Province being 6 mos. longer than in Virginia and more Northern Plantations, a planter can make more tar in any one year here with 50 slaves than they can do with double the number in those places, their slaves here living at very easy rates and with few clothes.[2]

The inclosed I received from M. Girard,[3] a French Prot-

---

[1] Dutch dollars, bearing as a symbol the lion of Brabant or of the Netherlands.

[2] This description of the naval stores business, then in its infancy, in Charles Town doubtless contributed a mite toward the splendid development it reached thirty or forty years later.

[3] Guerard.  See p. 143, note 1, *supra*.

estant living in Carolina. I find them very industrious and good husbands, but are discouraged because some of them having been many years Inhabitants in this Province are denied the benefit of being Owners and Masters of Vessels, which other the Subjects of His Majesty's Plantations enjoy, besides many of them are made Denizens.[1] If this Place were duly encouraged, it would be the most useful to the Crown of all the Plantations upon the continent of America. I herewith enclose to Your Lordships a Draft of the Town and Castle of St. Augustine, with a short description of it by a Gentleman who has been often there. It's done exactly true, more for service than for show. The Spaniards now, the French, if ever they get it, will prove dangerous neighbours to this Province, a thing not considered nor provided against by the Lords Proprietors. I am going from hence to Bermuda, with His Ma[tys] Commissioners, to administer the Oath to the Govr. of that Island, with a Commission for the Judge and other Officers of the Court of Admiralty erected there, from whence I believe it necessary to hasten to the Bahamas Islands, where a Brigantine belonging to New England was carried in as a wreck. The Master and Sailors being pursued by some persons who had commission from Govr. Webb,[2] believing they were chased by Spaniards, forsook their Vessel and went on shore among the Natives to save their lives.

All which is humbly submitted by

Your Lordship's

Most humble Servant,

ED. RANDOLPH.

The want of a small Vessel to support the loss of the Frigate, which was appointed by the Lords Commiss[rs] of the

---

[1] Many of the French Protestants, or Huguenots, were naturalized in England before coming to America, but in 1696 the General Assembly of South Carolina passed "An Act for Making Aliens Free" by which nearly all of the rest of them were naturalized. Many of the French Protestants had been serving in the General Assembly before that time and some of them were members of the same assembly that naturalized their countrymen. See *Journals of the Commons House of Assembly* for 1692, 1693, and 1696, and of the Grand Council for 1692, all recently printed by the Historical Commission of South Carolina and edited by the editor of this volume.

[2] Colonel Nicholas Webb, governor of the Bahama Islands.

Admiralty to transplant me from one Plantation to another, makes me stay a great while at one place for a passage to another, which is uncertain, difficult and dangerous.

I have by the extreme of cold last Winter in Maryland and Pennsylvania, and by my tedious passage in the Winter time from New York to this place, got a great numbness in my right leg and foot. I am in hopes this warm climate will restore me to my health. I have formerly wrote to your Board and the Commiss$^{rs}$ of H. M. Customs, the necescity of having a Vessel to transport me from one Plantation to another.

I humbly pray Your Lordships favour to direct that the little residence I am to make in these parts of the World, may be in this Province, and that a Vessel well manned may be sent me hither, which may answer all occasion, my intentions being not to lye idle, for when the Hurricane times come in these parts of the World, I can go securely to Virginia, Maryland and Pennsylvania and New England, without fear of being driven from those Plantations by North West Winds, and when they come I can pass from one Plantation to another without difficulty.

# REVEREND JOHN BLAIR'S MISSION TO
## NORTH CAROLINA, 1704

# INTRODUCTION

In 1703 the Society for the Propagation of the Gospel in Foreign Parts authorized John Blair to go as a missionary to the settlers of North Carolina, and he was, accordingly, ordained to the ministry for that purpose April 12, 1703. He set out for his mission in October following and on January 14, 1704, landed in Virginia; ten days later he arrived at his destination in North Carolina. He found the people among whom he labored backward in religious matters and little disposed to aid in the support of a minister of the Established Church—if of any at all. After a hard struggle for some months, during which he spent nearly all of the little bounties he had received from Queen Anne and other philanthropic sources, he returned to England and wrote a narrative of his experiences for the information of the Society. It is very indefinite as to the locality of his place of residence while in North Carolina, but from some slight indications given on that point it would appear to have been in the Pamlico settlement on Pamlico Sound.

Mr. Blair's narrative is preserved in London in the North Carolina letter book of the Society for the Propagation of the Gospel in Foreign Parts. A transcript of it has been printed in *The Colonial Records of North Carolina*, I. 600–603, which has been followed here.

# REVEREND JOHN BLAIR'S MISSION TO NORTH CAROLINA, 1704

I WAS ordained, in order to go to the plantations, 12th April, 1703, and then received the queen's bounty of £20, and, soon after, my Lord Weymouth's[2] bounty of £50; upon which I lived in England till the 1st of October following which, together with my fitting out for such a voyage and country, consumed the most part of my money. I had likewise £5 sent me by my lord of London to Portsmouth, and when I landed in Virginia I had no more than £25.

I landed in Virginia, 14th of January, 1704; and, as soon as I could conveniently travel, I waited upon the governor, and immediately after made the best of my way into the country where I was bound.

I arrived amongst the inhabitants, after a tedious and troublesome journey, 24th *ditto*. I was then obliged to buy a couple of horses, which cost me fourteen pounds,—one of which was for a guide, because there is no possibility for a stranger to find his road in that country, for if he once goes astray (it being such a desert country) it is a great hazard if he ever finds his road again. Beside, there are mighty inconveniences in travelling there, for the roads are not only deep and difficult to be found, but there are likewise seven great rivers in the country, over which there is no passing of horses, except two of them, one of which the Quakers have settled a ferry over for their own conveniency, and nobody but themselves have the privilege of it; so that at the passing over the rivers, I was obliged either to borrow or hire horses, which was both troublesome and chargeable, insomuch that

---

[1] Queen Anne's Bounty was instituted in 1704 for the benefit of the poorer clergy, the Queen appropriating to their relief a branch of her income which had originally come to the Crown from the "first-fruits and tenths" of church livings in Henry VIII.'s time.

[2] Viscount Weymouth, a benevolent privy-councillor of Queen Anne.

214

in little more than two months I was obliged to dispose of the necessaries I carried over for my own use, to satisfy my creditors.

I found in the country a great many children to be baptized, where I baptized about a hundred; and there are a great many still to be baptized, whose parents would not condescend to have them baptized with god-fathers and god-mothers.

I married none in the country, for that was a perquisite belonging to the magistrates, which I was not desirous to deprive them of.

I preached twice every Sunday, and often on the week-days, when their vestries met, or could appoint them to bring their children to be baptized.

I called a vestry in each precinct, in my first progress through the country, to whom I gave an account of my Lord Weymouth's charitable bounty in supporting my mission among them, and likewise of the good designs the honorable society had for them, as I was informed by Mr. Amy[1] that they had settled £50 per annum for the maintenance of two clergymen amongst them; and likewise a proposal that Dr. Bray[2] desired me to make to them, that, upon their procuring good glebes, he doubted not that there might be a settlement made for the advantage of the Church, such as there is in the island of Bermudas, viz., two slaves and a small stock in each precinct, and that to be continued good by the incumbent to his successor, which will be a lasting estate to the Church.

They have built in the country three small churches, and have three glebes.

In the three chief precincts, there is a reader established in each, to whom they allow a small salary, who reads morning and evening prayer every Lord's day, with two sermons, and I took care to furnish them with books from the library[3] before I came away.

I remained very well satisfied in the country till their Assembly sat, which was on 1st March, where I expected they

---

[1] An officer of the Society for the Propagation of the Gospel in Foreign Parts.

[2] Rev. Dr. Thomas Bray, who practically founded the Society for the Propagation of the Gospel in Foreign Parts and who for years labored assiduously for its success.

[3] Meaning no doubt the library which had been established in the province by the Society for Promoting Christian Knowledge, founded by Dr. Bray. See Steiner, in *American Historical Review*, II. 72.

would propose a settlement for my maintenance; and they taking no care of it, together with my then circumstances, which were but very indifferent, discouraged me very much, and occasioned my first thoughts of returning to England; for I was informed before I went thither that there was £30 per annum, settled by law,[1] to be paid in each precinct for the maintenance of a minister, which law was sent over hither to be confirmed by their lords proprietors, and it being supposed not to be a competency for a minister to live on, was sent back again without confirmation, whereof the Quakers took the advantage, and will endeavor to prevent any such law passing for the future, for they are the greatest number in the Assembly, and are unanimous, and stand truly to one another in whatsoever may be to their interest.  For the country may be divided into four sorts of people: first, the Quakers, who are the most powerful enemies to Church government, but a people very ignorant of what they profess.  The second sort are a great many who have no religion, but would be Quakers, if by that they were not obliged to lead a more moral life than they are willing to comply to.  A third sort are something like Presbyterians, which sort is upheld by some idle fellows who have left their lawful employment, and preach and baptize through the country, without any manner of orders from any sect or pretended Church.  A fourth sort, who are really zealous for the interest of the Church, are the fewest in number, but the better sort of people, and would do very much for the settlement of the Church government there, if not opposed by these three precedent sects; and although they be all three of different pretensions, yet they all concur together in one common cause to prevent any thing that will be chargeable to them, as they allege Church government will be, if once established by law. And another great discouragement these poor people have, is a governor who does not in the least countenance them in this business, but rather discourages them.[2]

Finding it impossible to travel through the country at that rate I began, I was resolved to settle in one precinct, but the people, all alleging that my Lord Weymouth's charity

[1] Act of 1701.

[2] Governor Henderson Walker (d. April 14, 1704) is probably meant.

was universally designed for the whole country, would not
consent to it; which bred some disturbance amongst them,
upon which I was advised, by some of the best friends of the
Church, to come over and represent their condition to the
honorable society, not only of their want of ministers but
likewise of inhabitants to maintain them; and their desires,
they complying with my necessities, was a powerful argument,
considering I was then reduced to my last stake, and knew
not where, or upon what account, to be further supplied.
Besides, such a solitary, toilsome, and hard living as I met
with there were very sufficient discouragements. I was distant from any minister one hundred and twenty miles, so that
if any case of difficulty or doubt should happen, with whom
should I consult? And for my travelling through the country,
I rode one day with another, Sundays only excepted, about
thirty miles *per diem* in the worst roads that ever I saw;
and have sometimes lain whole nights in the woods.

I will now endeavor to show you how inefficient a single
man's labors would be amongst so scattered a people. In the
first place, suppose him minister of one precinct (whereas
there are five in the country), and this precinct, as they are
all bounded with two rivers, and those rivers at least twenty
miles distant, without any inhabitants on the road, for they
plant only on the rivers, and they are planted at length upon
those rivers at least twenty miles, and to give all those inhabitants an opportunity of hearing a sermon, or bringing their
children to be baptized, which must be on the Sabbath, for
they won't spare time of another day, and must be in every
ten miles distant, for five miles is the furthest they will bring
their children, or willingly come themselves; so that he
must, to do his duty effectually, be ten or twelve weeks in
making his progress through one precinct.

You may also consider the distance that the new colony
of Pamtico is from the rest of the inhabitants of the country,
for any man that has tried it would sooner undertake a voyage
from this city to Holland than that, for beside a pond of five
miles broad, and nothing to carry one over but a small perry-
auger,[1] there are about fifty miles desert to pass through,
without any human creature inhabiting in it. I think it
likewise reasonable to give you an account of a great nation

[1] Periagua.

of Indians that live in that government, computed to be no less than 100,000,[1] many of which live amongst the English, and all, as I can understand, a very civilized people.

I have often conversed with them, and have been frequently in their towns: those that can speak English among them seem to be very willing and fond of being Christians, and in my opinion there might be methods taken to bring over a great many of them. If there were no hopes of making them Christians, the advantage of having missionaries among them would redound to the advantage of the government, for if they should once be brought over to a French interest (as we have too much reason to believe there are some promoters amongst them for that end by their late actions), it would be, if not to the utter ruin, to the great prejudice of all the English plantations on the continent of America.

I have here in brief set down what I have to say, and shall be ready to answer to any questions the honorable society shall think convenient to ask me concerning the country; and shall be both ready and willing to serve them anywhere upon such encouragement as I can live, according to my education, after my Lord Weymouth ceases to lay his commands on me.

I have made a considerable losing voyage of it this time, both by my troublesome travelling in America, and likewise by being taken into France, where I was a prisoner of war nine weeks, and was forced to make use of my credit for my sustenance; and have lived in the same circumstances since I came to England, without any manner of relief, which has been very troublesome to me, all of which has brought me considerably in debt, near £35, and now in no way to pay it, without my charitable benefactor or the honorable society judge my labors worthy a reward.

[1] This estimate is far in excess of the correct figure. There was no nation of Indians in that quarter at that time that contained more than a tenth of that number, and all neighboring tribes combined scarcely a fourth thereof. Mr. James Mooney, in *The Siouan Tribes of the East* (Washington, 1894), pp. 8–9, says: "On the lower Neuse and its tributaries, the Contentnea and the Trent, and extending up about as far as the present site of Raleigh, were the Tuscarora, the most important tribe of North Carolina east of the mountains. Before they rose against the whites in 1711 they were estimated at 1,200 warriors, or perhaps 5,000 souls, but their terrible losses in the ensuing war, amounting to 400 in one battle and 1,000 in another, completely broke their power."

PARTY-TYRANNY, BY DANIEL DEFOE, 1705

# INTRODUCTION

No sooner had the Lords Proprietors of Carolina effected a settlement in that part of the province subsequently known as South Carolina than it became an object of jealousy to the Spaniards in Florida, and several attempts to destroy it were made by them.[1] This hostile attitude of the Spaniards soon provoked a counter spirit in the people of South Carolina and a determination on their part to invade Florida and destroy St. Augustine at the first favorable opportunity.

Upon the death of Governor Blake, September 7, 1700, the Lords Proprietors' deputies met on the 11th of that month and elected ("according to the Instructions or Rules of Government from the Lords prop[rs]. to Coll Phill Ludwell") James Moore, one of the deputies, governor.[2] Governor Moore had for many years cherished an ambition to invade Florida. The opportunity came now while he was governor.

[1] See pp. 185, 186, 205, *supra;* and McCrady, *History of South Carolina under the Proprietary Government.*

[2] The account of the election of Moore given by various historians from Hewat to McCrady is entirely erroneous. The Proprietors having furnished a mode of procedure in instructions on the subject to Governor Ludwell it was strictly followed and the election of Moore was entirely consistent therewith. There were two landgraves and four other deputies at the meeting. The name of the senior landgrave in the province, Bellinger, was presented first and he received one vote, that of Landgrave Morton. Deputies LeNoble, Gibbes, Daniell, and Moore voted against him. The name of Landgrave Morton was then presented and he received the votes of Landgrave Bellinger and Deputies LeNoble and Gibbes, Deputies Daniell and Moore voting against him. Both landgraves were objected to on the ground that they had accepted offices from the Crown while still holding commissions as Lords Proprietors' deputies. There being no other landgrave in the province the deputies, following their instructions, proceeded to elect one of the deputies governor, and James Moore received a majority of the votes and was declared governor. ("Public Records of South Carolina," V. 70–71.)

He learned in 1702, before he had any knowledge of Queen Anne's declaration of war against Spain, that the Spaniards in Florida had planned to invade South Carolina by land with 900 Indians. The plot was discovered by friendly Creek Indians and disclosed to South Carolina traders in their nation. These traders gathered 500 Creeks and defeated the invaders. A land and naval expedition was then sent by the General Assembly of South Carolina to invade Florida. Governor Moore led the land forces and Robert Daniell, one of the Proprietors' deputies, led the naval armament, but they did not accomplish their undertaking and returned in disappointment.[1]

In January, 1703, the General Assembly met, and immediately entered into discussion of plans for again invading Florida, and for paying the expenses of the late expedition. A bill to raise £4000 was passed in the Commons House over the opposition of certain Dissenters in that body, who forthwith withdrew therefrom in anger. The next day they returned to the House and offered to resume their seats if the other members of the Commons House would join them in the assertion of their rights. The other members spurned their offers and insulted them. Their withdrawal broke a quorum and thereby estopped legislation that was very important for the welfare of the province. This enraged the populace of Charles Town and when the obstructing members appeared on the streets they were set upon by a mob. They sought redress at the hands of Governor Moore and other local officials, but obtained no sympathy. They then tried petitioning to the Lords Proprietors for redress at their hands. They sent one of their number, John Ash, to England to lay their petition before and plead their cause with the Lords Proprietors, but the Proprietors gave little attention to their complaint. Ash then began to prepare a pamphlet giving

[1] McCrady, *History of South Carolina under the Proprietary Government.*

the Dissenters' side of the controversy, but died before he had completed it. Ash's place was soon taken by Joseph Boone, another of the leaders of the Dissenters in South Carolina, who came with a new petition and new complaints to the Proprietors. He met with no better success in convincing the Proprietors of the wickedness of their government than had Ash. Boone next enlisted the sympathy of Daniel Defoe, the noted fiction-writer and publicist, who prepared the succeeding brief of the Dissenters' case for the information of Parliament. Defoe's case is based entirely on the *ex parte* statements of the discontented Dissenters, who, while respectable people, constituted a very small portion of the population of South Carolina. A decided majority of the people of the province were of the Church of England, and aligned with them were the French Protestants, several hundred in number, and a few Jews and persons of other religious persuasions; nor were all of the Dissenters in the province opposed to Governor Moore and his governmental policies. Defoe had never lived in South Carolina and was not familiar with conditions in the province. His narration of the preceding and current political history of the province, therefore, cannot be given full credence as such, although it is interesting. His pamphlet was printed in London in 1705, and has become the principal source for this episode in the history of South Carolina, notwithstanding the existence of the journals of the Commons House of Assembly of South Carolina, the correspondence of the public officials of the province, and the records of the Lords Proprietors of Carolina, all of which fail to sustain his and the Dissenters' statements concerning this noted controversy.

# PARTY–TYRANNY, BY DANIEL DEFOE, 1705

*Party-Tyranny, or an Occasional Bill in Miniature; as now Practiced in Carolina. Humbly offered to the Consideration of both Houses of Parliament. London, Printed in the Year 1705.*[1]

As it has been always the Care of the Commons of England, to Defend the English Subjects from all manner of Invasions of their Liberty; the Authors of this, thought it a Duty, and it seems to be the Duty of every part aggriev'd, to apply to their Common Remedy in all their Oppressions; where they have reason to expect Relief in all Cases that merit their Cognizance, and who are indeed proper Judges, whether the Cases of which they Complain, merit their Cognizance, or no.

The Doors of the House of Commons are ever Open to receive the just Complaints of the People, and no Man however Mean or Despicable he be, but has a full Liberty to bring his Grievances to their Feet, and has Reason to expect suitable Redress.

If it be the proper Business of the House of Commons, to Redress the Subject's Grievances, it must be the proper Duty of the Subjects, to lay that Grievance they Expect Redress in, before them: The House of Commons are but Men; they are a Select Number chosen from the General Body, to represent the whole, and due Deference ought to be paid to both their Dignity and Capacity; but still they are but Men, and cannot be supposed to know the Grievances of the Subject they should relieve, 'till they are laid before them, and till they are fairly and properly represented.

And this is both the Reason, and we hope the sufficient Justification of this Book: It contains a short, but true Abridgement of High-Church-Tyranny, it is an Occasional

---

[1] Title-page of original.

Bill in Miniature;[1] 'tis a Compendium of Various Kinds of Oppressions practised on the English Subjects, by Fellow-Subjects in the Face of that Government, which being Establish't on the Neck of Tyranny, has openly declar'd against all sorts of Invasion of English Liberty.

If any Man shall say this Matter is not Cognizable in Parliament, and that the People of Carolina are not represented here, having a Parliament of their own, by whom they are to be Determin'd, that they are therein entirely under the Government of themselves, and that these Oppressions are the Act and Deed of their own Representative, and therefore their own Act and Deed, I shall take leave to Answer.

'Tis true, by the Constitution of Carolina, they are under the Government of themselves, and perhaps if their Constitution were rightly Administred, it may be allow'd the best Settlement in America.  But as the Wisdom of their Constitution is known, and unquestion'd, without doubt those able Heads that settl'd their Government, did not forget, that even those Representative Assemblies, especially in the Infancy of the Government, might be corrupt, or might by Bribery or other ill Practices, be Modell'd and Influenc'd in Matters of Parties, to Oppress and Injure the People they acted for.  That especially in their Infancy and the Paucity of Electors, they might be Obtruded upon the People by Clandestine Methods, the Management and Artifices of Governors, and Men of Design, might have great Opportunities from the Power and Purse of the People to byass and awe the Elections; and having fill'd their Assembly with Men of their own Principles, all manner of Mischiefs might ensue to the Destruction of the Colony, Overthrow of the Settlement and Ruin of the Inhabitants.

And if any Man ask me, why then did they not make Laws, to direct the People in such Cases what to do, I cannot, but Answer for them, as I verily believe they would have Answered for themselves had they been alive.

That when any Body of Men Representative, or other Acting by, or for a Constitution, from whom they receive their

---

[1] The Occasional Bills of the period from 1702 to 1719 in English history were bills against occasional conformity to the Established Church, intended to prevent Dissenters from securing municipal office.

Power, shall Act, or do, or make Laws and Statutes, to do anything destructive of the Constitution they Act from, that Power is *Ipso facto* dissolv'd, and revolves of Course into the Original Power, from whence it was deriv'd.

From hence it must follow, that upon known Depredations of Common Liberty, Breach of the Capitulations of Government, between the Governors and the People of Carolina; the People without doubt, by Right of Nature as well as by the Constitution, revolves under the immediate Direction and Government of the English Empire, whose Subjects they were before, and from whom their Government was deriv'd.

It remains here, to lay down what these Capitulations I speak of are, by which the people of Carolina ought to be govern'd, and in the Breach whereof they are Oppress't; and then to descend to the black Relation, how those *Postulata* are broken and unregarded, how these people are Injur'd and Tyranniz'd over, what Redress ought to be given them by their Governours the Proprietors, How that Redress has been legally sought for, and humbly petitioned for but in Vain.

I shall then Examine, not only, how far the People have a Right to dispence the Engins of this Sub-Tyranny; but how far the Constitution it self is dissolved, and the People have a Right to Establish their being there so far as their Free-hold extends; Upon such Foundations of Justice and Liberty, as that it may no more be in the Power of Usurping Thieves and Oppressors, to injure and disturb them.

In Order to the first, the Reader may please to take the following Abridgement of the Constitution of the Collony, as the Ground Plot by which, tho' it be short, he will plainly Discover, upon what Exact Basis of Right and Property this Government was Erected, and how, plainly, by the Encroachments of the present Gentlemen, the People are Injur'd, the Constitution in it self Destroy'd and Inverted, and the People left.

> Free . . . To Choose for their Own share,
> What Case of Government they please to wear,
> If to this Lord, or that, they do Commit
> The Reins of Rule. . . .
> All Men are bound in Conscience to submit;

But then that Lord must give his free assent,
To Postulata's of the Government.
Which if he breaks, he Cuts off the Entail,
And Right retreats to it's Original.

## An Abridgement of the Settlement of Carolina.

To Understand the true Foundation and Establishment of the present Plantation of Carolina, it is necessary to Observe:

That this Colony, tho' discovered, and in part possest, even before that part of America, call'd Virginia, to which it is contiguous; yet lay for several Ages of Time unimprov'd and neglected, till about the Year        , When a particular Account of its Fertility, the wonderful agreableness of the Climate, the Pleasantness and Health of its Scituation, Advantages of Produce, Fitness for Trade, and all Manner of Improvement, being brought to some Gentlemen of Quality and Estates in England, they resolv'd to encourage the planting this Country, and in particular, resolv'd to settle it upon some better Foundations of Government, than the rest of the English Colonies seem'd to stand upon; as the only Thing, which added to the rest of its Advantages, wou'd best encourage the speedy Planting it, and draw Inhabitants in great Numbers from other Plantations to this New Settlement; These Gentlemen being truly sensible of that known and undisputed Maxim of Government, That the Number of Inhabitants, is both the Wealth and Strength of a Nation.

In Order to this, they first obtain a Grant of the Province from King Charles the Second, to them and their Heirs, as Absolute Lords and Proprietors of the Country.

But the Reader is desir'd not to forget, that this Grant or Charter of King Charles the Second, had two Restrictions or Saving Articles in it, which, indeed, were not Proviso's of Capitulation, but Proviso's of Necessity. I'll explain my self presently, the Salvo's were these,

1. Saving always the Faith, Allegiance, and Soveraign Dominion due to us, our Heirs, and Successors for the same. And,

2. Saving also the Right, Title and Interest, of all, and every our Subjects of the English Nation, which are now planted within the Limits and Bounds aforesaid.

See the Printed *Charter*, p. 3.

These I call Proviso's of Necessity, because nothing can depute more Power, than it possesses.

I.  The King could not part with the Allegiance and Dominion due to the English Crown, without consent of Parliament.  For,

1.  That had been, to have alienated Part of the English Government from the Crown.

2.  It had been, to consign some of his Subjects over to the Government of another Prince without their Consent.

II.  The King could not grant the Right, Title and Interest of those of his Subjects already planted there, for that was none of his own; and he could no more transfer their Property, than their Allegiance.

I bespeak the Reader, bearing with this Digression, as what he will see just Reason for, and a good use made of by and by: But for the present he may Observe.

1.  That the Government of Carolina is dependant upon England, and subject to the Laws, Government and Direction of the English Crown; and consequently their Grievances are cognizable in the Parliament of England.

2.  There were Inhabitants in Carolina before the Grant made to the present Proprietors[1] which Inhabitants had a Right both to the Government as well as Possession; which King Charles the Second, neither did, nor cou'd grant by Charter, or otherwise to any Body.

3.  As their Allegiance to the English Crown cou'd not be transfer'd by Gift or Charter, so neither could the Protection of the English Government be deny'd them; and therefore, the Parliament of England has an undoubted Right to redress their Grievances, and to relieve them against all the Oppressions of their pretended Governours of what kind soever.  And this is my Reason for the Argument.

This Charter is a Creation of the Proprietors, both Temporal and Spiritual Lords of the Country, and gives them full Spiritual Dominion, as to Building and Forming Churches, with the Patronage, and Advowsion of them, the Dedication, Consecration, but limited to the Rites of the Church of England; a Continued Badge of their Dependance on this Kingdom,

---

[1] At Chowan, in what is now North Carolina.  A few New Englanders had also tried to raise cattle on the Charles (Cape Fear) River, but did not effect a permanent settlement.

both in Spiritual Matters, as well as Temporal. The **Tenure** of this Regality is also held of the Mannor of Greenwich in the County of Kent, in Free and Common Soccage, paying to the Crown, as of the said Mannor, twenty Marks Yearly as a Quit-Rent, and a Fourth part of all Gold and Silver Oar, which shall be found.

Nor was the Proviso for the Right of the People already planted, or to be planted, at all forgot in this Charter of the King; for in the first Empowering Clause of the Charter, it is expressly said,

"To ordain, make, enact, and under their Seals to publish any Laws whatsoever. But how,

By and with the Advice, and Assent, and Approbation of the Freemen of the said Province, or the greater Part of them.
*Vide* the printed *Charter*, p. 4.

This is incerted to remind those Gentlemen, that Assembling the Freemen of Carolina to make Laws, etc., was not a Voluntary Act of their own Clemency, but what they were oblig'd to, by the very Charter from whence they derive their Authority.

Nor was it a Restriction of the meer Grace of the King, but according to the Native Right of the Freemen, Inhabitants of Carolina settled there before, provided for in the Clause before-mentioned, whose Right, even the King himself, had no Power to Dissolve or Transfer.

In making the Laws these Assemblies are empower'd to Enact and Execute, It is further Remarkable, and of which, I hope, good Use will be made, His Late Majesty Charles the Second, lays another Double Restriction.

1. "Provided such Laws be consonant to Reason.

2. "As near as may be conveniently, agreeable to the Laws of England."

His Majesty knew, that Law is the Result of Reason, and that the Sovereignty of Reason over all the Actions of Men, cannot be invaded, but that Laws offer'd by whatever Society of Men against Reason, are void of course, and therefore expressly prepar'd them to expect it.

In the next place, His Majesty plainly signifies, that all their Laws ought to be corresponding with the English Constitution, Convenience of the People, *Anglice,* The Publick Good

only excepted; by which is inferr'd, that Reason and the
Publick Good are the principal Ends of all Law, and are to
supersede all the Power granted to the Proprietors of Carolina,
as indeed they ought to do all Humane Power committed to
Man in the World.

Upon these and Sundry other Conditions was the first
Charter or Grant made to the Lords Proprietors of Carolina,
dated the 24th of March, 15 Car. II. A Second Grant or
Charter *verbatim* by the first, only Enlarging the Bounds, was
granted to the same Lords Proprietors, dated the 30th of
June 17 Car. II. and the Proprietors by these Two Charters
are, Edward, Earl of Clarendon; George, Duke of Albemarle;
William, Earl of Craven; John, Lord Berkeley; Anthony, Lord
Ashley, afterwards Earl of Shaftsbury; Sir George Carteret,
Sir John Colleton and Sir William Berkeley.

Pursuant to these Charters, The Proprietors went on with
the Settlement of this Colony, and knowing that on the good
Government of the Province, and the large Priviledges granted
to the Inhabitants, depended very much the Encouragement
to Strangers of all Nations, as well as to the English, to Transport themselves, Families, and Estates thither, and consequently the Prosperity of the Colony,

They form'd the Government of the said Province into a
Publick Instrument, which they call the Fundamental Constitution of Carolina, consisting of 120 Articles, which in the
last Article are declar'd, shall be and remain, the Sacred and
Unalterable Form and Rule of Government of Carolina for ever.[1]

These Articles are afterwards abridg'd into One and Forty,
containing the full Substance, Intent and Meaning of the
aforesaid One Hundred and Twenty, and being first sign'd
and sealed to by the Lords Proprietors, as the *Pacta Conventa* of Government, are presented to, and accepted by the
Freemen, Freeholders and Inhabitants, and agreed to be past,
in a Full and Free Parliament or Assembly, as the Sacred
and Unalterable Conditions, on which they Consent to be
Governed and Directed, and to which they submit.

[1] Of the various forms in which the Fundamental Constitutions exist, that
first printed was one (in 120 articles) bearing date March 1, 1669/70. This is
reprinted in *N. C. Col. Rec.*, I. 187-205, in Thorpe's *Federal and State Constitutions*, V. 2772-2786, in *Old South Leaflets*, no. 172, and elsewhere. The original draft, preserved among the Shaftesbury papers, is printed in the *Thirty-third
Report of the Deputy-Keeper of the Public Records* (London, 1872), pp. 258-269.

*An Abridgement of the Constitutions, Consisting of* 41 *Articles.*

The Preamble sets forth, That K. Cha. the IId. having Granted to the Proprietors the Province of Carolina, with all the Royalties Privileges, etc.,

For the better Settlement of the Government of the said Province, the said Lords Proprietors agree to the following Form of Government to be perpetually Establish't, and which they oblige themselves to in the most binding Ways that can be Devis'd.

The First five Articles contain the Regulation of Authority and Division of the Government into: 1. The Proprietors Court, to Consist of the Palatine, and seven Proprietors, and in the Absence of the Governor, and such Deputies as they Assign: This Court to have all the Supream Power Granted to the Proprietors in the Charter, as Calling and Dissolving Parliaments, Pardoning Offences, etc.

The 6th to the 19th Article regulates the Parliament, to Consist of the Proprietors or their Deputies by themselves; The Landgraves and Casticks[1] in the Upper-House, and Free-holders in the Lower-House; this is their King, Lords, and Commons, and the Manner Exactly Regulated to the Simily, with Limitations and Quallifications for Electing, and being Elected, and the Privileges and Office of each House settled.

To the 22d Article Exclusive is settled the Division of the Province into Counties, the Limitation of every ones Quantity in Possession, the Tryal of Causes and Crimes *per Pares*, the Choosing and Deputing the Governour, the Admitting Free-men, Establishing Religion, Churches, etc.

To the 38th Article they determine what Society of Men, and on what Terms shall be Esteemed a Church, and the Regulating Religious Matters, wherein the only Religious Quallifications, by which any Man is Admitted a Member of any Church, and of the Government are these two:

1. That he believes there is a God,
2. That God is Publickly to be Worshiped.

A Third Article Obliging all People to bear Witness in Cases Required to Truth, either by Oath or some Equivalent, is added.

[1] Cassiques.

The 39th Article is positive.

"No Person whatsoever shall Disturb, Molest, or Persecute another for his Opinion in Religion, or Way of Worship."

The two last Articles settle the Freemens Power over their Slaves, and the Form of Signing the Constitutions by all Persons admitted into Office or Trust.

And the Conclusion of these Articles are thus,

Those Fundamental Constitutions in Number Forty One, and every Part thereof shall be and remain the inviolable Form and Rule of Government of Carolina for ever.

Witness our Hands and Seals 11 April, 1698.

| | |
|---|---|
| BATH, *Palatine,*[1] | WILLIAM THORNBUGH, |
| A. ASHLEY, | for Sir John Colleton. |
| CRAVEN, | THO. AMY, |
| BATH for Ld. Cartaret, | WILLIAM THORNBURGH. |

These Constitutions I know have obtain'd upon the World, to be the Contrivance of the Old Earl of S——bury;[2] but I think, I have very good Authority, to assure the World Mr. Lock[3] had the Right of Parentage to the former; whether I ought to contend for either the Policy or Humane Understanding, in Right of either of these Great Men in the Contrivance or no, I shall not debate. I am certain of this, they handed the Infant Government into the World without Leadingstrings, and turn'd it loose before it cou'd stand alone; by which means, like young Romulus, it has got a Wolf to its Nurse, and is like to be bred up a Monster.

'Tis true, these Constitutions were not actually past in any Assembly, and so may be objected against, as not so binding as in other Cases they would be.

But they were sign'd by the Proprietors, and in the Infancy of the Settlement by the Inhabitants, as they came there to Settle; and were only referr'd to a Parliament or Assembly when the Colony was considerable enough to require it.

In these Parliaments, these People have always opposed passing the Constitutions, fearing without doubt, to come under the Fetters of the Law, and a just Government; and knowing the Measures they design'd to take, were destructive

---

[1] The eldest proprietor, at this time Lord Bath, was called the palatine.
[2] Shaftesbury.        [3] John Locke the philosopher.

of the very Being and Nature of the Government; and therefore being unwilling to have the Obstruction of any Settled Constitutions, they always rendred the Proposal contemptible, and banter'd the Colony with the frequent Attempts to pass them, laying them by, as useless Trifles not worth Notice, tho' they were indeed the Fundamentals of the Government.

It remains now to examine, how the Gentlemen now concern'd have acted in Correspondence to

1.  The Powers granted to the Proprietors,
2.  The *Pacta Conventa* with the People, and in this Enquiry it will come to be examin'd:
1.  Whether the Powers assembled there, have been summon'd according to the Constitution.
2.  Whether the Freeholders, and none but such have elected the Persons, who have imposed these Laws, and have had a Free Choice.
3.  Whether these Laws have the due Qualification requir'd by the Charter, *viz.*
1.  To be consonant to Reason.
2.  To the Utility of the Subject.
3.  To the Preservation of Right and Property: The Words expressly set down in the Charter.
4.  Whether if not, they are not void in their own Nature.
5.  Whether the Lords Proprietors not redressing these Abuses when humbly addrest to by the Inhabitants, have not broken the sacred, unalterable Conditions of the Government.
6.  Whether this Fracture of the Constitution, does not empower the Inhabitants of Carolina who purchas'd Estates, and settl'd there on these Conditions, and of whose Right his Late Majesty made such Provision in his Charter, have not a full Power to settle such other Government and Constitutions, as shall correspond with the Freedom and just Rights of the Province, tho' without the Consent of the said Lords.
7.  Whether all this Matter is Cognizable in the Parliament of England, and the Proprietors, of Carolina subject to such Determination as shall be made there.

It lies before us now, to Examine, How these Gentlemen have acted, in Correspondence to the Powers granted by the

Charters to the Propritors, and the Constitutions or *Pacta
Conventa* made with the People.

Before this is enter'd upon, I must determine, who I
mean by those Gentlemen; for this Paper, as 'tis a Complaint
of Fact, may be also expected to be a Charge against particular
Persons also.

To this is answer'd, The Proprietors in one Sence may
be the Persons charg'd here, as being answerable for all the
irregular Practices of those that act under them; since every
Man is really the Actor of what is done by his Authority,
and every Man is tacitely the Author of what is in his Power
to hinder, and which he ought to hinder.

But as here is no Need to fly to a speculative Charge,
when the Agents and Instruments of these Mischiefs are known
and plain, and to be found upon the Spot; so let the Charge
lye in its constructive Part where it will, 'tis plain, where it
more immediately lies, by the following Instances to which I
refer, and the Persons will be but too easily known there.

But yet this Account cannot pretend to clear the Proprietors, from being both Agents and Principals, at least
some of them, in that they have constantly had the particulars of these Things, laid before them in the humble Petitions
of the Inhabitants; which they to their great Charge and
Trouble, have sent over to England by Members of their own
Body, purposely Deputed as Embassadors to the Proprietors;
*viz.* John Ash, Esq; who died here in the Negotiation of those
Affairs, and is now succeeded by Mr. Jos. Boon, as will appear
in the Prosecution of this Paper.

The submissive Letters, the humble Applications, the Petitions and Remonstrances of the People of all Perswations,
and of the Conforming Minister of the Place, demonstrate, that
the Oppression is universal, the Grievance extraordinary, and
that the Proprietors have been duely inform'd of it all.

I think, it will most naturally occur, that if these Gentlemen, who, God knows, are ill qualified for Government, do not
redress the Grievances of the People, some Body else must;
and for that purpose, the present Application is made to the
Commons of England assembled in Parliament; where publick Grievances never fail of Redress, and where all sorts of
Tyranny has been the Sacrifice to Justice.

The Government of this Province has had the usual Misfortune of those People, who are left to the Conduct of Mercenaries; the Gentlemen-Proprietors, or Lords (call them what you will) are very honest Gentlemen; but are here plac'd above their Sphere; they are Gentlemen of Birth and Fortunes, and well enough instructed in Things within their Quality, but they never learnt to be kings; they have not taken in the Hint of *Pater Patriæ*, they don't know, that a King must be the Father of his People; and that there is a sort of Patriarcal Affection, as well as Obligation, between a King on the Throne, and the People He Governs, which obliges them to treat them with Gentleness, listen to their Complaints, and redress their Grievance; they need have gone no farther, than to their own Sovereign, to have seen a Pattern of this Pious Care, and have reflected, how Sollicitous Her Majesty appears for the General Good; how pleas'd and thankful, when Prosperity Crowns their Affairs; how affectionately Concern'd, when any Calamity attends Her People, either publick as in the Great Storm, or private in the Case of Trade; as in the Disaster of Mr. Pitkin's ill treating them: How concern'd did Her Majesty appear for the Widows and distress'd Families of the Seamen that perisht in the Storm! how bountifully relieve them! and the like. Whence does this proceed? God Almighty, for the Good of Nations, furnishes Princes, born to Crowns and Kingdoms, with the suited Affections for these Circumstances of Government, and thereby fullfils the promise of making them Nursing Fathers, and Nursing Mothers.

The Propriety-Monarchs are born without these Affections, like a Landlord to his Tenant, they have their Eyes upon the Rent; their Concern, if any, is not of Affection, but of Interest; they are Step-fathers and Strangers in the Government, and they have shown it; for their Ears have been stopt, and shut to the Complaints of their Oppress'd People; they govern them by Sub-Tyrants, and connive at their Tyrannies, because they are not furnished with the Affection of Love to the People they govern.

That this is no Scandal, and I hope, no needless Digression, I shall refer to the Judgment of the Impartial Part of Mankind, after Reading the true State of the Colony, as now suppress'd, and under the Government of a Party, and of the Tyranny practis'd there, and this will be best represented by themselves.

I shall then describe the true Posture of it, as it would reasonably be allow'd to be, under a State of Liberty and Encouragement; in the Result of which, the Imprudence and ill Policy, as well as Injustice of the Proprietors, will appear in suffering a flourishing Colony, thus to languish under their Hands.

The first thing I shall refer to for a Prospect of the Grievance before us, is the Representation of the Inhabitants, directed to the Proprietors, sign'd by above 100 of the principal Merchants, Freeholders and Planters, with several Members of the Assembly; and sent over by John Ash, Esq; who, with great Difficulty and Hazzard, got away to Virginia, where his Powers and Instructions were Convey'd after him; the Government there using all possible Endeavours to prevent him. The Address is as follows.


*To the Right Honourable John Granvill, Esq; Palatine,[1] and to the rest of the true and absolute Lords and Proprietors of the Province of Carolina.*

*The Representation and Address of several of the Members of this present Assembly return'd for Colleton County, and other Inhabitants of this Province, whose Names are hereunto Subscribed.*

*May it please your Lordships,*

Altho' the miserable Estate of this Colony will be sufficiently known to your Lordships, from the Relation of John Ash, Esq; who is fully intrusted by us to remonstrate our grievances to your Lordships; yet we think our selves exceedingly bound and obliged to lay before you, what we think does concern your Lordships Honours, and the Peoples Rights and Priviledges: For if the Question were about matters of small moment, we should be asham'd to be importunate, and unwilling to give the least trouble to your Lordships; but considering that the very Foundation of our lawful Rights, hath of late been struck at by Persons, who have more regard

---

[1] Granville, afterward Lord Granville, had succeeded Lord Bath as palatine.

to their private Interest than the Publick good, we humbly
conceive, that it cannot stand with the Duty we owe to our
selves as English-men, or to our Posterity, to sit down contented
with less than that which every Liege and Freeborn Subject
of the Crown of England may, and of Right ought to have.
And therefore least our silence should be prejudicial to so
important a Cause, we humbly crave your Lordships leave,
faithfully and impartially to represent to you the great and
notorious Violations and Infringments of our Laws and
Liberties, under which we suffer.

We shall go no further back, but date the unhappy Causes
and Grounds of our Complaints from, and immediatly after,
the Death of the late Governor Blake; for the Choice and
Election of a Governor to succeed him being intrusted with
your Lordships Deputies here, that Person amongst your said
Deputies who made the strongest party in the Councel, did
carry the Government, by perverting the Design, and breaking
through the Rules and Instructions agreed to by your Lordships for such Election.[1]   And this manifestly appear'd in
the unjust Election of the late Governor Moore, in prejudice
of Landgrave Morton's Title, who (after he was Elected by a
Majority of the Councel then present) was objected against
by the said Moore, and excluded, only because he had accepted of a Commission from the King:[2]   And as the said
Moore acquir'd and obtain'd the Government of this Province
by Fraud, Flattery and trifling Exceptions, as aforesaid, so
has he endeavour'd ever since to manage all things by base
and indirect Methods, and crafty Projects, which made his
Government miserably unfortunate to us all.   The great
and Personal Debts and Necessities which the said late Governour Moore had to struggle with, may well be thought to
have put him upon, and prompted him to Designs, to enrich
himself at the hazard of publick Peace and Welfare: And
because these his designs could not possibly be effected by

[1] They scrupulously followed the Proprietors' instructions, as the minutes
of the Council show.   If the proceedings were improperly recorded on the journal
it is strange that Landgraves Bellinger and Morton of the minority party made
no complaint of it.

[2] The same objection was made to Bellinger.   The objection was a valid
one; the logical position for loyal deputies of the Proprietors to take.

himself alone, he knew very well, that to engage the Council to his Interest, and to have an Assembly chosen to his liking, would be the way effectually to compleat and accomplish his Ends and Purposes; Thereupon 'tis manifest, there being Vacancies in the Council, for Persons fit and worthy to represent your Lordships, and your Lordships Pleasure not being then signifi'd and known therein, those very Vacancies were supply'd by such Persons whom he beforehand knew, and was well satisfy'd and assur'd, would be for his Use and Purpose; and it's as well known, that the Debates and Consultations of the Council have all along been carry'd on, and manag'd to the ends aforesaid.

And pursuant to his said Design, he did by indirect Practices endeavour, that such an Assembly might be chosen, as would be agreeable in their Temper and Disposition with his Designs and Resolutions; This was to be brought about, though the very Foundation of our English Rights and Liberties were undermined, and utterly subverted in the attempt.

I.   We therefore, in the first place, humbly represent to your Lordships, and we do Assert and Maintain, That it is one of the Fundamental Rights and unquestionable Priviledges belonging to Englishmen, That all Elections of their Representatives to serve in Parliament, ought to be free and indifferent, without any Prayer or Commandment to the contrary, and that no Alien born out of the Allegiance to the Crown of England, unless he be otherwise especially qualify'd, ought to Elect for, or be Elected to serve as a Member of Assembly;[1] all which, notwithstanding, at the Election of Members of Assembly to serve for Berkly County made in

---

[1] So early as 1692, perhaps earlier, six out of the twenty members of the Commons House were French Protestants who had settled in the province after the revocation of the Edict of Nantes, and their return had been made by a French Protestant sheriff.   Each subsequent House up to Moore's administration contained several French Protestants, and one, Henry LeNoble, who had anglicised his name to Noble, sat in Blake's council as a Proprietor's deputy and afterward participated in the election of Moore as governor and was a member of his council.   During the intervening years three Dissenters, Smith, Archdale, and Blake, governed the province.   It was only when a Churchman became the head of the government and his administration was supported by the Frenchmen that the Dissenters raised any serious objection to Frenchmen voting for officers and being elected to offices.

the Month of November, 1701, There were several great
Abuses made and committed, against the ancient Usages and
Customs of this Province, and contrary to Law, particularly
an Act Intituled, An Act for Regulating Elections, etc., and
to the great dissatisfaction, and manifest Prejudice of the
several Inhabitants of this Province, Candidates and others.
For so it was, may it please your Lordships, that at the said
Election, much Threatnings, many Intreaties, and other
unjustifiable Actions were made use of, and illegal and unqualify'd Votes given in to the Sheriff; and by him Receiv'd
and Return'd, particularly the Votes of very many unqualify'd
Aliens were taken and enter'd,[1] the Votes of several Members
of the Council were filed and Received, a great number of
Servants and Poor and indigent Persons, voted promiscuously
with their Masters and Creditors, as also several free Negroes
were Receiv'd, and taken for as good Electors as the best
Freeholders in the Province.[2]   So that we leave it with your
Lordships to Judge, whether admitting Aliens, Strangers,
Servants, Negroes, etc., as good and qualify'd Voters, can be
thought any ways agreeable to King Charles's Patent to
your Lordship's, or the English Constitution or Government.

II. We represent to your Lordships, that when at the
Meeting of the Assembly, divers Candidates, by Petition by
them Exhibited, pray'd to be heard against the Return of
the Sheriff for Berkly County of the Election aforesaid, and
insisted upon their Right, and that the Sheriff's Return was
false and illegal, and the said Assembly the better and more
impartially, to inquire into the ill Practices of the said Elec-

---

[1] It is not at all probable that there were "very many unqualify'd Aliens"
in South Carolina at the time.   The enabling act of 1696 had naturalized nearly
every alien in the province who had not been naturalized in England before settling in South Carolina, and had made it so easy for aliens to become citizens
that it is hardly likely that any settled colonists of alien birth had neglected to
become qualified electors, especially when it is shown by records that when a
Frenchman, who had not yet been naturalized, was elected to the Commons
House in 1692 he was not allowed to take his seat.

[2] An early example of pure democracy.   The only requirement prescribed
for an elector by the Fundamental Constitutions was that he own fifty acres of
land, or its equivalent in securities.   As every male settler, servants not excepted,
received fifty, or more, acres for settling in Carolina it is hardly likely that there
were very many illegal votes taken.

tion, did first of all resolve to begin upon Priviledges and Elections, that the late Governour Moore, to prevent such Inquiry, did several times Prorogue the said Assembly.[1]

III.  That when the said Assembly were at last suffer'd to sit, the Inquiry and Examination into the Sheriff's Return of the last Election was obstructed, and industriously prevented, by setting on foot an ill laid design of raising Forces to attaque St. Augustine.

IV.  That notwithstanding your Lordships repeated Commands to your Deputies, to procure a good regulation of the Indian Trade, on which our friendly Correspondence with all our neighbouring Indians, and the Peace and Safety of this Colony chiefly depends, yet the said late Governor Moore has been by his Artifices, the Chief (if not the Only) Occasion of obstructing the same, designing nothing less than ingrossing the same for himself and Accomplices; having already almost utterly ruin'd the Trade for Skins and Furs (whereby we held our chief Correspondence with England) and turn'd it into a Trade of Indian or Slave-making, whereby the Indians to the South and West of us are already involv'd in Blood and Confusion, a Trade so odious and abominable, that every other Colony in America (altho' they have equal temptation) abhor to follow.

V.  That the said late Governor Moore did grant Commissions to Anthony Dodsworth, Robert Mackoone, and others, to set upon, assault, kill, destroy, and take Captive as many Indians as they possible could, the Profit and Produce of which Indian Slaves were turn'd to his private use; whereas such undertakings, unjust and barbarous in themselves, will in all Probability draw upon us an Indian War, with all the dreadful Consequences of it.

VI.  We represent to your Lordships, that the late unfortunate, ill contriv'd, and worse Manag'd expedition against St. Augustine, was principally set on Foot by the said late Governor and his Adherents; and that if any Person in the

---

[1] From the journals of the Commons House it appears that this action was taken more because certain dissatisfied members of that house absented themselves from the meetings thereof and thereby prevented quorums than because of any effort to prevent inquiring into the behavior of the sheriff of Berkeley County.

said late Assembly undertook to speak against it, and to shew how unfit and unable we were at that time for such an Attempt, he was presently look'd upon, by them, as an Enemy and Traytor to his Country, and revil'd and affronted in the said Assembly, altho' the true Design of the Expedition, was no other then catching and making Slaves of Indians for private advantage, and Impoverishing the Country; And this will plainly appear, when your Lordships know that your Country is brought more in Debt at this time, and upon this occasion, then ever since its first Settlement, if we put all the Debts we have ow'd together; and that the Expedition was to enrich themselves will appear particularly, because whatsoever Booty, as rich Silks, great Quantity of Church-Plate, with a great many other costly Church Ornaments and Utensils taken by our Souldiers as [at] St. Augustine, are now detain'd in the Possession of the said late Governor and his Officers, contrary to an Act of Assembly made, for an equal Division of the same among the Souldiers.

VII. That the said Governor would have had the said Expedition against St. Augustine begun and undertaken before the War with Spain was Proclaim'd here; and this was vehemently urg'd by his Interest in the said Assembly, but with much ado, being put to the Vote, was carried in the Negative. And when at last the Expedition was Order'd, the Management of the said late Governor was such, in all its Steps, particularly in relation to his shameful retreat, and burning the Country's Vessels, that we are asham'd to mention the same till we have a Free Assembly, before which the matter may be fairly try'd, which is the only thing the said late Governor and his Adherents are most afraid of.

VIII. That in the said late Assembly, the Constitutions sent by Major Daniel were offer'd for their passing, Urg'd with great strength of Reason, for to have them Pass'd by Mr. Ash, but they were opposed by Mr. Trott, Mr. Howes, and others the said Governor's Creatures, and several reflecting words used by the said Trott and Howes concerning them, exposing the Constitutions as Ridiculous and Void in themselves, (thereby endeavouring, notwithstanding your Lordships care of us) to keep the People in an unsettl'd Condition, that from time to time, they might the more easily be imposed on by them.

IX.  That after the People Return'd from St. Augustine, the time for the said Assembly to meet, according to the last Prorogation, was just at hand; when they met, they went upon the Inquiry of the Charges the Country had been at in the said Expedition, and were upon Debate for the finding out Ways and Means for the Payment of the Countries Debts, for securing the Colony, for the settling of Elections for the future, and for granting as much Freedom to the French, and other Aliens, as could be granted by the Assembly, or the French reasonably expect.  A Bill for the better Regulating Elections, pass'd the lower House twice, and was sent up to the said Governor and Council, where it was rejected without so much as a Conference; upon which several of the Members, jealous of their Priviledges, and being so order'd by those that sent them, left the House, first entring their Protestation, a copy of which Mr. Ash has to shew your Lordships, and to which we refer You.

X.  But what we have yet to represent to your Lordships, makes very deep Impressions on us, and is not to be thought on by us, but with the greatest Regret and Concern.  For altho' the Members of the late Assembly, who Protested, and did leave the House as aforesaid (hoping that the next Day they might find things in better order, and some temperating Means found out, which might have given some tolerable Assurance of having their Liberties secur'd) went every one of them to the House on the Morrow, and frankly offer'd to sit longer, if the rest of the Assembly would joyn with them to Assert their Rights; but instead of any compliance, they were Abus'd, Revil'd, and treated with the most reflecting Language imaginable, very unbecoming an Assembly.  And we further Represent to your Lordships, that after such Abuse given them in the House, several of the said Members, *viz.* the said John Ash, Esq; Landgrave Thomas Smith, and others, were Assaulted and set upon in the open Street, without any Provocation or Affront by them given, or offer'd. The said Thomas Smith was set upon by Lieutenant Colonel George Dearsby,[1] who with his Sword drawn, and the Point

---

[1] A misprint for Dearsley.

held at the said Smith's Belly, swore he would Kill him, and if he had not been prevented, would have done the said Smith some considerable Mischief to the endangering of his Life. The said John Ash walking along the Street, was assaulted by a rude, drunken, ungovernable Rabble, headed, encouraged and abetted by the said Dearsley, Thomas Dalton, Nicholas Nary, and other Persons, Inhabitants, who set upon the said Ash, used him Villanously and Barbarously, and that Evening, when he the said Ash was retir'd into a Friend's Chamber for Security, the same armed Multitude came to the House where the said Ash was, and demanded him down, assuring him at the same time that they would do him no hurt, but only wanted to discourse with him, upon which Assurance he came down to them; who notwithstanding, being encourag'd and assisted by Captain Rhett, and others, drew him by Force and Violence on board his the said Rhett's Ship, reviling and threatning of him as they drag'd him along; and having gotten him on board the said Rhett's Ship, they sometimes told him they would carry him to Jamaica; and at other times threatning to Hang him, or leave him on some remote Island.

XI. That the said late Governor had the same day (immediately before the Riot began) treated a great many of the Persons concern'd therein, and used such Expressions to them, as gave them, next their drink, the greatest Encouragements for what they acted, by telling them, that the protesting Members would bring the People on their Heads for neglecting to pay the Country's Debts, which if it should happen, he knew not who could blame them; in the meantime he thank'd them for their close adherence to him in all his Concerns. And after the Riot began (of part of which he was an Eye-witness) having first drank with some of them, he withdrew himself out of the way, thereby giving them greater Incouragement to proceed in their Tumultuous Practices, and by his Example and Absence, discouraging the inferior Officers from executing their Duty.

XII. That whilst the said Riot continu'd, which was four or five Days, Landgrave Edmond Bellinger, who was a Justice of the Peace, there being no other to be seen that understood his Office, went out to Suppress and Record the aforesaid Riot, but the Rioters no sooner saw him, than they call'd him all the opprobrious Names they could think of, and the said Rhett came up to him, and struck him over the Head with his Cane, and continu'd beating and striking of him for a considerable time, as by the said Record herewith sent your Lordships, will more fully appear.

XIII.  That the said Rioters beat and abused Mr. Joseph Boone, and put him in danger and fear of his Life, without any Provocation by him given or offer'd; and that for four or five days successively, and at other times after, the said Rioters unusually Arm'd and Weapon'd, to the great Terror of the People, and frightned and terrify'd Persons, that they were forc'd to leave the Town, their Affairs and Interests exposed to the Mercy of a licentious Rabble.

XIV.  That some of the said Rioters, whilst the Riot was at the Church, went one Night to the House of John Smith, a Butcher in Charles Town; and there being a Woman big with Child in the said House, they with Force open'd the door, threw her down, and otherwise mis-used her, that she brought forth a dead Child, with the Back and Skull broken.

XV.  That the said John Ash, Thomas Smith, James Byres, Joseph Boon, and others, complain'd to the said late Governor and his Council, setting forth the Abuses and Barbarous Usages they had met withal from the aforesaid Rioters, and the Danger they were yet in, for that the said Rioters were still in Arms, etc., but they met with no other Satisfaction from them, then that the said late Governor shifted off the Matter; by saying, it was a Business fit for a Justice of the Peace; and being ask'd by James Byres, whether or not he look'd on himself, as Governor, oblig'd to keep the Peace of the Province?  He reply'd, that was a Question he was not oblig'd to Answer.

XVI.  That before the next Sessions of the Peace, holden for the said Province, Sir Nathaniel Johnson was proclaim'd, and took upon him the Government; and then Mr. Trott had a Commission to be Judge, and the said late Governor was made Attorney General; so that it was in vain to expect any Relief or Remedy here: However, the said Edmond Bellinger, did what in him lay, to have the said Riot inquir'd into, gave in the Record thereof to the Bench, and some of the Grand Jury urg'd to have it presented, but to no purpose.

for some of the Abettors of the Rioters being of the Jury, and making Friends there, stopt the whole Proceeding.

XVII. We further represent to your Lordships, that contrary to the Rights and Priviledges which we ought to Enjoy, the last Election of Members to serve for Berkly County, was manag'd with greater Injustice to the Freemen of this Province than the former; For at this last Election, Jews,[1] Strangers, Sailors, Servants, Negroes, and almost every French-man in Craven and Berkly County, came down to Elect, and their Votes were taken, and the Persons by them Voted for, were Return'd by the Sheriff, to the manifest wrong, and Prejudice of other Candidates.

Things standing with us, as is before faithfully represented to your Lordships, we thought it our Duty, since we can have no Remedy or Relief in Carolina, to apply our selves to your Lordships, whose Paternal care and Concern for us, we Question not, will be signally evidenc'd and extended unto us upon such occasions, and in such extremities: For when once our Lawful Rights and Priviledges are deny'd us, when Forreigners and Strangers shall make our Laws, when we can have no Protection from those who ought, and are Intrusted by your Lordships, to see the Laws executed, when, in a word, force is made the Arbiter of all differences, and all things reduc'd to a State of Confusion, it is surely a time, if ever there be one, for a People to Complain, and miserable are those Subjects, who must be Hector'd and Domineer'd over by their fellow Subjects, even by those who have hardly any other way to support their decay'd Fortunes, but at the Expence of the Publick. It may be worth your Lordships while, to Reflect what might have been the occasion, that so few Persons of Interest, Honor, and Education come amongst us,[2] and that good People go, and are going from

---

[1] There were at this time five or six wealthy and influential Jews among the leading merchants of Charles Town. Four of them had been included in the naturalization act passed in 1696, and the others were probably qualified also. Under the Fundamental Constitutions Jews were not denied the right of suffrage, and every Jew in Charles Town, so far as we are informed, had the required amount of property.

[2] The contemporaneous records show that an exceptionally large percentage of those who had previously settled in South Carolina were persons of interest, honor, and education. The government that they conducted, the trade they

us, when the Colony is in a thriving Condition; certainly it is because the English Liberties, that all Her Majesty's Subjects in all other Places in Her Dominions Justly claim, are notoriously trampl'd on, to the great discouragement of Settlers. As to the French, they have hitherto liv'd peaceably, and with due encouragement amongst us; but when we see and consider, that they are often made Tools of, and imposed upon, and perswaded by ill designing Persons here, to carry on sinister designs to the General disadvantage of the Country, and how easily they are drawn into Errors, by reason they have not a right understanding of our Language, and are ignorant of our Laws,[1] we can't imagine that we do them any hurt, by making good and wholesome Laws for us and them, since we Oblige them by no other Laws whatsoever, or upon any Account, than what we ourselves are Obliged by, and live under. What then have we to entreat for and pray of your Lordships? Nothing less, than that your Lordships would be pleased to establish the peace of this Colony on such a sure Foundation, that it may be beyond the Wit and Malice, and out of the Power of ill designing Men to disturb it for the time to come. And lastly, we on behalf of our selves and Her Majesty's leige Subjects, Inhabitants of this Province, do more especially pray and desire your Lordships, that you would be pleased to give directions for calling a free General Assembly, which will undoubtedly Assist your Lordships to Redress and Remove the Grievances aforesaid, settle the Peace and Prosperity of

built up, the wealth they accumulated, and the general ability and culture they displayed in various ways, would attest that, even if we had not a knowledge of their antecedents and connections.

[1] The greater part of the Frenchmen had been in the province upward of twenty years; some of them had been there a longer period, and many of them had lived in England or Ireland before settling in South Carolina. They had become thoroughly imbued with English ideas and ideals; many of them had joined the Church of England; some had already anglicised their names; many of them wrote excellent English and it is fair to assume that they also spoke it equally well; their children scarcely spoke French at all and it is doubtful if their grandchildren could speak it, save such as enjoyed the advantage of a private tutor at home or of schooling abroad. The evidence is that the Huguenots, who constituted but three or four per cent. of the population of South Carolina when they first reached the province, were almost immediately so thoroughly absorbed by the English as to lose very soon all of their French individuality save their family names; and even those were in many instances anglicised.

this Colony, and procure their chearful Obedience which
ought to be Render'd to your Lordships, under Her present
Majesty, carrying with it the offer of our Fortunes and best
endeavours for Her Majesty's and your Lordships Honours, as
a real Testimony of our thankfulness.

Carolina 26 June, 1703.

Sign'd by 150 of the Inhabitants.[1]

The Gentleman, who brought this, a Member of their
Parliament and Considerable Freeholder, faithfully deliver'd
it to His Excellence the Prince Palatine,[2] for such, I suppose,
he would be called, from whom how little Encouragement he
receiv'd, to hope for a Redress of the Grievances of the Countrey, he would have told the World if he had liv'd to finish
a Tract, which 'tis a great loss to the World he did not: Entituled *The present State of Affairs in Carolina;* Two Sheets
whereof were printed before he died;[3] but his Death has prevented what is but too imperfectly supplied by these Sheets,
for which the Author asks the Readers Charity; it being impossible he should be equally touch'd with a Sence of the
Miseries of the Colony, with One who had so great a share
as Mr. Ash, both of the Property and the Suffering.

The loss this Gentleman's Death was to the Collony, was
as to this Negotiation, as well as possible, supplyed by their
sending a second Agent to the Proprietors: *viz.* Mr. Joseph
Boon, by whom the following Petition was with like ill Success
brought to the Proprietors; the failing in which frequent
Application, causes this publick Appeal to the World for
the Justice of their Application to the Parliament of England;
where it is not doubted, they will meet with a suitable Assistance.

I think, I need add nothing to this melancholly Description
of the barbarous Treatment of this Innocent People, tho' I
could furnish the World with innumerable Particulars. Nor
cou'd I make a greater Satyr upon the Conduct and Character
of the Gentlemen Proprietors than to say, that all those
Humble Representations met with no Redress from them; but

[1] Reprinted in Rivers's *Sketch of the History of South Carolina,* pp. 453–460.

[2] Lord Granville.

[3] For this fragment, see the next division of this volume.

on the contrary, all Application to them has hitherto been fruitless, and has met with Repulses, too unbecoming the Reasonableness of their Cause, to say no worse of it.

The Petition of the Inhabitants brought over by Mr. Boon is as follows; and is Sign'd by above 180 Persons of the principal Freeholders of the Countrey.

*To His Excellency, John Lord Granville Palatine, and to the rest of the true and absolute Lords and Proprietors of the Province of Carolina.*

*May it please Your Lordships,*

By an Address sent your Lordships by John Ash, Esq; bearing Date the 26th of June, 1703, Several of the Inhabitants of this part of Your Province, set forth to Your Lordships the Undue Election of the present Assembly; and besides, the heavy Taxes they have laid on Us, and the severe Impositions on Trade (the Consequences of the vain Attempt on St. Augustine.)  We are more particularly to make our Complaints to Your Lordships, of the Great and Unparallel'd Breach they have made in the Charter, granted Your Lordships by K. Charles the II. and of our Priviledges therein contained.  The Assembly having been prorogued on the 10th of May; it was however called together by Proclamation, to Sit the 6th of April: And having continued together seven or eight Days, with little or no Business before them (to the great Surprize of the generality of the people) on a suddain, without any previous Notice, on the 4th of May a Bill was brought into the House (the Copy whereof We have herewith sent Your Lordships) to Exclude by a Sacramental Test, all Dissenters from Sitting in the Common's House of Assembly. This Bill was hurried on so, that on the 6th it Past the House; there being, after all their Endeavours, but Twelve for it, and Eleven against it; whereof several where Members of the Church of England.  In the Upper House, tho' it Past with less Opposition, yet the Landgrave Joseph Morgan[1] was deny'd the Liberty of Entring his Reasons for his Dissent.

<hr>

[1] Morton.

We are unable (My Lords) to describe, the Consternation
of the Generality of the People at these Violent Proceedings:
All moderate Persons are extreamly dissatisfy'd, and the Dissenters themselves under the last degree of Confusion and
Discontent; desiring, with Grief of Heart, that Your Lordships, in Your Great Wisdom and Goodness, will take Their
present Condition into Your Serious Considerations, and Order
a Repeal of the aforesaid Act, so Prejudicial to Their Libertys;
for which They humbly offer to Your Lordships these following Reasons.

1.  K. Charles the IId. having by His Charter to Your
Lordships, given His Subjects, the Freemen and Freeholders
of this Province by Themselves, or Their Delegates, the
Priviledge of Advising and Consenting with Your Lordships,
to all such Laws as shall be Made here; and the Dissenters
being a very large Part of the Freemen, and Freeholders, and
incouraged to Transport Themselves, Families, and Estates,
hither by the said Priviledges, are notwithstanding, Excluded
from the Priviledge of being Delegates, or Representatives of
the People in Their Assemblys by the said Act, to the Manifest Violation of the Charter.

2.  The Dissenters, in all the rest of Her Majesty's Govern-
ments in America, being by no Laws Excluded from being
Chosen into Assemblys in the respective Colonys, And the
Dissenters here, having a Right thereunto in this Govern-
ment, not only as Freemen, but by the Concessions in the
Charter, have the greater Reason to complain of Their present
Sufferings.

3.  We cannot too feelingly Assure Your Lordships, that
the said Act, tends not only to the great Prejudice, and utter
Discouragement of Her Majesty's good Subjects, the Dissenters here, in rending from them that fundamental Priviledge,
which They and Their Ancestors have peaceably Enjoy'd
ever since the First Settlement of this Colony; but will also
be a very great Discouragement to Them in Their several
Trades, and Employments, and a fatal Discouragement of
the further, and better Settlement of this Part of Your Lordships Province.

For a further Account of these Things, we refer Your Lordships to Mr. Joseph Boone, by whose Hands We send this to

Your Lordships, desiring You to give Credit to what he shall further Offer to Your Lordships, on Our Behalf. Wishing Your Lordships good Health and Prosperity, We are
Your Lordships<br>Most Humble, and most<br>Obedient Servants.

The Lady Blake Widow of the late Governor, at the same time took the freedom to represent to the Proprietors, the matter of Fact of this Proceeding in a most pathetick and extraordinary manner, by Letter as follows:[1]

*May it please your Lordships,*
The Share my Son has the Honour to have with your Lordships in the Propriety of this Province, together with the publick Concern I have for the Propriety thereof, oblige me at this time to give you this Trouble, and to lay before your Lordships a short Representation of the many Grievances the People are oppress'd with.

The precipitate and fatal Undertaking against St. Augustine, and the Consequences thereof carried on by a Party, have involv'd the Countrey in a Debt of about Ten thousand Pounds, to the Ruin of our Trade, the Loss of our Credit abroad,[2] and infinite Dissatisfactions at home.

Towards Satisfaction of which Debt, an Act was contriv'd for forcing the Currency of Bills of Credit to the value of Six thousand Pounds, these Bills were declared Current in all Payments, and the Refuser of them fineable in double the value of the Sum refus'd, whereby the boldest Stroke has been given to the Property of the Settlers in this Province, that

---

[1] Elizabeth (Axtell) Blake, widow of Landgrave Joseph Blake (who was one of the eight Proprietors at the time of his death in 1700) and daughter of Landgrave Daniel Axtell. Her father and her husband had both been Dissenters. Her father-in-law, Benjamin Blake, had been bitter in his criticisms of the Church of England in his lifetime. Her husband's first wife was a daughter of the first Landgrave Morton (the governor) and the sister of the then Landgrave Morton. Her prejudices, therefore, were strongly with the Dissenters. Her minor son, the second Landgrave Joseph Blake, owned one of the Proprietary shares in Carolina.

[2] Exaggerated views.

ever was known in any Country, not govern'd by arbitrary
Power: And the bad Consequences of this forc'd Currency
in Relation to Trade with Strangers are so great, that they
can scarcely be express'd, without being more prolix than
the Bounds of a Letter can allow.   Your Lordships very well
know, that if the Kingdom of England did not conceive such a
Method destructive of the Peoples Property, and of the
utmost Danger to Commerce, they cou'd not need any Pro-
jection of Ways and Means, for raising of what Money the
Government's Affairs do require,  But there has nothing of
this been weigh'd by your Lordships Deputies here, or by the
pack'd Members of our Commons House of Assembly: Besides
all this, the People are not satisfy'd how many Bills are
truly sent abroad; and the great Concern Mr. James Smith
*alias* Serureir,[1] (who cheated the Scot's Company of a considerable Sum of Money, and with his Keeper made his Escape
from London hither) had in this Contrivance, doth give a
Jealousie of indirect Practices therein so prevalent among the
People as must end in Confusion and Disorder.

Neither have they stopt here, but to our present Amazement, and the Increase of our Fears of their evil Designs for
the future, they have proceeded to pass an Act for the Exclusion of all Dissenters from their Right to sit in the Commons
House of Assembly, and obliging them to take the Sacrament
according to the Rites of the Church of England.   In the same

---

[1] James LeSerurier was the son of James LeSerurier, a merchant of St.
Quentin in northern France, who fled as a refugee to South Carolina after the
revocation of the Edict of Nantes.  The elder LeSerurier became a wealthy
merchant of Charles Town and his son became a merchant in London at some
time prior to May 21, 1697, the date of the making of the will of his father, which
was proved October 4, 1706.  His mother was Elizabeth Leger, of another of
the most prominent of the Huguenot families that settled in South Carolina.
Her will, which was made September 26, 1721, shows that she was then of the
parish of St. Anne, Westminster, England.  We are uninformed as to the merits
of these charges against the younger Serurier, but as he was a member of one of
the wealthiest and most influential of the Huguenot families and a brother-in-law
of Henry LeNoble (or Noble, as he had anglicised his name), another of the
most conspicuous of the Huguenots, who was then a Proprietor's deputy and a
member of the Grand Council and siding with the Church party, and as he continued to be highly regarded in South Carolina, it is likely that there was considerable partisan bitterness at the bottom of these charges.  The Scots Company
referred to is that which founded the unfortunate settlement at Darien.

Act inserting a Clause, to qualifie the most profligate of themselves for Admission into Assemblies by a Declaratory Oath, altho' they never take the Sacrament: This Act (after much under-hand Dealing) was pass'd in a hurry and carry'd by Twelve only against Eleven, the above Mr. Smith, who has neither Interest nor Reputation, being one of the Number of the Twelve.

By the Artifices of these Men, the honest and well-meaning People have been all along set against your Lordships Constitutions, they therefore seeing that by passing of them, their indirect and arbitrary Proceedings would be in a great Measure prevented; But now the Eyes of the People are somewhat more open'd, and they begin to be sensible of the Delusions and Oppressions they have been involv'd in. Your Deputies decline offering the Constitutions to the People, altho' your Lordships (as I am well inform'd) have often of late Commanded it of them.

I know, that there has already been made to your Lordships by Mr. John Ash, a Representation of the People's Sufferings here, and that there will be at this time, and upon this Occasion, a farther Account of these Affairs sent your Lordships by many of the good People in the Behalf of themselves and others, most sensibly affected with the Loss of these Priviledges, which by King Charles His Charter to your Lordships, has been the Right and Usage of their Ancestors and themselves, ever since the first Settlement of the Province: And my earnest Request to your Lordships is, That in your great Wisdom, you would be pleas'd to give them such a Hearing and speedy Redress, as may conduce most to the Glory of God, your Lordships Honour, and the Welfare and Prosperity of your Colony, and you will highly oblige

Your Lordships
Most Humble Servant.

It may be observ'd, That during the Negotiation of Mr. Ash, and the Interval before the sending Mr. Boon, the Party carried on their Excesses, and added to the Grievances Complain'd of before; by setting on foot that most barbarous and unheard of Law against the Dissenters mention'd in the above Letter and Address; the Copy whereof is as follows:

*An Act for the more effectual Preservation of the Government of this Province, by requiring all Persons that shall hereafter be chosen Members of the Commons House of Assembly, and sit in the same, to take the Oaths and subscribe the Declaration appointed by this Act; and to conform to the Religious Worship in this Province, according to the Church of England; and to receive the Sacrament of the Lord's Supper, according to the Rites and Usage of the said Church.*

As nothing is more contrary to the Profession of the Christian Religion, and particularly to the Doctrine of the Church of England, than Persecution for Conscience only, NEVERTHELESS,

*Whereas* it hath been found by experience, that the admitting of Persons of different Perswasions and Interest in Matters of Religion, to sit and vote in the Commons House of Assembly, hath often caused great Contentions and Animosities in this Province, and hath very much obstructed the publick Business; and whereas by the Laws and Usage of England, all Members of Parliament are obliged to conform to the Church of England, by receiving the Sacrament of the Lord's Supper, according to the Rites of the said Church,

*Be it therefore enacted,* by his Excellency John, Lord Granville, Palatine, and the rest of the true and absolute Lords and Proprietors of this Province, by and with the Advice and Consent of the rest of the Members of the General Assembly, now met at Charles-Town, for the South-West Part of this Province, and by the Authority of the same, That every Person that after the Ratification of this Act, shall be chosen a Member of the Commons House of Assembly that hath not, within the Space of Twelve Months before such his Election, receiv'd the Sacrament of the Lord's Supper, according to the Rites and Usage of the Church of England, as establish'd by Law, such Person after his Election, and before he be permitted to sit and vote in the said House, shall receive the Sacrament of the Lord's Supper, according to the Rites and Usage of the Church of England, in some publick Church, upon some Lord's Day, commonly called Sunday, immediately after divine Service and Sermon; and every of the said Persons, in open Assembly, in a full House duly sitting, with their Speaker in his Chair, shall deliver a Certificate of such his receiving of the said Sacrament as aforesaid, under the Hand of the respective Minister, or shall make proof of the Truth thereof by Two credible Witnesses at least upon Oath.

*But whereas* some Persons scruple the Receiving the Sacrament of the Lord's Supper, by reason they fear they are not rightly fitted and prepared to partake of that Ordinance, who do nevertheless, out of real Choice, conform to the Church of England, as establish'd by Law, and do sincerely profess the Same, and do not abstain from the Sacrament of the Lord's Supper, out of any Dislike to the Manner and Form of the Administration thereof, as used by the Church of England, and prescribed in the Communion-Office, in the Book of the Common-Prayer of the said Church,

*Be it therefore enacted* by the Authority aforesaid,  That every Person that after the Ratification of this Act, shall be chosen a Member of the Commons House of Assembly in this Province, in case he hath not received the Sacrament of the Lord's Supper, according to the Rites and Usage of the Church of England, as is before prescribed by this Act, then every such Person before he vote in the said Commons House of Assembly, or sit there during any Debate in the said House, after their Speaker is chosen, shall upon his Oath taken on the Holy Evangelists, declare as follows:

I, A. B., Do solemnly and sincerely, in the Presence of God, profess, testify and declare,  That I am of the Profession of the Church of England, as Establish'd by Law; and that I do conform to the Same, and usually frequent the said Church for the publick Worship of God; and that I do not abstain from the Sacrament of the Lord's Supper, out of any Dislike to the Manner and Form of the Administration thereof, as used by the said Church of England, and as it is prescribed in the Communion-Office, in the Book of Common-Prayer of the said Church; and that I am not, nor for One Year past, have not been in Communion with any Church or Congregation, that doth not conform to the said Church of England, nor received the Sacrament of the Lord's Supper in such Congregation; and that as a Member of this House of Assembly, I will endeavour the Good and Welfare of the said Church of England, as establish'd by Law: So help me God.

Which said Oath or Declaration of Conformity shall be solemnly and publickly made, and subscribed by every Member of the said Commons House of Assembly (that doth not produce a Certificate, or other Proof of his having received the Sacrament of the Lord's Supper, as before prescribed by this Act,) between the Hours of Nine in the Morning, and Four in the Afternoon, at the Table in the said House, and whilst a full House is sitting with their Speaker in his Chair: And every such Person that shall upon Oath make, and subscribe such Declaration of Conformity to the Church of England, is hereby declared to be sufficiently qualified to be a Member of the Commons House of Assembly, as if he had receiv'd the Sacrament of the Lord's Supper according to the Usage of the Church of England, as is above prescribed by this Act.

*And be it further enacted* by the Authority aforesaid, That all Persons that after the Ratification of this Act shall be chosen Members of the General Assembly, before they vote in the Commons House of Assembly, or sit there during any Debate in the said House of Commons, after their Speaker is chosen, shall on the Holy Evangelists take the Oaths appointed to be taken, instead of the Oaths of Allegiance and Supremacy by one Act of Parliament, made in the First Year of the Reign of the late K. William and Q. Mary, entituled. An Act for the Abrogating of the Oaths of Supremacy and Allegiance, and appointing other Oaths, and shall make and subscribe the Declaration appointed to be made and subscribed in the Act made in the Thirtieth Year of the Reign of the late King Charles the Second, entituled, An Act for the more effectual Preserving the King's Person and Government, by disabling Papists from sitting in either Houses of Parliament. And shall also take the Oath appointed to be taken by one Act of Parliament made in the First Year of the Reign of Her present Majesty, entituled, An Act to declare the Alterations in the Oath appointed to be taken by the Act, entituled, An Act for the further Security of Her Majesty's Person, and the Succession of the Crown in the Protestant Line; and for extinguishing the Hopes of the pretended Prince of Wales, and all other Pretenders, and their open and secret Abettors, and for declaring the Association to be determined; Which Oaths and Declaration in every succeeding Assembly shall be solemnly and publickly made and subscribed betwixt the Hours of Nine in the Morning, and Four in the Afternoon, by every Member of the Said Assembly, at the Table of the said House, and whilst a full House is sitting, with their Speaker in his Chair.

*And be it further enacted* by the Authority aforesaid, That if any Person, that shall hereafter be elected a Member of the Commons House of Assembly, shall presume to sit and vote in the said Commons House after their Speaker is chosen, before he hath received the Sacrament of the Lord's Supper, according to the Rites and Usage of the said Church of England, or upon Oath and subscribed such Declaration of Conformity to the Church of England as is prescribed by this Act, and hath also taken the Oaths, and made and subscribed the Declaration, as required by this Act; every Person so offending shall forfeit for the first time he shall so sit, the Sum of Fifty Pounds current Money of this Province; and for every Day after that he shall so sit, the Sum of Ten Pounds, the one half to the Palatine, and the rest of the true and absolute

Lords and Proprietors of this Province, to and for the Support of
the Government of this Province, and the contingent Charges
thereof, to be disposed of by Ordinance of the General Assembly;
and the other half to him or them that shall sue for the same within
Six Months after the Offence committed, by Action of Debt, Suit,
Bill, Plaint, or Information in any Court of Record in this Province, wherein no Essoign, Protection, Privilege, Injunction, or
Wager of Law, or Stay of Prosecution, by *Non Vult ulterius Prose-
qui*, or otherwise, shall be admitted or allow'd.

*And be it further enacted* by the Authority aforesaid, That in
case any Person shall be return'd a Member of the Commons
House of Assembly, who shall refuse to qualifie himself as required
by this Act, and so cannot be permitted to sit and vote in the said
House, that then in such Case it shall be lawful for those Members
of Assembly, that are qualified to sit and vote in the said House of
Assembly, to order the Sheriff of the County to lay the Poll or List
of the several Candidates, and the Numbers of them that voted for
each of the Candidates, and admit that Person or Persons, that
hath the greatest Number of Votes next to them, Members that
were return'd to sit and vote as a Member or Members of the said
Commons House of Assembly, provided they do qualifie themselves as is above directed by this Act: And in case there is not a
sufficient Number of the other Candidates, that are qualified, as
aforesaid, to fill up the Vacancies, that then a new Writ shall be
issued out for such Number as is so wanting.

Read Three times, and ratified in open Assembly, the Sixth
Day of May, Anno Domini, 1704.

N. JOHNSON,    THO. BROUGHTON,   JA. MOORE,
ROB. GIBBS,    HENRY NOBLE,    NICHOLAS TROTT.[1]

This is the famous Exclusive Act: A Law in it self so
ridiculous, so partial, so calculated for the Ruine of the Colony,
that nothing but mad Men, that depended upon being Superior
in Power to all humane Authority, the People should apply
to, would have ever brought upon the Stage of the World:
A Law that gives such a Test of its Makers, that it fills Strangers
with Amazement, at the Impudence of it, makes their own

---

[1] This Act proved the undoing of the theretofore victorious party, for the
manifest unfairness of the majority in resorting to so tyrannical a measure
(although the very inhibition the Dissenters had wished to put upon the Huguenots) not only solidified the Dissenters, but caused many Churchmen to join
them, and at the next election the Dissenters won.

Friends abandon them, and they that would advocate for the Thing in general, yet blush at the horrid Particulars.

A Law, that contrary to all Laws universally made, which, however ill design'd, have pretence of publick Good, has thrown off the very Mask of Modesty; and openly declares, no Villany can unqualify for a part in the Government, but a Conscientious Scruple may.

A Law that has the Impudence to declare War against the Christian Religion, and the Church of England, in the frontice Piece, and begins with a *Non obstante* to both of them.

That having first own'd what it Enacts, to be Unchristian and Hetrodox, has the face, to begin with a *Nevertheless* in Capital Letters, damning the Laws of God, and of the Church, as well as of the Country, to a positive Submission to a Rabble of Sham-Representatives.

A Law that, turning the first Paragraph into the Genuine English, which the Words will, without any straining, or partial Construction, bear, begins in this sense:

*Whereas* the Laws of God, the Laws of Nature and Reason, the Christian Religion, the Doctrine of the Church of England, and the Constitution of this Country, are directly against, and do clearly condemn the Law now making, yet in Defiance to them all, in order to carry on our own private Resolutions, for the Enriching our selves, and the Destruction of this Colony, we have resolved to Enact; *and be it Enacted,* etc.

Blush, Gentlemen-Proprietors, and be asham'd for your Petty Sub-Tyrants; that, like the Lord's Servants in the Gospel, beat and abuse their Fellow-Servants, and Eat and Drink with the Drunken, and with a Detestation suitable to your own Honour, and the Nature of the Crimes, publish your Dislike of these Things, and immediately apply your selves to reforming the Abuses of your Subjects, who, tho' in one Sense they are your Subjects, in another Sense, as Englishmen, are your Fellow-Subjects to the Crown and General Government of the English Empire, and that are under the Government of a Princess; Who, as She hates Tyranny in all its Parts, carefully avoids it in Her Own Administration, Vigorously struggles with it in Europe, and Fights to loose the World from General Bondage, will never suffer Her Own

Subjects to Tyrannize over one another, nor any part of Her People to oppress the rest. In Her Majesty's Equal Administration, you may assure your selves, these injur'd People will have Redress; and the barefac'd Villany, with which they have been thus treated, will ripen Matters so, for the Royal Justice, that it cannot Escape a Necessary Correction.

Prevent it, Gentlemen, by a timely Redress, and let Her Majesty see, that Her pious Examples of Peace will animate you, to extend it to all the parts of Her Subjects under your Direction; for certainly, when Her Majesty exhorts us all to Peace and Union, and promises Her Royal Favour to those that promote it, it cannot be understood, that all Her Majesty's Dominions should Enjoy it, but Carolina.

Hitherto you have seen the General Complaint of the Inhabitants of Carolina, and how they have been Tyranniz'd over, and barbarously treated in the Country.

I conclude this Treatise, by giving Account of the Reception they met with here, in their peaceable Application to their Palatine and Board of Proprietors for Redress.

Mr. Ash, as is related, being arriv'd here with the Remonstrance and humble Petition of the Inhabitants, apply'd himself in the Name of the People, by whom he was sent, to their Excellencies the Proprietors; and delivering his Petition, etc., found it was impossible to obtain any Redress; either for the publick, or his own private Abuses, which were intolerable; and therefore resolv'd to publish the Account, but dy'd before it was finished; and his Papers being sent over to his Relations there, were treacherously deliver'd to the Governor's Agents, whose Guilt Dictated to them, That they were exposed in them; and several private Letters of the Inhabitants to Mr. Ash, being among them, they are now prosecuting and insulting the said Inhabitants for those Letters, to terrify others from transmitting a true Account of the Oppressions practiced upon them.

As in the Interval of Mr. Ash's Negotiations, the Exclusive Bill was pass'd, as I have noted, and Mr. Boon sent over with it as before; he applyed himself to my Lord G——ll Palatine (as he calls himself) for all Men know that by the Right of the Constitution, even that Mock Title is none of his Due. Having laid the Case before his Excellence (as he loves to be

call'd) Mr. Boon desir'd a Board of the Proprietors might be
call'd, which his Lordship promised, but never perform'd
till after about 7 Weeks Attendance and Sollicitation.

At this Board, one Mr. Arsdale,[1] now a Proprietor, and
formerly the very well respected and upright Governor of
Carolina, vigorously opposed the passing this Exclusive Bill;
and gave such Reasons against it, as his Lordship, who all the
World knows, does not always make use of his Profound Skill
of Reasoning, not being able to Answer, had Recourse to the
true Methods of all Tyrants, positive Will, and answer'd in
this Arbitrary and Imperious Manner:

"Sir, You are of one Opinion, and I am of another, and
our Lives may not be long enough to End the Controversy.
I am for this Bill, and this is the Party that I will Head and
Countenance."

This is so much the Picture of the Answer of King James,
to the Humble and Peaceable Address of the Bishops, when
he sent them to the Tower;[2] that a Body would wonder the
Tale of one, should not warn his high Mightiness against the
Practice of the other.

But let us go on, and see how the sweet and delicious
Taste of Tyranny had swallow'd up all the Justice of this
Mountebank Prince.

Mr. Boon, the present Agent for the Oppress'd People, humbly mov'd his Excellence to be Heard by Council against this
Barbarous Act.   Hark now, Gentlemen, to the haughty Answer of an insulting, pedant Prince, to a Request so reasonable.

"What Business has Council here?   it is a Prudential Act
in me, and I'll do as I see fit; I see no Harm at all in the
Bill, and am resolv'd to pass it."

Accordingly, *Sic Volo, sic Jubeo*,[3] he Sign'd it that Day,
the Board consisting but of three Persons, and he having
Power by a Proxy for Two in himself; and tho' we must in
Justice acknowledge, that some of the Gentlemen Proprietors
were against it, yet by that Means they were over-rul'd and
the Bill pas't.[4]

---

[1] John Archdale.   He was a Dissenter.
[2] In 1688.                              [3] "So I will, so I order."
[4] There were eight shares.   Lord Granville voted his own share, that of
the minor Lord Ashley, and that formerly belonging to Seth Sothell.   Carteret,

By this Arbitrary Proceeding, the Liberties of Carolina are trampled under foot, and the People's Properties subjected to all manner of Insults and Oppression.

Mr. Boon had a Petition against this Bill to present him, sign'd by the principal Merchants of London, Trading to Carolina; but he saw himself foreclosed by absolute Power, and that he had to do with a Monarch, on whom the Cries and Prayers of his oppress'd Subjects made no Impression.

For this Cause, he now addresses himself to the Honourable House of Commons, and hopes, that from the Premises, it will be allow'd of, in behalf of the oppress'd People of Carolina, that they have not taken this Course but as the last Resort; all manner of humble, dutiful, and peaceable Application to their Governors, having been first in vain attempted, to obtain a just Redress.

What have the peaceable Subjects of this Province done, that they alone must be oppress'd, when all the rest of Her Majesty's People enjoy the Blessing of a Government, the best constituted, and under the best, most moderate, and most equal Administration in the World?

This Law in its Nature appear'd so black, that even in this very Assembly afterwards, *viz.* ———, Some Members mov'd to have it Repealed, and the Act pass'd to Repeal it in the Lower House, which they call         [1] but in the Upper House, where the Engines of this Confusion Sat, and had a more particular Influence, and which they call the Court of [2] there it was rejected *Nemine Contradicente.*

It would swell this Book too much, to give a particular Account of the flourishing Circumstances of this Colony before these things, and of the fatal Effects already felt on their Trade, especially on the Number of Inhabitants, which is allow'd by all, to be the Wealth, Strength, and Prosperity of a Country: These Proceedings not only discouraged People from going to Settle, where all things are in such Confusions, and Hurries, and where Men are not safe in their Houses and Families, nor in the Streets; but many Families (well settl'd and flourishing) daily Remove, and others are preparing to

Colleton, and Craven were the other shareholders voting. The shares of Archdale and young Blake were the two not voted.

[1] Blank.   The Commons House.                    [2] Palatine court.

quit the Place, chosing to abandon a Settlement, where their Industry is subjected to such Violences, and they are not sure to enjoy (peaceably) the Fruit of their Labour.[1]

There is yet another Scandal these Proceedings lye under, which carries in it some Reflection on the Great Persons concern'd; and that is, That these Proceedings, being Contemporary with Times of Occasional Bills, Tackings, dangerous Experiments, and the like in England, receiv'd their Life and Motion from the same Original, and prosecuted the same Design, being under the Power and Government of some of the same Persons. This Observation has several Aspects.

1. England may here see the Consequence of Tackings, Occasional Bills, etc., in Miniature, and what the Designs of the Party are in general, viz. the absolute Suppression of Property, as well as Religion; or in short, both Civil and Ecclesiastical Tyranny.

2. Carolina may have reason to think their Oppressions were at least encourag'd from the same Expectation they had of Success in the like Design here; and not expecting a Disappointment here, no wonder, if they acted as People that thought they should never give any Account, either to God or Man.

3. Her Majesty has here an Exceeding Testimony, to the Necessity of Party-Peace, which her Royal Wisdom Dictated before, was the only Happiness of Her People; and which the same Party of Men, were carefully destroying here, as these did there.

4. Here may be seen, the Great Assurance this Party acted with, that depending they should succeed here, durst attempt the persecuting their Fellow-Subjects there.

5. 'Tis plain, what is the Design of Occasional Bills in general; which, where they durst appear to show themselves, Demonstrate 'tis not to prevent Hypocrisy, but to plunder and destroy their Neighbours; and that any Man may come in to the Administration, let his Manners be never so corrupt, and that provided he be not tainted with the Sin of defending

---

[1] An exaggeration. No such condition existed at the time. A few people removed from Charles Town to other parts of the province in consequence of the dissensions, and business became a little stagnant because of the trouble with Spain.

his Liberty, nor with the Scandal of being a Man of Conscience, he is own'd fit to be a Member of this Society.

I believe, I may freely challenge all Mankind, ever since there were Governments in the World, to show a like Test of Qualification, where Men conscious to themselves, that if they lock't the door against Rogues, against profligate, unqualify'd Rakes, they should shut themselves out, open'd the Door to all that were scandalously unfit for any thing, and bolted it upon none but those who could not swear themselves regardless of Conscience.

But while we are hinting here at the People that push on these Extravagancies, we ought to clear the Church of England, as a Church, as far as possible, from the Guilt of an Action so Horrid.

For tho' here is a seeming Appearance for the Church of England, and some shew of Regard to her, yet as the Doctrine of the Church abhors such Practices, so the worthy and reverend Minister of the Church of England there, has shared with the deepest, in the Suffering Part, from the Violences and Fury of those People, because he would not joyn with them in the same Excesses, against the Laws of the Place, the Liberty and Religion of the Inhabitants, and the known Capitulations of the Government.[1]

Nor can they Charge this Gentleman with Phanaticism, or Partiality, who, 'tis known, was so far from that, that it was some time here before he could satisfy his Conscience to take the Oaths, and lost several Advantages because of it.

Yet this Gentleman abhorring such Unchristian Violences, and not being to be prevail'd upon to joyn with them, has been insulted by them in the most barbarous and villanous manner, even in the Streets, his Gown torn off from his Back, whipt with a Horse-whip, and in a most unseemly manner beaten and abused, as by his many and frequent Complaints made to the Proprietors (tho' never regarded) will appear.

Nor does their Rage end here; but the Party now are

[1] Rev. Edward Marston, of St. Philip's Church, opposed the unfair action of the provincial government in depriving Dissenters of the right to sit in the Commons House and became involved in quarrels with Governor Johnson and the Assembly. Mr. Marston's conduct in these quarrels was far from blameless. See McCrady's *History of South Carolina under the Proprietary Government*.

resolv'd to have him turn'd out, tho' he is marry'd, settled, and has a Family of Children upon the Place, depending upon his being fixed there for his Life; knowing that his blameless Conversation would be uncapable of forfeiting that Settlement.

It would require a History as large as the Rest of this Book, to set down the Barbarities this Gentleman has met with, and which he has fully represented to some Reverend Divines here; and perhaps Dr. S——hope [1] may better know, why no Redress is obtain'd for him, while an Ignorant, Illiterate, and Untaught Person, to say no worse of him, is encouraged and supported by this Party, to Insult and Depress the other.

Nor are their Proceedings altogether unlike what in former times was practised here, since they are now Erecting a little High Commission Court to Govern the Clergy, and to whom they shall be always subject; by which 'twill be always true, That when ever a Clergy-man has Courage, either to reprove their Vices, or oppose any of their Arbitrary Proceedings, they shall be lyable to the Censure of those very Men they ought to reprove.

This Gentleman was so far from obtaining any Redress in the Case we hint here, that to requite him, we are inform'd they resolve to have him out.

Nor is he the first, but two several Clergy-men before him have been so treated, turn'd out, and reduc'd, that both of them went distracted, and dyed in Misery and Distress.[2]

'Twould sully this Paper, and turn the sad Account to a History of Immoralities, to bring upon the Stage the Characters of the People: Men are best known by their Actions; and we leave this unparallel'd Act of Parliament as a Standard for them to be match'd by, if ever Providence should suffer a Society of such Men, to get Legislative Power into their Hands, in any part of the World.

If this be the Effect of Occasional Bills, and English Persecution, no wonder it was declar'd contrary to the Christian Religion; but sure these are the first Men that ever made a

---

[1] George Stanhope, dean of Canterbury.

[2] This statement is a gross perversion of facts; no such treatment was given to any ministers before Mr. Marston's day or after, and, therefore, there was no such resultant consequence.

Law, tho' it has been elsewhere push't at, with a *Nevertheless* upon its Title, to its being contrary to the Christian Religion.

It can therefore no longer be doubted, but when these things come to be consider'd in an English Parliament, such Redress will there be obtain'd, as may secure English Liberty, wherever it pleases God to establish English Government;

That no part of the Subjects of this Nation be oppress'd by others; and that while Great Men obtain the Liberty of their Estates, and the Property and Security of their Inheritances; they may not Erect Petty-Tyrannies under them, and skreen Men of profligate Principles, from the Resentment of the Government;

That Men may not be wheedled in by the pretence of a free Possession of Estate and Liberty, and on Condition of a just Government; first, to wander into remote Wildernesses with their Estates and Families, then industriously Plant, Cure, Manage and Improve their Estates, and at last, have their Labours discourag'd by Tyrannick and Barbarous Insults, their Estates sunk and lessen'd, by being subjected to Arbitrary Taxations, for the Executing improbable and preposterous Projects, and their Persons unqualify'd without a Crime, to appear in the Assembly of their Country, where all these Injuries might, in a legal manner, be redress'd and repair'd.[1]

---

[1] The following pamphlet relating to this question was subsequently published: *The Humble Address of the Right Honourable the Lords Spiritual and Temporal in Parliament Assembled, Presented to Her Majesty on Wednesday the Thirteenth Day of March, 1705, Relating to the Province of Carolina, and the Petition therein mentioned, With Her Majesties most Gracious Answer Thereto.* (London, Printed by Charles Bill, and the Executrix of Thomas Newcomb, deceas'd, Printers to the Queens most Excellent Majesty, 1705, folio, 4 pp.)

The first two pages consist of the title-page and order to print, dated March 13, 1705; page 3 contains the Address of the Lords and the Queen's answer, and page 4 "The Humble Petition of Joseph Boone Merchant on behalf of himself and many other Inhabitants of the Province of Carolina, and also of several Merchants of London, Trading to Carolina, and the Neighboring Colonies of Her Majesty in America." The latter has been reprinted in Rivers's *Sketch of the History of South Carolina*, pp. 461–463. There are seventeen signatures to it and of these Boone was the only man whose name is in the least conspicuous in the records of the day.

THE PRESENT STATE OF AFFAIRS IN
CAROLINA, BY JOHN ASH, 1706

# INTRODUCTION

DURING the seven years preceding the death of Governor Joseph Blake in September, 1700, South Carolina was governed by three governors who were all Dissenters. Upon the death of Blake the Lords Proprietors' deputies met to choose a governor. Under the mode of procedure laid down by the Proprietors for such elections Landgrave Joseph Morton, a Dissenter and a son of a former governor of the province, was, in right of being a landgrave, entitled to the preference over the untitled deputies, provided he obtained a majority of the votes of the deputies and no valid objection were raised against him by any deputy. On the ballot for Morton he received three votes for governor and two were cast against him. Deputies Moore and Daniell objected to him on the ground that he had accepted the appointment from the Crown as judge of the admiralty in South Carolina while still holding a commission from the Proprietors as a deputy. This being a valid objection, and no one dissenting but Morton, the deputies proceeded to the election of one of the untitled deputies and James Moore was elected.

Moore had come into the province about 1675 and shortly afterwards married Dame (Margaret Foster) Yeamans, widow of Sir John Yeamans, a former governor of the province. During the first few years of his residence he managed plantations for Dame Yeamans and Captain William Walley, but later he engaged in trading with the Indians, at which he became very enterprising and successful. As that branch of business in Carolina was a constant source of quarrels and bickerings in both private and official sources, due primarily to the unre-

liable character of the Indians, Moore made many enemies
and was often the target for personal abuse.  He proved himself to be a valuable man to the province, however, and the
Proprietors frequently honored him with their commands.

No sooner had Moore been elected governor, however,
than the greatest aspersions yet cast upon his character were
hurled at him.  His former enemies were reinforced by a
faction who had become dissatisfied over his defeat of Morton
for governor.  The fact that he was of the faith of the Church
of England was sufficient to arouse the jealousy of the Dissenters, who had hoped for a continuation of their party in
power by the election of Morton.  Chance had put Dissenters
at the head of the government since the spring of 1692, Thomas
Smith and Joseph Blake having been elected by the deputies
by virtue of being landgraves and Archdale and Blake (second
term) assuming the government in right of being Proprietors.
This was the first real test of strength between Churchmen and
Dissenters and when the latter lost they began to raise dissensions.  The quarrel finally waxed so warm that the minority
faction sent an agent to England to lay their grievances before
the Proprietors, Parliament, or the Crown, whichever would
heed their prayers.  This agent was John Ash, a member of
the Commons House for Colleton County, who theretofore had
played no conspicuous part in the affairs of the province.
Not meeting encouragement from the Proprietors, Ash prepared for publication a statement of the Dissenters' side of the
controversy and had had two pages of it printed when he
died.  His statement of the case is an impassioned one and
plainly shows his bias, is filled with personal abuse of and sar-
castic references to the party in power, vitiates the truth in
so many particulars as to render it unreliable in any, and
should not be taken too seriously by students of the history of
South Carolina.

# THE PRESENT STATE OF AFFAIRS IN CAROLINA, BY JOHN ASH, 1706

*The Present State of Affairs in Carolina, by John Ash, Gent.,*
*Sent by several of the Inhabitants of that Colony, to deliver*
*their Representation thereof to, and seek Redress from, the*
*Lords Proprietors of that Province : Together with an Ac-*
*count of his Reception, by the Honourable the Lord Gran-*
*vill, their Palatine, President, or Chief of the Proprietors.*

On the Death of Joseph Blake, Esq; Governour, and one
of the Proprietors of Carolina, the Proprietors Deputies met,
according to their Instructions in such Cases, proceeded to
elect a new Governour; and by them Landgrave Joseph
Morton was Elected Governour. But James Moor, Esq; one
of the said Deputies, knowing the Party he had amongst
Deputies, and nothing regarding how Disloyal, how Derogatory
from the just Right of the English Throne that Objection was,
objected against the said Landgrave Joseph Morton, That he
the said Joseph Morton had made a Breach of the Trust
reposed in him by the true and absolute Lords and Proprietors,
etc. by accepting of a Commission for Judge of the Admiralty
from King William, when at the same Time he had a Commission from the said Proprietors for the said Office, in whom the
Disposal of the same was: Now, besides the Disloyalty of
this Objection, it was also false; for it appears not by the
Charter, That the Proprietors can impower any one to try
Persons for Facts committed out of their Dominions, and
which is necessary for such Judge; yet such was his Interest,
that on this his Objection, Landgrave Morton was rejected,
and the said James Moore Elected and declared Governour.
Of this Landgrave Morton Inform'd, and Complain'd to the
Proprietors, but to no purpose.

The Power thus boldly gotten, Mr. Moore resolves to make
the best use of it: and therefore finding himself too poor, even

with the Countenance of his Office, to make any considerable
Profit of the Indian Trade, he lays a Design of getting it wholly
into his Power. This he attempted by getting a Bill brought
into the Assembly at the latter end of the Year 1700, Intituled, A Bill for Regulating the Indian Trade, but so contriv'd as to have made him wholly Master of it. But Mr.
Robert Stephens, Mr. Trott (then no Courtier) and some others
so plainly shew'd its ill Aim, that it was thrown out of the
Assembly,[1] as it was again in the beginning of the Year 1701.
On which Mr. Moore perceiving, That that Assembly could not
be prevailed with to answer his Ends, he dissolved the Assembly,
and about the latter End of that Year a new one was chosen,[2]

[1] The contemporaneous records show that there was a necessity for the regulation of the Indian trade. What Governor Moore's plan was is not revealed by
the journal of the Commons House, but the following report, made to the House,
November 13, 1700, and the only action taken on the subject, shows nothing to
warrant the above statement:

"Reported from the Committe, ord[rd] to Attend the Governo[r], by Ralph
Izard Esq[r]: That his Hon[r] hath Considered of Severall Methods, for the Regulation of the Indian Trade But This House haveing Thoughts To make this a
short Sessions, The Time will be to short to make an Act for Regulateing that
Trade, Therefore if This House will appoynt a Committe To Consider of such
methods as may be Thought necessary for makeing that Trade secure to the
Publick Betweene this sessions and the next adjournm[t] he will Assist therein and
order Those Indian Traders Down that have opprest the natives, and keepe
them here till said Adjournment, or Take security for their Appearance and
Allso Give orders, To severall of the Indian Kings to be here Likewise."

On the 15th the House "Ordered That Ralph Izard Esq[r]: and m[r] Robert
Stevens be a Committe to Prepare a Bill for the Regulateing the Indian Trade
[and several other bills] against the next meeting after this Sessions," and the
next day the House adjourned for the session.

[2] No session was held at the beginning of 1701, the next session convening
January 7, 1701/2, and there was, therefore, no dissolving of the Assembly nor
election of a new House in that year. In a message to the Commons House
January 15, 1701/2, Governor Moore made the following recommendation:
"That you Consider of a way to remove the abuses done to the Yamasee Indians
by them that live among and Trade with them, and of makeing them Easie in
Our Neighbourhood and friendship, So as that they may not have reason to
return to the Spaniards.

"That you think of some way to prevent the Tallabooses and other Indians
now our friends their trade and acquaintance with the ffrench till some way may
be found to secure us from the dangers and Mischiefs which that Trade and
acquaintance will bring on us.

"That you think of some way to Confirm the Cussatoes w[th] live on Ochasa
Creek and the Savannos in the Place they now live in, and to Our friendship

at the Election of which, tho' the Right of Electing be by the Charter in the Freeholders only, he so Influenc'd the Sheriff, that Strangers, Servants, Aliens, nay Malatoes and Negroes were Polled, and Returns made accordingly. Such as at the Place opposed those Practices, were abused, nay, assaulted by Mr. Moore's Favourites. By this Means, having got several into the Assembly, of neither Sense nor Credit, but such as would Vote as he would have them, he there kept them from being thrown out on the Petition of those who were unjustly excluded by their being Return'd, by repeated and strangely procur'd Adjournments and Prorogations, until the Proclamation of our New War with France and Spain arriv'd.[1]

they being the Only People by whom Wee may expect Advice of an Inland Invasion."

After various discussions, during which the House several times called upon Governor Moore for papers and advice, it was finally resolved: "That a Bill be Prepared against next Sitting Wherein provision may be taken that Indian Traders shall pay for Lycences and that a Clause be added to send a Commissary or two to the Southward and that there be a perticular Care Taken of the Yammassees, And allso that there be provission in the said Act Concerning all Debts of the Indians."

That resolution was adopted January 29 and closed legislation relating to Indian affairs for the session. On February 3 the House adjourned till the first Wednesday in September. On February 12 writs for a new election were issued to the sheriffs under the hand of Governor Moore and Deputies Daniell, Bellinger, Noble, Dearsley, and Parris, the election to be held March 11 and the new assembly to convene April 1. It is evident, therefore, that Moore's plan, if he had one, for controlling the Indian trade, had nothing to do with the dissolution of the House or the issuing of writs by the governor and deputies for a new election.

[1] The high sheriff of Berkeley County, holding the election at Charles Town for Berkeley and Craven counties, returned the twenty having the highest vote as follows: Dr. Charles Burnham 392, Capt. John Guppell 357, Major Charles Colleton 340, Col. Thomas Broughton 250, Capt. Job Howes 227, William Smith (merchant) 226, John Buckley 224, Col. Stephen Bull 221, Landgrave Thomas Smith 221, George Logan 218, Nicholas Trott 218, Serurier Smith 217, Capt. John Godfrey 217, Capt. James Risbee 217, Capt. David Davis 216, Henry Wigington 212, Richard Beresford 212, Major Benjamin Waring 208, Capt. George Smith 204, Major William Smith 200. He further reported that Capt. Abraham Eve had received 199 votes and that there were "Tenn Moore Votes for him and Major Wᵐ Smith which were objected against as unquallified to Vote, which is Humbly Submitted to the House to Judge of whether Unquallified or not. Therefore Returne the said Capt Eve."

Almost immediately upon organizing the House proceeded to consider the contest, Joseph Boone, Robert Fenwick, and John Croskeys being the contestants of the seats of Major Benjamin Waring, Major William Smith, and Richard

Then possessing the People by Stories with hopes of mighty Plunder, he got a Design that he had proposed to the Assembly before, of going against St. Augustin, a Fort belonging to Spain, a little to the Southward of Carolina, to be approved, tho' in truth it was no more than a Project of Freebooting under the specious Name of War, for neither the Preparation nor the Performance will permit any one to believe it was meant for any other Purpose, or the least Good of the Colony.[1]

However, it was approved, and Two Thousand Pounds were raised to equip his Honour and his Comrades out for their beloved Exercise of Plundering, and Slave-catching. This they performed well enough, but carrying on the Pretence too far, and coming to sit down before the strong Castle of St. Augustin, while they were sending their Plunder to Jamaica by their trusty Officers, under Colour of seeking Supplies, sending for Bombs and Mortars, in the midst of all their Riot and Misrule, they were alarm'd by the coming of Four Vessels into the Harbour, in which were (they say) 200 Enemies. At first, being encouraged by Wine up to a Height above performing any Thing, the General Moore resolves bravely to put on Board his Eight Vessels then riding in the Harbour, all their Goods and Plunder, and with his few Men about 500, Fight thro' the Enemy, and so come Home. But the Pillow, which often lets out Heat to make way for Caution, changed this his Resolution; So the next Day, having destroyed as many of his own Ships, and as much of his War Stores and

Beresford. It will be observed that no contest was made of the election of George Smith, who received fewer votes than either Beresford or Waring. He was a Dissenter, a brother of Landgrave Thomas Smith. The House, however, ordered him to withdraw also during the investigation. The House then summoned all of those whose right to vote had been challenged to appear on Monday, April 6, and "Shew what Right they have to voting," naming them in the resolution. On that day no quorum appeared. The journal shows that it was the desire of Governor Moore for the House to meet and proceed with business, but that his enemies desired neither to transact the business for which the House was called nor to hold the investigation of the election which they had demanded. As almost every voter named as unqualified could have shown his right to vote, as can still be shown by extant records, the charges would have fallen. After war was declared against Spain Governor Moore was able to get the House to work and it soon found too much real work to do to bother with a trumped up contest.

[1] See pp. 221, 222, *supra*.

Provisions as the haste they were in would allow, he retreats with such Caution and Dispatch, that he lost not one Man by the Enemy.

This Expedition, whatever the Governour or General (if you please) got by it, brought a Debt on the Country (besides the 2000 *l.* first raised) of near 6000 *l.*, for the Payment of which (and Security of the Country, as was said) the Assembly was called; they enquire into the Debt, bring in a Bill to raise the Sum, consider of defending the Southward open to the Enemy; but of that the Courtiers made but a Jest, even in the House, and it yet is (as I hear) neglected; as also a Bill for Regulating Elections for the Future, for to the Breaches of the Freeholders Rights, our present Miseries they saw were plainly owing, nor had those Members, who sat by Means of those illegal Practices, the Courage to oppose it; so it past the Assembly, but being sent up to the Governour in Council it was there thrown out; on which Fifteen Members (the Assembly consists of Thirty) left the House, resolving no longer to cover with their Authority the Pernicious Practices of the Ministry, since nothing useful for the Country could be obtained.

On this several of Mr. Moore's Favourites, after having been treated by him (and thereunto encourag'd, as is said) headed the Rabble, and in a riotous Manner, sought after (threatning openly to murther them) several Persons thought the chief Opposers and Mislikers of Mr. Moore's Management; some they met with, Members of the Assembly, one Deputy, several rich Merchants, and good Planters, Confining, Striking and Abusing them; and for several Days continuing these Disorders, particularly breaking open a House one Night on a poor Woman, and so abusing her, that thereupon she brought forth a dead Child, whose Scull, Arm, and Back-bone was broken, and one Eye forc'd out of its Head, as the Chyrurgion, who delivered her, deposed; but this Violence not producing that Submission as was expected, that Assembly was Dissolv'd.

Of this Riot, Complaint was several times, while it lasted, made to Mr. Moore; but he would not try to suppress it, nor, when in some Measure over, would he take any Care that they should be Prosecuted; nor so much as oblige such of them, as Landgrave Thomas Smith regularly demanded Security of the Peace from, to give the same: Nay, one Mr. Stephens, who was not in Town then, but heard he was named by the Rioters as one of the proscribed, going with several who had been injur'd, to see how Mr. Moore would receive them, was, while sitting by Mr. Moore at his own Table, by a Servant of Mr. Moore's pull'd backwards by the Hair of his Head, struck and wounded, and all only for his impertinent Curiosity, as he was told on that Occasion. He desires the Governour to bind this his Servant to his good Behaviour, and oblige him to appear to answer this Action at the next Sessions, but nothing was done. The now Governour, Sir Nathaniel Johnson, was hereby oblig'd to take on him the Government. To him immediately the Injur'd apply'd for Justice, but are denied; and, tho' the Grand Jury, a little after he took on him his Office, after having receiv'd a Record of the Riot from Landgrave Bellinger on his own View, and on his Examination of Witnesses and Depositions in relation to the Outrage committed on the Woman with Child, presented it to the Court as a great Grievance, that this Riot was not looked into, nor the Rioters prosecuted, yet no Justice against them could be obtain'd, the Judge giving for Answer, *It was before the Council his Superiors.* The present Governour, That it was an Action done before his coming to the Government, that he thought the time of Prosecution lapsed, but would take care the like should be no more.

Then a new Assembly was called, and at the Election for Berkley and Craven County, (for in Colleton County there was no Opposition) the Violences in Mr. Moore's Time, and all other illegal Practices were with more Violence repeated and openly avow'd by the present Governour and his Friends. On this Joseph Morton and Edmund Bellinger, Landgraves, and Deputies of the Lords Proprietors, all the other Members of Colleton County, and several of the greatest Worth and Reputation in Berkeley County prevail'd with me to come for England, and represent to our Proprietors our miserable State; which (when I should be gone, for before they durst not) they said they would write down, subscribe, and with Letters of Credence, send to me to Virginia, where they knew I was to wait for Convoy. This they did, and I receiv'd them, and not only what they promised, but an Account of what extraordinary Advances the late and present Governours made, by help of their new Assembly, to their desired absolute and tyrannick Power, and particularly their Practices on one John Martin, to squeeze from him 60 *l.* for the present Governour, whereas the other had been content with Fifty, for that Favour, which they would perswade John Martin was necessary for him: But he thought this too oppressive, so makes his Escape, not daring to stay in that Country. But before he goes, discovers a Design Mr. Moore had of Employing him the said John Martin in a private Trade with the French, in which its more then likely others were to be concern'd. 'Tis true, I can't, by the Evidence I have here, legally convict them of this Design of holding Commerce with Her Majesty's Enemies; but I think the original Letter I have of Captain Moore's to John Martin, the strange Bond on the Breach of their Confederacy, by the present Governour extorted from John Martin's Brother Patrick, and his Securities, of which I have a Copy, as also the Illustration of some obscure Expressions in the Letter made by John Martin himself, which are that the Respects to be sent by Mr. Valentine the Jew,[1] was the 60 *l.* required, Our Business, the private Trade with the French, will hardly let one doubt but they had such a Design.

The Treacheries, Oppressions and Hostilities committed by J. Moore, Esq; on the Natives before this our War with Spain, and which now under that Colour, tho' on such as are neither subject to them, nor have injur'd us, much increased, are Acts so barbarous, so inconsistent with the Profit and Safety a good Correspondence with them would afford us, that I dare but mention it, lest it let me into a Description too large for this Paper; nor for the same Reason can I here give a full Account of that partial Prosecution which the same James Moore, as Attorney-General, made against one Alford——his Servant or Trader, accus'd of having hir'd and assisted an Indian Slave in Murthering his Master John Henry, Servant or Trader to Mr. James Stanyarn, not for any Quarrel that was between them, but only to remove a too successful Competitor in that Trade of which the Grand Jury held at Charles Town in           [2]last complain'd, desired the Tryal therefore

---

[1] Simon Valentyn, a wealthy and respected Jew who at that time was a merchant in Charles Town.           [2] Blank in original pamphlet.

to be deferr'd till the Witnesses wanting might be present, and the Indian, who, confessing the Fact was condemn'd, might till the Tryal should be over, be Repriev'd; all which the said James Moore with heat opposed, tho' the Judge thought it reasonable, and answer'd their Desire.

To confirm and strengthen the Truth of this my Relation, I have thought fit to offer to the Reader the Representation as drawn by those who sent me, whose Names are Subscrib'd; as also the Minutes of the Election of Mr. Moore, and the Message from the Grand Jury to the Court about the Riot.

A NEW DESCRIPTION OF THAT FERTILE
AND PLEASANT PROVINCE OF CAROLINA,
BY JOHN ARCHDALE, 1707

# INTRODUCTION

SIR WILLIAM BERKELEY, one of the original Proprietors of Carolina, died July 13, 1677. By his will he devised his share in Carolina to his widow. On May 20, 1681, she sold it to John Archdale, of England, who took the title in the name of his son Thomas. Subsequently Dame Berkeley married Philip Ludwell and, disregarding her former sale to Archdale, she and her husband in 1682 joined in another sale of the share in Carolina to Thomas Amy in trust for four of the other Proprietors: the Duke of Albemarle, the Earl of Craven, Lord Carteret, and Sir John Colleton. Subsequently, in 1705, the four *cestuis que trust* executed a deed to John Archdale of the same share—the legal title still remaining in Amy.

Notwithstanding the complications over the title, Archdale was all along recognized as a Proprietor, and in 1695, when the Proprietors were responding to a popular demand in South Carolina that one of their number be sent over as governor, he was prevailed upon by the other Proprietors to accept the governorship. When he arrived in South Carolina and claimed the governorship in right of being a Proprietor his right was readily recognized by Governor Blake, who relinquished the office to him. He assumed the government at a time when patience and forbearance were necessary. The people had had turbulent times with the government from 1686 to 1692, and were just recovering from their troubles. James Colleton (governor from 1686 to 1690) had been arrogant and tyrannical and the people had finally arisen against him and expelled him from the province, and Seth Sothell, a

Proprietor, coming upon the scene just then was recognized as governor.

Sothell was neither broad enough nor intelligent enough to cope with the situation, and there was soon almost as much dissatisfaction with his administration as there had been with Colleton's. The Proprietors forced him out in 1692, and appointed Col. Philip Ludwell, of Virginia, to succeed him. Conditions improved during the next three years under Ludwell, Landgrave Thomas Smith, who succeeded Ludwell, and Landgrave Joseph Blake, who succeeded Smith, but many of the people believed that a proprietor could settle their differences and bring about better feelings, and so it came to pass that Proprietor Archdale was persuaded to become governor.

Archdale was a Quaker, and a man of tact and ability. He patiently strove to establish harmony between discordant elements, to materially advance the welfare of the province and to improve the condition of the Indians. He succeeded to a marked degree in almost all of his endeavors. Having accomplished the object of his mission to South Carolina, he returned to England in 1696, leaving Landgrave Joseph Blake once more at the head of the government. Blake was prudent and wise and succeeded in keeping the province in the condition in which Archdale left it, but unfortunately he died in 1700, and upon the election of James Moore as his successor new troubles arose that were not allayed for seven or eight years. While the factional strife was on, Archdale, the good Friend, stepped into the breach once more and tried to pour oil on the troubled waters. He adopted the plan of publishing a pamphlet, wherein he gave a brief sketch of Carolina, a more extended account of his administration and achievements therein, and an exhortation to the warring factions to come together. His pamphlet was first printed in 1707 and has since been reprinted several times. In 1836 it was included by B. R. Carroll in his *Historical Collections of South Carolina.*

Archdale's name has been preserved in South Carolina in the name of one of the oldest and most picturesque streets of Charleston.

# A NEW DESCRIPTION OF THAT FERTILE AND PLEASANT PROVINCE OF CAROLINA, BY JOHN ARCHDALE, 1707

*A New Description of that Fertile and Pleasant Province of
Carolina: with a Brief Account of its Discovery, Settling,
and the Government Thereof to this Time. With several
Remarkable Passages of Divine Providence during my Time.*
By John Archdale: Late Governour of the same.
London, Printed for John Wyat, at the Rose in St. Paul's Church-
yard, 1707.[1]

## To the Courteous Readers.

I FIND myself under an Obligation to Apologize for some
part of the ensuing Treatise that seems to Applaud my own
Actions in Carolina; but I desire you to consider, that a sort
of Necessity draws from me this Description and Account
of the Government of Carolina: And I can assure the Reader
that I write not to Introduce my self again, as Governour of
the same; (yet my Opinion and Judgment is, that a Moderate, Discreet Man from England, which now yields many a
one, such a one that hath not been concerned in their Broils,
would be their most suitable Governour, when it shall seem
proper to remove the present one) For I believe no Entreaties
could move me to it; but I write to give the Country it self
its true and due Praise, and to clear my self from the Malitious
Aspersions of some that feared my antient Treatment of the
People would revive again their Affections to me, to ruin
their present Designs; for the moderate Party Politickly
spreading a Report, as they thought that I was coming over
to redress the Grievancies of the Country; they thereupon
contrived an Act to Fetter my Power, by putting it out of

[1] Title-page of the original

my Power for two Years to call a New Assembly; but no such Act being approved on here, their Fetters would have proved like Sampsons Cords, easily broken asunder; But this may be of great Benefit to many Readers, in Considering the mutability of humane Affairs; That I, that had so large Powers from the Lords Proprietors, which I entirely exercised for the Peoples Good; should as an ungrateful requital be so Crampt by their Power, as not to be capable to Redress their Solid Grievances: For I believe, I may at the least truly declare, that not one Inhabitant in four, would have Signed that Excluding Act, which had not the Queen declared Null and Void, would have speedily ruined that Colony: For it was not the meer Mob that was against it, like that generally in the Scotland Petitions,[1] but the most considerable Persons of the place that removed with free Estates into those Parts; so I shall dismiss my Reader, to the Consideration of what I have written, with this Further Remark of the Learned and pious Bishop of Salisbury,[2] who by his Travels observed that the most Fertile Soile of Italy, under the Ecclesiastical State of Rome, was by ill Government so Decay'd; that the Grisons Country tho naturally far more Barren, yet became more Fruitful and Pleasant than the other, through the free and generous Government Administred in that State: Who in his Travels was no Disgrace to the Protestant Clergy of the Church of England, and whose Moderation hath appeared unto all Men. That the Reader may see the Moderation of the Sober, moderate Church-men and Dissenters in a free Assembly, I think good to Conclude with the Clause of a Militia Act, which runs thus;

*And whereas there be several Inhabitants call'd Quakers, who upon a Conscientious Principle of Religion, cannot bear Arms, and because in all other Civil Matters they have been Persons Obedient to Government, and very ready to disburse their Monies in other necessary and publick Duties. Be it therefore Enacted, that all such whom the present Governour John Archdale Esq; shall judge that they refuse to bear Arms on a Conscientious Principle of Religion only shall by a Certificate from him be Excused.*

[1] Against the Episcopal Church in Scotland.
[2] Gilbert Burnet, the historian.

## A Description of Carolina.

BEFORE I give a particular Description of Carolina, I think good to make some general Remarks on the Divine Providence of the Almighty and Omniscient God, who hath so stated the various Scenes of Nature, as to accomplish his Divine Will in fulfilling whatsoever stands recorded in the Holy Scriptures: Now that Scene of Divine Providence which seems to be appropriated to our Times, is the dawning Day for the Accomplishment of various Promises, not only that Christ should be given as a Light to enlighten the Gentiles, and to be the Glory of his People Israel, which Glory is not yet revealed, as hinted at by Paul, Rom. 10. But again, Psal. 2. That God will give unto Christ the Heathen for his Inheritance, and the utmost Parts of the Earth for his Possession; as also, Isa. that the Earth shall be filled with the Knowledge of God, as the Waters covers the Seas; and Dan. 12. that many should run too and fro, and Knowledge should be increased in the Earth; with many more Promises of the like Nature, which plainly intimates, That the Mysteries of the Kingdom of God are to be unsealed in the last Days: To the which that Excellent Poet Davies[1] intimates in Queen Elizabeth's Days, in these Words,

> O thou bright Morning Star, thou rising Sun,
>   Who in these latter Days hast brought to light,
> Those Mysteries that since the World begun,
>   Lay hid in Darkness and eternal Night.

And because in all the Grand Scenes of Divine Providence, some preparative Stroakes are generally made as Preludiums to what is quickly to ensue, the Art of Printing, to beget Knowledge, hath been reserved for this last Age; as also the Compass to convey Knowledge, as aforesaid; and the Discovery of Gunpowder hath been another Medium to subdue Millions of People that lay under a Barbarous and Brutish State: As for Example, in Mexico, where was a Temple dedicated to their chief Idol larger than Paul's[2] whose Walls

[1] Sir John Davies, *Nosce Teipsum.*
[2] *I.e.*, St. Paul's Cathedral in London.

were two Inches thick bespread or beplaister'd with Human
Blood, sacrificed to their Deities or Devils: And although I
cannot excuse the Barbarity or Cruelty of the Spaniards
towards them, yet, as on God's part, it was justly brought
upon them, who thereby gave them their own Blood to drink,
in lieu of what they had most barbarously shed of their Neighbours. And indeed, Providence seemed wholly to design this
Bloody Work for the Spanish Nation, and not for the English,
who in their Natures, are not so Cruel as the other; witness
the Inquisition, its Cruelty being most establish'd in Spain.
And, courteous Readers, I shall give you some farther Eminent Remark hereupon, and especially in the first Settlemeent
of Carolina, where the Hand of God was eminently seen in
thining the Indians, to make room for the English. As for
Example in Carolina, in which were seated two Potent Nations,
called the Westoes, and Sarannah,[1] which contained many
Thousands,. who broke out into an unusual Civil War, and
thereby reduced themselves into a small Number, and the
Westoes, the more Cruel of the two, were at the last forced
quite out of that Province, and the Sarannahs continued
good Friends and useful Neighbours to the English. But
again, it at other times pleased Almighty God to send unusual Sicknesses amongst them, as the Smallpox, etc., to lessen
their Numbers; so that the English, in Comparison to the
Spaniard, have but little Indian Blood to answer for. Now
the English at first settling in small Numbers, there seemed a
Necessity of thining the barbarous Indian Nations; and
therefore since our Cruelty is not the Instrument thereof, it
pleases God to send, as I may say, an Assyrian Angel to do
it himself. Yet will I not totally excuse the English, as being
wholly clear of the Blood of the Indians in some Respects,
which I at present pass over. But surely we are all much to
blame, in being so negligent of executing the proper Means
for their Soul's Salvation, which being a gradual Work, the
introducing a Civilized State would be a good and stable Preparatory for the Gospel State; even as the Divine Hand of
Providence prepared us by the Romans, as all Historians
mention that relate to us. I shall farther add one late more
immediate Example of God's more immediate Hand, in making

[1] Savannah.

a Consumption upon some Indian Nations in North Caralina, and that was in my time at the River Pemlicoe, and some Nations adjoyning: This is a late Settlement, began about eight Years since.  When I was in the North about eleven Years since, I was told then of a great Mortality that fell upon the Pemlicoe Indians; as also, that a Nation of Indians called the Coranine, a bloody and barbarous People, were most of them cut off by a neighbouring Nation: Upon which I said, that it seemed to me as if God had an Intention speedily to plant an English Settlement thereabouts; which accordingly fell out in two or three Years, although at that time not one Family was there.  I shall make one more general Remark, before I come more particularly to treat of Carolina; and that is, in short, to give an Account how this vast Continent of America was discovered, that lay hid for many Ages.  The Reader may reasonably guess, that before the Knowledge of the Compass, Navigation was very imperfect, as also the Knowledge of the Globe; yea, so Ignorant was former Ages that one Vigilius, a Gentleman of Italy, was adjudged a Heretick, for affirming Antipodes; so that the Providential seeming Casualty of Human Affairs, appeared rather to make the Discovery, than any premeditated Skill or Art of Man. For, according to the best Accounts, a certain Spanish Colonel sailing into the West Ocean towards the Isles of the Canaries, by a forcible continued Easterly Wind, the Vessel was drove upon the American Coast; but being ill provided for such a Voyage, by Hunger and Hardship all died save the Pilot and three or four more; who afterwards returning back, came to the Maderaes, and after that died at the House of one Christopher Colon or Columbus, born in the Territory of Genoa; and the said Pilot left him his Maps and Cards of his Voyage; and he himself having some Skill in Navigation, was much affected with the Relation, and was very desirous to prosecute the same; but wanting of Wealth to get Shipping, and Protection from some European King, to secure the Riches he should come to possess, he first made an Essay by his Brother Barthor Colon upon Henry VIIth of England, at that time a Wealthy Prince; but he rejecting the same as a fantastical Matter, as the Discoveries both of Nature and Grace are at the first looked upon by most; for the Beginning of the Reformation quickly succeeding this grand Discovery of the New World, was as lightly esteemed at first in the Spiritual Appearance of it.  But Colon or Columbus, not wholly daunted at the first Repulse, was introduced into the Favour of the King and Queen of Spain, about *Anno* 1490, the same Year that the Moors lost Granada, their principal Hold at that time in Spain; and then he was furnished with three Ships, and departed for the Indies in the Kalends of September, 1491, and fell in first with the Canaries, not long before discovered, *Anno* 1405, inhabited by savage and wild People; he sailing thence 33 Days, and discovering no Land, his Men mutinied, and designed to cast him into the Sea; but he with gentle Words and large Promises, appeased their Fury, and putting them off some few Days, he discovered Land, so long looked for; and so by Degrees settled the same, as Historians at large declare.

Now, candid Readers, I have introduced you into the general Discovery and Spanish Settlement in America; I shall now proceed to shew unto you the Occasion of the Settlement of Carolina, that lies in the very Heart of America.

I have hinted how Henry the VIIth having lost the Opportunity of possessing the Spanish Mines of Mexico, the Fame of which raised up the Spirit of the said Henry to get some Share in this American Continent; he therefore, about *Anno* 1500, furnished Sr. Sebastian Cabot with Shipping, who was born at Bristol, though his Father was a Venetian, to make a farther Discovery, who fell upon the Coast of Florida, and having sailed along the Continent a considerable way North-East, returned again, but made no Settlement that time.   And although the English were the first Discoverers of this Noble and Fertile Tract of Land, from the Latitude of 25 to 36½; yet was no Colony planted in it, till several of the English Nobility stir'd up with a pious Zeal, to propagate the Christian Religion; and with a Heroick Spirit, to enlarge the Dominion of the Crown of England, procured a large and ample Patent, with extraordinary Privileges both for themselves, and the People that would Plant and Inhabit them, as appears by the Patent of Cha. II. unto George Duke of Albermarle, Edw. E. of Clarendon, W. Earl of Craven, John Lord Berkley, Anthony Lord Ashley, now E. of Shaftsbury, Sir George Cartwright,·

<hr />

¹ Carteret.

after that Lord Cartwright, and Sir John Colleton Knight and Baronet, who were thereby created the true and absolute Lords and Proprietors of the Province of Carolina, and the same to be held *in Capite* of the Crown of England, to Them, their Heirs, and Assigns for ever; which said Province begins at the Latitude of 29 Degrees, and reaches to the Latitude of 36½ North Latitude; and the said Province is to enjoy all the Privileges and Liberties that the Bishop of Durham hath or ought to have. These aforesaid Lords therefore enter'd into a joynt Stock, and fitted out Ships on their own proper Charges, to transport People and Cattle thither, to the Value of about 12000 Pounds, besides several Thousands laid out by single Proprietors, to advance the Colony; and all their Rents and Incomes have since the Beginning been also expended in publick Services.

I shall now come to the particular Description of the Country itself, and that not by a bare Report, but as an Eye Witness. I have hinted how Sir Sebastian Cabot, at the Charge of Henry VIIth, first discovered that part of the Continent which is called Florida, which begins at Cape Florida, in the Latitude of about 25, and runs North East to 36½. Now Carolina only is its Northern Part, *viz.* from 29 Degrees to 36½, and is indeed the very Center of the habitable Part of the Northern Hemisphere; for taking it to be Habitable from the Equinoctial to 64 Degrees, the Center of Carolina lies in about 32, which is about the Middle of 64, lying parallel with the Land of Canaan, and may be called the Temperate Zone comparatively, as not being pestered with the violent Heats of the more Southern Colonies, or the extream and violent Colds of the more Northern Settlements. Its Production doth answer the Title of Florida, *quia regio est Florida*, being indeed a most Fertile and flourishing Region, every thing generally growing there, that will grow in any Parts of Europe, there being already many sorts of Fruits, as Apples, Pears, Apricocks, Nectarines, etc., and they that once tast of them, will for the future despise the watry and washee Tast of them here in England; yet doth their Plenty make them the Food of the Swine of their Country; for from a Stone in 4 or 5 Years they come to be bearing Trees of a considerable Bigness; likewise all sorts of Grain, as Wheat, Barly, Peas, etc., and I have measured some Wheat Ears 7 or 8 of my Inches long. It produces also Rice the best of the known World, being a Commodity for Returns home; as also Pitch, Tar, Buck, Dear, Bear-Skins, and Furs, though the last not so good as the Northern ones: And it hath already such Plenty of Provisions, as Beef, Pork, etc., that it furnishes in a great measure, Barbadoes, Jamaica, etc. The Natives are somewhat Tawny, occasioned, in a great measure, by Oyling their Skins, and by the naked Raies of the Sun: They are generally very streight Bodied, and Comely in Person, and quick of Apprehension; and I believe, if managed discreetly, may many of them, in a few Years, become Civilized, and then very capable of the Gospel of Christ. The Indians are great Hunters, and thereby not only serviceable to kill Dear, etc., for to procure Skins for Trade with us, but those that live in Country Plantations procure of them the whole Dear's Flesh, and will bring it many Miles for the Value of about six Pence, and a wild Turky of 40 Pound, for the Value of two Pence Engl. Value. There is also vast Quantities or Numbers of wild Ducks, Geese, Teal, and exceeding Plenty of Fish, etc., and that which makes Provisions so cheap, is the shortness of the Winter, where they need not to mowe for Winter Fodder, and so can employ their Hands in raising other Commodities as aforesaid. It is Pity they should be farther thin'd with Civil Quarrels, being their Service is in all Respects so necessary: And indeed I my self their late Governour, prevented the Ruin and Destruction of two small Nations. The Manner of it was thus;

Two Indians in drinking Rum quarelled, and the one of these presently kill'd the other; his Wife being by, immediately, with a Knife, smote off his Testicles, so as they hung only by a Skin: He was pursued by my Order, I happening to be then that way, being about 16 Miles from Town, and was taken in a Swamp, and immediately sent to Custody into Charles Town; and the Nation to whom the slain Indian belonged unto, was acquainted with it, whose King, etc., came to the Governour, and desired Justice on that Indian; some of the Indian's Friends would have brought him off, as is usual; But nothing but his Life would satisfie that Nation, so he was ordered to be shot by the Kinsman of the murthered Indian. Before he went to Execution, the Indian King to whom he belonged, told him, that since he was to die, he

would have him to die like a Man: and farther he said, I
have often forwarn'd you of Rum, and now you must lose
your Life for not taking my Council; I hope it will be a warning
to others.   When he came to the Tree, he desired not to be
tyed to it, but to stand loose, for, said he, I will not budge
or stir when he shoots me; so he was shot in the Head, and
immediately died.   Now the Manner of the Indians in such
Cases, is to War one Nation against the other to revenge
any Blood-shed; and being ordered Satisfaction this way, no
War ensued.

The Soil of Carolina near the Sea is of a Sandy Mould,
appearing ten times more Barren than it proves to be: Yea,
there is vast Quantities of Vines in many Parts on the Sea
Shore, bearing multitude of Grapes, where one would wonder
they should get Nourishment.   But farther distant up in the
Country, the Land is more mixed with a blackish Mould,
and its Foundation generally Clay, good for Bricks, it is
beautified with odoriferous and fragrant Woods, pleasantly
green all the year; as the Pine, Cedar, and Cypress, insomuch,
that out of Charles-Town for three or four Miles, call'd the
Broadway, is so delightful a Road and Walk of a great breadth,
so pleasantly Green, that I believe no Prince in Europe, by
all their Art, can make so pleasant a Sight for the whole Year:
in short, its natural Fertility and easy Manurement, is apt to
make the People incline to Sloth; for should they be as Indus-
trous as the Northern Colonies, Riches would flow in upon
them: And I am satisfied, that a Person with 500*l.* discreetly
laid out in Old England, and again prudently managed in
Carolina, shall in a few Years, live in as much Plenty, yea
more, than a Man of 300*l.* a Year in England; and if he continue Careful, not Covetous, shall increase to great Wealth
as many there already are Witnesses, and many more might
have been, if Luxury and Intemperance had not ended their
Days.   As to the Air, it is serene and exceeding pleasant, and
very healthy in its natural Temperament, as the first Planters
experienced, seldom having any raging Sickness but what
has been brought from the Southern Colonies, by Vessels
coming to the Town, as the late Sickness may intimate; to
the which may be added the Intemperance of too many:
What may properly belong to the Country, is to have some

gentle touches of Agues and Feavers in July and August, especially to New-comers. It hath a Winter Season to beget a new Spring, and thereby the Air is made more suitable to our Temperament. I was there, at twice, five Years, and had no Sickness, but what once I got by a careless violent Cold: And indeed, by my Observation, I did perceive that the Feaver and Agues were generally gotten by carelessness in their Cloathing, or Intemperance as aforesaid. What I write is not to encourage any to depend upon Natural Causes, but prudently to use them with an Eye to God, the Great Lord of the Universe and Disposer of all Humane Affairs; yet hath he justly and wisely decreed, that such as every one sows, such shall he reap.

Carolina also abounds with many Rivers, now found to be more Navigable than was at first believed;[1] and it was prudently contriv'd, not to Settle at the first, on the most Navigable, but on Ashly and Cooper River, whose Entrance is not so bold as others, nor having so much Water; so that the Enemy and Pirates, etc., have been dishearten'd from disturbing the Settlement until this Year where they were repuls'd with the loss of about Three Hundred Men.[2] The New Settlers have now great Advantage over the first Planters, being they can be furnish'd with Stocks of Cattle and Corn, etc., at reasonable Rates: As also, they have an advantage in seating a new River with Indians at Peace with them, and the choice of the best Land: And I understand two New Rivers are about seating one in the South, the other in the North;[3]

[1] The possibilities of some of them, so far as navigation is concerned, have not yet been determined. Although the width and depth of the Edisto above Jacksonborough and of its two upper forks are sufficient to accommodate steamers they do not ply their waters because of the snags and sandbars that obstruct the channels.

[2] This reference is to the invasion by a French fleet in August, 1706. After several days of fighting, the militia troops of South Carolina defeated the French, inflicting severe losses upon them. The most conspicuous defender of the province was Col. William Rhett, who had been greatly maligned a few years before by the Dissenter faction in local politics. See McCrady's *History of South Carolina under the Proprietary Government*, pp. 396–401.

[3] New London, or Willtown, on the Edisto, to the South, had been established for several years. See *The South Carolina Historical and Genealogical Magazine*, X. The second reference is to James Town (French) on the Santee River. (*Ibid.*, IX.)

and if it please God that the Union succeed with Scotland, the principal place in Carolina, call'd Port-Royal, may be seated with English and Scots in a considerable Body, because 't is a bold Port, and also a Frontier upon the Spaniard at Augustine, which is but a weak Settlement, about 200 Miles to the South West of it. The Scots did, about 20 Years since, begin a Settlement with about 10 Families,[1] but were disposs'd by the Spaniards. O how might the Scots, that go now as Switzers[2] to serve Foreign Nations, how might they, I say, strengthen our American Colonies, and increase the Trade of Great Britain, and enrich themselves both at Home and Abroad. I could plainly demonstrate what a great Advantage Carolina is to the Trade of England, by consuming our Commodities from Home thither, and by bringing great Duties to the Crown, by importing Goods or Commodities thence: For Charles-Town Trades near 1000 Miles into the Continent; but to enlarge thereupon, would too much enlarge this Treatise: But notwithstanding all the Discouragements it hath met withal, which are many, yet 17 Ships this Year, came laden from Carolina with Rice, Skinns, Pitch and Tar, etc., in the Virginia Fleet, besides several straggling ones: And indeed London would be much too big, if it were only the Metropolis of England, if it were not also the Metrop-

---

[1] This settlement was effected by Lord Cardross in 1685, and was destroyed by Spaniards in 1686. (See p. 205, *supra*.) The following warrant shows who composed the colony:

" Carolina SS.

"You are forthw[th] to cause to be admeasured and laid out unto Henry Lord Cardross eight hundred and fifty Acres of Land being so much due to him for the Arriveall of himself, william Stevenson, Peter Allen, Alexand[r] M[r]tis, James Martine, Carpenter and Martha his Wife, James Martine Junio[r], Anna Martine, Deborah Martine, Priscilla Martine, Charles Campble, Mary Huttchison, Martha Martine, spinster, Moses Martine, mary Martine, Mary Foulton, and James Foulton, in some convenient place not yett laid out or m[r]ked to be laid out for any other person or use observeing the Lords Propriet[rs] instruccons bearing date the 21[th] day of Septemb[r]. 1682 and A Certificate fully specifying the scituacon and bounds thereof you are to returne to us w[th] all convenient speed and for y[r] so doeing this shall be y[r] sufficient Warr[t]. Dated this 6th day of Octob[r]. 1685.

To Stephen Bull Esq[r]                          JOSEPH MORTON
  Surveyo[r] Gen[ll]                             ROB[T]. QUARRY
                                                 PAUL GRIMBALL
                                                 JOHN FFARR"

[2] *I. e.*, mercenaries like the Swiss.

olis of America.  I wish I could write as large in the Propagation of the Christian Religion amongst the Natives, but the Gospel Spirit is not yet so gloriously arisen, as to seek them more than theirs, as Paul intimates: Yet I believe, that in time Trade may be a means, to introduce the Gospel both in the West and East Indies, with some other Discoveries that are a breaking forth in Nature, as the Time and Season for it ripens.

And, Christian Reader, since I am fallen upon this Subject, which is one great Branch of the Patent, as hinted before, which was to propagate the Gospel of Christ; I doubt there hath been a great defect therein, so shall give a brief Essay to answer that pious Clause aforesaid.

And because the Patent is granted for Propagating the Gospel; and the most peculiar Obligation consequentially thereby lies on those of the Church of England: I shall in the first place give my Advice to them on the Indians behalf: I do therefore adjudge it reasonable and just, that a certain Portion of Land be set apart for that use, to be added to a proportionable Income from the Society *ad Propagandum fidem*, to be prudently administered to Missionaries who have Zeal, Courage and Fidelity for such a Work; and that the Government, on no pretence of their Service in the Plantations, divert them from their Commissionated Service; for if so, a lazy Spirit will quickly lay hold on them, and Flesh and Blood will plead for ease; for Hardships and Perils will attend them: Wherefore, as Christ said, 'T is prudent first to count the Cost before they enter into the Work.  In the next place I advise, That such Missionaries be well skill'd in Chymistry, and some natural Genius to seek the Virtues in Herbs, Metts and Minerals, etc., and the prudent Conduct of such Skill, might introduce them into a good Opinion with the Indians; and let them understand that we were once such as themselves, but were by a Noble Heroick Nation reduc'd into a Civiliz'd State; and then had the Gospel preach'd to us by Just and Holy Men who sought our Salvation with the hazard of their Lives, etc.  Let them have sent with them (and if not far from the English) some English Children, to introduce familiarity with the Indian Children, that so they may be brought to learn Letters, etc.

I remember I have read in History of a Welsh Prince, who advised his Sons, ready to Quarrel about the Division of his poor and barren Lands, that they should sail to the Westward, where they would meet with better Land, and Territories large enough for all their Posterities.

Now I may apply this spiritually; If Christian Magistrates and Ministers would forsake their Quarrels for poor Trifles and barren Opinions, and encourage each other to plant substantial practicable Truths; they may now sail East or West, and meet with People to make a plentiful Harvest on, both in a Temporal and Spiritual respect, which should redound more to their Glory and Advantage, than all their Unchristian Quarrels and Practices to promote unfruitful Doctrines that are computed to have shed more Christian Blood than all the Heathenish Ten Persecutions. I hope the Reader will not think this Mixture of Spirituals with Temporals improper or impertinent, since the original Design of the Patent was the Promotion of both.

I shall next proceed to treat of the Government, as granted by King Charles II. to the Eight Lords Proprietors aforesaid, who again, by common consent, center'd that Power in Four of them, *viz.* in a Palatine of their own election, and Three more who were impower'd to execute the whole Powers of the Charter, and is call'd a Palatines Court; their Deputies in Carolina executing the same, as from their Principals they are directed: For each Proprietor hath his Deputy there. The Charter generally, as in other Charters, agrees in Royal Privileges and Powers; but especially at that time it had an Over-plus Power to grant Liberty of Conscience, altho' at Home was a hot Persecuting Time; as also, a Power to Create a Nobility, yet not to have the same Titles as here in England, and therefore they are there by Patent, under the Great Seal of the Provinces, call'd Landgraves and Cassocks,[1] in lieu of Earls and Lords: and are by their Titles to sit with the Lords Proprietors' Deputies, and together make the Upper-House, the Lower-House being elected by the People; and these Landgraves are to have four Baronies annex'd to their Dignities, of 6000 Acres each Barony; and the Cassocks two

---

[1] Cassiques.

Baronies, of 3000 [1] each; and not to be separated away by
Sale of any part; only they have power to let out a third
Part for three Lives, for to raise Portions for younger Children. And many Dissenters went over, Men of Estates, as
also many whom the variety of Fortune had engaged to seek
their Fortunes, in hopes of better Success in this New World:
And truly such as better improved their new Stock of Wit,
generally had no cause to repent of their Transplantation into
this Fertile and Pleasant Land: Yet had they at first many
Difficulties and Dangers to cope withal, and therefore the
most desperate Fortunes first ventured over to break the Ice,
which being generally the Ill-livers of the pretended Church-
men, altho' the Proprietors commissionated one Collonel
West their Governour, a moderate, just, pious and valiant
Person; yet having a Council of the loose Principled Men,
they grew very unruly, that they had like to have Ruin'd
the Colony, by Abusing the Indians, whom in Prudence they
ought to have obliged in the highest degree, and so brought
an Indian War on the Country,[2] like that in the first Planting
of Virginia, in which several were cut off; but the Governour
by his Manly prudence, at last, extinguish'd the same in a
great measure, and so left Matters a little better settled to
Governour Jos. Morton, in whose time General Blake's
Brother,[3] with many Dissenters came to Carolina; which
Blake being a wise and prudent person, of an heroick temper
of Spirit, strengthen'd the Hands of sober inclined People,
and kept under the First Loose and Extravagant Spirit; but
not being able to extinguish it, it broke out and got head
in the Government of James Coletin of Barbadoes, and Sir
Peter Colleton's Brother: And this Party grew so strong
among the Common People, that they chose Members to
oppose whatsoever the Governour requested; insomuch that
they would not settle the Militia Act, tho' their own Security

---

[1] A barony consisted of 12,000. Each landgrave was entitled to four baronies
and each cassique to two.

[2] The Churchmen in whom the Quaker Archdale could see so much evil,
were, as a rule, the ablest and most progressive men in the province, and their
treatment of the Indians had not nearly so much to do with bringing on the war
as had the inborn treachery of the Indians.

[3] Benjamin Blake.

(in a Natural way) depended on it. And the grounds of
their farther Strength, was by reason of the Discontent the
People lay under about the Tenure of their Lands, and payment of their Quiterance¹ which was afterwards rectified by
me. After Colleton² succeeded one —— Smyth,³ a wise and
sober, moderate and well-living Man, who grew so uneasy
in the Government, by reason that he could not satisfy the
People in their Demands, that he writ over *An.* 1694, "That
it was impossible to Settle the Country, except a Proprietor
himself, was sent over with full power to Heal their Grievances,
etc." And now let the Reader consider, that the ensuing
Account hath been for several Years supprest by me, least I
should thereby seem to exalt my own Actions; but there is
now at this Juncture some more than ordinary Cause so to
publish the same as follows: For the Proprietors took Governour Smyth's Letter under Consideration; and the Lord
Ashly was pitch'd upon by all the Lords, who was then in
the Country, a Person every way qualified for so Good a
Work;⁴ who desired to be excused, because his Fathers
Affairs lay upon his Hands; upon which Account I was then
pitch'd upon, and intrusted with Large and Ample Powers;
and when I arriv'd, I found all Matters in great Confusion,
and every Faction apply'd themselves to me in hopes of Relief;
I appeased them with kind and gentle Words, and so soon
as possible call'd an Assembly to whom I spoke as follows:

*Friends and Representatives of the People.*
The Occasion of my coming hither I think good to acquaint
you withal at this time, that so you may the better judge of the
Proprietors and my own Intentions in this my Undertaking.
There came various Letters from Carolina, signifying the great
Discontent and Division the People lay under; but especially one

----

¹ Quit-rents.
² The objection to Colleton was not due to any turbulent spirit in the people,
but to their love of liberty and constitutional government. Colleton totally dis-
regarded the constitution and the law and was arrogant and tyrannical, and the
people revolted against his government and drove him from the province.
³ Thomas Smith.
⁴ This Lord Ashley was afterward the third earl of Shaftesbury, the celebrated
philosophical writer. His grandfather, the first earl and original Proprietor, was
dead; his father was an invalid.

dated presently after Sir Peter Colleton's Death; wherein it was intimated, That except a Proprietor himself came over, it was impossible to reconcile the Matter; so the Lord Ashley was nominated, but his Affairs not permitting, the Matter was moved to me; and after a very mature Deliberation, and by the Encouragements of several Carolinians then in England my Going was concluded on; and they have endued me with a Considerable Power of Trust, and I hope I shall faithfully and impartially answer their Expectations: And I believe I may appeal to your Serious Rational Observations, whether I have not already so allay'd your Heats, as that the distinguishing Titles thereof are much wither'd away; and I hope this Meeting with you, will wholly extinguish them, so that a solid Settlement of this hopeful Colony will ensue, and by so doing, your Posterity will bless God for so Happy a Conjunction; and the Proprietors will not repent of this Great Trust reposed in me, nor my self repine at the many Dangers and Hardships I have undergone to my arrival hither: And now you have heard of the Proprietors Intention of sending me hither, I doubt not but the Peoples Intentions of Choosing you were much of the same nature; I advise you therefore, to proceed soberly and mildly in this weighty Concern; and I question not but we shall answer you in all Things that are reasonable and honourable for us to do: And now Friends, I have given you the reason of my Coming, I shall give you the Reasons of my calling you so soon, which was the consideration of my own Mortality, and that such a considerable Trust might not expire useless to you; for my Commission is recorded to be no President[1] to future Governours: as also a late Petition of many of the Inhabitants of this Colony: I hope the Consideration hereof will quicken and direct you into a speedy Conclusion of what the People may reasonably expect from you; and I hope the God of Peace will prosper your Counsels herein.

*The Assembly reply;*

*To the Right Honourable John Archdale Esq; Governour of Carolina.*

*May it please your Honour,*
    We heartily thank Almighty God for your Honours Safe Arrival in this Place, after so many Difficulties and Dangers, mention'd in your Honours most acceptable Speech; and we return your Honour our most sincere and hearty Thanks for the Progress your Honour has already made since your Arrival towards the Settle-

[1] Precedent.

ment of this Place; but our most particular Thanks again are for your candid Expressions, and the good Favour and great Kindness shewn to the People of this Place; and do assure your Honour, That we on our Parts, will heartily endeavour to give our utmost Assistance to the attaining your so much desired Wish, the perfect Settlement of this Place, which will redound to the Honour of the Lords Proprietors and the Happiness of the People.

But, Courteous Readers, after this fair Blossoming Season to produce Peace and Tranquility to the Country, some endeavour'd to sow Seed of Contention, thereby to nip the same; insomuch that they sat Six Weeks under Civil Broils and Heats; but at length recollecting their Minds into a cooler Frame of Spirit, my Patience was a great means to overcome them; so that in the conclusion all Matters ended amicably, as the Address intimates.

*The Humble Address and Recognition of Thanks by the Commons assembled in Charles-Town. To the Right Honourable the True and Absolute Lords Proprietors; and to the Right Honourable John Archdale, Esq; Governour of Carolina.*

*Right Honourable,*
     We the Representatives of the Free-men of South Carolina, being profoundly sensible of your most gracious Inclinations, Condescentions and Honours in Commissionating and Investing the Right Honourable John Archdale, Esq; Governour, with such large and ample Powers for the encouragement of us the Inhabitants of this your Colony, which was so highly necessary conducing to the Peopling, Settling and Safety thereof, do most humbly Recognize, and most sincerely and cordially thank your Lordships for the same, and for the Remission of some Arrears of Rents, the undeniable manifestation of your Honours Paternal care of us, living in this your Colony: And we the Commons now assembled, no less sensible of the prudent, industrious and indefatigable Care and Management of the said Powers by the Right Honourable Joh. Archdale Esq; do in most humble Manner acknowledge the same; and that we doubt not but that the Fruits thereof will be the Peace, Welfare, and Tranquility, Plenty, Prosperity and Safety of this Colony and the People therein; For the Acts of Grace you have so seasonably condescended unto, have removed all former Doubts, Jealousies, and Discouragements of us the People; and hath laid a firm and sure Foundation on which may be erected ॰

most glorious Superstructure to the Honour of the Lords Proprietors and you our Governour, which we do, and forever shall be obliged most heartily to own as the Production of the Wisdom, Discretion, Patience and Labour of the Honourable John Archdale, Esq; our Governour; of whom we the Commons request, to return this our Recognition of Thanks to your Lordships; and we shall humbly pray, etc.

JONATHAN AMERY,[1] Speaker.

But it may be queried by the Reader, But what was the Effect of all this? To the which I answer, That the Fame hereof quickly spread it self to all the American Plantations, as several Letters I receiv'd intimated; among which I shall mention One from New-England, from a single Person of Note there, on the behalf of a Number of People, and is as follows, bearing Date from Ipswich 26th June, 1696.

*Great Sir,*
   I had not thus boldly intruded my self in this manner, or been the least Interruption to your publick Cares, but that I am commanded to do this Service for a considerable Number of Householders, that purpose (with the Favour of God's Providence, and your Honours Countenance) to Transport themselves into South Carolina: For we having heard the Fame of South Carolina, as it now stands Circumstanced with the honour of a true English Government, with Virtuous and Discreet Men Ministers in it, who now design the promoting of the Gospel for the increase of Virtue amongst the Inhabitants, as well as outward Trade and Business· and considering, that the well Peopling of that Southern Colony of the English Government or Monarchy may, with God's Blessing, be a Bulwark (a) to all the Northern Parts, and a Means to gain all the Lands to Cape Florida (which are ours by the first Discovery of Sir Sebastian Cabot, at the Charges of K. Henry VII, to the Crown of England; and being credibly inform'd of the Soil and Climate, promise, that all adventurers, with the Favour of God, shall reap Recompence as to Temporal Blessings.
   *Sir,* These and such like Reasons have encouraged and produced the aforesaid Resolutions: And farther, Sir, your great Char-

---

"(a) It is remarkable that the French Landed at Sewee, where many of the New-England Men were planted, and beat off the French, and killed many of them, and this was Ten Years after this Letter." (Note in original.)

[1] Amory.

acter doth embolden us, for it is such as may be said, without Flattery, as was said of Titus Vespasian, that noble Roman, *Ad gratificandum assiduus Natura fuit:*[1] So praying for Blessings upon your honourable Person, Concerns and Province, I rest, etc.

Now that the Reader may plainly discern, that the Almighty and Omnicient God, takes cognizance of Human Affairs, and directs them by a wise and prudent Chain of Causes, I shall relate some remarkable Passages that happened quickly after that I entered upon the Government, which was the 17th of August, 1695. There is a Nation of Indians call'd the Yammasees, who formerly liv'd under the Spanish Government, but now live under the English, about 80 Miles from Charles-Town. Some of these Indians going a Hunting, about 200 Miles to the Southward, met with some Spanish Indians that lived about Sancta Maria, not far from Augustine, the Seat of the Spanish Government; and taking them Prisoners, brought them Home, designing to sell them for Slaves to Barbadoes or Jamaica as was usual; but I understanding thereof, sent for their King, and ordered him to bring these Indians with him to Charles-Town, which accordingly he did: There were three Men and one Woman; they could speak Spanish, and I had a Jew for an Interpreter, so upon examination I found they profess'd the Christian Religion as the Papists do; upon which I thought in a most peculiar manner, they ought to be freed from Slavery; and thereupon order'd the King to carry them to Augustine, to the Spanish Governour with a Letter, desiring an Answer relating to the receit of them; who having receiv'd them, sent me the following Letter: So far as relates to this Affair, I copy it forth:

*Sir,*
I have receiv'd your Letter with the four Indians, three Men and one Woman, being the same that were taken from a Town of my Jurisdiction; and I do promise, If ever it lies in my power to manifest a reciprocal Kindness, I shall gratefully do the same; and shall always keep and observe a good Correspondence and Friendship with you, as our Soveraigns at home, being in strict Alliance and Amity expect from us, etc.

---

[1] "He was by nature assiduous in obliging."

After this he sends over an Indian civilized King, with a fresh return of Thanks, but complains of Mischief done to his Indians by some of our Indians; to the which I answered,

That I knew nothing before, and did not approve of it; and found, on Enquiry, that the Indians call'd the Apalachicoloes had kill'd three Churchcates, and were conducted by White Men; but I have taken care for the future, by sending an Express to command them, that they do not commit any Acts of Hostility on any of your Indians, and do expect there be given the like Orders to your Vassals: And surely you cannot be ignorant of the Temper of the Indians as well as my self, how hard a matter it is to keep them from taking Revenge for any Injuries received, to the third and fourth Generation; making personal Murders oftentimes National Quarrels; notwithstanding which, I hope to prevent it for the future, being that they live in great Obedience to our Government; but if they should happen to do any small Mischief to each other, I desire you not to send any more White Persons amongst them, least you thereby make the Quarrel National. I do assure you that nothing shall be wanting on my part to maintain a good Amity and Friendship with you, and I doubt not of the same on your part: So wishing you Health and long Life;
I am
your assured Friend
Jo. ARCHDALE.

Now to shew the Providence of God in the Affair of transmitting the Indians back, as I intimated before, it happened that some few Months after that an English Vessel from Jamaica, bound to Carolina, was Cast-away to the Southward of Augustine amongst barbarous Indians, who in a wonderful manner were preserv'd from being murdered by them, so that they came at last to Augustine; and when the Spanish Governour heard of it he sent them all things necessary, retaliating my Kindness in a peculiar manner. Two of these were call'd Robert Barrow and Edward Wardell, publick Friends,[1] Men of great Zeal, Piety and Integrity.

Another eminent Remark of Divine Providence was as follows: One Colonel Bull of the Council, trading with some Northern Indians near Cape Fear, told me that those Indians

---

[1] *I. e.*, Quaker ministers.

desired to come under the English Government; the Reason of it was this; some of our Neighbouring Indians had killed and taken Prisoners some of the Cape Fear Indians, and sold them for Slaves; and complaining to the Traders, they told them, that if they came under the English Government the other Indians durst not touch them: So they came, and I told them that I had heard of their barbarous Cruelty on Men Cast-away on their Coast; I therefore now expected a Civil Usage from them, to any that should unhappily be Cast-away on their Coast; which they promised, and faithfully perform'd, as follows.

For about Six Weeks after a Vessel coming from New-England with 52 Passangers, was Cast-away at Cape Fear, who finding that it was the Place of savage Indians, despaired of their Lives; but being willing to preserve Life as long as they could, they Trench'd themselves in, and took some provisions with them: The Indians quickly came down, and with Signs of Friendship, laying their Hands on their Breasts, invited them out, and shew'd them Fish and Corn: But they, not willing to trust them, kept still in their Retrenchment till Famine began to creep on, and then, like the Samaritan Lepers, in the 2 *Kings*, vii. Chap. who being like to perish with Famine, ventured to go to the Host that beseiged Samaria, as at large is there related: So these being ready to starve, some few ventured out to the Indians, who received them kindly and furnish'd them with Provisions for the rest, who thereby being embolden'd, came all forth, and were by the King at his Town well treated; and four or five of them came to Town, and I procured a Vessel to fetch them to Charles-Town, which is about 100 Miles from thence, and all came safe but one Child that died. But now I shall wind up and conclude the Scene of my Government, having settled the Country; I returned for England, being not sent for Home, and left one Blake [1] Governour, who became a Proprietor,

---

[1] As Joseph Blake was a landgrave his selection to succeed Archdale was a mere form. In 1698 he purchased from the Lords Proprietors the forfeited share in Carolina of John, Lord Berkeley, who had failed to keep up his assessments. He had been commissioned governor by the Proprietors without first securing the assent of the Crown and for that reason the Crown would not recognize him as governor until the Proprietors explained that he was acting governor in the

and continued to manage Matters to the general satisfaction
of the Country for about four or five Years, but then dying,
the Lords Deputies chose one Capt. More for Governour, until
the Lords should Commissionate one from England. In his
time began the War with France and Spain; and being a
Man of an active spirit, and hoping to advance his Fortune
by an Exploit against Augustine, without any Orders from
England,[1] he proposed his Mind to an Assembly, who con-
descending thereunto, he march'd against Augustine, took the
Town, the Inhabitants, with their Substance, flying into the
Castle, and they having no Mortars could not bring them to
yield; but the Besieged sending to the Havanah, a Spanish
Town on Cuba, procured 4 or 5 small Men of War, who came
to their Relief before Major Daniel could come from Jamaica,
who was by Governour More sent thither for Mortars; and
so More was forc'd to break off the Siege, and return to Charles-
Town; which vast expence upon such an Infant Colony, was
ready to make a Mutiny among the People; for many Vessels
had been press'd to that Service, which being burn'd by the
Governour's Order, because they should not fall into the
Spaniards Hands, the Masters demanded Satisfaction; and an
Assembly being call'd, great Debates and Divisions arose,
which, like a Flame, grew greater and greater: In the midst
of which, Sir Nath. Johnson's Commission came for to be
Governour, who by a Chimical Wit, Zeal and Art, transmuted or turn'd this Civil Difference into a Religious Controversy;[2] and so setting up a Standard for those call'd the
High-Church, ventured at all to exclude all the Dissenters out
of the Assembly, as being those principally that were for a
strict Examination into the Grounds and Causes of the Mis-

right of a Proprietor under the Fundamental Constitutions. After that the oath
was administered to him by Edward Randolph, an officer of the Crown. See p.
204, *supra*.

[1] Archdale, like all of Moore's Dissenter critics, ignores the fact that an
attempt had been made by the Spaniards with Indian allies to invade South
Carolina. See p. 222, *supra*.

[2] Sir Nathaniel was not responsible for the religious turn of the trouble.
The Dissenters drew the religious lines at the outset, and the Churchmen, an-
gered to the extreme by the Dissenters' pestiferous conduct, and taking advantage of the power brought by their repeated successes, went to the extreme of
adopting a tyrannical plan for excluding Dissenters from the Commons House.

carriage of the Augustine Expedition; which was, after great
Complaints of undue Elections, and by the great Subtilty and
Activity of the Governing Party, carry'd by one Man, to
exclude the Dissenters by a more severe and rigid Exclusion,
than the Occasional Bill design'd here in England, to the
which I refer the Reader; and was afterwards, by the general
Complaint of that Party to the House of Lords, adjudged so
severe and illegal, as to cause an Address to the Queen, which
she was pleased to accept, and to command the Lord's Proprietors not to suffer the same to be further put in execution,
and declared the same Law void and null; as also an Act to
establish the Church of England there, and a Maintenance for
the same; which, notwithstanding its splendid gloss, savour'd
so much of a persecuting Spirit, and of a haughty Dominion
over the Clergy it self, that it was declared void and null
by the Queen's gracious and prudent Command to the Lord's
Proprietors; which I hope will so far allay and cool that fiery
Spirit in the Government, as to make room for a more peaceable and healing Spirit, when any one not concern'd in the
Broils arrives, Commissionated for that End and Purpose:
And indeed they have been fairly alarum'd by the late Assault
upon them by the French and Spaniards; in which affair
Sir Nath. Johnson, as a Souldier, behaved himself with great
Courage and Prudence; but that is not a sufficient Qualification to reconcile intestine Heats and Broils, which, like a
Canker, will enfeeble the vital Spirit of that Colony; for the
united strength of those term'd the High-Church and Dissenters, are little enough to secure the same: And beside, the
immediate Hand of God by the late Pestilential Feaver, is not
only a sign of His Displeasure against their Unchristian Broils,
but it hath thereby so weakened and thined the People, that
it seems impossible for the High-Church to be a sufficient
Strength to support that Colony, it being the Southern Bulwark of our American Colonies on that vast Continent.[1]

[1] The Church Act of 1704 was rejected by the Proprietors because it contained so many objectionable features as to make it obnoxious to the Crown,
but in 1706 another act, freed of those objectionable features, was passed establishing religious worship in the province in accordance with the tenets of the
Church of England. This act proved a great blessing to the province, and was
an agency for the more rapid development thereof. It gave an impetus to education and culture, and its influence for good was far-reaching and permanent.

It is stupendious to consider, how passionate and preposterous Zeal, not only vails but stupifies, oftentimes, the
Rational Powers: For cannot Dissenters Kill Wolves and
Bears, etc., as well as Church-men; as also Fell Trees and
Clear Ground for Plantations, and be as capable of defending
the same generally as well as the other.  Surely Pennsylvania can bear witness to what I write; and Carolina falls
no way short of it in its Natural Production to the industrious
Planter: But our late Accounts intimate the Repeal of the
two former Laws, which may be a preparatory Stroak, if discreetly managed, to allay their Annimosities.  I would not
be supposed to Justify every Step of the Dissenters which they
made in these Broils, being their first Agent seem'd not a Person suitably qualified to Represent their State here, not that
he wanted Wit but Temper, which is a necessary Qualification
in Persons in that Employ: But it is not my Business to
Open the Sore, but to Heal it, if possible; and now[1] we are
like to have some considerable Numbers of Scotch Britains,
Men generally Ingenious and Industrious, who are like to
disperse themselves into our American Colonies, who are a
People generally zealous for Liberty and Property, and will
by no Perswasion be attracted to any part where their Native
Rights are invaded, or who rather expect an Enlargement
thereof in a Wilderness Country, than an Abridgement
thereof, as that prudent Management of William Penn hath
establish'd in his Colony, and was first intended for Carolina,
in a Scheme laid by the Earl of Shaftsbury, etc., but secretly
over-thrown by that Party of High pretended Church-men
that have lain Latent from the Beginning, as I have before
intimated.  Our Colonies are very weak at this time, but the
Divine Hand of Providence seems to be ready to supply our
Deficiency by a Union, contrary to that Spirit that hath
wrought the Dissentions in Carolina.  Now if the Reader be
so curious as to Query how I did so speedily and solidly Heal
their former Annimosities, as I have before intimated, I shall
gratify his Curiosity herein: My Power was very large, yet
did I not wholly exclude the High-Church Party at that time
out of the essential Part of the Government, but mix'd two
Moderate Church-men to one High-Church Man in the Council,
whereby the Ballance of Government was preserved peaceable

[1] By reason of the union of England and Scotland, 1707.

and quiet in my Time, and so left and continued several Years, whilst Blake whom I left Governour lived. And the said Blake, though accounted in some measure a Dissenter, yet did he procure the Act for about 150*l*. a Year to be settled on a Church of England Ministry, which continues to this Day. And indeed in such Mixture as I have intimated, the High-Church Party was useful to me, being Men of good Parts, very useful under Good Conduct; their Advice being by me found very necessary in many particular Cases.

But to proceed farther in this Treatise, the Design whereof is to make Carolina a suitable Bulwark to our American Colonies: I can farther plainly demonstrate, that False Measures have been taken for that Infant Settlement that should have been Strengthen'd with Encouraging Terms, for all sorts of Dissenters to enjoy Liberty and Property in whatsoever their laborious Hands Improves from a Wilderness possess'd by Wolves, Bears and barbarous Indians, who ruin'd themselves, by intestine Wars, to make room for us; and we more Foolish, because more Capacitated by Human Policy to strengthen our selves against a Foreign Power, yet suffer a sort of Transmigration of the Wolfish and Brutish Nature to enter our Spirits, to make our selves a Prey to our Enemies, that seek to Revenge themselves for our foolish Attempt and unchristian Usage on the Inhabitants of Augustine, where the Plunder of their Churches or Places of Worship intailed on it such a Curse, that much of it fell into the Hands of the French, the Ship being taken near England, and the whole Design of it for Negroe Slaves, ruin'd thereby.

Now as some there seeks to set up a sort of an arbritrary Vestry to inhance the Labours of the Industrious Dissenters, who have enough to do to maintain their own Ministry; how unreasonable doth it look to force Maintenance from them, by excluding their true Representatives, to compass so foolish a Design in the most untimely Season that possibly could happen to that Country; for one of the most considerable amongst them writ over to his Friend in England, That without that Excluding Act they could not have obtain'd the other. Now as the Civil Power doth endanger it self by grasping at more than its Essential Right can justly and reasonably claim; so the High-Church by over-toping its Power in too great a Severity, in forsaking the Golden Rule of doing as they would

be done by, may so weaken the Foundation of the Ecclesiastical
and Civil State of that Country, that so they may both sink
into a ruinous condition by losing their Main Sinews and
Strength, which (as Solomon saith) lies in the multitude of its
Inhabitants: And this I am satisfied in, and have some experi-
mental reason for what I say, That if the extraordinary Fertility and Pleasantness of the Country had not been an alluring
and binding Obligation to most Dissenters there settled, they
had left the High-Church to have been a Prey to the Wolves
and Bears, Indians and Foreign Enemies: But I hope now
they will see their Folly, and embarque in one common Interest, and thereby they will reap the Benefit of our Union
at Home, by Numbers of Industrious and Ingenious Scottish
Britains, who otherwise will never come to be imposed upon
by a High-flown Church Party; and without such a Strength
I see not how it can stand long, let the Government be in any
Hand whatsoever. I have discharged my Conscience in a
Christian and truly British Spirit, that desires nothing more
than the Spiritual and Temporal Welfare of Great Britain;
and hope, pray for, and cordially desire the long and pros-
perous Reign of our most gracious Queen, whom the Divine
Hand of Providence hath placed on the Throne, to be as a
Nursing Mother to all Her Children committed to Her Charge.
And I also heartily wish that the inferior Sphere of the Royal
Power committed in Trust to the Lords Proprietors of that
Province of Carolina, may Govern it with a measure of the
same Prudence, Justice, and truly Christian Affection, as She
more imediately Governs the entire Body of Her Subjects.

Now since the Reader may expect the Names of the present Proprietors, they are as follows;

JOHN Lord GRANVILL, Palatine.

| | |
|---|---|
| John Lord Cartwright, | Sir John Colleton, Baronet, |
| William Lord Craven, | Jos. Blake, Esq;[1] |
| Maurice Ashley, Brother | Nicholas Trott,[2] Esq; |
| and Heir Apparent to | John Archdale. |
| the Earl of Shaftsbury, | |

[1] Joseph Blake, the then Proprietor, was at that time about six years of age.
[2] The original share of the Earl of Clarendon was sold after the earl's death
to Seth Sothell. Sothell died about 1694, intestate and without heirs, and his

I am now willing to give my Advice to heal up the present Breaches, Rents and Divisions amongst the Inhabitants of Carolina; and I am somewhat encouraged hereunto by the Good Success I formerly had amongst them, as I have at large declared; and I have Reasons, both Spiritual and Temporal for this my Admonition.  On a Spiritual Account I would have all to consider that their Lot is fallen, by the Divine Hand of Providence, into the American Canaan, a Land that flows with Milk and Honey; which ought to be a pressing Engagement on every Soul to bless God in a most peculiar manner for those Temporal Enjoyments that many other Nations and Provinces want the Benefit of: And let them consider, that altho' God had some peculiar Love for the Children of Israel, yet they held their Land of Canaan on Terms and Conditions; and their Disobedience and Neglect of God's Laws, occasion'd God to remove them out of the same; Yet before He utterly Excluded them, he brought various Corporeal Punishments upon them to alarum them to Repentance, and a forsaking of the Evil of their Ways: And when His Chastising Hand did not prevail upon them, their Utter Destruction immediately ensued.  Now it is apparent that God has brought a Pestilential Fever amongst the Carolinians, that hath swept away many in the Town, which ought to stir up a Considerati[on] in the Remainder of them, that it is His infinite Mercy that hath spared them: Let them also consider that God hath shaken the Rod of his Power over their Heads by a Foreign Enemy, which many times is an Occasion to Unite, not only to a General and Common Defence, but also it creates an Affection where before it was wanting: But if upon these and the like Considerations, no Good Effect ensue thereby, it is then a dangerous Prognostick that more severe Judgments will follow.  It is recorded in the Holy Scriptures; O that Men would consider their Ways; for the Act of Consideration is much in the Soul's power; and is one of the Powers being purchased by Christ for us after the Fall, whereby a Capacity comes to be awaken'd in us, to choose the Good

share was sequestered by the other Proprietors under provisions of the Fundamental Constitutions and assigned to Thomas Amy, September 29, 1697.  Upon the marriage of Amy's daughter with Nicholas Trott, of London, cousin of Judge Nicholas Trott, of South Carolina, Amy assigned him the share in Carolina as a marriage portion.

and refuse the Evil; and I believe the Soul never exerts it, but that some secret Concomitancy of God's Power is witness'd thereby to the benefit of every such Soul. One thing more I would lay to their Consideration, That by intestine Quarrels and Annimosities they loose the essential Badge of Christianity, and so can never be Instruments to propogate the Gospel amongst the Heathen, who will never be won to the Gospel of Peace by the Banner of War. Much more might be said on a Spiritual Account, but this at present may suffice: I shall now proceed on a Temporal Account, to reason them into a Unity; and that is first, because their own Lives will be more comfortable under a friendly Conversation; and, secondly, it will encourage others to come amongst them, which will wonderfully strengthen the Colony and increase Trade, and make their Lands of considerable more value.

Now, altho' I seem principally to lay the Occasional Quarrel on the High-Church Party, yet I would not be so understood as to clear the other in all respects; for in Heats and Annimosities many unjustifiable Words and Actions may arise and be committed: I am satisfied whence the original Spring of them arose, but because they are generally dead on both sides, Christian Charity forbids the raking into their Ashes; and 't is pity their Quarrels should surrvive them: They shall never find Fewel here, so far as lies in my power. I can truly say, I write with Love and Affection to the whole Body of the Inhabitants; having been so considerable a Promoter of Planting the said Colony with Men of Piety and Industry, and that brought considerable Free Estates with them, insomuch that were they all removed again out of it, whose coming thither I occasion'd, it would be a thin Colony: I could name them, but forbear at present: So I am not for excluding any, as I have hinted; for I am satisfied that it is possible to Reconcile and Unite them, there being a great President[1] of Wisdom and Christian Affection in the Governing Powers at Home in the Union of 2 Kingdoms into 1 Common Interest,[2] for the Strength and Advantage of both, and Disadvantage of our Enemies Abroad and at Home: And I can truly say, I rejoyce to see effected what for some Years I have

[1] Precedent.
[2] The Union of England and Scotland had been effected on March 6, 1707.

so much desired, and so earnestly endeavoured, in my Capacity and Station, upon all argumentative Occasions; which have not been a few, and with considerable Persons of eminent Quality, who have not despised the Reasons I have given for the same.

Since I wrote the former Part I understand that Silk is come unto great Improvement, some Families making 40 or 50*l.* a Year and their Plantation Work not neglected; little Negro Children being serviceable in Feeding the Silk-worms, etc. And I must give Sir Nathaniel Johnson the Reputation of being the principal Promoter hereof, and of a considerable Vineyard also. I further understand, That the Inhabitants work up the Silk into Druggets mix'd with Wool, which is an excellent Wear for that Country: And so advantageously is the Country scituated, that there is little or no need of Providing Fodder for Cattle in the Winter; so that a Cow is grased near as cheap as a Sheep here in England; but all these Natural Conveniences and Benefits may be blasted through imprudent Discouragement, that may hinder fresh Inhabitants from coming amongst them. O what need is there of Wisdom to nourish up an Infant Colony with all sorts of industrious People, as is in a great measure presidented in Pennsylvania, etc., and was the Beginning of the Carolina Settlement; and I hope will be the future Method to strengthen the same: And hereby the Design of the Patent will be truly answer'd which is the Propagation of the Gospel of Peace among the Heathen, and the Enlargement of the Dominion of the Crown of England, which is now already spread many Hundred of Miles to the Westward; which Design was ingeniously laid and begun by Governour Blake in his Time. And that discret Preparative Stroak of Trade that he begun, which if prudently and wisely managed, it may beget such a Familiarity and Interest with the Indians, as in time to introduce a Spiritual Benefit by the Preaching of the Gospel of Christ among them:[1] For God oftentimes by the wise adapting

---

[1] While there is very little evidence of any increase of "Spiritual Benefit" having come to the Indians by this "Stroak of Trade," it did greatly expand Charles Town's trade, so that within a few years its traders were going as far as the Mississippi River and Indians were bringing skins and furs all the way from the Great Lakes and Canada.

of Temporal Causes, makes them to co-operate for the production of Spiritual Benefits: And so the Romans by a Civil Taxation fulfilled the Prophecy of Christ to be Born at Bethlehem; and this Taxation figured forth Christ who was to lay a Spiritual Yoke on all the Sons of Men: For Taxation imports the Yoke of the Civil Power upon them.

Since what I have before written the former mention'd Acts that gave so bad an Influence on the Carolina Affairs, are both of them actually repealed, so that once more there seems to present it self a fair Prospect for an amiable Reconciliation, if true and proper Method be pursued for the encouragement of all that desire to retire into this New World to lead an industrious, quiet, godly and sober Life, without that disquieting and turmoiling Care which naturally attends most European Affairs. Now, candid Readers, I shall Conclude with what our blessed Lord and Saviour hath intimated, That the Harvest is great and the Labourers few, and that it is our Duty to pray to the Lord of the Harvest that he would be pleased to send more Labourers into the Harvest, *Matth. 9.* Chap. 37, 38. Ver. Now these Labourers seems to me to be such as will take Pains and venture their Lives for to propagate the Gospel of Christ amongst these barbarous Nations, which God, as I have before intimated, hath discovered in this last age of the World: And it is my Belief, that Christ will intercede to have this Prayer answered, and will incline the Hearts of many to begin this glorious Work.[1]

---

[1] The Society for the Propagation of the Gospel in Foreign Parts sent Rev. Samuel Thomas to South Carolina in 1702 as a minister to the Yemassee Indians, but he found the task such an impossible one that he gave it up and labored most usefully among the whites. See *The South Carolina Historical and Genealogical Magazine*, IV., V.

FROM THE HISTORY OF THE BRITISH EMPIRE
IN AMERICA, BY JOHN OLDMIXON, 1708

# INTRODUCTION

In 1708 John Oldmixon, Whig pamphleteer and historical writer, published in London a work entitled *The History of the British Empire in America*, two chapters whereof deal with South Carolina. The first chapter deals with the history of the province and the second with its geography. The former consists of a desultory and frequently erroneous history of the province up to the administration of Governor James Moore (1700–1703), followed by another lengthy brief in behalf of the Dissenter faction in the political controversy that had just shaken the province, the greater part of the chapter being devoted to that one episode. Nothing new was added to that controversy save a few lively imaginings, while many whole passages were inaccurately repeated from the earlier pamphlets by Defoe, Boone, and Archdale. The geography is also quite erroneous. Not only did the writer confuse names and places, but put in some topographical features that had no existence.

Oldmixon stated in his preface that he had read each chapter of his book to inhabitants of the colonies that he wrote of, and that every statement he had made had been acknowledged to be correct, and that his statements could be relied upon. So far as South Carolina was concerned, it is evident that whoever he read that part of his history to—if he really read it to anyone from South Carolina—was as ignorant of the subject as Oldmixon himself was. It is quite evident that the latter had never been to South Carolina and had very little information respecting it save what he had acquired from the several pamphlets relating to the political controversy between the Dissenters and the Churchmen during the administrations of Moore and Johnson.

A new edition of Oldmixon's work, with a few unimportant additions, was published in 1730, and in 1836 B. R. Carroll reprinted the chapters on South Carolina in his *Historical Collections*.

# FROM THE HISTORY OF THE BRITISH EMPIRE IN AMERICA, BY JOHN OLDMIXON, 1708

## THE HISTORY OF CAROLINA

## CHAPT. I

*Containing an Account of the Discovery and Settlement of this Province, and of all the Wars, Factions, Disturbances, and other Events there, from that time to the present.*

WE are not ignorant of the pretences of the concern'd in this Province, who affirm, 'twas discover'd by Sebastian Cabot. Mr. Archdale, one of the Proprietors, in his printed *Description of Carolina*, says, Henry the VIIIth about the Year 1500. furnish'd Sir Sebastian Cabot with Shipping, (He was born at Bristol, tho his father was a Venetian,) to make a discovery; and he fell upon the Coast of Florida, and having sail'd along the Continent a considerable way North-East, return'd. But this does not appear in any authentick Historian; nor that Sir Sebastian Cabot ever got so far to the South.

Carolina is the Northern part of the vast Region of America, which was discover'd by John Ponce de Leon, in the year 1512. He made Land about 30 Degrees from the Æquator, near the River of San Mattæo, the most Southerly part of this Province. He sail'd thither from the Island of Porto Rico, and gave the Country the Name of Florida, for that the Face of it has the Resemblance to a continual Spring.[1]

---

[1] "Castell, of America." (Marginal note in the original, referring to W. Castell, *A Short Discoverie of the Coasts and Continent of America*, London, 1644.)

The Spaniards, who passionately desir'd to secure it to themselves, eight years afterwards sent Vasquez de Ayllon to make a further discovery of it, as belonging to Charles V. in whose Name de Leon had taken Possession of it. He came upon the North Coast, and call'd the North North-West River by the Name of Jordan. He did nothing memorable, except this infamous Action, of inviting many of the Natives aboard his Ships, where when he had got them, he hoisted Sail, and carry'd them into miserable Bondage.

In the Year 1526. Charles V. Emperor of Germany and King of Spain, sent Pamphilio Narvesi[1] to Florida, who stay'd so long in the South-West part of this Country, which is the most barren, that, says my Author, they were fain to eat one another, his Crew having spent their Provisions.

Ten years afterwards Ferdinando de Soto came hither in the search of Gold and Silver Mines, having a little Army of 900 Foot, and 500 Horse. Himself, and three Parts of his Soldiers, dy'd, either thro' Want, or by Sickness, or the Indians; and the rest were led back by Lewis Moscos to New Spain, tho not without great Difficulty, for the Natives setting upon them several times in their march, kill'd all that fell into their Hands.

This unfortunate and expensive Expedition so discourag'd the Spaniards, that for several Years they made no more Attempts in these Parts, and indeed they search'd no further than that Part of the Continent which lies opposite to the Gulph of New Spain, and not within and beyond the Streights of Bahama, which includes that part of the Country we are now treating of, and which is the most fertile and rich, abounding in several merchantable Commodities.

The French perceiving the Spaniards neglected this long Tract of Land, Admiral Coligny, in the Reign of Charles IX. procur'd two of the King's Ships to be sent thither, the Command of which he gave to Jean Ribaut, who after a Voyage of Two Months, arriv'd at the River of Dolphins, between that of San Mattæo, and that of May, lying about the 30th Degree.

The next River to that of May, he call'd the Seine. The next to that, the Somme; then the Loire; then the Charente, and the Garonne. At the Mouth of Albemarle River, then

---

[1] Pánfilo de Narvaez.

call'd the Great River; the Port being safe and commodious,
he built a Fort, which he called Charles Fort, and gave it the
Name of Port Royal, in 32 Degrees of Latitude, bordering on
Virginia, now North Carolina, where the first Settlement was
made by any European Nation.[1]

The Civil Wars raging in France, Ribaut's soldiers mutiny'd
for want of Supplies. The Natives, 't is true, were very kind
to them, out of Hatred to the Spaniards; but they could not
furnish them with many Necessaries which they wanted; and
the Admiral was so engag'd in Politicks at home, that he had
not Leisure to provide for the Wants of his Colony. So
Ribaut having made some Discoveries in the North-East part
of Florida, return'd to France, and in his Return, if Credit
may be given to an Old Author,[2] his Company were reduc'd to
such Extremity, that they kill'd and eat one of their own Men;
and probably would have done so by others, had they not
accidentally met with an English Ship, the Master of which
furnish'd them with some Provisions. A peace being concluded 2 Years after in France, between the Papists and the
Protestants, Coligny, who was then in Favour at Court, procur'd other Ships to be sent to this Country, which was now
call'd Carolina, from Fort Charles, as that was from the French
King.[3] The Command of those Ships, and the Men aboard,
was given to Lewis Laudoner,[4] who was order'd to carry on
the Settlement. He arriv'd here the 20th of June, 1564.
with 3 Ships, and was kindly receiv'd by the Indians, but could
find no Gold and Silver Mines, tho he spent much Labour
and Time in search after them. His Provisions being almost
all gone, and the Natives either unable, or unwilling to furnish him with more, Laudoner resolv'd to return also to
France; and as he was preparing to depart, Jean Ribaut
arriv'd with 3 Ships, which had so good an Effect on the In-

---

[1] Charles Fort, or Arx Carolina, was not at the mouth of the river which
the author calls Albemarle or Great (Broad), but was on an island formed by
that river, Port Royal River, which empties into it some distance above its mouth,
and Pilot's Creek, which connects the two rivers.

[2] Castell, according to a note by Oldmixon in his original work.

[3] There is nothing in evidence to show that the country was ever called Carolina prior to the patent to Sir Robert Heath, October 30, 1629.

[4] René Laudonnière.

dians, that they seem'd to be as welcome to them as to the French. The Kings of Homoloa, Seravatri, Almacam, Malica, and Castri, waited upon Ribaut, to congratulate his Arrival, and promis'd to conduct him to the Apalatæan Mountains, which part Carolina from Virginia.

The French conceiv'd great Hopes of this Settlement, but all vanish'd on the Arrival of the Spaniards, who with a Squadron of Ships and Land Forces, drove the French out of their Forts, kill'd Ribaut, and 600 Men, after having given them Conditions of life, and oblig'd Laudoner, with a few of his Countrymen who remain'd alive, to return to France.[1]

The French King took no notice of this Act of Violence committed on his Subjects, because they were Protestants; and indeed 'tis thought Coligny intended by this Settlement, to secure a Retreat for himself, and his Brethren of the Reform'd Religion, in case they were conquer'd in France. Peter Melanda[2] commanded the Spaniards, who dislodg'd the French, and so provok'd the Indians by his Cruelty and Injustice, that they were very ready to revenge themselves when Opportunity offer'd, as it did not long after; for Capt. De Gorgues,[3] a French Gentleman, at his own cost, fitted out three stout Ships, and with 280 Men sail'd to Carolina, where he took the Fort, and put all the Spaniards within it to the Sword. They had built two other Forts, which he easily reduc'd, and serv'd the Garrisons as he did that of Fort Charles. He demolish'd them, and was assisted by the Kings of Homoloa, and Seravatri.

The French travell'd into the Dominions of the great King of Apalacha,[4] near the Mountains, where they converted many Indians to Christianity. These Indians were more civil than those to the Northward, their King's Dominions larger, and their Manners, in a great measure, resembled the Mexicans.

We do not find that Monsieur de Gorgues made any Settlement here; or that the Spaniards attempted to recover the Country; which from the Year 1567, lay deserted by all

---

[1] This second French settlement was not on Carolina soil, but in Florida.
[2] Pedro Menéndez.                    [3] De Gourgues.
[4] "Dav. *of Kid*, p. 247." (Note in original, meaning to refer to John Davies of Kidwelly, *History of the Caribby Islands*, London, 1666, a translation from the French of César de Rochefort, or Francisco Raymundo.)

European Nations, till the Reign of King Charles II. of England.[1]  In the Year 1622. several English Families flying from
the Massacre of the Indians in Virginia and New-England,
were driven on these Coasts, and settled in the Province of
Mallica, near the Head of the River of May, where they acted
the Part of Missionaries among the Mallicans and Apalachites.
The King of the Country is said to have been baptiz'd; and
in the Year 1653. Mr. Brigstock, an Englishman, went to
Apalacha, where he was honourably entertain'd by his Countrymen, who were there before him; and from his Relation
of the Country ours is taken.

It will not be unacceptable to the Curious, to see a Description of Carolina, as it was before the English settled there,
which we find very distinctly in a Discourse, Printed A. D.
1644.  The nearest River of any Note, to Virginia, falling into
the Sea, is the Jordan, which lies in 32 Degrees; from whence,
about 20 Leagues downwards to the South, is the Promontory
of St. Helen, near Port-Royal, which the French chose for
the best and surest Place to begin their Plantations.[2]  Between
the River Jordan and St. Helens, are Oristanum, Ostanum,
and Cayagna; Oristanum lying 6 Leagues from St. Helens;
Ostanum 4 Leagues from Oristanum; and Cayagna 8 Leagues
from Ostanum.  From St. Helens to Dos Baxos Haven is
5 Leagues.  From thence to the Bay de Asapo, 3 Leagues;
thence to Cafanusium 3, to Capula 5, to Saron 9, to S. Alcany
14, and to S. Peter 20 Leagues, lying in 31 Degrees of Latitude.
The next Place is San Mattæo, 4 Leagues from St. Peter.

'Twill be difficult for an Inhabitant of the present Carolina,
to reconcile all these Names to the Modern, and the old Description to the New; wherefore we shall not pretend to it,
at least but occasionally, and where we can be almost sure
that we are in the right.

This Country having been abandon'd by all European
Nations, for near 100 years, it seemed reasonable then, that
any one who would be at the Expence of settling upon it,
and cultivate it, should possess it; and the Pretence of Sebastian Cabot's discovering it, gave the Crown of England a
Title to it, which King Charles II. asserted: For some Noble-

---

[1] "Ibid."   (Note in original.)
[2] "Castell, p. 33."   (Note in original.)

men and Gentlemen begging it of him, he made a Grant of it, by a Pattent, bearing date the 24th of March, 1663, to Edward Earl of Clarendon, then Lord High Chancellour of England, George Duke of Albemarle, William Lord Craven, John Lord Berkley, Anthony Lord Ashley, Sir George Carta-ret, Sir William Berkley, and Sir John Colliton: "Who," to use the Words of the grand Charter, "being excited with a laudable and pious Zeal, for the Propagation of the Gospel, begg'd a certain Country in the Parts of America not yet cultivated and planted, and only inhabited by some barbarous People, who had no Knowledge of God, etc., wherefore the King granted them all that Territory in his Dominions in America, from the North End of the Island called Lucke-Island, which lies in the Southern Virginian Sea, and within 36 Degrees of N. Latitude; and to the West as far as the South Seas; and so Southerly, as far as the River San Mattæo, which borders on the Coast of Florida, and is within 31 Degrees of North Latitude, and so West, in a direct Line, as far as the South Seas aforesaid:" With all Royal Fisheries, Mines, Power of Life and Limb, and every thing necessary in an absolute Propriety, paying a Quitrent of 20 Marks Yearly.

We are not to enter into the Merits of the Cause, nor inquire by what Right King Charles became possess'd of this Province, and Carolina to be a part of his Dominions in America; 'tis enough for us, that he gave the Proprietaries such a Charter, and that they proceeded towards a Settlement by virtue of it: which was in a few Years effected. Whatever has been said of the French and Spaniards, 'tis but just, that if one Nation does not think a Country worth cultivating, and deserts it, another, who has a better Opinion of it, may enter upon it, by the Law of Nature and Reason.

The Proprietaries, after they had got their Charter, gave due Encouragement for Persons to settle in this Province, and there being express Provision made in it for a Toleration, and Indulgence to all Christians in the free Exercise of their Religion, great numbers of Protestants, Dissenters from the Church of England, retir'd thither.

This Toleration appears so firm by this Charter, that we wonder any Palatine could presume to break in upon it. The King granted the Proprietaries full and free License,

Liberty and Authority, by such legal Ways and Means, as they shall think fit, to give unto such Person and Persons, inhabiting, and being within the said Province, or any Part thereof, who really in their Judgments, and for Conscience sake, cannot, or shall not conform to the Liturgy, Form and Ceremonies of the Church of England, and take and subscribe the Oaths, and Articles, made and establish'd in that behalf, or any of them, such Indulgences and Dispensations in that behalf, for, and during such Time and Times, and with such Limitations and Restrictions, as they, etc., shall think fit.

Let us now see what the Proprietaries did, pursuant to the Power the King had invested them with, to grant Liberty of Conscience. We cannot have a better Authority than the *Case of the Dissenters in Carolina*, publish'd lately by a gentleman of this Province.[1]

The first Proprietors were so sensible that nothing could people that Province, and enrich it, but an universal and absolute Toleration, that they made the most express and ample Provision for such a Toleration that ever was made in any Constitution in the World, as may be seen in the 96, 101, 102, 106 Articles of the Fundamental Constitutions: Which provide, as the Lords Proprietors word it in those Constitutions, That "since the Natives of that Place, who will be concern'd in our Plantations, are utterly Strangers to Christianity, whose Idolatry, Ignorance, or Mistake, give us no Right to expel or use them ill, and that those who remove from other Parts to plant there, will unavoidably be of different Opinions concerning Matters of Religion, the liberty whereof they will expect to have allow'd them; and that it will not be reasonable for us, on this account, to keep them out; therefore, that sure Peace may be maintain'd, amidst the Diversity of Opinions, and our Agreement and Compact with all Men may be duly and faithfully observ'd, the Violation whereof, upon what Pretence soever, cannot be without great Offence to Almighty God, and great Scandal to the true Religion which we profess: And also that Jews, Heathens, and other Dissenters, from the Purity of the Christian Religion, may not be scar'd, and kept at a Distance from it, but by having an Opportunity of acquainting themselves with the Truth and Reasonableness of its Doctrines, and the Peaceableness and Inoffensiveness of its Professors, may by good Usage and Persuasion, and all those convincing Methods of Gentleness and Meekness,

[1] The margin refers to pp. 27, 36, of Defoe's pamphlet of that title.

suitable to the Rules and Designs of the Gospel, be won over to embrace, and unfeignedly receive the Truth." Therefore the said Constitutions provided for their Liberty, but declar'd, "That no Person above seventeen Years of Age, shall have any Benefit or Protection of the Law, which is not a Member of some Church or Profession, having his Name recorded in some one religious Record."[1]

Thus did these Lords Proprietors take care, that Persons of all Professions in Religion should be protected and secur'd in the free Exercise of them; and the Reader thus prepossess'd with the Laws of the Country, on which the Government of the Colony is intirely founded, will be the better able to judge of the Principles of those Men, who, in the Sequel of this History, we shall find endeavouring to over-turn the most considerable Articles of these Fundamentals; for great Numbers of Protestant Dissenters from the Church of England, removing with their Families to Carolina, when there were so many Inhabitants, that a Form of Government was necessary, the Proprietaries agreed on that abovemention'd, call'd, the Fundamental Constitutions, consisting of 120 Articles, sign'd by the Duke of Albemarle, then Palatine of the Province; the Lord Craven, the Lord Ashley, Sir John Colleton, the Lord Cornbury, the Lord Berkley, Sir George Cartaret, the 1st of March 1699.[2] Which Constitutions, as is expressed in the last Article, *shall be, and remain the sacred and unalterable Form and Rule of Government in Carolina for ever.*

They were drawn up by that famous Politician the Earl of Shaftsbury, one of the Proprietors, and the only one that could be suspected of having the least Inclination to favour the Dissenters. The first Article of these Fundamentals, is, that a "Palatine shall be chosen out of one of the Proprietaries, who shall continue during Life, and be succeeded by the eldest of the other Proprietaries." The Palatine has the executive Power in most Cases, and the rest of the Proprietaries have their Places and Privileges. Mr. Archdale, in the before-mention'd treatise says,

They center'd all their Power in four of them, *viz.* in a Palatine of their own choosing, and three more, who were authoris'd

---

[1] Oldmixon's quotation is not perfectly accurate.

[2] Misprint for 1669; the reference is to the second or revised constitution, dated March 1, 1669/70. Cornbury was the son of Clarendon, now in exile.

to execute the whole Powers of the Charter. This is call'd the
Palatine's Court; and their Deputies in Carolina execute it as they
are directed by their Principals.[1]

By the Fundamental Constitutions, there are to be three
Hereditary Noblemen in every County, one call'd a Landgrave, and two call'd Cassiques. The Parliament consists of
the Proprietors, or their Deputies, the Governour and Commons; and by the Fundamentals should have 25 Landgraves,
and 50 Cassiques to make a Nobility: But the Number of
Landgraves and Cassiques is very small, and they are not
summon'd to make an Upper-house, on that Account; so the
Governour and the Proprietors Deputies arrogate that Title.
The Commoners are chosen by the Free-holders of every
County, as the Commons in England; and all were at first to
sit in one House, and have equal Votes. This Parliament
should meet once in every two Years, and oftener, if Occasion
require. The Courts of Justice are, besides those of the
Palatine's Court, the Chief Justice's Court, the High-Constable's
Court, the Chancellor's Court, the Treasurer's Court, the
Chamberlain's Court, the High-Steward's Court: Besides
which, there are the Great Council and the Hundred Courts.
Mr. Archdale, on this head, tells us,[2]

The Charter generally, as in other Charters, agrees on Royal
Privileges and Powers, but especially at that Time it had an over-
plus Power to grant Liberty of Conscience, tho at home was a hot
persecuting Time; as also a Power to create a Nobility, yet not
have the same Titles as here in England: And therefore they are
there by Pattent, under the Great-Seal of the Province, call'd Landgraves and Cassiques, in lieu of Earls and Lords, and are by their
Titles to sit with the Lords Proprietors Deputies, and together
make the Upper House, the Lower House being elected by the
People. These Landgraves are to have four Baronies annex'd to
their Dignities, of 6000 Acres each Barony; and the Cassiques two
Baronies, of 3000 each, and not to be divided by Sale of any Part.
Only they have Power to let out a third Part for three Lives, to
raise Portions for younger Children.

Every County has a Sheriff and four Justices of the Peace.
Every Planter pays 1d. an Acre Quit-Rent to the Proprie-

taries, unless he buys it off. All the Inhabitants and Freemen, from 16 to 60 Years old, are bound to bear Arms, when
commanded by the Great Council.[1]

The Proprietaries enter'd into a Joint-Stock, and fitted
out Ships on their own proper Charges, to transport People
and Cattle thither, which Expence amounted to 12000*l.*
besides as much or more disburs'd by single Proprietors to
advance the Colony; and all their Rents and Incomes have
since the Beginning been laid out in publick Services.

Many Dissenters of good Estates went over, and many
other Persons in hopes to mend their Fortunes. And if they
could tell how to improve the Opportunities that were put
into their Hands there, they had seldom any Reason to repent
of going thither.

Tho the Difficulties and Dangers they met with at first
were a little discouraging, all free Persons, who came over,
were to have 50 Acres of Land for themselves, 50 more for
each Man-Servant, and 50 more for each Woman-Servant
Marriageable; and not Marriageable, 40 Acres. Each Servant out of his or her Time was to have 50 Acres, paying the
Quit-Rent of 1*d.* an Acre.

The Proportion of Land was much greater by the first
Instructions which the Proprietaries sent their Governours,
but they afterwards thought fit to reduce it to the present
Allotment. Some Gentlemen who did not care to be liable
to the Yearly Quit-Rent of 1*d.* an Acre, bought their Lands
out-right.

The common Rate of purchasing now, is 20*l.* for a 100
Acres, and 10*s.* a Year Quit-Rent. The Proprietors, in all
their Leases, never forget to except all Mines, Minerals, and
Quarries of Gemms and precious Stones.

Things being thus establish'd, the Lords Proprietaries
appointed Col. William Sayle, to be Governour of their Province, about the Year 1670.[2] The first Plantations that came

---

[1] Grand Council.

[2] The Proprietors sent a commission for a governor of South Carolina to Sir
John Yeamans, of Barbados, in 1669, with the fleet bearing the first settlers for
South Carolina, leaving the place for the name blank, and requested him to fill
in the blank with his own name if he desired the position, or with that of someone
else in case he did not desire it. Sir John selected Col. William Sayle, of Bermuda.

to any Perfection, were about Albemarle and Port-Royal Rivers.[1] But Ashley and Cooper Rivers drew People that way, for the Convenience of Pasture and Tillage, for which Reason that Part of the Country became most inhabited.

In 1671. The Proprietors sent Cap. Halsted with a Supply of Provisions and Stores for the Colony, and created James Cartaret, Sir John Yeomans, and John Lock, Esq; Landgraves.

The Constitutions having been found deficient in some Cases, Temporary Laws were added, and the Form of Government settled thus.

A Governour named by the Palatine.

A Council consisting of
- 7 Deputies of the Proprietors.
- 7 Gentlemen chosen by the Parliament.
- 7 of the eldest Landgraves and Cassiques.

An Admiral.  
A Chamberlain.  
Chancellor.  
Chief-Justice.  
Secretary.  
Surveyor.  
Treasurer.

High-Steward.  
High-Constable.  
Register of Births, Burials, and Marriages.  
Register of Writings.  
Marshal of the Amiralty.

All which were nominated by the Proprietors respectively. The *Quorum* of the Council were to be the Governour and 6 Councillors, of whom 3 at least were to be Proprietors Deputies; and because there were not Inhabitants to make a Parliament, according to the *Fundamental Constitutions*, 'twas order'd to consist of the Governour, the Deputies of Proprietors, and twenty Members chosen by the free-holders; of whom ten were to be elected by Berkley's County, and ten by Colliton County; which number was encreas'd, as more Counties were laid out, and more People came to settle in the Province.

---

[1] No settlement "that came to any perfection" was made about either of those rivers. The first settlers were intended for a settlement at Port Royal, but after reaching that point they changed their plans and settled on the west bank of the Ashley River. They stayed at Port Royal only two or three weeks, and made no settlement.

The Temporary Laws were made in the Year 1671. At which time William, Earl of Craven, was Palatine. On which Office he enter'd, after the Death of the Duke of Albemarle; who, as has been said, was Palatine, when the *Fundamental Constitutions* were sign'd, but dy'd soon after. In the same Year Cap. Halsted was order'd to make Discoveries up Ashley River, and a Model of a Town was sent, which it will be well, if the People of Carolina are able to build 100 Years hence, but the Proprietaries, as appears by their Constitutions and Instructions to their Governours, thought 'twas almost as easy to build Towns, as to draw Schemes.

The next Governour to Col. Sayle was Sir John Yeomans, Baronet; in whose time many of the before-mention'd Transactions happen'd, but we have not been able to distinguish the Events in his Government from those in Sayle's.[1]

About the Year 1680. the Proprietaries made Joseph West, Esq; one of the first Planters, their Governour.[2] He was a Man of Courage, Wisdom, Piety, and Moderation: And such an One was necessary in his time; for tho many Dissenters had fled from the Rage of their Enemies in England, yet there were not wanting Men of other Principles, who by Factions disturb'd the Peace of the Infant-Colony. Mr. Archdale's Word will, in this case, be more acceptable to the Reader:[3]

The most desperate Fortunes first ventur'd over to break the Ice, which being generally the ill Livers of the pretended Churchmen, tho the Proprietaries commissionated one Col. West their Governour, a moderate, just, pious, and valiant person; yet having a Council of the loose principled Men, they grew very unruly, and had like to have ruin'd the Colony, by abusing the Indians, whom in Prudence they ought to have oblig'd in the highest degree, and so brought an Indian War on the Country, like that in the first planting of Virginia, in which several were cut off; but the Governour, by his manly Prudence at least in a great measure extinguish'd the Flame, which had a long time threatned the Dissolution of the Colony.

[1] Joseph West served as governor for over a year between Sayle and Yeamans. He succeeded Sayle March 4, 1671, and was superseded by Yeamans April 19, 1672.

[2] West succeeded Yeamans August 13, 1674, and served to June, 1682.

[3] See p. 295, *supra*.

The two Factions were that of the Proprietaries and that of the Planters, like Court and Country Party in England. This Division got to such a Head, that one Mr. John Culpeper, was sent Prisoner to England, with a Charge of High-Treason against him, for raising a Rebellion in Carolina; for which he was try'd at Westminster-Hall, and upon hearing the Matter, it appear'd only to be a disorderly Quarrel among the Planters and Inhabitants of the Province, so he was acquitted.

Col. West held a Parliament in Charles Town, A. D. 1682. In which several Acts were pass'd and ratify'd by him, (Andrew Percivall, Esq; William Owen, Esq; and Maurice Matthews, Esq; Deputies of the Proprietaries); as, "An Act for High-ways, for suppressing Drunkenness and profane Swearing, for Observation of the Lord's Day, and for settling the Militia."[1]

'Twas in this Governour's Time, that the Westoes, a Nation of the Indians, were troublesome to the Colony, and attempted the Subversion of this hopeful Settlement, as the Act of Parliament to raise Money for repelling them words it. There was not much Blood shed, or Money spilt; for 4 or 500 *l.* paid the Charge of the War, and other publick Expences.

The Lords Proprietaries erected a Commission for Maurice Matthews, Esq; William Fuller, Esq; Jonathan Fitz, Esq; and John Boon, Esq; to decide all Causes between the English and Indians. And Mr. West is charg'd with dealing in Indians: For which, and opposing the Proprietaries Party, he was remov'd, in the Year 1683. and Joseph Moreton, Esq; appointed Governour in his stead.[2]

'Twas about this time, that the Persecution rais'd by the Popish Faction, and their Adherents, in England, against

---

[1] Sessions of Parliament, or, as it soon came to be known, the General Assembly, in which legislation had been enacted, had been held almost every year from 1671.

[2] Landgrave Joseph Morton superseded West in June, 1682. The charge against West of dealing in Indian slaves was not a valid one, and the real reason of his removal was doubtless to make room for Morton, whose influence at that time was in demand. He was an influential Dissenter. Some Dissenters, fearing a Popish successor to Charles II., were leaving England. Axtell, Morton, and Blake had induced many to settle in South Carolina. As governor, Morton would induce many more to come. By this policy the Proprietors gave the Dissenters a position in South Carolina politics that eventually split the people of the province into two bitter factions.

the Protestant Dissenters, was at the height; and no Part
of this Kingdom suffer'd more by it than Somerset-shire.
The Author of this History liv'd at that time with Mr. Blake,
Brother to the famous General of that name, being educated
by his Son-in-law, who taught School in Bridgwater,[1] and
remembers, tho then very young, the Reasons old Mr. Blake
us'd to give for leaving England: One of which was, That
the Miseries they endur'd, meaning the Dissenters then, were
nothing to what he foresaw would attend the Reign of a Popish
Successor; wherefore he resolv'd to remove to Carolina: And
he had so great an Interest among Persons of his Principles,
I mean Dissenters, that many honest substantial Persons
engag'd to go over with him.

I must prevent all prejudice to what I have said, by
declaring that this book is written by one who is not himself
a Dissenter, but verily believes, the true Church of England
is the most orthodox, and the most Pure Church in the World.
And by the true Church of England, he understands all those
who live up to the doctrine it professes; who by their Piety,
Charity, and Moderation, are Ornaments of our Holy Religion,
and who do not blindly espouse a Name out of Interest, or
from the Impressions of Education; who pity, and not hate,
such as dissent from them; who are loyal to their Prince,
submissive to their Superiours, true to their Country, and
charitable to all: Of such a temper is every true Church-man;
and may their number daily encrease, till we are all of One
Mind, and One Religion, as we have but One God, and One
Saviour.

If the reader will pardon this Digression, he shall have no
more; and so much 'twas necessary to say, that he may
not think, whatever is said of Mr. Blake, or his Brethren, is
out of respect to his Profession, but as a Christian: For tho
I doubt not there may be many good Christians of the same
principles, I should esteem them more, if they would be con-
vinc'd, and conform; that the Union so often recommended
by our Gracious and Glorious Queen Anne, may be universal.

I say the more of Mr. Blake, because his Family is one
of the most considerable in this Province; where he arriv'd

---

[1] The only son-in-law of Benjamin Blake of whom we can now cite a record
was William Dry, who married his daughter Elizabeth Blake.

in the Year 1683.[1] with several other Families, the followers
of his fortune. What Estate he had in England, he sold,
to carry the Effects along with him; and tho the Sum was
not many Thousands, if it did at all deserve the plural Number; yet 'twas all that his great Brother left him, tho for
several Years he commanded the British Fleet; and in a
time when our Naval Arms were victorious, and the treasures
of New-Spain seldom reach'd home.

By Mr. Blake's Presence in Carolina, the Sober Party,
we call them so in opposition to Mr. Archdale's Ill Livers,
began to take Heart, and the other to be discourag'd in their
irregular Courses. The Gentleman I just mention'd, in his
*Description of Carolina*, writes thus:[2] "In Governour Moreton's time, General Blake's Brother, with many Dissenters,
came to Carolina; which Blake being a wise and prudent
Person, of an heroick Temper of Spirit, strengthened the
Hands of sober inclin'd People, and kept under the first loose
and extravagant Spirit," etc. The Governour, as we are told,
marry'd Mrs. Elizabeth Blake,[3] his Daughter; and by this
Alliance, the Strength of their Party was so encreas'd, that
we hear little of the other till Mr. Colliton's government.

There being some Complaints against Mr. Matthews, and the
other Commissioners for deciding Causes between the English
and the Indians, they were discharg'd and the Commission
abrogated. The Lords Proprietaries order'd the Indians 400
Miles from Charles Town, to be taken into their protection.

---

[1] On March 28, 1683, the Grand Council directed the surveyor-general to
lay out 1000 acres to Benjamin Blake "being soe much purchased by him from
the right hono[ble]: the pallatine and the rest of the Lords and absolute Proprieto[rs]:
of this province a conveyance under their hands and Seales bearing date th sixth
day of June Anno Dni 1682."

[2] See p. 295, *supra*.

[3] Oldmixon was confused in this matter, as in others. Elizabeth, daughter
of Benjamin Blake, married William Dry (p. 330, note 1). Governor Morton's
will shows that his wife's name was Elinor. It also contains a mention of a
brother-in-law Edward Bowell. Being an old man himself he was necessarily
much older than any child of Benjamin Blake. It is possible that Elinor was
a second wife whom he married late in life and that she was Benjamin Blake's
daughter and that Bowell was brother-in-law by another connection, but it is
more likely that Oldmixon's confusion was due to the fact that the first wife of
Benjamin Blake's son Joseph was Deborah, daughter of Governor Morton. In
his will, made in 1685, Governor Morton mentions his daughter Deborah Blake.

The County of Berkley, between Stono and Sewee, was
now laid out; and soon after Craven County, on the North
of Berkley; and Colliton County, on the South: All which
Counties were divided into Squares of 12000 Acres, for the
several Shares of the Proprietaries, Landgraves and Cassiques.

Mr. Moreton, at his entering upon his Office, call'd a Parliament, which met in Form, and pass'd several Acts; as,
"For raising 500*l*. for defraying the Publick Charge of the
Province; for regulating the Surveyor General's Fees; for
raising the Value of Foreign Coin; for Trial of small and
mean Causes under 40*s*. for Damages of protested Bills of
Exchange; for ascertaining Publick Officers Fees; to suspend Prosecution for Foreign Debts; to inhibit the trading
with Servants or Slaves; for laying out, and making good
High-ways; for preventing the taking away Boats and Canoos;
for marking of all sorts of Cattle; to prevent unlicens'd Tav-
erns and Punch-houses, and ascertaining the Rates and Prices
of Wine, and other Liquors; to prevent Runaways." All
which Acts were sign'd by Joseph Moreton, Esq; Governour,
John Godfrey, Esq; John Boon, Esq; James Moor, Esq;
Maurice Matthews, Esq; Andrew Percival, Esq; Arthur
Middleton, Esq; Counsellors and Deputies; and Mr. Joseph
Oldys, Clerk to the Parliament. At this time, Robert Gibs,
Esq; was Treasurer of the Colony; John Moor, Esq; Secretary; John Boon, Esq; Robert Daniel, Esq; Mr. Bernard
Schinkingh, Mr. Peter Hearn, and Cap. Florence O'Sullivan,
were appointed Commissioners for stating and passing the
Publick Accounts. Maurice Matthews, Esq; was also Sur-
veyor-General. The Trade of dealing in Indians continu'd,
and several of the Proprietors Deputies were concern'd in it:
Whether the Governour, Mr. Moreton, favour'd it or not, we
cannot undertake to determine. 'Tis certain, he did not long
enjoy his Office; For it appears by the Copies of the Original
Instructions sent by the Proprietaries to his Successor, that
in the following Year the Pallatine made Sir Richard Kyrle
Governour. He was a Gentleman of Ireland; and dying
within the Year, Joseph West, Esq; was again chosen Governour by the Council; and being a Man of great Interest,
the Proprietaries thought fit to confirm him in his Govern-

ment:[1]  But they turn'd out Maurice Matthews, Esq; James
Moor, Esq; and Arthur Middleton, Esq; from being Deputies
and Councillors, for disobeying their Orders, and sending
away Indians.  They also displac'd their Secretary John
Moor, Esq; and put Rob. Quarry, Esq; in his Place.

Thus we see the Latter has enjoy'd honourable Offices
many Years in the American Colonies; with the Interest of
which he must, by this means, be very well acquainted.

In Mr. West's second Government, the Right Honourable
the Lord Cardrosse remov'd to Carolina, and, with ten Scots
Families, settled at Port-Royal, esteem'd the most convenient
Place in this Province for Commerce, as being the best Port.
The Lord Cardrosse having been disgusted with the Govern-
ment of the Province, for some ill Usage he met with, return'd
to Scotland, and the Spaniards dislodg'd the Scots who had
seated themselves on that fine River.  This Lord was of the
House of Buchan, and in King William's Reign enjoy'd the
Title of Earl of Buchan.

Dissenters continuing to come hither from all Parts of
England, the Colony thriv'd and encreas'd in Numbers and
Riches.

James Colliton, Esq; of Barbadoes, Brother to Sir Peter
Colliton, Baronet, a Proprietary, being honour'd with the Title
of Landgrave, left the Island he liv'd in, and transported
himself and Family to Carolina, where he seated himself at
old Charles Town, on Cooper-river, built a handsome House
there; and being made Governour,[2] his Seat is to this day
call'd the Governour's House.  Had this Gentleman had as
much Honour and Capacity as his Brother Sir Peter, we
should have had no Occasion to Excuse our selves for keeping
to the Truth of History in his Behalf.  One of his Successors
writes in this Manner of his Government:[3]  "The Party Governour Moreton had gone a great way in suppressing, grew

[1] Upon the death of Kyrle the Council chose Robert Quary as governor.  He
was superseded by West, under appointment by the Proprietors, in the spring of
1685.

[2] Joseph West retired from the governorship toward the end of 1685 and was
succeeded by Joseph Morton, who was succeeded by Landgrave James Colleton
in 1686.

[3] "Mr. Archdale's *Description of Carolina.*"  (Note in margin of original.
See pp. 295, 296, *supra.*)

now so strong among the Common People, that they chose
Members to oppose whatsoever the Governour requested;
insomuch that they would not settle the Militia Act, tho
their own Security depended on it, and that it would be
Grounds of their further Strength." The reason of the Discontent the People lay under, were Disputes about the Tenure
of their Lands, and Payment of their Quit-rents, which were
not settled till Mr. Archdale's Government.

Mr. Colliton call'd a Parliament, A.D. 1687. This Assembly
not liking the Proprietaries *Fundamental Constitutions;* and
thinking they could supply the Deficiencies in them, appointed
a Committee to examine them: And these Gentlemen drew
up a new Form of Government, differing in many Articles
from the former; to which they gave the Title of Standing
Laws, and Temporary Laws. This Committee were James
Colliton, Esq; Governour, Paul Grimball, Esq; and William
Dunlop, Esq; Deputies; Bernard Schinking, Thomas Smith,
John Farr, and Joseph Blake, Esqs; Commoners. But neither
the Lords Proprietaries, nor the People of Carolina accepted
of them; and thus the *Fundamental Constitutions* keep their
Ground to this Day.

Mr. Colliton gave such Discontent in his Administration,
that he was banish'd the Province; a fate few Governours of
Colonies were ever so unhappy as to meet with.

Mr. Archdale tells us, Mr. Smith succeeded Mr. Colliton,
and that he succeeded Mr. Smith; but then the latter must
have been twice Governour: For we find several other Gentlemen, who had that Title and Office before the Year 1694.
when Mr. Archdale says, Governour Smith wrote over to the
Proprietaries, to advise them to send one of their Number to
Carolina. For Col. Robert Quarry was Governour about the
year 1690. After him, Mr. Southwell. And in the Year
1692. Col. Philip Ludwell held this Government. In which
'tis certain, he was succeeded by the above-mention'd Thomas
Smith, Esq; Landgrave of this Province.

We are not doubtful of any Error in this Order of the
Governours, except in Mr. Southwell's; our informations
having been uncertain as to him.[1]

---

[1] Sothell succeeded Colleton, Ludwell Sothell and Smith Ludwell. Oldmixon's guesswork was not accurate.

"Mr. Smith," says Mr. Archdale, "was a wise, sober, well-living Man; who grew so uneasy in the Government, by Reason he could not satisfy People in their Demands, that he wrote over, *Anno*. 1694 'It was impossible to settle the Country, except a Proprietary himself was sent thither, with full Power to hear their Grievances.'" The Proprietaries took Governour Smith's Letter into Consideration, and the Lord Ashley was pitch'd upon by all the Lords as a Person every way qualify'd for so good a Work; but he desir'd to be excus'd, on Account of his particular Affairs in England. Upon which Mr. Archdale, was chosen by the Proprietaries, to be sent over with large and ample Powers. Which having receiv'd, he embark'd and sail'd to Carolina. When he arriv'd, and enter'd upon the Government, in August, 1695. he found all Matters in great Confusion, and every Faction apply'd themselves to him, in hopes of Relief. In order to which he summon'd an Assembly, and made a kind Speech to them. The Parliament chose Jonathan Amary Esq; to be their Speaker; and having presented a dutiful Address to the Governour, proceeded to do Business. But the Divisions among them were so great, that had not Mr. Archdale exercis'd a great deal of Patience, neither his Power as Governour, nor his higher Title of Proprietary, could have brought that Assembly to any Temper; which he at last effected, and the Disorders of the Province were remedy'd.

The Parliament presented an Address of Thanks to the Governour, to be transmitted to the Proprietaries, and all things ended well. In his time the Tammasees,[1] an Indian Nation, who formerly liv'd under the Spanish Government, and now under the English, made an Incursion into the Territories of another Indian Nation, near Sancta Maria, not far from St. Augustino, took several Prisoners, and intended to sell them for Slaves at Barbadoes, or Jamaica, as had been usual among them. Mr. Archdale hearing of it, sent for the King of the Tammasees, and order'd him to bring those Indians to Charles Town, which he did. They were Papists; and the Kings of England and Spain being at that time Confederates, the Governour gave the King of the Tammasees Orders to carry them to St. Augustino, with a Letter to the Governour;

---

[1] Yemassees.

which may serve to give us an Idea of the Power of an Indian King, who receives Orders from a Governour of a small Province, as Carolina was then at least, whatever it is now.

The Spaniard who commanded in St. Augustino, return'd Mr. Archdale a Letter of Thanks; and not long after another Indian King was sent by the Spanish Governour, with a Letter of Complaint, of wrong done the Spanish Indians by those ally'd to the English.

The Spanish Indians were called Churchcates; of whom the Apalachicoloes, English Indians, had kill'd three. The Governour commanded that Nation, and all others depending on the English, to forbear molesting those within the Spanish Jurisdiction; which had so good an Effect, that when Mr. Robert Barrow, Mr. Edward Wardell, and other Englishmen, were afterward cast away to the Southward of Augustino, the barbarous Indians offer'd them no hurt; and when they arriv'd at that Town, the Governour supply'd them with all Necessaries.

Col. Bull, one of the Council, and a greater Trader with the Indians, engag'd that Nation which dwelt about Cape Fear, to submit to the English, who however were afraid to trust them; for a Vessel coming from New-England, being shipwrack'd on that Coast, the Passengers, to the Number of 52, despair'd of their Lives from those Barbarians, but resolv'd to defend themselves as well as they could: Accordingly they entrench'd in their little Camp. The Indians came down, and by Signs of Friendship invited them to come forth; which they were afraid to do. At last, when their Provisions were almost all spent, some of them ventur'd out, were kindly receiv'd, and furnish'd by the Indians with Necessaries. The King invited them to his Town, treated them; and 4 or 5 of them travelling to Charles Town, gave the Governour notice of their Misfortunes; which hearing, he sent a Ship to fetch the rest; and they arriv'd safely at the Capital of Carolina.

In Mr. Archdale's Time, two Indians quarrelling in their Drinking, one of them presently kill'd the other; whose Wife being by, immediately dismember'd the Murderer, to revenge her Husband's Death, cutting off his Privities with a Knife. The Governour happening to be near the Place where the Murder was committed, order'd the Criminal to be pursu'd.

He was taken in a Swamp about 16 Miles from the Town; to which he was sent under a Guard. The Nation to whom the slain Indian belong'd, hearing of his Death, their King came to Mr. Archdale, and desir'd Justice upon the Murderer. Some of whose Friends would have bought him off as usual; but nothing less than his Death would satisfy the injur'd Nation; and, according to the Custom of his Country, the Governour order'd him to be shot by the Kinsman of the Deceas'd. As he was leading to Execution, his King came to him, and bid him die like a Man, since he must die, adding, he had often forewarn'd him of Rum, the Liquor which he was drunk with when he kill'd the Man, and now he must loose his Life for not taking his Council.

When he came to the Tree, he desir'd not to be ty'd to it, but to stand loose, saying, I will not stir when he shoots me. So he was shot in the Head, and fell down dead.

This Piece of Justice hinder'd a War between the Nations to which these two Indians belong'd. The Indians inhabiting the Country about the River Pemlico, were almost all consum'd by a Pestilential Disease, while this Governour was in Carolina; and the Coranines, a bloody and barbarous People, were most of them cut off by a neighbouring Nation.

In his Time several Families remov'd from New-England, to settle at Carolina, and seated themselves on the River Sewee, in North Carolina. These are all the Events which happen'd during Mr. Archdale's Government, at least he has thought fit to communicate no more to the Publick; and as inconsiderable as they may appear to some Persons, who are us'd to turn over the Græcian and Roman Histories, if they will give themselves the Trouble to examine the Affairs of these two Empires, they will find them as trivial, in the beginning at least, if they can distinguish the History from the Fable.

We cannot expect much Business in the Infancy of a Colony; and yet Carolina is not so young, but Factions have been as rampant there, as if the People had been made wanton by many Ages of Prosperity.

Mr. Archdale, to use his own Phrase, Return'd for England, being not sent for Home. And Joseph Blake, Esq; Son of the before-mention'd Mr. Blake, being become a Proprie-

tary,[1] was look'd upon as the fittest Person to succeed him in
his Government; in which Office he behav'd himself to the
Satisfaction of the Country, which he govern'd with equal
Prudence and Moderation.

In his time, Major Daniel brought from England new
Constitutions, consisting of 41 Articles, wherein as ample
Provision was made for Liberty of Conscience, as in the
Fundamental Constitutions. These new Laws were call'd,
the last Fundamental Constitutions, and sign'd by John Earl
of Bath, Palatine; Anthony Lord Ashley, the Lord Craven,
the Lord Cartaret, the Earl of Bath, Sir John Colliton, William Thornburgh, merchant, Thomas Amy, and Wil. Thornburgh; but they were never confirm'd in Parliament at
Carolina.

Mr. Blake, tho he was himself a dissenter, finding there
was no settled Maintenance for the Church of England minister, procur'd an Act of Assembly (in which there were a
great Number of Dissenters) for the settling a very convenient
House with a Glebe, two Servants, and 150*l.* per Annum
upon the Minister of Charles Town for ever. 'Twas by his
Influence that Act past, and he gave his Assent to it; he, as
Governour, having a negative Voice to all Bills. His Lady
also was one of the greatest Benefactors towards the Ornaments of the Church. And this Friendship deserv'd a more
grateful Return than they met with from those who succeeded in the Government.

Mr. Blake dying about the Year 1700. after he had been
Governour 4 or 5 Years, the Proprietaries Deputies met,
according to their Instructions in such Cases, and proceeded
to the Election of a new Governour; which Post is generally
conferr'd on the eldest Landgrave, if there 's no Objection
to him, and no Person sent from England with that Character.

Joseph Moreton Esq; being the eldest Landgrave,[2] was
elected Governour by the Deputies: but Capt. James Moor,

[1] Blake did not become a Proprietor for two years after becoming governor.
Landgrave Thomas Smith, who had died in 1694, had willed him his patent as
landgrave, and, being in the Council, he was, as a landgrave, chosen governor
by the Council. The Proprietors also issued him a patent as landgrave.

[2] Edmund Bellinger was the oldest landgrave and was ballotted for first,
but received but one vote out of five members of the Council voting, and the
same objection was raised to him that was made against Morton.

one of these Deputies, knowing the Party he had among them, objected against Mr. Moreton, as if he had made a Breach of the Trust repos'd in him by the true and absolute Lords and Proprietaries, by accepting of a Commission from King William, to be Judge of the Admiralty, when he had at the same time a Commission from the Lords Proprietaries for the same Office.

Tho this Objection was answer'd by Mr. Moreton's Friends;[1] "That it did not appear by the Charter, the Proprietaries can empower any one to try Persons for Facts committed out of their Dominions, which is necessary for such a Judge;" and the Proprietaries could not grant it; yet such was Mr. Moor's Interest, that on this his Objection Mr. Moreton was set aside, and his Opponent Mr. Moor chosen Governour. Mr. Moreton inform'd and complain'd to the Proprietaries, but was never redrest.

From this Election I date the Rise of all the Misfortunes that have since befallen this Colony, and that have given the Government of England so much Trouble.

The Earl of Bath was dead, and his Son, John Lord Granville, lately advanc'd to the House of Peers, was Palatine. All the World knew how zealous that Gentleman had been for promoting a Bill against Occasional Conformists in England, and that he shew'd his Aversion to Dissenters even in the Court of Stannaries in the West,[2] while he was Warden. The Bitterness of his Spirit appear'd in the Speeches he made to the Representatives of that Court; and was such, that he was not long employ'd by a Government, which is founded on Principles of Justice and Moderation; which has in all things promoted Union, and which has united the Hearts of all the Subjects of the British Empire more than all the Princes could do since the Conquest, and many Ages before it.

In an ill time therefore did this Palatine countenance the Divisions in Carolina, by encouraging this and the succeeding Governour in their vain Endeavours, to establish that for a Law there, which had been rejected with such Marks of Abhorrence in England by our Illustrious Representatives.

[1] Landgrave Morton alone offered a protest against the validity of the objection offered to him by Deputies Daniell and Moore.

[2] The court having jurisdiction over the region of tin mines in Cornwall.

Mr. Moor was easily confirm'd in his new Dignity by the Palatine; and as he is said to have sought after it, to enrich himself, so he made use of it to that end, he being in mean Circumstances, if the Representation of the principal Inhabitants of the Colony does not deceive us.

Let us give the Reader the proper Words, that we may not be accus'd of Partiality, which we detest in all things that hurt the Truth. But we know very well, that Faction will often accuse Fact of Partiality; and an Historian may write Things true, and yet by writing the Truth only of one Side, and concealing what is to its Disadvantage, it may give a plausible Appearance to a bad Cause; wherefore we solemnly declare, that after a full Enquiry we have not been able to learn any thing that could excuse the Disorders we are about to relate, and vindicate the Administration in Carolina, while the Lord Granville was Palatine. Whether that Lord or his Governours ought to be blam'd most, let the World judge.

Mr. Moor, says the author of the above-mention'd Representation,[1] having thus boldly gotten the Government, resolv'd to make the best use of his Authority, and finding himself too poor, with the Countenance of his Office, to make any considerable Profit of the Indian Trade, he laid the Design of getting it wholly into his Power. He to that end procur'd a Bill to be brought into the Assembly, then sitting, for regulating the Indian Trade: which Bill was so drawn, that had it past, he would have engross'd all that beneficial Commerce. But Mr. Robert Stephens and Mr. Nicholas Trott (who had not then forsaken the Country Interest) and some others, so plainly shew'd the ill Aim of that Act, that 'twas thrown out of the Assembly: Which Mr. Moor dissolv'd, perceiving they would not answer his Ends.

We do not think our selves oblig'd to keep to the Words of this Representation, which are too rough in some Places; but we keep religiously to the Sense; and having refer'd the Reader in the Margint to our Authority, he cannot suppose we endeavour to impose on him.

The Governour call'd a new Assembly about the latter end of the Year 1701. At the choosing of which, tho the Right of Electing be in the Freeholders only, he so influenc'd

[1] *"Case of Diss. in Car.*, p. 29, 30." (Note in original.)

the Sheriff, that Strangers, Servants, Aliens; nay, Malatoes and Negroes were poll'd, and return'd.

Such as at the Place of Election oppos'd these Practices, were abus'd, and some assaulted by Mr. Moor's Favourites. By this means having got several into the Assembly, Men of no Sense and Credit, who would vote as he wou'd have them; he there kept them from being thrown out, on the Petition of those who were unjustly excluded.

Colliton County sent a Representation against him to the Palatine, containing in Substance the same, as that we have spoken of before; therefore we cannot suspect the Truth of it.

When the Governour was afraid any of the Members [1] he was sure was in his Interest would be turn'd out, on Petitions,[2] he prorogu'd the Assembly: And when at last they were suffer'd to sit, the Inquiry into the Sheriff of Berkley County's Return was obstructed, by setting on foot an ill contriv'd Design of raising Forces to attack St. Augustino, a Fort belonging to the Spaniards, to the Southward of Carolina. If any Member of the Assembly undertook to speak against it, and to shew how unable the Province was at that time to undertake such an Expedition, he was presently look'd upon by him, and his Adherents, as an Enemy and Traitor to his Country;[3] and accordingly revil'd and affronted; tho the true Design of the Expedition, as the Representation from Colliton County tells us, was no other than catching and making Slaves of Indians for private Advantage.  He would have had this Military Enterprize been undertaken before the War with Spain was proclaim'd; but the Assembly carry'd that in the Negative.

Before we treat of this Expedition, we must observe what past further in the Assembly.  Mr. John Ash, one of the Members, propos'd to have the last Fundamental Constitu-

---

[1] "*Ibid.*, p. 34."  (Note in original.)

[2] There was no reason for Moore's party to fear investigation; there was no prospect of any of their number being turned out, and the journal shows that Moore prorogued the House from time to time because no quorum could be obtained because the Dissenters absented themselves to prevent Moore's measures from being adopted, and perhaps because they realized that an investigation of their charges of fraud would show that there had been little, or no, fraud.

[3] "P. 35."  (Note in original.)

tions, which Mr. Daniel brought over, confirm'd; but he was oppos'd by Mr. Trott and Mr. How, the Governour's Creatures.[1]

This Mr. Trott had himself been Governour of Providence,[2] and behav'd himself so arbitrarily, that he was complain'd of to King William some Years before. Trott and How expos'd the Constitutions as ridiculous; and the Country was thus left in an unsettled Condition.

There's one Article in this Representation which is very extraordinary: That the said late Governour Moor did grant Commissions, to Anthony Dodsworth, Robert Mackoone and others,[3] to set upon, assault, kill, destroy, and take as many Indians as they possibly could; the Profit and Produce of which Indian Slaves were turn'd to his private Use. Whereas such Undertakings, unjust and barbarous in themselves, will in all Probability draw upon us an Indian War.

We have said enough to give an Idea of the Condition the People of Carolina were in under such a Government, and have taken it all from Memorials presented by their Agents to the Lords Proprietaries. The next thing that comes in our way is the War of Augustino.

Two Thousand Pounds were rais'd by an Act of the Assembly, to defray the Charge of this Expedition. The Governour prest as many Merchant Ships as were necessary to transport the Troops he intended to embark; who were order'd to rendezvous at Port Royal.

The Number of Men which were listed for this Enterprize were 1200, 600 English, and 600 Indians. Col. Moor took the Command on himself, as General of all the Forces that should be rais'd within the Limits of his Government.

Col. Rob. Daniel, a very brave Man, commanded a Party who were to go up the River in Periaga's,[4] and come upon Augustino on the Land side, while the Governour sail'd

---

[1] "*Ibid.*" (Note in original.)

[2] New Providence or Nassau in the Bahamas. But the Nicholas Trott who had been governor of that island was not the Nicholas Trott who now held high position in South Carolina. Nicholas Trott of London, the son-in-law of Thomas Amy (see p. 307, note 2 *supra*), was the man who had been governor of New Providence.

[3] "*Coll. County Repr.*, Article 5." (Note in original.)

[4] Periaguas.

thither and attack'd it by Sea. They both set out in August, 1702. Col. Daniel in his Way took St. John's, a small Spanish Settlement; as also St. Mary's, another little Village, belonging to the Spaniards. After which he proceeded to Augustino, came before the Town, enter'd and took it; Col. Moor not being yet arriv'd with the Fleet.

The Inhabitants having notice of the Approach of the English had pack'd up their best Effects, and retir'd with them into the Castle, which was surrounded by a very deep and broad Moat.

They had laid up Provisions there for 4 Months, and resolv'd to defend themselves to the last Extremity. However Col. Daniel found a considerable Booty in the Town. The next Day the Governour arriv'd, and a Council of War was immediately call'd, in which 'twas resolv'd to land.

Accordingly the Governour came ashore, and his Troops following him, they entrench'd, posted their Guards in the Church, and block'd up the Castle. The English held the Possession of the Town a whole Month, but finding they could do nothing for want of Mortars and Bombs, they dispatch'd away a Sloop for Jamaica; but the Commander of the Sloop, instead of going thither, came to Carolina, out of Fear or Treachery. Finding others offer'd to go in his stead, he proceeded in the Voyage himself, after he had lain some time at Charles-Town.

The Governour all this while lay before the Castle of Augustino, in Expectation of the Return of the Sloop: Which hearing nothing of, he sent Col. Daniel, who was the Life of the Action, to Jamaica, on the same Errand.

This Gentleman being hearty in the Design, procur'd a Supply of Bombs, and return'd towards Augustino. But in the mean time two Ships appear'd in the Offing, which being taken to be two very large Men of War, the Governour thought fit to raise the Siege, and abandon his Ships, with a great Quantity of Stores, Ammunition, and Provision, to the Enemy. Upon which the two Men of War enter'd the Port of Augustino, and took the Governour's Ships. Some say he burnt them himself. Certain it is, they were lost to the English, and that he return'd to Charles-Town over Land, 300 Miles from Augustino. The two Men of War that were thought to be so large, prov'd to be two small Frigats, one of 22, and the other of 16 Guns.

When Col. Daniel came back to Augustino, he was chas'd, but got away; and Col. Moor retreated with no great Honour homewards. The Periagas lay at St. John's, whether the Governour retir'd, and so to Charles Town, having lost but two Men in the whole Expedition. Arratommakaw, King of the Yanioseaves, who commanded the Indians, retreated to the Periagas with the rest, and there slept upon his Oars, with a great deal of Bravery and Unconcern. The Governour's Soldiers taking a false Alarm, and thinking the Spaniards were coming, did not like this slow Pace of the Indian King in his Flight; and to quicken him in it, bad him make more Haste: But he reply'd, No; tho your Governour leaves you, I will not stir till I have seen all my Men before me.

The First Representation, call'd also, *The present State of Affairs in Carolina*,[1] reflects a little too bitterly on Col. Moor on this Head; and one would suspect the Truth of what it contains, if it was not confirm'd by the second. We are told there, They sent Plunder to Jamaica by their trusty Officers, under colour of seeking Supplies, and sending for Bombs and Mortars. Which is a malicious Turn given by Col. Moor's Enemies to Col. Daniel's going to Jamaica, who by the Dispatch he made there shew'd he went really for Mortars; and had the Governour staid till he had return'd, the Castle of Augustino had perhaps now been in English Hands; for the Spaniards had not above 200 Men aboard the two Frigats.[2] This Expedition, as unfortunate as it was in it self, was much more so in the Consequence of it; for it brought a Debt of 6000*l.* on the Province. The Assembly had been under a Prorogation during the Governour's Absence, and when he return'd they met. The first thing they went upon, was to raise Money to pay off the Debt above-mention'd, and then they took into Consideration the Danger of the Country, as it lay expos'd to the Southward. But while these Bills

[1] "*Coll. County Repr.*, p. 30." (Note in original.)

[2] And just as Governor Moore was misrepresented about the plunder he sent to Jamaica by Daniell just so was he misrepresented in other respects. The failure of his expedition was due to cowardice or traitorousness on the part of some of his officers, as is even here partially shown by Oldmixon.

were passing, another for the better regulating Elections,
pass'd the Lower House twice, and was sent up to the Governour and Council, by whom 't was rejected without so much
as a Conference.   Upon which several of the Members, jealous
of their Privileges, and being so order'd by those that sent
them, enter'd their Protestation, and left the House;[1] but
return'd the next Day, offering to sit longer if the rest of the
Assembly would join with them, in asserting their Right.   The
Whole Assembly consists of but 30 Members, and 15 of them
protested against the irregular Proceedings of the Governour.
Instead of tempering Matters, when they return'd to the
House, they were abus'd and treated with the most scandalous
Reflections, unbecoming an Assembly that represented a
whole Province.   And as they were insulted within doors,
they were assaulted without; for a Day or two after Lieut.
Col. George Dearsby drew his Sword upon Thomas Smith,
Esq; a Landgrave, and once Governour of the Colony,[2]
threatning his Life.   John Ash, Esq; a Member of the
Assembly, was not only abus'd in the Streets by a Company
of Drunken Fellows, but forc'd aboard a Ship belonging to
Cap. Rhett, and threatned to be hang'd, or sent to Jamaica,
or left on some Desart-Island.   This Mr. Ash is the Man who
was employ'd as Agent for the People of Carolina, to represent their Grievances in the first Memorial, call'd, *The Present
State of Affairs in Carolina*; and the Persons who thus barbarously treated him, were George Dearsby, Nicholas Nary,
Thomas Dalton, and others, whom, says the Representation
of Colliton County, Article xi. the Governour had treated
immediately before the Riot began, and us'd such Expressions
to them, as gave them, next their Drink, the greatest Encouragements for what they acted; telling them,[3] The Protesting
Members would bring the People on their Heads for neglecting
to pay the Country's Debts.   After the Riot began, of Part
of which he was an Eye-Witness, having first drunk with some
of them, he withdrew himself out of the way.   This Riot con-

---

[1] "See the *Representation of the Members of Colliton County*." (Note in
original.)

[2] This Landgrave Thomas Smith (1664–1738) was the son of the former
governor, who died in 1694.

[3] "P. 36." (Note in original.)

tinu'd 4 or 5 Days; and Edmund Bellinger, Esq; a Landgrave, and Justice of Peace, attempting to suppress it, was call'd opprobrious Names by the Rioters, and Rhett can'd him for a considerable time. The Rioters assaulted Mr. Joseph Boon, a Merchant, deputed by Colliton County, to present the above-mention'd Second Representation to the Palatine and Lords Proprietaries, and put him in Danger and Fear of his Life, without any Provocation. The same they did by Mr. James Byres; who with the rest complain'd to the Governour; and receiving no Satisfaction, they ask'd him, whether he did not look on himself, as Governour, oblig'd to keep the Peace of the Province: The Governour reply'd, *That's a Question I am not oblig'd to answer.* He told them, 'twas a Justice of Peace's Business.

The Rioters went one Night to the house of one John Smith, a Butcher in Charles-Town, and forcing open the Door, threw down a Woman big with Child, and otherwise misusing her; she brought forth a dead Child, with the Back and Skull broken. These Instances are enough to shew any Man the Temper of this Governour and his Party; who were the same that stickled so much for the unhappy Bill we must speak of in the Sequel of this History. What follow'd upon this Riot, is told us in a late Tract, which I shall make use of in the Author's own Words,

As this Riot was rais'd encourag'd and countenanc'd by the said Governour and Council;[1] And as no Assistance could be obtain'd to quell it, so all Methods to enquire into, and punish it, have been render'd ineffectual, and the Course of Justice intirely stop'd. For Sir Nathaniel Johnson was made Governour in the Room of the said Moor. The said Governour Moor was presently made Attorney General; and Mr. Trott, another of the chief Abettors of the Riot, the Chief Justice of the Common Pleas; who in this Province is sole Judge. Sir Nathaniel Johnson was General of the Leward Islands, in the Reign of the late King James; but he quitted his Government upon the Revolution, and retir'd to Carolina, where he liv'd privately till the Death of the late King James. Upon which he first took the Oaths to the Government; and some time after was made Governour of the Province. And he has since his being Governour appointed such Sheriffs, as pre-

[1] "*Case of Dis. in Car.*, 19." (Note in original.)

vent all Prosecutions of this Riot at their Assizes or Quarter Sessions (which are the only Courts of Justice in this Province) where
Crimes of this Nature can be try'd; and where the said Mr. Trott
is sole Judge, by returning such Jurors as were known Abettors of
the said Riot: So that there is a total Failure of Justice, and nothing
but Corruption in the whole Frame and Administration of Government.

Colliton-County Representation tells us particularly, that
Mr. Bellinger did what in him lay to have the said Riot inquir'd into.  He gave in the Record of it to the Bench; and
some of the Grand Jury urg'd to have it presented, but to
no purpose.  The first Representation informs us, that the
Grand Jury presented it to the Court as a great Grievance,
that the Riot was not look'd into, and the Rioters prosecuted;
yet no Justice against them could be obtain'd; the Judge
giving for Answer, 'Twas before the Council, his superiors:
The present Governour, That it was an Action done before
his coming to the Government; that he thought the time of
Prosecution laps'd, but would take care the like should be no
more.

This Answer had in the last part of it a Face of Moderation;
and such an Air was necessary, because an Assembly was
about being elected.  "The Conspirators," as my Author
terms them,[1] "saw that a new Parliament might set all things
to rights again, and therefore when the time of a new Election
came, which, according to their Constitution, is once in two
Years; they resolv'd to procure a Commons House of Assembly of the same Complexion with the former, and by more
illegal Practices.  If those they had us'd in the former Elections would not do their Business, their Designs took Effect;
and such a Commons House of Assembly was return'd, as
fully answer'd their Expectations."

The first Representation brought over by Mr. Ash, informs us,  That at the Election for Berkley and Craven
County, the Violence in Mr. Moor's Time, and all other illegal
Practices, were with more Violence repeated, and openly
avow'd by the present Governour, and his Friends.

The second Representation adds, Jews, Strangers, Sailors,
Servants, Negroes, and almost every Frenchman in Craven

[1] "*Ib.*, p. 20."  (Note in original.)

and Berkley Counties, came down to elect, and their Votes were taken, and the Persons by them voted for, were return'd by the Sheriffs.

The Assembly meeting, chose Job How, Esq; to be their Speaker, and this was that Parliament, who, to oppress the Protestant Dissenters, brought in a Bill contrary to the first and last Fundamental Constitutions, to the true Interest of the Colony, and the right of every Freeholder there. 'Twas entitl'd, An act for the more effectual Preservation of the Government, by requiring all Persons that shall hereafter be chosen Members of the Commons House of Assembly, and sit in the same, to, etc., and to conform to the religious Worship in this Province, according to the Church of England, and to receive the Sacrament of the Lord's Supper according to the Rights and Usage of the said Church.

Every Dissenter that was turn'd out of the House, by virtue of this Act, made room for the most bigotted of the Faction to get in; for it provided, that the Person who had the most Votes next to such Dissenter, should be admitted in his place; and those that oppos'd the Dissenters being generally, according to the before-mention'd Author, Men of violent and persecuting Principles, the Faction secur'd the Power in their own Hands.

There were 12 Members for this Bill, and 11 against it, in the Lower House; and in the Upper, Joseph Moreton, Esq; a Landgrave, and one of the Proprietary's Deputies was deny'd the Liberty of entering his Protest against it. The Bill pass'd the 6th of May, A. D. 1704. and was sign'd by Sir Nathaniel Johnson, Col. Thomas Broughton, Col. James Moor, Robert Gibbs, Esq; Henry Noble, Esq; Nicholas Trott, Esq;

The Governour and Proprietaries Deputies, upon passing this Act, allarm'd all the Dissenters, who according to the Orthodox Minister of Charles Town, the Reverend Mr. Marston's Letter to the Reverend Dr. Stanhope,[1] are the soberest, most numerous, and richest People of this Province; and this Assembly was compos'd of many Men of very loose and corrupt Morals.

We have shewn in the Beginning of the History of Carolina, that by the Fundamentals of the Province, the Dis-

[1] "*Case of Diss.*, part 2, p. 57." (Note in original.)

senters could not be justly excluded from any Rights of the
Members of it; we have shewn here what a sort of Convention,
and by what Government countenanc'd, this Assembly was;
and there's no need of exaggerating Matters, to make the
thing look black; wherefore we shall proceed in our History.

It cannot be imagin'd that a People who had been us'd
so ill, wou'd sit still, and tamely bear such barbarous Usage:
especially considering those that were concern'd in the Riot
were some of the worst, and those that suffer'd by it, some
of the best Men in the Province.

Col. Joseph Moreton, and Edmund Bellinger, Esq; Land-
graves, and Deputies of the Lords Proprietaries, all the other
Members of Colliton County, and several of the greatest
Worth and Reputation in Berkley County, prevail'd with
Mr. Joseph Ash to come for England, to represent the miser-
able State of the Province to the Proprietaries.

The Faction being apprehensive of their Danger in such
a Proceeding, did their utmost to prevent Mr. Ash's Voyage;
and 'twas not without the greatest Difficulty that he got
away from Carolina to Virginia, where his Powers and Instructions were convey'd to him, as Agent for the Gentlemen and
Inhabitants above-nam'd.

Coming to England, he apply'd himself to the Lord Granville, then Proprietary of the Province: But finding he was
entirely in the Interests of the prevailing Party in Carolina,
he despair'd of seeing the Grievances he came to complain of,
redress'd: He therefore drew up the first Representation, often
cited in this Treatise, printed a Sheet of it, and intended to go
through with it; but dy'd before he could finish it; and his
Papers, after his Death, were betray'd into his Enemies Hands.

How this Agency was lik'd in Carolina, we may suppose;
and that the Author of *The Case of the Dissenters in Carolina*,
does not impose upon us, in telling us, The Governour and
his Agents prosecuted and insulted several of the Inhabitants,
and particularly Landgrave Smith, on the account of some
private Letters which they sent to the said Ash, while he was
in Virginia and England, and which were found among the
Papers betray'd to the Governour's Agents.

Mr. Ash may probably represent Things with too much
Partiality, especially if what Mr. Archdale says of him be

true;[1] "Their first Agent seem'd not a Person suitably qualifiy'd to represent their State here, not that he wanted Wit, but Temper."

What Share the Governour had in this Business, appears also in the same Tract.[2] "Sir Nathaniel Johnson by a Chymical Wit, Zeal, and Art, transmuted or turn'd this Civil Difference into a religious Controversy; and so setting up a Standard for those called High Church, ventur'd at all to exclude all the Dissenters out of the Assembly, as being those principally that were for a strict Examination into the Grounds and Causes of the Miscarriage of the Augustino Expedition."

The Party did not stop here; for on the 4th of November an Act past, and was sign'd by the Governour, and the Deputies above-nam'd; entitl'd, "An Act for establishing Religious Worship in this Province, according to the Church of England; and for the erecting of Churches for the Publick Worship of God, and also for the Maintenance of Ministers, and the building convenient Houses for them." [3]

Which Act Mr. Archdale acquaints us, "notwithstanding its splendid Gloss, savour'd of a persecuting Spirit, and of a haughty Dominion over the Clergy itself; for they set up a High Commission Court, giving them Power to place and displace Ministers, and act much in the Nature of the High Commission Court erected by King James II. in England." These Commissioners were Sir Nathaniel Johnson, Thomas Broughton, Esq; Col. James Moor, Nicholas Trott, Esq; Col. Robert Gibbes, Job How, Esq; Ralph Izard, Esq; Col. James Risbee, Col. George Logan, Lieut. Colonel William Rhett, William Smith, Esq; Mr. John Stroude, Mr. Thomas Hubbard, Richard Beresford, Esq; Mr. Robert Seabrook, Mr. Hugh Hicks,[4] John Ashby, Esq; Capt. John Godfrey, James Serurier, alias Smith, Esq; and Mr. Thomas Barton.

It will not be improper to give a Character of this James Serurier, who has been mightily employ'd by the present Government in Carolina; and we cannot do it better, than in using the same Words Mrs. Blake, Mother of the Proprietary Joseph Blake, Esq; writes to the Lords Proprietaries.[5]

---

[1] "*Description of Carolina*, p. 25." (Note in original.)
[2] "P. 23." (Note in original.)     [3] "P. 24." (Note in original.)
[4] Hugh Hext.     [5] See p. 250, *supra*.

Towards the Satisfaction of the Augustino Debt, an Act was contriv'd, for forcing the Currency of Bills of Credit to the Value of 6000*l*. These Bills were declar'd current in all Payments, and the Refuser of them sueable in double the Value of the Sum refus'd; whereby the boldest Stroke has been given to the Property of the Settlers in this Province, that ever was known in any Country not govern'd by Arbitrary Power. And the bad Consequences of this forc'd Currency, in Relation to trade with Strangers, are so great, that they can scarcely be exprest. But there has nothing of this been weigh'd by your Lordship's Deputies here, or by the pack'd Members of our Commons House of Assembly. Besides all this, the people are not satisfy'd how many Bills are truly sent abroad; and the great Concern, Mr. James Smith, alias Serurier (who cheated the Scots Company of a considerable Sum of Money, and with his Keeper made his Escape from London hither) had in this Contrivance, gives a Jealousy of indirect practices.

By this the Reader understands what Inconveniences the Augustino Expedition brought upon the Colony, and what sort of Persons were Promoters of this Occasional Bill in America. But to shew that this Faction in the Assembly had nothing less in their View, than the real Advancement of Religion, and the Church of England;[1] the Reverend Mr. Edward Marston, minister of that Church in Charles Town, was censur'd by them, for three Passages of a Sermon preach'd there by him; two of which Passages were not in the said Sermon; and that which was amounted to no more, than that the Clergy had a Divine Right to a Maintenance. They depriv'd him of his Salary settl'd on him by Act of Parliament, and of 50*l*. besides due to him by an Act of Assembly: Tho the chief Reason was his having visited Mr. Landgrave Smith, when he was in Custody of a Messenger, being committed by the Commons House, and living Friendly with the Dissenters.

Of this Assembly the same Reverend Divine says, "They made some very odd and unjustifiable Laws, which have occasion'd great Feuds and Animosities here."[2] And in his Representation to the Lords Proprietaries; "Most of the late Members of Assembly have been constant Absenters from

[1] "*Case of Diss. Car.*, p. 23." (Note in original.)
[2] "See his letter to Dr. Stanhope, Part 2, p. 57." (Note in margin of original, with subsequent references to pp. 62, 63, 67, 60, 58.)

the Holy Sacrament: So 'tis no Wonder they have inserted an absurd Oath in a late Act, etc. I cannot think it will be much for the Credit and Service of the Church of England here, that such Provisions should be made, for admitting the most loose and profligate Persons to sit and vote in the making of our Laws, who will but take the Oath appointed by the late Act." And of the High Commissioners 'tis said, "Eleven of the Twenty were never known to receive the Sacrament of the Lord's Supper."

And that this furious Faction were no Friends to the Church of England is plain, by their Design to wrest the Ecclesiastical Jurisdiction out of the Hands of the Right Reverend Father in God, Henry Lord Bishop of London.[1] Mr. Marston being threaten'd in Col. Risbee's House, "That at the next Sessions of Assembly he should see the Bishop of London's Jurisdiction abolish'd there." And of this Carolina Parliament he adds further, "Our Lower House of Assembly imprison by a Vote of the House, *sine die*, and bid Defiance to the *Habeas Corpus* Act, tho made in Force there by an Act of Assembly." The Governour was very "cholerick with the Minister, because he had made Landgrave Smith a Visit, at the House of the Messenger; and a Bully lash'd him causelesly with his Whip, and tore his Gown from his Back. His Creatures also in the Assembly were the Occasion of his Sufferings."

If I am accus'd of being partial in representing this Matter, I answer, that besides the Memorials publish'd by the Agent of Carolina, Mr. Archdale's Tract and others, I have diligently inquir'd into the Truth of the Fact, and have not been able to learn the least hint that makes against it, or vindicates the Party that is complain'd of, and were powerfully protected by the Lord Granville; notwithstanding it was made out to him, that the Assembly in passing the Occasional Bill in Carolina,[2] were guilty of the most notorious ill Practices, and were Men of corrupt Principles and Manners. That Bill was brought into the House the 4th of May, and carry'd so precipitately, that it past the 6th, four Days before the time to which they were prorogu'd. There never were above 23 Members present, from the 26th of April to the 6th of May.

[1] Bishop Henry Compton.        [2] "Part I., p. 38." (Note in original.)

There was but one more for it than against it; and of the latter many were Members of the Church of England.

There's one thing very remarkable in the Act, which is the Stile: "Be it enacted, by his Excellency John Lord Granville, and the rest of the true and absolute Lords and Proprietors of Carolina," etc. A Stile never assum'd by them till very lately.[1] From whence we may observe how pleas'd that Faction is every where with the Despotick and Absolute Power, insomuch as to usurp the Name, when they cannot obtain any thing more. *The Case of the Dissenters in Carolina*, is so full of Irregularities in the Course of this Affair, that we must refer the Reader to it. We have taken the most material, and now are to see what was done in England relating to this Matter.

The principal Merchants in London trading to Carolina, drew up a Petition to the Lord Granville against passing this Act, or to order its Repeal. Which Petition they lodg'd with Mr. Boone, the Agent of Carolina, who solicited the Palatine seven Weeks before he could prevail to have a Board of Proprietaries call'd.

Mr. Archdale, one of the Proprietaries, oppos'd the ratifying of the Bill against the Dissenters at the Board, and with such solid Reasons, that 'tis amazing to find the Palatine make this short Answer to all of 'em: "Sir, you are of one Opinion, and I am of another; and our Lives may not be long enough to end the Controversy: I am for this Bill, and this is the Party that I will head and countenance."

What other Tone could he have talk'd in had he been Sultan of Carolina? Mr. Boon pray'd he might be heard by Council. The Palatine reply'd, "What Business has Council here? It is a prudential Act in me; and I will do as I see fit. I see no harm at all in this Bill, and am resolv'd to pass it." He should have added, *Car tel est notre Plaisir*.[2]

As all Methods to procure Justice from this Board were ineffectual, in the Case of the Dissenters, the same were

---

[1] The earliest original acts of the General Assembly of South Carolina now in possession of the state of South Carolina were enacted in 1690 (Sothell's administration) and they are worded in exactly that "stile," save that "William Earl of Craven Palatine" appears instead of "John Lord Granville."

[2] The customary subscription of the edicts of the kings of France.

they in Mr. Marston's Case, and the Abuses he met with from the Party, the Lord Granville was resolv'd to head and countenance. And what that Party was in England, and how they have seen their unreasonable Attempts baffl'd and exploded, is too well known, to need any Remembrance here.

The Bill which occasion'd all the Complaints in Carolina, having past thus illegally and arbitrarily, the Dissenters in this Province *being notoriously known to be above two thirds of the People*,[1] and the richest and soberest among them, according to Mr. Marston's Evidence, 'twas not likely that they would suffer themselves to be insulted and persecuted without seeking Redress. The very Assembly who past the Bill, about half a year afterwards past another to repeal it, when the House was full; but it was lost in the Upper House; and the Governour, in great indignation, dissolv'd the Commons House, by the Name of the Unsteady Assembly.[2] The Society for propagating the Gospel in America and elsewhere, meeting in St. Paul's Church, taking the Act for the Establishing Religious Worship, etc., into Consideration, resolv'd not to send or support any Missionaries in that Province, till the said Act, or the Clause relating to the Lay Commissionaries, was annul'd.

There being no Hopes of any Redress of the Grievances the Inhabitants of this Colony suffer'd in Carolina, nor from the Lords Proprietaries in England, they resolv'd to bring the Matter before the House of Lords in England, not doubting but to have entire Justice done them by that august Assembly; where the Language of their Palatine was never heard from the Throne, at least in this Reign, or the last; both which are the Glory of the British Annals.

Mr. Boon was not only empower'd by the principal inhabitants of Carolina to act as their Agent, but he was assisted in his Agency by several eminent Merchants of London, who sign'd the Petition to the House of Lords; as Mr. Micaiah Perry, Mr. Joseph Paice, Mr. Peter Renew, Mr. Christopher Fowler, and others.

The Effect of which was, after a full hearing of the Cause at the Lord's Bar, that most Honourable House, who have

[1] "P. 12." (Note in original.)        [2] "P. 41." (Note in original.)

done such great Things for the Liberties of England, voted an Address to the Queen, in behalf of the Province of Carolina: But the Reader cannot be better satisfy'd, than to have it in their own Words; by which the State of the Case will be best seen.[1]

The House having fully and maturely weigh'd the Nature of these two Acts, found themselves oblig'd in Duty to Your Majesty, and in Justice to your Subjects in Carolina (who by the Express Words of the Charter of Your Royal Uncle King Charles II. granted to the Proprietors, are declared to be the Liege People of the Crown of England, and to have Right to all the Liberties, Franchises, and Privileges of Englishmen, as if they were born within this Kingdom: And who by the Words of the same Charter, are to be subject to no Laws, but such as are consonant to Reason, and as near as may be to the Laws and Customs of England) to come to the following Resolutions.

First, That it is the Opinion of this House, that the Act of the Assembly of Carolina, lately pass'd there, and since sign'd and seal'd by John Lord Granville, Palatine, for himself, and for the Lord Cartarett, and the Lord Craven, and Sir John Colliton, four of the Proprietors of that Province, in order to the ratifying it, entitled, "An Act for the establishing Religious Worship in this Province, according to the Church of England, and for the erecting of Churches for the publick Worship of God, and also for the Maintenance of Ministers, and building convenient Houses for them," So far forth as the same relates to the establishing a Commission for the displacing the Rectors or Ministers of the Churches there, is not warranted by the Charter granted to the Proprietors of that Colony, as being not consonant to Reason, repugnant to the Laws of this Realm, and destructive to the Constitution of the Church of England.

Secondly, That it is the Opinion of this House, That the Act of the Assembly of Carolina, entitled, "An Act for the more effectual Preservation of the Government of this Province, by requiring all Persons that shall hereafter be chosen Members of the Commons House of Assembly, and sit in the same, to take the Oaths, and subscribe the Declaration appointed by this Act, and to conform to the Religious Worship in this Province, according to the Rites and Usage of the said Church," lately pass'd there, and sign'd and

---

[1] "*The Humble Address of the Right Honourable the Lords Spiritual and Temporal in Parliament assembled, Die Martii 12, 1705.*" (Note in original; see also p. 264, note 1, *supra*.)

seal'd by John Lord Granville, Palatine, for himself, and the Lord
Craven, and also for the Lord Cartarett, and by Sir John Colliton,
four of the Proprietors of that Province, in order to the ratifying
of it, is founded upon Falsity in Matter of Fact, is repugnant to the
Laws of England, contrary to the Charter granted to the Proprietors
of that Colony, is an Encouragement to Atheism and Irreligion,
destructive to Trade, and tends to the depopulating and ruining
the said Province.

   May it please your Majesty;

   We your Majesty's most dutiful Subjects, having thus humbly
presented our Opinions of these Acts, we beseech your Majesty to
use the most effectual methods to deliver the said Province from
the arbitrary Oppressions, under which it now lies; and to order
the Authors thereof to be prosecuted according to Law.

To which Her Majesty was graciously pleas'd to answer:

   I thank the House, for laying these Matters so plainly before
me; I am very sensible of what great Consequence the Plantations
are to England, and will do all that is in my Power to relieve my
Subjects.

   It appear'd to the House, that some of the Proprietors
absolutely refus'd to join in these Acts.   This Matter being
referr'd to the Lords of the Committee of Trade, they examin'd into it; and finding all the Fact charg'd upon the
Promoters of these Bills, true, represented to Her Majesty,
the 24th of May, 1706,   That the making such Laws is an
Abuse of the Power granted to the Proprietors by their Charter,
and will be a Forfeiture of such Power.   They further humbly
offer'd to her Majesty, That she would be pleas'd to give
Directions for re-assuming the same into her Majesty's Hands
by *Scire Facias*, in her Majesty's Court of Queen's Bench.
Which Representation was signed by the Right Honourable
the Lord Dartmouth, the Honourable Robert Cecil, Esq;
Sir Philip Meadows, William Blathwayte, Esq; Matthew
Prior, Esq; and John Pollexfen, Esq.

   On the 10th of June, her Majesty was pleas'd to approve
of the said Representation; and accordingly having declar'd
the Laws mention'd therein to be *null* and *void*, did Order,
That for the more effectual Proceeding against the said Charter
by way of *Quo Warranto*, Mr. Attorney, and Mr. Solicitor

General do inform themselves fully concerning what may be most necessary for effecting the same.

Thus did our most Gracious Sovereign hear the Cry of the Oppress'd, right the Innocent, and do Justice on the Oppressor. For no Distance of Country can put any of her Subjects out of her Protection; nor no Difference of Opinion (provided they are kept within the Bounds of Duty and Religion) prevent her favouring alike all her People, and doing her utmost to make them all happy, as the infinite God has made her Reign to her self, and her Empire in a distinguish'd manner.

The Assembly which pass'd these two memorable Acts were dissolv'd in the following Year, and a new one summon'd to meet at Charles Town. At the Election, Craven and Berkley Counties were so streightned by the Qualifying Act, that they had not 20 Men to represent them, unless they would choose a Dissenter, or a Man not fit to sit in the Assembly. Nineteen of the Party against the Occasional Bill were chosen, and one Mr. Job How was elected by the Interest of the Goosecreek Faction, a Branch of the former. The French, who were Free-holders, voted for them, being induc'd to it, by a Frenchman's being set up for a Candidate. They also procur'd Masters of Ships, particularly Cap. Cole, who lay in the Harbour, to vote on their Side. This Election was made in the Town, and the Faction gave out, an Assembly was chosen, who would repeal the Church-Act, and not pay the Augustino Debt, threatning if they did, the House and Town should quickly be too hot to hold them.

In Colliton County, there were but 14 Men would qualify themselves: Therefore none of the Dissenters appear'd, and there were but 10 Votes out of 200 that appear'd at the Election. The 10 Electors voted for 14 Candidates, and the Sheriff return'd 10 that had the Majority of Votes.

On Jan. 2. 1705. the Members met, but not enough to make a House, and choose a Speaker. Mr. Stephens, one of the Members, ask'd Mr. How, in the Governour's Presence, to attend; but he refus'd. Before Night the House was compleat, and waited on the Governour, and ask'd if he would direct them to choose a Speaker? He Answer'd, he thought 'twas too late, but if they would venture they must do it with speed, for he was not well, and 'twould endanger his Health to sit up. So they presently chose Mr. Seabrook, and presented him to the Governour; who approv'd of the Choice.

The next Day the House met, the Speaker in the Chair, and the Members were call'd upon to qualify themselves: Six did, and three more were ready to do it, and Debates arising about Qualifying, the House adjourn'd.

The House meeting again, a Report was, as 'tis said, industriously spread, that the Members had forfeited 50*l.* a Man for adjourning before they were qualify'd. Mr. How and Mr. Wiggington attended in their Places, and offer'd to qualify themselves; but Mr. Bornwell coming with a Message, the House waited on the Governour; who spoke to this Purpose:

*Gentlemen,*

   You are building on a wrong Foundation, and then the Superstructure will never stand; for you have dissolv'd your selves by adjourning, before there was a competent Number of Members to adjourn, and I cannot dissolve you if I would, you not being a House. All this I know very well, as being my self many Years a Member of the House of Commons in England; and therefore as I am Head, I would advise you to go back no more to the House, but go every Man about his own Business: For if you should persist in settling and making Laws, besides incurring the Penalties of the Act, the Laws would be of no force, etc.

The Speaker refus'd to return to the Chair, and the Members dispers'd. The Governour and Council disowning the Assembly, Mr. Wiggington declar'd, 'Twas his Opinion the House was dissolv'd. But their Dissolution was aggravated, by the Pleasure the Government took in making them *Felo de se,* their own Murderers.[1]

Then another Assembly was call'd, the Choice of which was carry'd on with greater Violence than the former. Job

---

[1] The journal prior to January 31, 1704/5, has been lost, but if the above statement is correct the General Assembly which met on the 2nd was dissolved after several days, new writs were issued, a new election was held, and the new House met *before* January 31st—all with a haste that was not duplicated on any other occasion in the history of the province, so far as is shown by authentic records.

How, Esq; was chosen Speaker, and the Members for the most Part qualify'd themselves according to the Qualifying Act. The Faction had not then heard of the Proceedings against them in England, which indeed were not come to a Conclusion. They continu'd their Irregularities as if they were the most innocent Men in the Province, and the only true Patriots. They pass'd an Act for their Continuance two Years after the Death of the present Governour, or the Succession of a new one: The Reason is told us in the Preamble, "Whereas the Church of England has of late been so happily establish'd among them, fearing by the Succession of a new Governour, the Church may be either undermin'd, or wholly subverted, to prevent that Calamity befalling them, be it enacted," etc. Mr. Job How, Speaker of the Assembly, dying some time after, Col. William Rhett was chosen in his Place. But what has been since done in these Affairs, we know not more than in general, that the two Acts have been repeal'd, and the Party who drove things on with such Fury, have entirely lost their Credit, and that the Proprietaries are oblig'd to them for the cause now depending; wherein if they are cast, the Government of the Province will be forfeited to the Crown. They may thank themselves for it, or at least their late Palatine the Lord Granville; for since the foregoing Pages were written, that Lord dy'd.

How things may be manag'd now, is not difficult to be foreseen, from the good Intelligence between the Persons we have just mention'd; and the Fall of this Faction is a terrible Example to all Colonies, not to let any Prejudice or Passion hurry them on to do things which they cannot answer to their Superiours in England.

'Tis not yet known who will be Palatine of this Province, there being some Disputes in the Succession. 'Tis suppos'd the Lord Craven will succeed the late Lord Granville, who assign'd his Propriety to the Duke of Beaufort.

## CHAPT. II.

*Containing a Geographical Description of Carolina; as also an Account of the Climate, Soil, Product, Trade, First Inhabitants, etc.*

'Tis very well known, that the Province of Carolina has been a long time divided into two separate Governments, the one call'd North Carolina, and the other South Carolina; but the latter being the more populous, goes generally under the Denomination of Carolina, and as such we have treated of it in the foregoing Pages. The Proprietaries of North Carolina are the Proprietaries of South Carolina; tho the Governours are different, in other things they are exactly the same  And we shall put them together in the Geographical Description; as also in our Account of the Climate, Soil, Product, Trade, first Inhabitants, etc.

Carolina, as has been said, contains all the Coast of North America, between 31 and 36 Degrees of Northern Latitude. Its breadth is not to be computed, King Charles II. having granted the Proprietors all the Land Westward in a direct Line from the above mention'd Degrees to the South Seas. 'Tis in Length three hundred Miles. Its Situation is most convenient for Trade, the Coast pleasant and safe, not stormy, or frozen in the Winter.

As to the Climate, Mr. Archdale says of it, Carolina is the Northern Part of Florida, *viz.* from 29 Degrees to 36½, and is indeed the very Center of the habitable Part of the Northern Hemisphere; for taking it to be habitable from the Equinoctial to 64 Degrees, the center of Carolina lies in about 32. which is about the middle of 64, lying Parallel with the Land of Canaan, and may be called the temperate Zone comparatively, as not being pester'd with the violent Heats of the more Southern Colonies, or the Extremes and violent Colds of the more Northern Settlements. Its Production answers the Title of Florida, quia Regio est Florida. Carolina North and South is divided into 6 Counties; of which two are in North Carolina, Albemarle and Clarendon;

and four in South, Craven, Berkley, Colliton, and Cartarett Counties.[1]

The first is Albemarle County, to the North, bordering on Virginia. 'Tis water'd by Albemarle River; and in this Part of the Country lies the Island Roanoke, where Philip Amidas and Arthur Barlow, whom Sir Walter Rawleigh sent to Virginia, landed. This County may be said to belong to Virginia, as New England, etc., did, which justifies King Charles's Grant. When Carolina was first settled, Albemarle was more planted than any of the other Counties, and consisted of near 300 Families. But the Plantations upon Ashley River in time grew upon it so much, that most of the Planters here remov'd thither. This River is full of Creeks on both Sides of it, which for Breadth deserve the Name of Rivers, but they do not run far into the Country. At Sandy Point, it divides it self into two Branches, Noratoke and Notaway; and in the North Point lives an Indian Nation, call'd the Mataromogs. Next to Albemarle is Pantegoe River; between them is Cape Hattoras, mention'd in the History of Virginia. Next to it is Neuse River. The Coranines, an Indian Nation, inhabit the Country about Cape Look out.

Next to Albemarle is Clarendon County; in which is the famous Promontary, call'd Cape Fear, at the Mouth of Clarendon River, call'd also Cape Fear River. Hereabouts, a Colony from Barbadoes formerly settled. The Indians in this Neighbourhood are reckon'd the most barbarous of any in the Province. The next River is nam'd Waterey River, or Winyann, about 25 Leagues distant from Ashley River: 'Tis capable of receiving large Ships, but inferior to Port Royal, nor is yet inhabited. There's another small River between this and Clarendon River call'd Wingon River, and a little Settlement honour'd with the Name of Charles Town, but so thinly inhabited, that 'tis not worth taking Notice of. We come now to South Carolina, which is parted from North by Zantee River.[2] The adjacent Country is call'd,

---

[1] *"Des. of Car.*, p. 6." (Note in original. See p. 288, *supra*.) The name of Carteret County was changed to Granville after Archdale's time as governor.

[2] The Cape Fear River was called the Charles at the time of the settlement of the Barbadian colony thereon. The Wateree River is a branch of the Santee. Winyah Bay indents the coast just above the mouth of the Santee. There is no

Craven County; it is pretty well inhabited by English and French; of the latter there's a Settlement[1] on Zantee River, and they were very instrumental in the irregular Election of the *Unsteady Assembly*. The next River to Zantee is Sewee River;[2] where some Families from New England settled: And in the Year 1706, the French landing there, they were vigorously oppos'd by this little Colony; who beat off the Invaders, having forc'd them to leave many of their Companions dead behind them. This County sends 10 Members to the Assembly. We now enter

Berkley County, passing still from North to South. The Northern Parts of this Shire are not planted, but the Southern are thick of Plantations, on Account of the two great Rivers, Cooper and Ashley. On the North Coast there's a little River call'd Bowal River; which, with a Creek, forms an Islands, and off the Coasts are several Isles, nam'd the Hunting-Islands, and Sillivant's Isle. Between the latter and Bowal River, is a Ridge of Hills; which, from the Nature of the Soil, is call'd the Sand-Hills.[3] The River Wando waters the North-West Parts of this County, and has several good Plantations upon it, as Col. Daniel's on the South Side, and Col. Dearsby's lower down on the North. It runs into Cooper River, near the latter, and they both unite their Streams with Ashley River at Charles Town. The late Assembly enacted, "That a Church should be built on the South-East of Wando River, and another upon the Neck of Land, lying on the North-West of Wando," but we do not see that this Act was obey'd.[4]

Charles Town, the Capital of this Province, is built on a

such river as the Wingon between Winyah and North Carolina. Two rivers run into Winyah Bay from that territory: the Peedee and the Waccamaw. There was no Charles Town then in Carolina other than that between the Ashley and Cooper rivers. The Barbadian settlement on the Cape Fear had been called by that name, but it had been abandoned before the Ashley River settlement was effected.

[1] On this French settlement, James Town, see Mr. H. A. M. Smith in *The South Carolina Historical and Genealogical Magazine*, IX. 220–227.

[2] Seewee is not a river, but a bay.

[3] There is no river in that quarter and there are no such sandhills as are here described. All of the coastal islands just to the northward of Charleston are sandy and the wind piles this sand into dunes, but there are no hills near that coast.

[4] Churches were built in both parishes about that time.

Neck of Land between Ashley and Cooper Rivers, but lying most on Cooper River, having a Creek on the North Side, and another on the South. It lies in 32 Deg. 40 Min. N. Lat. 2 Leagues from the Sea. It is the only free Port in the Province, which is a great Discouragement to it, and a vast Injury to Trade: "'Tis fortify'd more for Beauty than Strength." It has 6 Bastions, and a Line all round it. Towards Cooper River are Blake's Bastion, Granville Bastion, a Half Moon, and Craven Bastion. On the South Creek are the Pallisades, and Ashley Bastion; on the North a Line; and facing Ashley River are Colliton Bastion, Johnson's cover'd Half-Moon, with a Draw-bridge in the Line, and another in the Half-Moon, Carterett Bastion is next to it. If all these Works are well made, and can be well mann'd, we see no Reason why they should not defend as well as beautify the Town; which is a Market Town, and thither the whole product of the Province is brought for Sale. Neither is its Trade inconsiderable; for it deals near 1000 Miles into the Continent: However, 'tis unhappy in a Bar, that admits no Ships above 200 Tuns. Its Situation is very inviting, and the Country about it agreeable and fruitful: The High-ways extremely delightful, especially that call'd Broad-way, which for three or four Miles make a Road and Walk so pleasantly green, that,[1] says my Author, I believe no Prince in Europe, by all his Art, can make so pleasant a Sight for the whole Year. There are several fair Streets in the Town, and some very handsome buildings; as Mr. Landgrave Smith's House on the Key, with a Drawbridge and Wharf before it; Col. Rhett's on the Key: also Mr. Boon's, Mr. Loggan's, Mr. Schinking's, and 10 or 12 more, which deserve to be taken Notice of. As for publick Edifices, the Church is most remarkable: 'Tis large and stately enough; but the Number of the Professors of the Anglicane Worship encreasing daily, the Auditory begin to want Room, and another Church. This is dedicated to St. Philip; and by the Act, which appointed the High Commission Court, 'twas enacted, "That Charles Town, and the Neck between Cooper and Ashley River, as far up as the Plantation of John Bird, Gent. on Cooper River, inclusive, is, and from henceforth shall for ever be a distinct Parish, by the Name of St. Philip's in

[1] "Archd., p. 9." (Note in original. See p. 290, *supra*.)

Charles Town;" and the Church and Cæmetry then in this Town were enacted to be the Parish Church and Church-Yard of St. Philip's in Charles Town. Mr. Williams was the first Church of England Minister in Carolina: A Person of whom since Mr. Marston has said so much, we shall say no more. One Mr. Warmel was sent over after him. The Reverend Mr. Samuel Marshal was the first establish'd Minister at Charles Town; and his Successor was Mr. Edward Marston, the present Rector of St. Philip's; he came over seven Years ago. Mr. Kendal, Minister of Bermudas, was invited to this Colony; and Mr. Corbin, an Acquaintance of Mr. Marston's, coming by chance, he got him settl'd in this Province.

The Society for Propagating the Gospel sent over one Mr. Thomas, to convert the Roman Catholick Indians; *but he did not obey his Mission.*[1] On the contrary, 'twas by his Influence on some Men of Interest here, that Mr. Kendal was displac'd: Upon which he went distracted.

Mr. Warmell was also us'd so ill by him, that he also dy'd distracted; and Mr. Corbin was forc'd to leave the Colony, by the causeless Quarrels of the Inhabitants; in which the Dissenters had the least Hand. 'Twas by their Procurement that the 150*l*. a Year, etc., was settled on the Orthodox Minister of this Church. The Church stands near the cover'd Half Moon.

There's a Publick Library in this Town, and a Free-School has been long talk'd of: Whether founded or not, we have not learn'd. The Library is kept by the Minister for the time being. It owes its Rise to Dr. Thomas Bray; as do most of the American Libraries, for which he zealously solicited Contributions in England.

Not far off, by Cartarett Bastion, is the Presbyterian Meeting-house; of which Mr. Archibald Stobe is Minister.[2] Between Colliton and Ashley Bastion is the Anabaptist Meeting-house, Mr. William Screven Minister. The French Church

---

[1] "See Mr. Marston's Letter to Dr. Stanhope, Part 2, *Case of Dissent.*, p. 58." (Note in original.) The contemporaneous records on both sides of the ocean show Rev. Samuel Thomas to have been a splendid man, whose work in South Carolina was of great benefit to the people. The statement that he caused these two ministers to die distracted is absurd.

[2] Archibald Stobo, an ancestor of former President Roosevelt.

is in the Chief Street: Besides which there is a Quakers Meeting-house, in the Suburbs of it, properly so call'd, on the other Side of the Draw-bridge, in the Half Moon, toward Ashley River.

To the Southward is the Watch-house; and the most noted Plantations in the Neighbourhood of Charles Town, are Ferguson's, Underwood's, Gilbertson and Garnett's.

We may see by this Description that the Town is full of Dissenters, and would flourish more, were not the Inhabitants uneasy under the Government there. For one may imagine they who fled from England, to avoid Persecution, cannot be well pleas'd to meet with it in America; or to cross the Atlantick, to live under Oppression abroad, while their Relations and Friends at home enjoy all the blessings of a peaceful and gentle Administration.

There are at least 250 Families in this Town, most of which are numerous, and many of them have 10 or 12 Children in each; in the whole amounting to about 3000 souls.

In Charles Town the Governour generally resides, the Assembly sit, the Courts of Judicature are held, the Publick Offices are kept, and the Business of the Province is transacted.

The Neck of Land between Cooper and Ashley Rivers is about 4 Miles over; and the Banks of both of these are well planted. The chief Settlements on Cooper River are Mathew's, Green's, Gray's, Starkey's, Grimboll's, Dickeson's, and Izard's; the latter on Turkey Creek. About a Mile from thence is the mouth of Goose-Creek, which is also very well planted. Here Mr. William Corbin above-mention'd liv'd, and had a Congregation of Church of England Men; and one of the Churches propos'd to be built by the Assembly which pass'd the two fatal Acts we have spoken of, was to be erected.[1]

Mr. Thomas, a Missionary sent by the Society beforemention'd, settled here, by Capt. How's and Col. Moor's Sollicitations; as did Mr. Stackhouse, and the Reverend Dr. Lejau.

Mr. Marston in his Letter to the Reverend Dr. Stanhope, accuses Mr. Thomas of being the Occasion of the ill Usage that made Mr. Kendal run distracted. He Complains he never

---

[1] There had been a church there so early as 1702. The new church was commenced soon after the passage of the Church Act of 1706 and was finished about 1711. It still stands—one of the oldest church edifices in America.

had University Education, saying, That the best Service
your Society can do this young Man, Mr. Thomas, is, to
maintain him a few Years at one of our Universities, where
he may better learn the Principles and Government of the
Church of England, etc., and some other useful Learning,
which I am afraid he wants.

Sir John Yeaman's, and Mr. Landgrave Bellenger's Plan-
tations are here; as also Col. Gibbs's, Mr. Schinking's, and
Colliton's Company. Between this and Back River are Col.
Moor's and Col. Quarry's plantations.

Back River falls into Cooper River, about 2 Miles above
Goose Creek, and its Western Branch a little higher. Here
another Church was propos'd to be built. The most noted
Plantations are Capt. Comming's, and Sir Nathaniel Johnson's,
bordering on the Barony of Mr. Thomas Colliton.

We must now take a View of Ashley River, where we
first meet with Mr. Landgrave West's Plantation on one
side,[1] and Col. Gibbs's on the other. Mr. Baden's over against
Col. Godfrey's; Mr. Simond's opposite to Dr. Trevillian's; and
Mr. Pendarvis's to Mr. West's, Mr. Colliton's to Mr. Marshal's,
and others, almost contiguous.

This Part of the Country belongs to the Lord Shaftesbury.
On the South-West of Ashley River is the great Savana.
One of the Churches intended to be erected in this County,
was to have been built on Ashley River.

Dorchester is in this Shire, bordering on Colliton County.
'Tis a small Town, containing about 350 Souls. There's a
Meeting-House belonging to the Independants, the Pastor of
which is Mr. John Lord.[2] Next to it is Stono River, which
divides Berkley from Colliton County, To which we must now
proceed, observing only that Berkley County sends ten Members to the Assembly. The same does,

Colliton County; which Stono River waters, and is join'd

---

[1] Landgrave Joseph West had long since died. On March 7, 1691/2, Miles
Forster, of the "Citty of New Yorke Merchant Sole Executor of the Last Will and
Testament of Joseph West, Esq late of the s⁴. Citty deceased and formerly of
South Carolina" executed a power of attorney to Thomas Smith of South Caro-
lina to recover all property belonging to West's estate in South Carolina. (Rec-
ords of the Register of the Province of South Carolina, 2, 200–201.)

[2] See p. 196. note 1, *supra*.

by a Cut,[1] near Mr. Blake's Plantation, to Wadmoolaw River. The North-East Parts of this Division of the Province is full of Indian Settlements; and the Stono and other Rivers, form an Island, call'd Boone's Island, a little below Charles Town, which is well planted and inhabited. The two chief Rivers in this County are North Edistow, and South Edistow. At the Mouth of the Latter is Col. Paul Grimboll's Plantation; and for two or three Miles up the River, the Plantations are thick on both sides, as they continue for three or four Miles higher on the North-side, and branching there, the River meets with the North Edistow.

Two Miles higher is Wilton, by some call'd New London, a little Town, consisting of about 80 Houses.[2] Landgrave Moreton, Mr. Blake, Mr. Boon, Landgrave Axtel, and other considerable Planters, have Settlements in this Neighbourhood, which is Sir John Colliton's Precinct.

A Church was to have been built on the South-side of the Stono, had that Project gone on, and the Act taken effect. This County has 200 Freeholders, that vote in Election for Parliament Men. There 's an Orthodox Church in this Precinct, of which Mr. Williams is Minister.

Carterett County is not yet inhabited, but is generally esteem'd to be the most fruitful and pleasant Part of the Province; this and Colliton County are distinguish'd from the other by the Name of the Southward. In it is the great River Cambage, which joining with the River May, forms with the Sea Island Edelano.[3]

The country upon the River May was inhabited by the Westoes, an Indian Nation already mention'd. There's a pleasant Lake and Valley in it; and the first English that came to Carolina, thought of settling hereabouts; but the Indians advis'd them to the contrary, because the Harbour of Port Royal was the finest in Florida, and would have tempted the Spaniards to disturb them.

[1] New Cut.

[2] See Mr. H. A. M. Smith's article on Willtown or New London in *The South Carolina Historical and Genealogical Magazine*, X. 20–32.

[3] There was no river Cambage. Possibly the Combahee was meant, but that does not unite with what was then called the May (Savannah). There was no Island Edelano. It is difficult to tell whether the writer meant Edisto Island or St. Helena Island. In either case he was wrong.

The Scots settled here, under the Lord Cardross, but were soon forc'd to abandon their Settlements, as has been elsewhere hinted. Port Royal River lies 20 Leagues from Ashley River, to the South, in 31 Degrees, 45 Minutes, North Latitude. It has a bold Entrance, 17 Foot low Water on the Bar. The Harbour is large, commodious, and safe for Shipping, and runs into a fine fruitful Country, preferable to the other Parts of Carolina. It spends its self, by various Branches, into other large Rivers. This Port is not 200 Miles from Augustino, and would be a great Curb to the Spaniards there, where their Settlement is not very considerable.

Next to it is the River of May, and then San Mattæo; which is the last of any Note in the English Florida, a Name this Province highly deserves.

The Air of this Country is healthy, and Soil fruitful,[1] of a sandy Mould, which near the Sea appears ten times more barren than it proves to be. There's a vast Quantity of Vines in many Parts on the Coasts, bearing abundance of Grapes, where one would wonder they should get Nourishment. Within Land the Soil is more mix'd with a blackish Mould, and its Foundation generally Clay, good for Bricks.

Its Products are the chief Trade of the Inhabitants, who send it abroad, according as the Market offers; and 'tis in demand in America or Europe. But the Chief Commerce from hence is to Jamaica, Barbadoes, and the Leward Islands. Yet their Trade to England is very much encreas'd; for notwithstanding all the Discouragements the People lie under, seventeen Ships came last Year, laden from Carolina, with Rice, Skins, Pitch, and Tar, in the Virginia Fleet, besides stragling Ships.

Its principal Commodities are Provisions, as Beef, Pork, Corn, Pease, Butter, Tallow, Hides, Tann'd Leather, Hogshead and Barrel Staves, Hoops, Cotton, Silk; besides what they send for England. Their Timber Trees, Fruit Trees, Plants, and Animals, are much the same with those in Virginia; in which History may be seen a large Account of them: But

---

[1] "Arch., p. 8." (Note in original. See p. 288, *supra*.)

since Mr. Archdale has been a little particular in his, and has added a short Description of the Natives, etc., we will communicate what he says to the reader.[1]

'Tis beautify'd with odoriferous Woods, Green all the Year; as Pine, Cedar, and Cypress. 'Tis naturally fertile, and easy to manure. Were the Inhabitants industrious, Riches would flow in upon them; for I am satisfy'd, a Person with 500l. discreetly laid out in England, and again prudently manag'd in Carolina, shall in a few Years live in as much Plenty, as a Man of 300l. a Year in England; and if he continues careful, not covetous, shall increase to great Riches, as many there are already Witnesses, and many more might have been, if Luxury and Intemperance had not ended their Days.

As to the Air, 'tis always serene, and agreeable to any Constitutions, as the first Planters experienc'd. There's seldom any raging Sickness, but what is brought from the southern Colonies; as the late Sickness was, which rag'd, A. D. 1706. and carry'd off abundance of People in Charles Town, and other Places.

Intemperance also has occasion'd some Distempers. What may properly be said to belong to the Country is, to have some gentle Touches of Agues and Fevers in July and August, especially to new Comers. It has a Winter-Season, to beget a new Spring. I was there, adds my Author, at twice, five Years, and had no Sickness, but what I got by a careless violent Cold; and indeed I perceiv'd that the Fevers and Agues were generally gotten by Carelesness in Cloathing, or Intemperance.

Everything generally grows there that will grow in any part of Europe, their being already many sorts of Fruits, as Apples, Pears, Apricocks, Nectarines, etc. They that once tast of them, will despise the watry washy Tast of those in England. There's such Plenty of them, that they are given to the Hogs. In 4 or 5 Years they come from a Stone to be bearing Trees.

All sorts of Grain thrive in Carolina, as Wheat, Barley, Peas, etc. And I have measur'd some Wheat-ears 7 or 8 of our Inches long. It produces the best Rice in the known World, which is a good Commodity for returns Home; as is also Pitch, Tar, Buck, Doe, Bear Skins, and Furs, though the last not so good as the Northern Colonies.

It has already such Plenty of Provisions, that it in a great measure furnishes Barbadoes, Jamaica, etc. There are vast Numbers of wild Ducks, Geese, Teal; and the Sea and Rivers abound

[1] "P. 9, p. 7." (Note in original. See pp. 290, 291, 288, 289, 291, *supra*.)

in Fish.   That which makes Provisions so cheap, is the Shortness
of the Winter: For having no need to mow for Winter Fodder, they
can apply their Hands in raising other Commodities.

The Rivers are found to be more navigable than was at first
believ'd; and t'was then prudently contriv'd, not to settle on the
most navigable; but on Ashley and Cooper River, those Entrances
are not so bold as the others; so that Enemies and Pirates have
been dishearten'd in their Designs to disturb that Settlement.

The new Settlers have now great Advantages over the first
Planters, since they can be supply'd with Stocks of Cattle and Corn
at reasonable Rates.

I shall conclude this Account of Carolina, with an Extract
of a Letter from thence, from a Person of Credit; in whose
Words I communicate it to the Publick:   He Speaks of the
Southward.

The many Lakes we have up and down breed a Multitude of
Geese, and other Water-Fowl.   All along Port-Royal River, and
in all this part of Carolina, the Air is so temperate, and the Seasons
of the Year so regular, that there's no Excess of Heat or Cold,
nor any troublesome Variety of Weather: For tho there is every
Year a kind of Winter, yet it is both shorter and milder than at
Ashley or Cooper River; and passes over insensibly, as if there
was no Winter at all.   This sweet Temperature of Air, causes the
Banks of this River to be cover'd with various Kinds of lovely Trees;
which being perpetually green, present a thousand Landskips to the
Eye, so fine, and so diversify'd, that the Sight is entirely charm'd
with them.   The ground is very low in most Places near the River;
but rises gradually, at a distance, with little Hills, adjoining to
fruitful Plains, all cover'd with Flowers, without so much as a Tree
to interrupt the Prospect.   Beyond these are beautiful Vales,
cloath'd with green Herbs, and a continual Verdure, caus'd by the
refreshing Rivulets that run through them.   There are a great
many Thickets, which produce abundance of Simples.   The
Indians make use of them for the Cure of their Diseases.   There
are also Sarsaparilla, Cassia Trees, Gumms, and Rosin, very good
for Wounds and Bruises; and such a prodigious Quantity of
Honey, which the Bees make every where, that the Store of it is
not to be exhausted.   Of this they make excellent Spirits, and
Mead as good as Malaga Sack.[1]   The Bees swarm five or six
times.   There's a kind of Tree, from which there runs an Oil of

[1] Sherry.

extraordinary Virtue, for the Curing Wounds. And another Tree, which yields a Balm, thought to be scarce inferior to that of Mecca.

Silk is come to a great Improvement here, some Families making 40 or 50 Pound a Year, and their Plantation Work not neglected, their little Negro Children being serviceable in feeding the Silk-Worms. And we must do Sir Nathaniel Johnson the Justice, to own he has been the principal Promoter of this Improvement, as also of Vineyards. He makes yearly 3 or 400*l.* in Silk only.

But 'tis objected, Since the Climate is so proper, since Grapes are so plentiful, and the Wine they make so good, why is there not more of it? Why do we not see some of it?

To which I answer, That the Inhabitants either think they can turn their Hands to a more profitable Culture, or impose upon us in their Reports; for I would not think them so weak, as to neglect making good Wine, and enough of it, if they could, and thought it worth their while.

They manufacture their Silk with Wool, and make Druggets. The French Protestants have set up a Linnen Manufacture; and good Romalls[1] are made here.

A French Dancing-Master settling in Craven County, taught the Indians Country-Dances, to play on the Flute and Hautboit, and got a good Estate; for it seems the Barbarians encourag'd him with the same Extravagance, as we do the Dancers, Singers, and Fidlers, his Countrymen.

Tho we have said enough of the Virginian Indians, who are much the same with the Carolinian; yet since we find Mr. Archdale speaks of them in particular, let the Reader see what he has said of 'em.

Providence was visible in thinning the Indians, to make Room for the English. There were two potent Nations, the Westoes and Sarannas, who broke out into an usual Civil War before the English arriv'd; and from many Thousands reduc'd themselves to a small Number. The most cruel of them, the Westoes, were driven out of the Province; and the Sarannas continu'd good Friends, and useful Neighbours to the English. It pleas'd God also to send

---

[1] Kerchiefs or small shawls.

unusual Sicknesses among them; as the Small-Pox, etc.[1] The Pemlico Indians in North Carolina, were lately swept away by a Pestilence; and the Caranine, by War. The Natives are somewhat tawny, occasion'd chiefly by oiling their Skins, and by the naked rays of the Sun. They are generally streight body'd, comely in Person, quick of Apprehension, and great Hunters; by which they are not only very serviceable, by killing Deer, to procure Skins for Trade with us; but those that live in Country-Plantations procure of them the whole Deer's Flesh, and they will bring it many Miles for the Value of about 6d. and a wild Turkey of 40 Pound, for the Value of 2d.

They have learn'd one of their worst Vices of the English, which is, Drinking; and that occasions Quarrels among them, one of which we have mention'd in the time of Mr. Archdale's Government. As to what he would excite us, to their Conversion to Christianity, 'tis a Project which, like a great many other very good ones, we rather wish than hope to see effected.

Mr. Thomas was sent to instruct the Yammosees in the Christian Religion, and had an Allowance of 50l. a year from the before-mention'd Society, besides other Allowances: But finding it an improper Season, his Mission is respited; the Reason is, those Indians revolted to the English from the Spaniards; and not being willing to embrace Christianity, 'tis fear'd they would return to their old Confederates, if any means were made use of to that purpose.

This Country is in a very flourishing Condition; the Families are very large, in some are 10 or 12 Children; and the Number of Souls in all is computed to be 12000. The Children are set to Work at 8 Years old. The ordinary Women take care of Cows, Hogs, and other small Cattle, make Butter and Cheese, spin Cotton and Flax, help to sow and reap Corn, wind Silk from the Worms, gather Fruit, and look after the House. 'Tis pity this People should not be easy in their Government; for all their Industry, all the Advantages of the Climate, Soil, and Situation for Trade, will be useless to them, if they live under Oppression; and Pennsylvania will have no occasion to complain, that she tempts away her Inhabitants; being a new Beauty, a fairer, and consequently a powerful Rival.

[1] "P. 2, 3." (Note in original. See pp. 285, 289, *supra*.)

We shall conclude this History and Account of Carolina, with a List of the present Proprietaries, and chief Officers of this Colony.

William Lord Craven,
Henry Duke of Beaufort,
The Honourable Maurice
   Ashley, Esq; Brother to
   the Earl of Shaftsbury,
John Lord Cartarett,     }Proprietaries.
Sir John Colliton, Baronet,
Joseph Blake, Esq;
John Archdale, Esq;
Nicholas Trott, Esq;

Sir Nath. Johnson, Governour, sallary 200*l.* a Year.

Col. James Moor,
Col. Thomas Broughton,
Col. Rob. Gibbs,
Mr. Nich. Trott,     }Counsellors.
Mr. ——. Ward,
Mr. Hen. Noble,

Speaker of the Assembly, William Rhett, Esq.
The Secretary, —— Ward, Esq; his Salary 60*l.* a Year.
The Chief Justice, Mr. Trott, 60*l.*
The Judge of the Admiralty-Court, Col. James Moor, 40*l*
Surveyor General, —— How, Esq; 40*l.*
Attorney General, Col. James Moor, 60*l.*
Receiver General, the same, 60*l.*
Naval Officer, Mr. Trott, 40*l.*
Collector of the Customs, Col. Thomas Broughton.
Agent for the Colony in England, Mr. Joseph Boone.

# INDEX